Advanced ICD-10 for Physicians Including Worker's Compensation and Personal Injury

Advanced ICD-10 for Physicians Including Worker's Compensation and Personal Injury

By
Eugene Fukumoto

CRC Press
Taylor & Francis Group
Boca Raton London New York

CRC Press is an imprint of the
Taylor & Francis Group, an **informa** business
A PRODUCTIVITY PRESS BOOK

CRC Press
Taylor & Francis Group
6000 Broken Sound Parkway NW, Suite 300
Boca Raton, FL 33487-2742

Printed on acid-free paper

International Standard Book Number-13: 978-1-138-03290-3 (Hardback)

Library of Congress Cataloging-in-Publication Data

Names: Fukumoto, Eugene, author.
Title: Advanced ICD-10 for physicians including worker's compensation and personal injury / Eugene Fukumoto.
Description: Boca Raton : Taylor & Francis, 2017. | "A CRC title, part of the Taylor & Francis imprint, a member of the Taylor & Francis Group, the academic division of T&F Informa plc." | Includes bibliographical references.
Identifiers: LCCN 2016040423| ISBN 9781138032903 (paperback) |
ISBN 9781315317342 (ebook)
Subjects: LCSH: Nosology--Code numbers--Problems, exercises, etc. | Medical records--Code numbers--Case studies.
Classification: LCC RB115 .F85 2017 | DDC 616.001/2--dc23
LC record available at https://lccn.loc.gov/2016040423

Visit the Taylor & Francis Web site at
http://www.taylorandfrancis.com

and the CRC Press Web site at
http://www.crcpress.com

MIX
Paper from responsible sources
FSC® C013056

Printed and bound in Great Britain by
TJ International Ltd, Padstow, Cornwall

Contents

Preface

The implementation of ICD-10 is the biggest change that Eugene Fukumoto has seen in over 30 years of billing and coding. It will be a continuing challenge to make this transition. It is very important that providers understand that their documentation is key and that they have to know that their documentation must support claims submitted.

The changes in ICD-10 are especially daunting for Worker's Compensation and Personal Injury because of the specific knowledge of injury codes required, as well as the medical-legal complications.

There are conflicting statements in ICD-10. On the one hand, there is a statement that there is no national mandatory ICD-10 External Cause reporting, unless it is required per state-based reporting mandate. On the other hand, many of the ICD-10 codes, such as sprains, are S codes, which by definition are External Cause codes.

We don't know how claims will be processed, but it is very important that providers be aware of these conflicting statements. Med-legal issues will probably require case law for resolution.

Eugene Fukumoto has spent most of his career in medical billing and collecting. As we transition into ICD-10, he saw a need to train doctors and their staff on how to get the bill "out the door." That is the purpose of this book, to help your entire staff understand ICD-10 and how it is used with CPT codes, the CMS Form 1500, and the documentation in the patient's status.

Once you go through the step-by-step process, the Six-Category System, and work with Eugene's examples, it will make it very clear. Eugene and his team are here to help you beyond the book, as well, with online training, blogs, and other tools.

The intention is to give you a credible book with a simple system to make the actual billing process easier.

Simply put, what Eugene is trying to accomplish here is to help you "get the bill out the door"!

Dr. Donna Meeks
Dr. Dan Farris

Preface

Acknowledgments

The author would like to thank the following people for their support and contributions to this book.

Dr. Michael Smith, Orthopedic Surgeon
Harvard Fellow
Past President of the California Society of Industrial Medical Specialists
Independent Medical Evaluator

Dr. Vincent Sghiatti, Family and General Practice
UCLA Fellow
Board Certified in Family Practice
Pennsylvania State University, College of Medicine

Dr. Donna Meeks, **Dr. Dan Farris**, DC
Created one of the largest Chiropractic clinics in California
Opened the first California sleep laboratory with a neurologist for Worker's Compensation per the American Medical Association Guides
Created MF University for online training/live seminars for MDs, attorneys, and DCs

Other Books by Eugene Fukumoto

Conquering ICD-10—For Chiropractors
Conquering ICD-10—For Family Physicians and General Practice
Conquering ICD-10—Worker's Compensation and Personal Injury (First Edition)

Online Courses by Eugene Fukumoto:
(Sponsored by MF University)
Conquering ICD-10: Module 1
Conquering ICD-10: Module 2—Advanced Concepts

For more info, visit Eugene at:
www.icd10center.com
www.mededonline.myicourse.com
www.dctodconline.myicourse.com
www.legaledonline.myicourse.com

Disclaimer

The purpose of this book is to educate the physician, as well as the billing and coding staff, on ICD-10, so that they can properly document all necessary information to accurately and thoroughly complete the billing process. Also, it is intended to give the physician an understanding of the proper implementation of ICD-10 and the possible repercussions of improper coding regarding all insurance billing, including Medicare, Group Insurance, HMOs, Worker's Compensation, and Personal Injury.

The ICD-10-CM Draft Release is not complete and is still evolving. This is another reason why you should be cautious about using the free ICD-9 to ICD-10 crossover packages. There are 21 sections now in ICD-10 and it is being revised as we speak, so you may be able to use a free crossover today, and next week it will be different.

This book was prepared as a service to the providers and billing and coding staff and is not intended to grant rights or impose obligations. This book may contain references or links to statutes, regulations, or other policy materials. The information provided is only intended to be a general summary. It is not intended to take the place of either the written law or regulations. We encourage readers to review the specific statutes, regulations, and other interpretive materials for a full and accurate statement of their contents.

Chapter 1

Chapter One

Introduction to ICD-10, Including Worker's Compensation and Personal Injury

The purpose of this book is to educate physicians on ICD-10, so that they can properly document all necessary information that the billing staff will require to accurately and thoroughly complete the billing process. Also, it is intended to give physicians an understanding of the proper implementation of ICD-10 and the possible repercussions of improper coding regarding all insurance billing, including Medicare, Group Insurance, HMO's, Worker's Compensation, and Personal Injury.

Updated coding for the ICD-10-CM book, 2017 edition, was analyzed for the creation of this book.

To the best of our knowledge, the first edition of this book was the first publication regarding ICD-10 and its use in Worker's Compensation and Personal Injury.

This book starts with an overview in Chapter 2 of the basic concepts of ICD-10. As you progress through the book, greater detail and explanation are given. This book was designed to give you more complex situations as you progress. Therefore, it is advised that you start at the beginning and read through the entire book.

Although this book includes discussion of ICD-10 as it applies to all types of insurance billing, Worker's Compensation and Personal Injury are especially complex due to the differences in State law and the fact that ICD-10 concepts have yet to be examined by legal authority. There may be many differences of opinion about how claims should be coded and/or submitted.

ICD-10 edits are complex and have not been strictly enforced. Therefore, we are uncertain of how claims will be processed under different circumstances and with different insurance company policies, or even differences in State laws.

On a positive note, ICD-10 gives the doctor more flexibility regarding injury and diagnostic coding.

ICD-10

The International Classification of Diseases and Related Health Problems, 10th Revision, is a coding system developed and maintained by the World Health Organization. The purpose of this code set is to serve as a tool for the classification of morbidity data for indexing medical records, medical care review, as well as a basis for health statistics. ICD-10-CM is the United States' Clinical Modification of the World Health Organization's ICD-10.

Annual modifications are made to ICD-9-CM and ICD-10-CM by the *Coordination and Maintenance Committee* (C&M). The Committee is made up of representatives from two Federal Government Agencies, the National Center for Health Statistics and the Centers for Medicare and Medicaid Services. *Everyone who is covered by the Health Insurance and Portability and Accountability Act (HIPAA) must to use ICD-10*, not just those who submit Medicare and/or Medicaid claims.

The change in title from "International Classification of Diseases" to "International Classification of Diseases and Related Health Problems" shows that the scope of the classification has moved beyond the classification of disease and injuries to the coding of ambulatory care conditions and risk factors frequently encountered in primary care. Please note that V codes and E codes in ICD-9 are no longer supplemental, nor optional. They have been modified and incorporated into the main body of ICD-10 in Chapters 19 and 20.

One of the fundamental goals of ICD-10 is to provide greater Data Granularity. Granularity means a greater level of detail to support improved clinical outcomes and more cost-effective disease management.

It also means that providers must document at a level to support the Granularity. Billing and support staff must have the appropriate level of documentation in order to meet the increased coding requirements. This includes proper injury coding for Worker's Compensation and Personal Injury.

It is important to understand that the ICD-10 coding system was not designed with the U.S. Health Care Reimbursement system in mind. This means that many compatibility issues exist. It is like trying to fit a square peg into a round hole at certain times when using ICD-10 for billing purposes. We have created a 6 Category System that helps handle these incompatibilities when dealing with Injury Coding.

Reasons to Avoid Relying on GEM Software

The current viewpoint of many physicians is that the change to ICD-10 is relatively easy because of the existence of *General Equivalency Mapping* (GEM) software. There are many published articles that state the same. GEM refers to software that allows users to enter an ICD-9 code and get a display of an ICD-10 code or codes that can be used in lieu of the ICD-9 code. *This is a big mistake*, especially for Injury Coding.

External Cause codes are used when a patient is injured or adversely affected by an external cause such as a fall during employment activities. These codes are in a separate chapter. As an example, using a GEM tool, you may enter ICD-9 code 722.1—Disc herniation. Using an online crosswalk tool can lead you to M51.26—Other intervertebral disc displacement, lumbar region. A more appropriate code in Worker's Compensation might be S33.0—Traumatic rupture of lumbar intervertebral disc. An example of the complete code is

> S33.0XXA Traumatic rupture of lumbar intervertebral disc—Initial encounter
>
> *Excludes 1—Rupture or displacement (nontraumatic) of intervertebral disc NOS (M51.-)*

Providers must be cognizant that their documentation must support the code(s) used. They must also know that the use of codes other than External Cause codes can be interpreted as conditions that are not a result of a work-related, or accident activity.

External Cause codes may, at a future point in time, require the use of activity and place of occurrence codes. These specify what the patient was doing to cause the injury and where the injury occurred. GEM tools do not help in determining these codes.

Another reason for being cautious about using GEM tools is that the ICD-10-CM Draft Release is not complete and is still evolving. ICD-10 is being revised as we speak. You may be able to use a GEM crosswalk today and next week it will be erroneous.

Chapter 2

Chapter Two

Structural Overview of the ICD-10-CM Book

The ICD-10-CM book is divided into three basic sections:

1. An Introduction with instructions/guidelines
2. Volume 2, which is in four parts
   a. Alphabetic Index to Diseases—listed alphabetically by condition (not by anatomical site)
   b. Table for Neoplasms
   c. Table of Drugs and Chemicals
   d. Alphabetic Index to External Causes of Injury
3. Volume 1—Tabular List of Diseases

Worker's Compensation and Personal Injury practices will mainly be working with many of the subsections due to the wide scope of services.

Please note that Chapter 20 – Volume 1 deals with all external causes of injury, including poisoning, auto-accidents, falls from horses, and so on.

At first, it can be a bit confusing to navigate through the book *ICD-10-CM Draft Release Expert Edition*. Here are some important locations for certain items:

In the "Alphabetic Index to Diseases," muscle strains are listed under "Injury," subcategory "Muscle," while sprains are listed under "Sprains."

Categories S10 to S19 are for injuries to the neck area.

When looking for "cervical, sprains and strains," or any other condition of the neck area, this is where you go.

S20 to S29 is injuries to the thorax area.

When looking for "thoracic, sprains and strains," or any other condition of the thoracic area, this is where you go.

S30 to S39 is injuries to the lumbar area.

When looking for "lumbar, sprains and strains," or any other condition of the lumbar area, this is where you go.

Please note that the above codes start with an S, thus indicating a condition as a result of injury. Similar diagnoses also exist under the M codes, which do not necessarily imply injury.

Code Structure Basics

ICD-9 codes contain from three to five numeric (N) digits. ICD-10 codes have valid codes containing three to seven **characters** (alpha and numeric, A/N, not just digits).

ICD 9 Format						*ICD-10 Format*							
N	N	N	.	N	N	A	N	A/N	.	A/N	A/N	A/N	A/N
—	—	—	.	—	—	—	—	—	.	—	—	—	—

The first character in ICD-10 is always a letter. The second is always a number. The third character can be alpha or numeric. There is a period after the third character if there are more than three characters. Characters after the first three can be alpha or numeric. If a code requiring a seventh character is not six characters in length, then a placeholder, X, must be used to fill the empty character fields.

For example, S33.8XXA—Sprain of other parts of lumbar spine and pelvis—Active Care:

The first character can use any letter with the exception of U, which is currently not used, but may be in the future. The use of an alpha character means that there can be up to 26 characters instead of just 10 when using numeric codes.

ICD-9 and ICD-10 both have a Table of Contents. In ICD-9, the Table shows a Tabular List of 17 diseases and two supplemental classifications: V codes and E codes.

In ICD-10, there are 21 disease classifications listed, which incorporate ICD-9 V codes and E codes. "External caused injuries" and "external causes of morbidity" (ICD-9 E codes) are concentrated in Chapters 19 and 20 in ICD-10. Factors Influencing Health Status (ICD-9 V codes) are concentrated in Chapter 20.

Using ICD-10 Overview

Billers and coders would use ICD-10 in a manner similar to using ICD-9. You would look in the Table of Contents for the major category. You can also use the Alphabetic Index to determine specific codes.

The major obstacle for billers and coders are as follows:

1. Many ICD-9 codes do not have a one-to-one crosswalk to ICD-10. Many codes have multiple possible choices.

2. There are over 400 instances where a single ICD-9 code can map to more than 50 ICD-10 codes.*
3. There are over 200 instances where a single ICD-9 code can map to more than 100 ICD-10 codes.*
4. ICD-10 represents an increase of over 700% in the number of codes versus ICD-9.
5. Medical records may not contain the necessary information to properly choose the correct ICD-10 code(s).

*Note: *These statistics were published by the CMS, April 2013 in an article "General Equivalence Mapping Frequently Asked Questions."*

Example in coding:
ICD-9 Description
846.0 Lumbosacral (Joint) (Ligament) Sprain

Reviewing the Alphabetic Index in ICD-10, we find:
ICD-10 Description
S33.9 Sprain, lumbosacral

The ICD-10 Alphabetic Index directs you to an S code. S codes are used for Injury, Poisoning and Certain Other Consequences of External Causes. In effect, you are directed to the ICD-9 equivalent of an E code.

It should be noted that ICD-10 has a separate Alphabetic Index to External Causes. A review of this index shows that there are no direct references to S codes. Rather, you are directed to the circumstances of an accident (for example, a motorcycle collision), which are specified by Y and V codes, which further describe the **circumstances** of the injury.

Whenever an S code is assigned, you should also have an external cause of morbidity 'Y' code, which are found in Chapter 20.

The lack of a one-to-one relationship should be a red flag that using a simple crosswalk tool will not allow you to understand ICD-10.

Chapter 3

Chapter Three

Components of ICD-10 and Their Usage

ICD-10 is basically an update of ICD-9. Many of the features of ICD-9 appear in ICD-10.

Both have an Alphabetic Index to Disease and a Tabular List of Diseases, which are used in a similar manner.

The major differences are that, in ICD-9, the Tabular Index contains 17 categories of diseases, which are numerically identified, and two categories of Supplemental Classifications (V and E codes). In ICD-10, the Tabular List includes 21 categories, including two for External Causes and one for Factors Influencing Health Status and Contact with Health Service.

E codes in ICD-9 become Y, W, and X codes in ICD-10. V codes in ICD-9 become Z codes in ICD-10. ICD-9 codes have three to five numeric digits while ICD-10 codes have three to seven alpha-numeric characters from A00- to Z99-.

The first three characters in ICD-10 are essential subdivisions of the disease classification, for example, "R10 Abdominal and Pelvic Pain". Four-character subcategories are subdivisions of three-character categories and define their Axis of Classification.

Axis of Classification refers to how disease can be arranged in ICD-10. They can be arranged by etiology (cause), anatomy, or severity.

Anatomy is the primary Axis of Classification, and the most commonly used.

For example:

R10.1 Pain localized in the upper abdomen

Then, further classification is noted in the fifth character.

R10.10 Upper abdominal pain, unspecified
R10.11 Right upper quadrant pain
R10.12 Left upper quadrant pain
R10.13 Epigastric pain

Severity is another Axis of Classification.
For example:

G44.0 Cluster headaches and other trigeminal autonomic cephalgias (TAC)
G44.201 Tension-type headache, unspecified intractable
G44.209 Tension-type headache, unspecified, not intractable

It is important that the doctor indicates the severity of the condition, as office staff may need this information in order to properly code and bill.

Etiology (cause) is the final Axis of Classification.
For example:

G44.5 Complicated headache syndromes
G44.51 Hemicrania continua
G44.52 New daily persistent headache (NDI)
G44.53 Primary thunderclap headache
G44.59 Other complicated headache syndrome

For cases where the doctor is uncertain of the specificity of the Axis of Classification, the ICD-10 uses the fourth character to state this. An 8 is used to signify "other specified," and 9 is used to signify "unspecified."
For example:

R10 Abdominal and pelvic pain
R10.8 Other abdominal pain
R10.9 Unspecified abdominal pain

Five- and six-character subdivisions are used as follows:
The fifth character can be used to provide a second Axis of Classification.
For example:

R10.81 Abdominal tenderness
R10.82 Rebound abdominal tenderness

The sixth characters can be used to further subdivide fifth-character classifications for greater specificity.
For example, anatomical location:

R10.811 Right upper quadrant abdominal tenderness
R10.812 Left upper quadrant abdominal tenderness
R10.813 Right lower quadrant abdominal tenderness
R10.814 Left lower quadrant abdominal tenderness

R10.815 Periumbilic abdominal tenderness
R10.816 Epigastric abdominal tenderness
R10.817 Generalized abdominal tenderness
R10.819 Abdominal tenderness, unspecified site

Five- and six-character subdivisions are presented in their natural sequence.

When they occur, seventh characters in ICD-10-CM are listed in a table and referenced in the instructions for that code.

One of the uses for the seventh-character code is to identify the status of the current condition under care for that specific encounter.

For example:

M48.50 Collapsed vertebra, not elsewhere classified, site unspecified
M48.50XA Initial encounter for fracture

Seventh-character codes describe Encounter Status, which can vary based on specialties. For Worker's Compensation and Personal Injury, the most common characters will be A, D, and S.

Initial encounter refers to the initial treatment for the condition. Some services such as physical therapy may require a series of treatments to treat a condition. All of these treatments will fall under the initial or current treatment classification. Each of those encounters would be classified as "Initial" and use a seventh character of A.

Subsequent encounter refers to seeing a patient after initial treatment has ended. In other words, the initial treatment was completed for that condition, but the patient was seen subsequently. Subsequent encounters use a seventh character of D. An example could be a post-operative visit 2 months post-surgery.

Please note: Aggravations of an old injury are treated as new initial encounters and NOT subsequent encounters.

Sequelae are the residual effects (conditions produced) after the initial acute phase of an illness or injury. There is no time limit as to when the sequelae can appear. They can appear early, as with a stroke, or can occur years later, as in arthritis following an injury. Sequelae use a seventh character of S.

For example, wrist fracture, which resulted in arthritis of the wrist:

M19.032 Primary osteoarthritis of the left wrist
S52.532S Colles fracture of the left radius

First, you list the specific type of sequela (arthritis). Next, you list the injury code with the seventh character S to signify it is the cause of the sequela. In this case, the sequela is arthritis.

There can be other variant uses of seventh-character codes. For example, for fractures they have the following:

1. Initial encounter for closed fracture (Seventh Character 'A')
2. Initial encounter for open fracture type I or II (Seventh Character 'B')
3. Initial encounter for open fracture type IIIA, IIIB or IIIC (Seventh Character 'C')
4. Subsequent encounter for closed fracture with routine healing (Seventh Character 'D')

Here, in addition to classifying whether it is an Initial encounter or a Subsequent encounter, the fracture type is specified as a separate seventh-character code.

The S52.9 subcategory lists these and others. You must familiarize yourself with these and other seventh-character codes based on your specialty. S52 is for fracture of forearm.

Please note: There are other uses for the seventh character, such as for the Coma Scale for traumatic brain injury, acute cerebrovascular disease, or sequelae of cerebrovascular disease codes. These are not discussed directly in this publication. Other seventh-character codes are shown in the Glossary.

External Causes

Chapter 20 of the ICD-10-CM book, External Causes of Morbidity (V00–Y99), permits the classification of environmental events and circumstances as the cause of injury and other adverse effects. When a code from this section is applicable, it is intended that its use is secondary to a code from another section. Most often, the condition will be classifiable to Chapter 19, "Injury, Poisoning, and Certain Other Consequences of External Causes (S00–T88)."

In other words, an S or T code has a secondary code to indicate the circumstance(s) of the injury. This is very important for Workers Compensation and Personal Injury cases.

For example:

S23.8XXA Sprain of other specified parts of thorax
V42.5 Car driver injured in collision with two- or three-wheeled motor vehicle in traffic accident

Combination Codes

A Combination Code is a single code used to classify two diagnoses, or a diagnosis with an associated manifestation or complication. Assign only the Combination Code that fully identifies the diagnostic conditions documented.

For example:

M54.4 Lumbago with sciatica

Please note: Although "lumbago" is currently a seldom-used term, it is used in the ICD-10-CM and therefore will be used in this book.

If you use a General Equivalency Mapping (GEM) tool to look up sciatica ICD-9 code 724.3, you may be directed to M54.30. When you review this code in ICD-10, you will find exclusions, for example, "Lesions of sciatic nerve (G57.0)" and other exclusions including "Sciatica with lumbago (M54.4-)." ICD-10 lists three five-character codes:

M54.30 Sciatica, side unspecified
M54.31 Sciatica, right side
M54.32 Sciatica, left side

If you use a GEM tool to look up lumbago ICD-9 code 724.2, you may be directed to M54.5, where ICD-10 lists the following:

M54.5 Low back pain, which excludes low back strain (S39.012)
M54.5 also excludes lumbago with sciatica M54.4-

Please note: Strain and sprain are now differentiated.

A review of M54.4 shows the following:

M 54.40 Lumbago with sciatica, unspecified side
M54.41 Lumbago with sciatica, right side
M54.42 Lumbago with sciatica, left side

Again, if both sides are affected, you must list both M54.41 and M54.42.

The important point is that M54.4- is a *Combination Code*. When both sciatica and lumbago occur simultaneously, you must use the Combination Code, and not the two separate codes (M54.3- and M54.5), unless there are specific Exclusions.

Specialty Crosswalk Enclosed

It would not be possible to crosswalk all ICD-9 codes to appropriate ICD-10 counterparts without an accurate understanding of all the possible alternatives. In order to assist users in this process, we have included a crosswalk for Worker's Compensation and Personal Injury. The enclosed crosswalk lists commonly used ICD-9 codes for your specialty crosswalked to ICD-10 codes. This crosswalk lists notations that describe potential problem areas and other information.

Please note: These crosswalks are not a GEM tool. They are designed specifically for Injury Coding. They are to be used to get you from an ICD-9 to the proper category of ICD-10 coding, and not the specific complete code itself. Crosswalks are located in the Appendix.

Instructional Notations

It is necessary to have a copy of the ICD-10-CM book. You should always read the notes at the beginning of each of the three- and four-character subdivisions. These provide specific diseases that are not included in the subdivisions. They also provide other data such as age and gender specificity.

You will see the notation, "Includes." This note appears immediately under a three-character code title to further define, or give examples of, the content of the category.

For example:

V06 Pedestrian injured in collision with other non-motor vehicle
Includes collision with animal-drawn vehicle, animal being ridden, non-powered streetcar

You will also see the notation, "Excludes." Unlike ICD-9, ICD-10 has two types of "exclude" notes. Each type has a different definition for use, but they are all similar in that they indicate that codes excluded from each other are independent of each other.

Excludes 1: A Type 1 Excludes note is a "pure" exclude. It means "Not Coded Here." An "Excludes 1" note indicates that the code excluded should never be used at the same time as the code that is above the "Exclude 1" notation. An "Excludes 1" is used when two conditions cannot occur together, such as a congenital form versus an acquired form of the same condition.

For example:

M88 Osteitis deformans (Paget's disease of bone)
Excludes 1: Osteitis deformans in neoplastic disease (M90.6)

Excludes 2: A Type 2 Excludes represents "Not Included Here." An example note indicates that the condition excluded is not part of the condition it is excluded from, but a patient may have both conditions at the same time. In other words, do not assume that the main diagnosis includes as part of its definition the excluded diagnosis. When an "Excludes 2" note appears under a code, it is acceptable to use both the code and the excluded code together.

For example:

S60.2 Contusion of wrist and hand
Excludes 2: Contusion of fingers (S60.0-, S60.1-)

Therefore, if you have a patient who has both a contusion of the wrist and hand, and a contusion of the finger, then you need to use both the S60.2 code and the appropriate S60.0- and/or S60.1- codes.

"Code First/Use Additional Code" notes (etiology/manifestation paired codes): Certain conditions have both an underlying etiology and multiple body system manifestations due to the underlying etiology. For such conditions, ICD-10 has a coding convention that requires the underlying condition be sequenced first, followed by the manifestation.

Whenever such a combination exists, there is a "use additional code" note listed with the etiology code, and a "code first" note listed with the manifestation code. The instructional notes indicate the proper sequencing order of the codes, etiology followed by the manifestation.

In most cases, the manifestation codes will have in the code title "in diseases classified elsewhere."

Manifestation codes are never used as "first-listed" or "principal diagnosis" codes. They must be used in conjunction with the underlying condition code and must be listed following the underlying condition.

For example:

D77 Other disorders of blood and blood-forming organs in diseases classified elsewhere

First, code the underlying disease such as:

Amyloidosis (E85-)
Congenital early syphilis (A50.0)
Echinococcus (B67.0–B67.9)
Malaria (B50.0–B54)
Schistosomiasis [bilharziasis] (B65.0–B65.9)
Vitamin C deficiency (E54)

Brackets are used in ICD-10 to enclose synonyms, alternative wording, or explanatory phrases.

Manifestation codes are backed by blue highlights and describe the manifestation of an underlying disease, not the disease itself.

Secondary Only Diagnosis Edits

Certain codes may not be used as first-listed (principal) codes, rather only as secondary codes. These are not manifestation codes, but are flagged with a Maroon Flag and the number 2.

For example:

Z86.010 Personal history of colonic polyps 2

When an instructional note appears under a three-category code, it applies to all codes within that category. An instructional note under a specific code applies only to that single code.

Z Codes and Their Importance in Worker's Compensation and Personal Injury

Z codes are used for "Factors Influencing Health Status and Contact with Health Services (Z00–Z99)." Basically, these replace V codes in ICD-9.

Z codes represent reasons for encounters. A corresponding procedure code (CPT or Medicolegal codes) must accompany a Z code, if a procedure is performed. Z codes can be used in any health care setting, but it is up to the carrier's discretion on its use in Group Insurance or Medicare cases. There are different categories of Z codes as follows:

1. **Status codes** to indicate that a patient is either a carrier of a disease or has the sequelae or residual of a past disease or condition. This includes the presence of prosthetic or mechanical devices resulting from past treatment. Status may affect the course of treatment and its outcome. A status code is different from a history code. A history code indicates that the patient no longer has the condition.
2. **History (of):** There are two types of history Z codes: personal and family.
3. **Screening** is the testing for disease or disease precursors in a seemingly well individual so that early detection and treatment can be provided for those who test positive for the disease (e.g., screening mammogram). Should the condition be discovered during the screening, then the code for the condition may be assigned as an additional diagnosis or replace it.

   In ICD-9 there are multiple V codes such as "V04.1 Need for prophylactic vaccination and inoculation against smallpox," "V04.2 against measles," and so on. In ICD-10, these have all been replaced by a single code, "Z23 Encounter for immunization." The type of vaccination is shown by the CPT procedure code(s).
4. **Observation:** There are two observation Z code categories. They are used in very limited circumstances when a person is being observed for a **suspected condition that is ruled out**. They are not for use if an injury or illness or any signs or symptoms related to the suspected condition are present. In such cases, the diagnosis/symptom code is used with the corresponding external cause code. Observation codes are used as principal diagnosis only.
5. **Counseling:** Z codes are used when a patient or family member receives assistance in the aftermath of an illness or injury, or when support is required in coping with family or social problems. They are not used when the counseling component is part of the procedural description.
6. **Routine and administrative examinations:** The Z code allows for the description of encounters for routine examinations, such as check-ups, or examinations for administrative purposes, such as pre-employment physicals. Pre-existing and chronic conditions and history codes may also be

included as additional codes, as long as the examination is for purely administrative purposes, and not focused on a particular condition.

A common use would be for routine general medical examinations. These are coded with Z00.00 Encounter for General Adult medical examination without abnormal findings. In ICD-9 the code for this is V70.0.

7. **Encounters for Medical Observation:** As an example, "Z04.2 Encounter for examination and observation following work accident," or "Z04.3 Encounter for examination and observation following other accident."
8. **Nonspecific:** Z codes should be limited to those instances when there is no further documentation to permit more precise coding.

   An example would be if a pregnant patient is seen for a reason(s) unrelated to the pregnancy, the code "Z33.1 Pregnancy state, incidental" would be appropriate.

One of the major concerns for doctors working in Worker's Compensation is to establish that this is a work-related injury. For example, if they use an M code, this is not always classified as an injury code. Insurance carriers may interpret or automatically consider it as a non-Worker's Compensation case. Therefore, we need to find ways to establish that this is a Worker's Compensation case. Z codes and Y codes can be used toward this end.

One way this could be done is the use of "Z04.2 Encounter for examination and observation following work accident." This is used when an evaluation and management CPT code is billed.

For Personal Injury, you could use "Z04.1 Encounter for examination and observation following transport accident," or "Z04.3 Encounter for examination and observation following other accident."

A Basic Seven-Step Process for Diagnostic Coding

You cannot assume that you can take your diagnosis from the Alphabetic Index of Diseases Volume 2. You use it to find a possible basic code. Then you go to the Tabular List Volume 1 to confirm and define the proper ICD-10 code.

Here are the steps to follow:

Step 1: Go to the Alphabetic Index of Diseases Volume 2 and find your general condition and the corresponding ICD-10 code listed for that condition.

Step 2: Follow the corresponding code listed in Volume 2, and find its listing in the Tabular List Volume 1.

Step 3: Use the Tabular List to find the proper code, taking into consideration such things as notations, laterality, additional character requirements for specificity, and so on. (Please note: We have included crosswalks and notations at the end of this book for your convenience.)

Step 4: If necessary, go to the Alphabetic Index Volume 2 section on Alphabetic Index to External Causes.
Step 5: Find the code corresponding to the general cause of injury (not the Place of Occurrence, External Cause Status code, or Activity code, which will be covered later in our Six-Category System) for the condition in the Alphabetic Index Volume 2 section on Alphabetic Index to External Causes. In some cases, the cause of injury is solely due to an activity, and in such cases, an Activity code can be used in place of a General cause of injury code. We give an example of this in our sample case in the next section.
Step 6: Follow the corresponding code listed in Volume 2, and find its listing in the Tabular List Volume 1.
Step 7: Use the Tabular List to find the proper code, taking into consideration such things as additional character requirements for specificity, and so on.

This Seven-Step Process works well for Medicare or Group Insurance cases. But, if you are working up a Personal Injury or Worker's Compensation case, it is best to use our Six-Category System, which we will discuss in Chapter 4 (Figure 3.1).

A Basic Seven-Step Process Case Example

A patient comes into your office and complains of right elbow pain after a morning of shoveling snow off his driveway. You diagnose right elbow sprain. These are the seven steps to take you to the proper ICD-10 code for your diagnosis.

Step 1: Go to the Alphabetic Index of Diseases Volume 2 and find "Sprain." We see that there is a subcategory for "Elbow" and the corresponding ICD-10 code is S53.40.
Step 2: Now we go to the Tabular List Volume 1 and find the general description of S53.40.
Step 3: Use the Tabular List to find the proper code. Below the general code of S53.40, you find additional subcategories and classifications. For this example, we will choose to leave it as "Unspecified sprain of elbow S53.40" and add the sixth category of right elbow, thus using S53.401. For this diagnosis, a seventh category is required. We will choose A for "Initial Encounter." So, the final code to be used is S53.401A.

Please note, under category S53.-, there are "Includes" and "Excludes" listed. We need to be aware of these. For example, in this case, there is an "Excludes 2," which means that if the listed diagnosis is present, they should all be listed. In this case, the "Excludes 2" is "strain of muscle, tendon, fascia at forearm level (S56.-)." This means that if both conditions are present, then both codes should be listed.

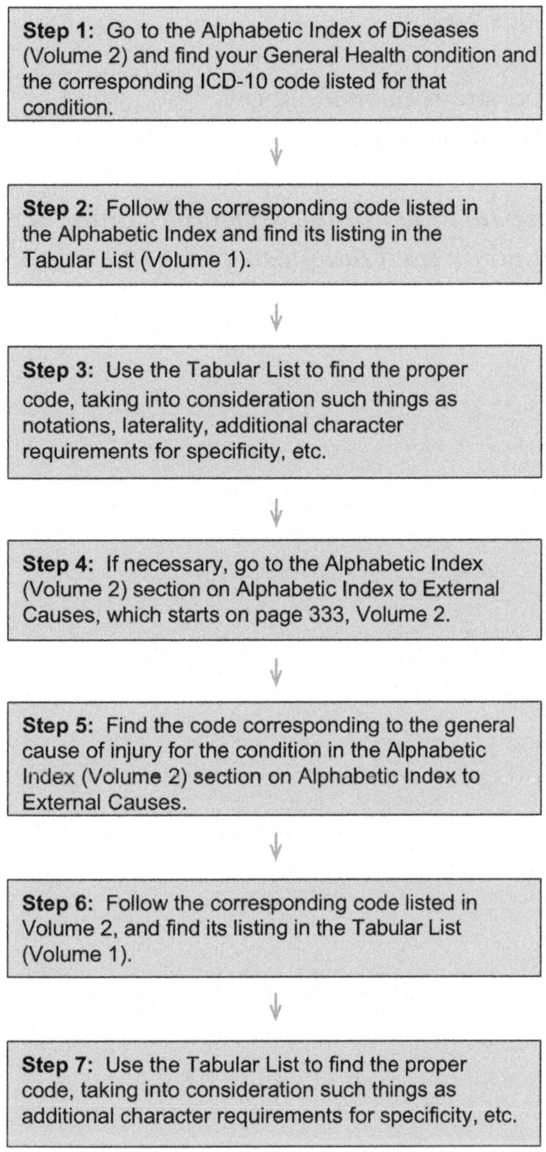

Figure 3.1 Seven-step process.

Step 4: Since this is an S code, we need to go to the Alphabetic Index Volume 2. There are two sections of concern here, one for the Alphabetic Index of Diseases and one for the Index to External Causes of Injury. It is the Alphabetic Index to External Causes of Injury we need to go to, and find the corresponding cause of the injury or activity.

Step 5: We find the code corresponding to shoveling snow, ICD-10 code Y93.H1. As mentioned before, here is a situation where an Activity code can be used to indicate the cause of injury.

Step 6: We now need to find Y93.H1 in the Tabular List Volume 1, section 20.

Step 7: We use the Tabular List to find the proper code. We note that it just states Y93.H1. No further specificity is required for this code and no further instructions are shown at the beginning of this section.

Hence, our two codes are:

S53.401A Unspecified strain of right elbow
Y93.H1 Activity, snow shoveling

Please note: We have included in the appendix common crosswalks and notations for the most commonly used diagnosis codes at the end of this book for your convenience.

Chapter 4

Chapter Four

Overview of Six-Category System for Injury Coding

We would like to introduce you to a Six-Category System of coding. ICD-10 was not designed with the United States reimbursement system in mind. Issues and incompatibilities could occur with the reimbursement system, particularly for Worker's Compensation and Personal Injury. In addition, the incredible detail and comprehensiveness of the CM book makes it very difficult to determine a starting point and system to correctly and completely code for injuries.

That is why we have created this Six-Category System and the Seven-Step Process to help you work through injury coding.

Injury coding is completely different from Non-Injury coding. There are many more decisions that need to be made in regard to Worker's Compensation and Personal Injury. The standard code that you would use, for example with Medicare health conditions, may not be an injury code, and could cause havoc in the Worker's Compensation and Personal Injury arena. We are trying to avoid electronic edits that would deny your reimbursement and put your patient's case at risk. We want to limit the chance of denied claims.

This Six-Category System is our method to further this goal.

There are six separate categories of diagnosis codes in ICD-10, which need to be addressed when coding injuries.

These are:

Category 1: Z codes
Category 2: Health Condition codes
Category 3: External Cause codes
Category 4: Place of Occurrence codes
Category 5: Activity codes
Category 6: External Cause Status codes

First, we will discuss each category and give an explanation. Then, in the section titled Six-Category System: Step-by-Step Process, we will give examples.

Our first category is "Z" codes. These are defined as "Factors influencing health status and contact with health services (Z00-Z99)." This is in Chapter 21 of the CM book.

Z codes represent reasons for encounters, for example, when a person who may or may not be sick encounters the health services for some specific purpose, such as to receive limited care or service for a current condition.

Injury coding may focus more on the first portion of this chapter, codes Z00 through Z13, specifically Z04.

Z04 is defined as "Encounter for examination and observation for other reasons." This has an "Includes" notation stating it includes "Encounter for examination for medicolegal reasons." It goes on to say that this category is also for use for "Administrative and legal observation status."

Of the Z04 codes, we are mainly concerned with Z04.1, Z04.2, and Z04.3.

Z04.2 is the code we would use for a Worker's Compensation case. It is defined as "Encounter for examination and observation following work accident." Thus, by using this code and listing it first, we are designating this case as a Worker's Compensation case.

For Personal Injuries, we have Z04.1 and Z04.3.

Z04.1 is defined as "Encounter for examination and observation following transport accident." Thus, we would use it for our Personal Injury cases involving transport vehicles, for example, cars and buses.. Z04.3 is defined as "Encounter for examination and observation following other accident." This code would be used for all other Personal Injury cases not involving transport vehicles. Thus, by using these codes and listing them first, we are designating this case as a Personal Injury case.

The next category, or Category 2, is the Health Condition codes section. Health Conditions are what we usually think of when referring to diagnoses: that is, the health condition for which the patient is seeing the doctor, for example, fracture of a bone, laceration, or a posttraumatic stress disorder.

This is a very large section of the CM book, and it will take some effort and time to get familiar with this section. This category of codes is broken up into Sections A through T in the Tabular List (Volume 1) of the CM book, which is covered in Chapters 1 through 19.

Here, we show the complete list of different sections for the Health Condition codes.

The CM book has color-coded tabs labeled by such categories as:

Neoplasms: orange
Endocrine, Nutritional, and Metabolic: green
Circulatory System: yellow
Musculoskeletal System and Connective Tissue: red
Injury, Poisoning and External Causes: red

(Please note the actual title should be ""Injury, Poisoning and Consequences of External Causes.")

External Cause of Morbidity codes are covered in Chapter 20. They are broken up into four sections:

1. External Cause codes
2. Place of Occurrence codes
3. Activity codes
4. External Cause Status codes

External Cause of Morbidity codes are intended to provide data for injury research and evaluation of injury prevention strategies.

Morbidity can be defined as, "a diseased state, disability, or poor health," or "the quality of being unhealthful, morbid, sometimes including the cause." Additional definitions include, "the incidence of a disease, as a rate of a population which is affected," "an occurrence of illness or disease, or a single symptom of that illness," and "adverse effects caused by a medical treatment such as surgery."

All of these definitions are encompassed by codes in the External Cause of Morbidity section of the ICD-10-CM book.

The ICD-10-CM book states: *There is no National requirement for mandatory ICD-10-CM external cause code reporting. Unless a provider is subject to a state-based external cause code reporting mandate or these codes are required by a particular payer, reporting of ICD-10-CM codes in Chapter 20, External Causes of Morbidity, is not required.*

The ICD-10-CM book may state this, but we do not know what the Worker's Compensation and Personal Injury carriers will expect, or require. At any time, any one of the 1600 carriers could make this part of their policy requirements, and you may not even be aware that this is the reason your claims are being denied. Therefore, it is our belief that they will eventually incorporate this coding and, thus, providers should implement it from the beginning.

The ICD-10-CM book also states "providers are encouraged to voluntarily report external cause codes, as they provide valuable data for injury research and evaluation of injury prevention strategies."

The term "External Cause" seems to be used within the ICD-10-CM book to refer to three separate sections. Those sections are:

1. External Cause codes: These are the true External Cause codes and part of the section External Cause of Morbidity.
2. The other External Cause of Morbidity codes: These are Place of Occurrence codes, Activity codes, and Status codes.
3. Chapter 19 Injury, Poisoning, and Certain Other Consequences of External Causes.

The provider needs to be aware of this loose use of the term "External Cause" and determine which actual section the ICD-10-CM book is referring to.

The External Causes of Morbidity codes should never be sequenced as the first-listed or principal diagnosis.

Now, let's discuss each of the four sections of External Cause of Morbidity codes separately.

Our Category 3 is the External Cause codes section. These include V, W, X, and Y00 to Y84.9 codes and starts in Chapter 21.

These codes capture how the injury or health condition happened (e.g., cause), as well as the intent (e.g., unintentional or accidental; or intentional, such as suicide or assault). These codes tell you what actually caused the health condition, or how the health condition came about, for example, slip and fall, or vehicular accident.

An External Cause code can never be a principal (e.g., first-listed) diagnosis.

Where a code from this section is applicable, it is intended that it shall be used secondarily to a code from another chapter of the classification indicating the nature of the condition.

Most often, the condition will be classifiable to Chapter 19, Injury, Poisoning and Certain Other Consequences of External Causes (S00-T88). Other conditions that may be stated to be due to external causes are classified in Chapters 1 through 18. For these conditions, codes from Chapter 20 should be used to provide additional information as to the cause of the condition.

This category has an implied intent. You may see intent referred to in other publications, so we will discuss that here as well.

There is the implied intent under the heading "accidents." This is actually an implied lack of intent. This applies to all codes defined as an "accident."

Two other categories of intent are "self-harm" and "assault" (Figure 4.1).

Self-harm external cause codes are covered in sections X71 to X 83.
Assault external cause codes are covered in sections X92 to Y08.
Events of undetermined intent are in section Y20 to Y33.
Other categories of intent are covered in Y35 to Y84.

Category 4 is the Place of Occurrence codes section. They are designated by the three-category codes, "Y92 Place of occurrence of the external cause."

This category is for use, when relevant, to identify the place of occurrence of the external cause. That is to say, this code may not always be relevant, but we recommend you use it whenever possible to avoid computer edits. In Worker's Compensation cases and Personal Injury cases, the place of occurrence is ALWAYS relevant.

The ICD-10-CM book states in Chapter 20 that the place of occurrence should be recorded only at the initial encounter for treatment. It is our view that it should be recorded for all encounters, primarily because multiple facilities are seeing portions of your paperwork, and are not necessarily always seeing the initial encounter paperwork.

V00-X58	Accidents
V00-V99	Transport accidents
V00-V09	Pedestrian injured in transport accident
V10-V19	Pedal cycle rider injured in transport accident
V20-V29	Motorcycle rider injured in transport accident
V30-V39	Occupant of three-wheeled motor vehicle injured in transport accident
V40-V49	Car occupant injured in transport accident
V50-V59	Occupant of pick-up truck or van injured in transport accident
V60-V69	Occupant of heavy transport vehicle injured in transport accident
V70-V79	Bus occupant injured in transport accident
V80-V89	Other land transport accidents
V90-V94	Water transport accidents
V95-V97	Air and space transport accidents
V98-V99	Other and unspecified transport accidents
W00-X58	Other external causes of accidental injury
W00-W19	Slipping, tripping, stumbling and falls
W20-W49	Exposure to inanimate mechanical forces
W50-W64	Exposure to animate mechanical forces
W65-W74	Accidental non-transport drowning and submersion
W85-W99	Exposure to electric current, radiation and extreme ambient air temperature and pressure
X00-X08	Exposure to smoke, fire and flames
X10-X19	Contact with heat and hot substances
X30-X39	Exposure to forces of nature
X52, X58	Accidental exposure to other specified factors
X71-X83	Intentional self-harm
X92-Y08	Assault
Y21-Y33	Event of undetermined intent
Y35-Y38	Legal intervention, operations of war, military operations, and terrorism
Y62-Y84	Complications of medical and surgical care
Y62-Y69	Misadventures to patients during surgical and medical care
Y70-Y82	Medical devices associated with adverse incidents in diagnostic and therapeutic use
Y83-Y84	Surgical and other medical procedures as the cause of abnormal reaction of the patient, or of later complication, without mention of misadventure at the time of the procedure
Y90-Y99	Supplementary factors related to causes of morbidity classified elsewhere

Figure 4.1

Regardless of the number of External Cause codes (Category 3) assigned, there should be only one Place of Occurrence code.

The Place of Occurrence codes are broken up into four- and five-digit categories that can be quickly scanned to guide you to the more specific six-digit codes.

Category 5 is the Activity codes section, designated by the three-digit code Y93.

Assign a code from category Y93, Activity code, to describe the activity of the patient at the time that the injury or other health condition occurred.

An activity code is used only once, at the initial encounter for treatment, but, once again, we recommend you use it whenever possible for the same reasons stated previously regarding place of occurrence.

Only one code from Y93 should be recorded on a medical record.

Category Y93 is provided to indicate the activity of the person seeking health care for an injury or health condition. External Causes, as discussed in Category 3, are what actually caused the injury, while Activities are what the patient was doing at the time the External Cause caused the injury. For example, the patient may have been involved in the "activity" of "food preparation" when the "external cause"—"slipping and falling"—took place.

In the beginning of the Y93 section, there is an index of all the four-digit subcategories. This allows you to quickly determine which four-digit code applies to your case, and then you can quickly determine the higher specificity code by going to that four-digit code section.

The final category is Category 6, External Cause Status codes section. These are designated as "Y99 External cause status."

A single code from category Y99 should be used in conjunction with the External Cause code(s) assigned to a record to indicate the status of the person at the time the event occurred.

There are five choices in this category, all of which are four-digit codes. The most commonly used codes for Worker's Compensation and Personal Injury are:

Y99.0 Civilian activity done for income or pay—which can be used for Worker's Compensation
and
Y99.8 Other external cause status (includes Activity Not Elsewhere Classified)—which can be used for Personal Injury
The other Status codes are:
Y99.1 Military activity
Y99.2 Volunteer activity
Y99.9 Unspecified external cause status

The ICD-10-CM book states that the External Cause, Place of Occurrence, Activity, and External Causes Status codes should be used in conjunction with each other. This is why we have included all four in our system for coding injuries.

Six-Category System: Step-by-Step Process

Now, we will discuss the step-by-step process of coding for each of the six categories. It is important that we include all six categories when coding injuries.

Category 1: Find the Correct Z Code

The possible Z codes for a personal injury are Z04.1 and Z04.3.

Z04.1 Encounter for examination and observation following transport accident
Z04.3 Encounter for examination and observation following other accident

If we have a Worker's Compensation case, then we would use "Z04.2 Encounter for examination and observation following work accident."

Category 2: Find the Correct Health Condition Code(s)

Here, we utilize the first three steps from our Seven-Step Process, reviewed previously in Chapter 3 (Figure 4.2).

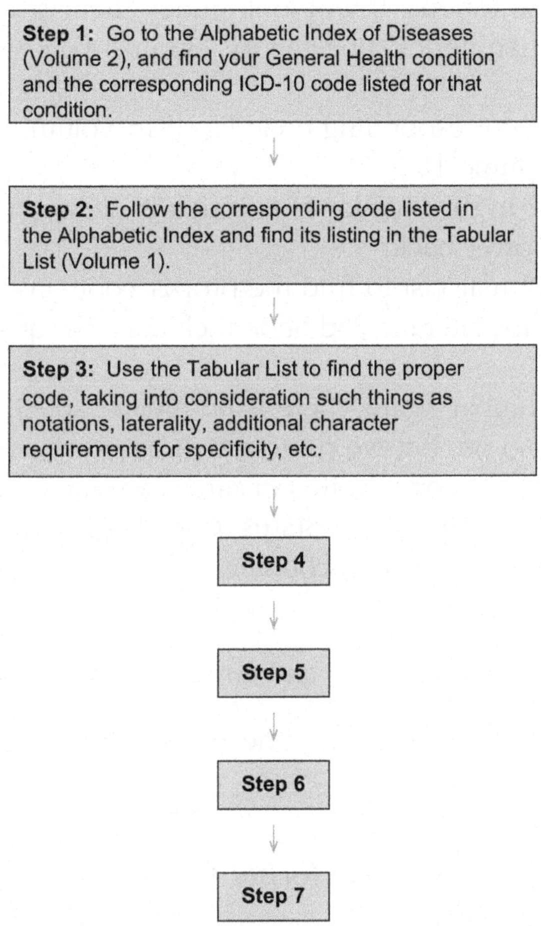

Figure 4.2 Seven-step process.

Those steps are:

Step 1: Go to the Alphabetic Index of Diseases (Volume 2) and find your general health condition and the corresponding ICD-10 code listed for that condition.

For example, let's say we have lumbar strain. Go to Volume 2, Alphabetic Index of Diseases, and you will find "strain." Within this category you find "low back S39.012."

Please note, this section of the Alphabetic Index of Diseases has a limited number of strain classifications. If you look under "Injury," and then under subcategories "Muscle," then under subcategory "Strain," you will find a more extensive list of strains.

Step 2: Follow the corresponding code listed in Volume 2, and find its listing in the Tabular List (Volume 1).

So, we find S39.012 in the Tabular List, which is defined as "Strain of muscle, fascia and tendon of lower back."

Step 3: Use the Tabular List to find the proper code, taking into consideration such things as notations, laterality, additional character requirements for specificity, and so on.

In this case, with lumbar strain, there is no greater specificity as far as anatomical location, and so on, but we must remember to review the guidelines at the beginning of the sections. In this instance, we must include a seventh-character code to indicate Encounter Status. Our choices are A, D, or S. For our example, we will use A for initial encounter.

Thus, our code becomes:

- S39.012A Strain of muscle, fascia, and tendon of lower back—initial encounter

You would repeat this process for all necessary Health Condition codes for the case.

Category 3: Find the Correct External Cause Code(s)

Here, we utilize the next four steps from our Seven-Step Process reviewed previously (Figure 4.3). Those steps are:

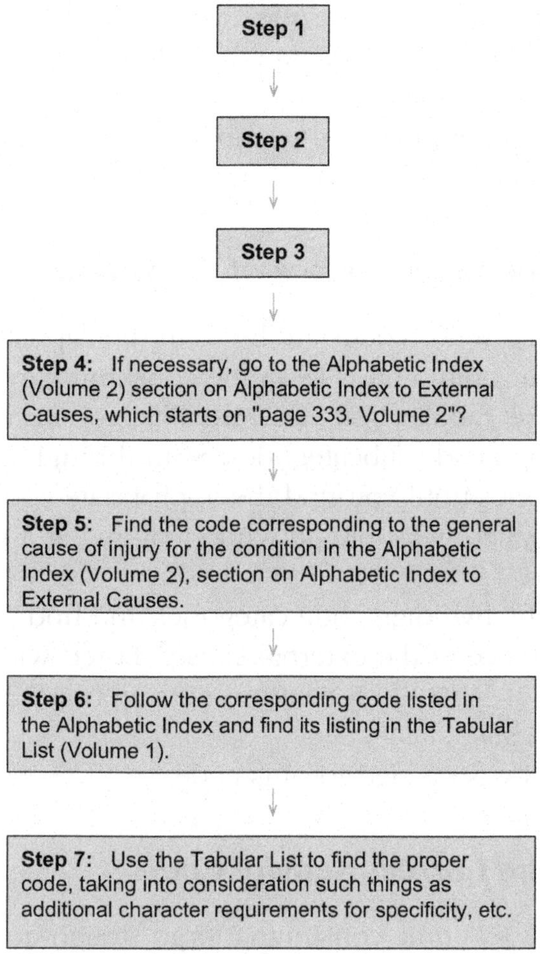

Figure 4.3 Seven-step process.

Step 4: If necessary, go to the Alphabetic Index (Volume 2) section on Alphabetic Index to External Causes.

Step 5: Find the code corresponding to the general cause of injury for the condition in the Alphabetic Index to External Causes.

Let's assume our patient injured his low back when he slipped without falling and, more specifically, while walking down a staircase. We look under "slipping" in the Alphabetic Index to External Causes and find "slipping." In the subcategories, we find "slipping without fall" and further defined by "Stepping from one level to another W18.43."

Step 6: Follow the corresponding code listed in Volume 2, and we find its listing in the Tabular List (Volume 1). We find W18.43.

- W18.43 Slipping, tripping and stumbling without falling due to stepping from one level to another

Step 7: Use the Tabular List to find the proper code, taking into consideration such things as additional character requirements for specificity, and so on.

Once again, in this case, we must include a seventh-character code to indicate Encounter Status. Thus, our code becomes:

- W18.43XA Slipping, tripping, and stumbling without falling due to stepping from one level to another—Initial encounter

Category 4: Find the Correct Place of Occurrence Code

Although Place of Occurrence codes are listed in the Alphabetic Index to External Causes, in our opinion it is less time consuming to go straight to Section Y92 of Volume 1 of the Tabular List. Here, the Place of Occurrence codes are broken up into five-digit code subcategories. Scan through the possible choices of five-digit subcategories until you find the appropriate code.

Let's assume our patient was injured while working at a nursing home, specifically in the kitchen.

We scan through the five-digit code categories and find "Y92.12 Nursing home as the place of occurrence of the external cause." Listed within this category is a more specific coding of "Y92.120 Kitchen in nursing home as the place of occurrence of the external cause."

No further specificity is needed for this code.

Category 5: Find the Correct Activity Code

Once again, we find it less time consuming to go straight to Section Y93 of Volume 1 of the Tabular List, where the Activity codes are listed. There is a useful index on the first page, which we can use to guide us to the appropriate four-digit code. Once we have that, we use it to find the more specific code, if applicable.

For our example, we find "Y93.G Activities involving food preparation, cooking and grilling."

Once in that section, we find further specification of the Activity. For our example, we will use "Y93.G9 Activity, other involving cooking and grilling."

No further specificity is required.

Category 6: Find the Correct Status Code

Again, we go straight to Section Y99 of Volume 1 of the Tabular List, where the External Cause Status codes are listed. There are only five categories of four-digit codes to choose from.

As stated previously, the most commonly used codes for Worker's Compensation and Personal Injury are:

Y99.0 Civilian activity done for income or pay—which can be used for Worker's Compensation

and
Y99.8 Other external cause status (includes Activity Not Elsewhere Classified)—which can be used for Personal Injury

In our example, it is a Worker's Compensation case, and therefore we would use:

- Y99.0 Civilian activity done for income or pay

Here is a basic flowchart of the Six-Category Process for injury coding. Please take a moment to review (Figure 4.4).

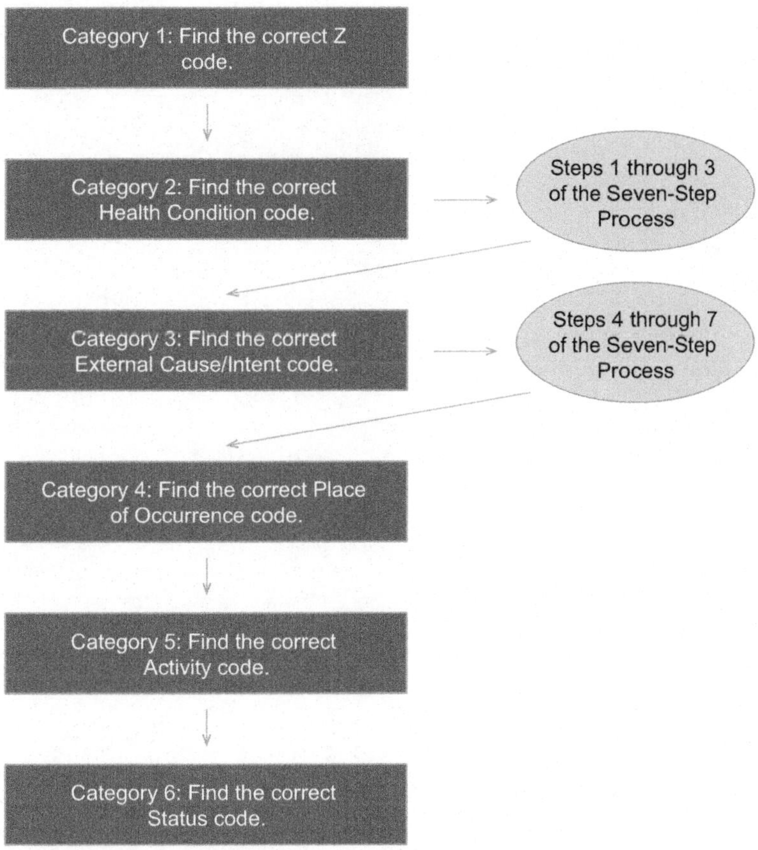

Figure 4.4 Injury coding.

Note: All accidents involving vehicles, whether motorized or not, are found under the subheading "Accident Transport."

In the ICD-10-CM book, it states text as shown in Figure 4.5

d. ***Place of Occurrence, Activity, and Status Codes Used with other External Cause Code***
When applicable, place of occurrence, activity, and external cause status codes are sequenced after the main external cause code(s).

Figure 4.5

Chapter 5

Chapter Five

Combination Codes

One reason for more ICD-10 codes than for ICD-9 codes is that ICD-10 has been expanded to facilitate the identification of associated complications, with what are called Combination Codes. A Combination Code is a single code used to classify two diagnoses, or a diagnosis with an associated manifestation or complication. You should assign only the combination code that fully identifies the diagnostic conditions that are being documented.

Combination Codes pose difficulties that did not exist in ICD-9 because they represent multiple codes in ICD-9, or codes that include manifestations and/or complications. The reason for Combination Codes becomes evident if you review statistics from some Centers for Medicare and Medicaid (CMS) (*Office of Information Products and Data Analytics, Medicare & Medicaid Research Review 2013: Volume 3, Number 3*), as follow.

"It is estimated that one in four Americans have at least two chronic conditions that require ongoing medical care. Over two-thirds of Medicare beneficiaries in traditional Medicare, also known as fee-for-service, have two or more chronic conditions. The co-occurrence of chronic conditions has far-reaching implications for treatment, coordination of care, and health care costs. About one in seven (14%) of traditional Medicare patients have six or more chronic conditions, accounting for almost half of total Medicare spending."

Combination Codes appear throughout ICD-10. Providers should try to identify them for their practices in order to preclude problems associated with using GEM (General Equivalency Mapping) tools in converting ICD-9 codes to ICD-10 codes.

The Alphabetic Index of Diseases will indicate combination codes by referring to subterm entries. For example:

Lumbago, lumbalgia M54.5
    with sciatica M54.4

This is another reason why it is important to look at the Alphabetic Index first when going through your code determination process.

The Alphabetic Index of Diseases also includes helpful hints, like sub-terms such as "with," "due to," "in," or "associated with" to denote when a combination code may be applicable.

A Combination Code indicates that there is/are co-morbidities assumed to be present and the correct ICD-10 code *must* be selected to identity the co-morbidity.

As an example, it is very common to see claims for office visits with a diagnosis of diabetes as follows:

CPT 99213 Office visit, established patient
ICD-9 Diagnosis 250.00 Diabetes without mention of complication or manifestation

This type of claim will probably not be paid in ICD-10 for the following reasons:

1. Every diabetes mellitus diagnosis code is now a combination code.
2. Every type of diabetes must be identified as Type 1, Type 2, secondary, or due to an underlying condition or induced by drug or chemical, or pregnancy induced.
3. If the type is not specified, the default is Type 2, which may or may not be correct.
4. Based on the ICD-10 code, the provider may be directed to use an additional code(s) to identify manifestation, for example, diabetic glaucoma (H40–H42).
5. For diabetes due to an underlying condition, you must first code the underlying condition, such as cystic fibrosis (E84.-).
6. For drug or chemical induced diabetes mellitus, you must first code the poisoning due to drug or toxin (T36–T65). This category also requires the adverse effect, if applicable, to identify the drug (T36–T50).
7. If there is Insulin Use, you must specify this by adding code Z79.4.
8. Every diabetes code that applies to the patient condition should be listed. Therefore, if a Type 2 patient also has manifestations due to drug(s) or chemical(s), all applicable codes should be listed.

Not all diagnosis codes present the issues shown for diabetes. However, it is important that the provider's staff identify combination codes and other potential problem areas.

Due to the complexity of diabetes codes, flowcharts are provided to assist you in determining the correct diagnosis codes.

In our view, ICD-10 has two main types of Combination Codes. Those that are organized in a "flowchart"-type format, like diabetes and rheumatoid arthritis, and those Combination Codes that are found individually, or as a small group, throughout the ICD-10 CM book.

For example:

J35.01 Chronic tonsillitis
J35.02 Chronic adenoiditis
J35.03 Chronic tonsillitis and adenoiditis

The next section gives examples for many of the specialties that show differing issues and complications of coding with combination codes in ICD-10.

Cardiovascular System

One ICD-10 Code Representing Two ICD-9 Codes

The ICD-10 text shows certain codes such as I25.11-, which list multiple ICD-9 codes below them preceded by a + sign. The Combination Code is a combination of the ICD-9 codes, for example:

I25.110 Atherosclerotic heart disease of native coronary artery with unstable angina pectoris
+ 411.1 Intermediate coronary syndrome (414.01)
+ 414.01 Coronary atherosclerosis of native coronary artery (411.1)

One ICD-9 Code Translating into Three ICD-10 Codes

Combination Codes clearly demonstrate problems in using GEM tools to convert ICD-9 codes to ICD-10 codes. A GEM tool found on the Internet shows the conversion of ICD-9 code 414.1 to:

I25.3 Aneurysm of heart

and

I25.41 Coronary artery aneurysm

and

I25.42 Coronary artery dissection

As you can see, the ICD-9 code of 414.1 is fairly nonspecific. ICD-10 breaks this into multiple possible codes for increased specificity.

A problem can arise when trying to use a GEM tool to convert the ICD-9 code of 414.01 to an ICD-10 code. In the GEM tool we used, it gave us "I25.10 Atherosclerotic heart disease of native coronary artery without angina pectoris, but we did not indicate whether angina pectoris was present or not. You may inadvertently include that in the diagnosis, even though it is not present in your patient, by using a GEM tool in this manner. This is the increased specificity and use of combination codes of ICD-10, which requires us to confirm that the data in the descriptive portion of the ICD-10 accurately represent the patient's diagnosis.

The GEM tool provided the following ICD-9 conversion of 414.01 to "I25.10 Atherosclerotic heart disease of native coronary artery without angina pectoris."

As shown, the GEM tool has problems with Combination Codes.

Dermatology/Family Practice and Others

A review of ICD-10 shows that there are a great number of Combination Codes. Some of them are clearly stated to be Combination Codes in the ICD-10-CM book.

For example, L89 has the following statement in the guidelines directly following its listing in the ICD-10-CM book: *Codes from category L89, pressure ulcer, are combination codes that identify the site of the pressure ulcer as well as the stage of the ulcer.*

In this case, the first ICD-9 code is the "site of the pressure ulcer" and the second ICD-9 code is the "stage of the pressure ulcer." For example:

707.03 Pressure ulcer, lower back
707.21 Pressure ulcer, stage 1

These are represented by the single code in ICD-10 of "L89.131 Pressure ulcer of right lower back, stage 1."

Note: As you can see, there is even greater specificity of location in ICD-10, by signifying it as "right" lower back.

In this example of a Combination Code, ICD-10 can interpret it being a Combination Code for two different reasons. One, because two ICD-9 codes are combined into one ICD-10 code; OR, because it is a diagnosis (pressure ulcer) with an associated manifestation or complication (stage of ulcer).

It should be noted that although the explanatory notes prior to this subsection state they are Combination Codes, not all the codes have the combining ICD-9 codes below them because there were no equivalent ICD-9 codes to combine per se. For example:

L89.221 Pressure ulcer of left hip stage 1

Emergency Medicine/Hospitalist

Most codes in Chapter 19 Injury, Poisoning and Certain Other Consequences of External Causes (S00-T86) can be considered Combination Codes in Emergency Medicine, because the nature of these injuries cannot be easily diagnosed or specified, for example:

S06.318 Contusion and laceration of right cerebrum with loss of consciousness of any duration with death due to other cause prior to regaining consciousness

Endocrinology/Gastroenterologist

Intraoperative complications of the endocrine system are described with subcategory E36- codes, for example:

> E36.01 Intraoperative hemorrhage and hematoma of an endocrine system organ or structure complicating an endocrine system procedure

Geriatrics

When osteoporosis occurs with current pathological fractures, there are specific Combination Codes for these, for example:

> M80.061- Age-related osteoporosis with current pathological fracture, right lower leg

It is combining two diagnoses, osteoporosis and pathological fracture.

Internal Medicine/General Practice

The ICD-10-CM book states: "Combination codes for MRSA infections when a patient is diagnosed with an infection that is due to methicillin resistant staphylococcus aureus (MRSA), and that infection has a combination code that includes the causal organism (e.g., sepsis, pneumonia) assign the appropriate combination code for the condition."

"A41.02 Sepsis due to methicillin resistant staphylococcus aureus" is a combination code because it identifies the type of MRSA (methicillin resistant *Staphylococcus aureus*) and the type of infection.

Another example of a Combination Code is "J35.03 Chronic tonsillitis and adenoiditis."

ICD-10 clearly differentiates between tonsillitis and adenoiditis, but it also recognizes that both can occur at the same time.

> J35.01 Chronic tonsillitis
> J35.02 Chronic adenoiditis
> J35.03 Chronic tonsillitis and adenoiditis

Oncology

Many codes used by oncologists are Combination Codes because they specify the type of neoplasm, site, and other specific information, for example:

> C82.21 Follicular lymphoma grade iii, unspecified, lymph nodes of head, face and neck

These codes are combining "Site of lymphoma" and "Grade of lymphoma."

Ophthalmology

In ophthalmology, "Glaucoma secondary to eye trauma codes (H40.4-)" are Combination Codes. For example:

> H40.31 Glaucoma secondary to eye trauma, right eye

Another example:

> H40.41X1 Glaucoma secondary to eye inflammation, right eye, mild stage

Please note: These codes show greater specificity by specifying the disease (glaucoma), the eye (right or left), and a seventh character used to specify the stage of glaucoma (0–4). An X is used as a place holder for the sixth character.

In the case of subcategory H40.4, the ICD-10 book has no notation that these are Combination Codes even though they clearly meet the definition. If you look up glaucoma in the Alphabetic Index of Diseases, it uses the terms "due to" and "with," which we stated earlier is an indication that these are Combination Codes.

Orthopedics

Orthopedists must be aware that there are Combination Codes for knee injuries that differentiate current versus old tear or injury, for example:

> M23.211 Derangement of anterior horn of medial meniscus due to old tear or injury, right knee

This is a Combination Code because it is combining the "derangement" and the "old knee injury/tear."

Pain Management Specialist

Pain is a complex subject for which we have created a separate pain-discussion chapter. Like other specialties, it has specific combination codes, such as:

> T88.52X- Failed moderate sedation during procedure

This is a Combination Code as it codes "sedation" and the complication of failure.

Pediatrics

As with family and general practices, this specialty deals with many conditions and Combination Codes throughout ICD-10 such as:

E10- Type 1 Diabetes was previously known as juvenile diabetes because it is usually diagnosed in children and young adults
G40.B01 Juvenile myoclonic epilepsy, not intractable, with stable epilepticus

Podiatry

This specialty treats feet and their ailments and has relevant Combination Codes such as:

I70.25 Atherosclerosis of native arteries of the extremities with ulceration

Primary Care

Gout

Chronic gout (M1A-) codes are Combination Codes because they specify the disease type, for example, idiopathic, anatomic location, and whether or not there is tophus, for example:

M1A.3111 Chronic gout due to renal impairment, right shoulder with tophus

Please note: This is an unusual use of the seventh-character code to specify the presence or absence of tophus.

Lumbago and Sciatica

When both lumbago and sciatica occur together in a patient, there is a specific Combination Code to be used.

M54.41 Lumbago with sciatica, right side
+ 724.2 Lumbago (724.3)
+ 723.3 Sciatica (724.2)

Obstetrics and Gynecology

Diabetes in Pregnancy

Diabetes mellitus codes are generally in subcategory E08-E13; however, there is a major exception for diabetes mellitus when it occurs in pregnant women. This is a major complication and ICD-10 calls for codes from this section to be followed by the appropriate code(s) from E08-E13.

Codes in Section O24- are Combination Codes because they describe the condition (pregnancy), the diabetes type, and the trimester, for example:

O24.111 Pre-existing diabetes mellitus, Type 2, in pregnancy, first trimester

Complications Specific to Multiple Gestation (O31-)

Codes in subcategory O31- are Combination Codes because they specify the specific problem and trimester, and the seventh character specifies the specific fetus, for example:

O31.01 Papyraceous fetus, first trimester, fetus 1

Here, we have a case where the code is specifying pregnancy, and a complication of the pregnancy, and thus falls under the definition of Combination Code.

Maternal Care for Malpresentation of Fetus (O32-)

Codes in subcategory O32- are Combination Codes because they specify the type of malpresentation and the specific fetus, for example:

O32.1X3 Maternal care for breech presentation fetus 3

Psychiatry and Psychology

ICD-10 Chapter 5 contains diagnosis codes for mental and behavioral disorders. A large number of these are Combination Codes, such as:

F13.151 Sedative, hypnotic or anxiolytic abuse with sedative, hypnotic or anxiolytic-induced psychotic disorder with hallucinations
F10.250 Alcohol dependence with alcohol induced psychotic disorder with delusions

Physical dependence and addiction often result in mental illnesses, and therefore often involve Combination Codes.

Pulmonology

There are many Combination Codes that may be relevant for Pulmonary Function Testing including:

C34.81 Malignant neoplasm of overlapping sites of right bronchus and lung

The ICD-10-CM book states: "Primary malignant neoplasm overlapping site boundaries: A primary malignant neoplasm that overlaps two or more contiguous (next to each other) sites should be classified to the subcategory/code .8 (and 'overlapping lesion'), unless the combination is specifically indexed elsewhere."

Radiology

This specialty has many applicable diagnosis codes used to identify and treat diseases. An example of Combination Codes is:

M61.311 Calcification and ossification of muscles associated with burns, right shoulder

Rheumatology and Related

Systemic lupus (M32-) has Combination Codes with combining ICD-9 codes listed. These include:

M32.11	Endocarditis in systemic lupus erythematosus
+ 424.91	Endocarditis in disease classified elsewhere (714.0)
+ 710.0	Systemic lupus erythematosus (424.91)

And M32.12-M32.15

It could be argued that many "Rheumatoid arthritis with rheumatoid factor (M05-)" codes are also Combination Codes, because they specify anatomic sites and list type of rheumatic disease, such as lung disease, vasculitis, and polyneuropathy. An example is as follows:

M05.571 Rheumatoid polyneuropathy with rheumatoid arthritis of right ankle and foot

This ICD-10 code cross-references the following ICD-9 codes using a GEM tool.

357.1 Neuropathy in collagen vascular disease

and

714.0 Rheumatoid arthritis

Since ICD-9 codes in different subsections appear, this would indicate a combination.

Urology

N49.3 Fournier gangrene appears with specific ICD-9 codes as follows:

+ 728.86 Necrotizing fasciitis and
+ 785.4 Gangrene (728.86)

Since this often occurs with diabetes, it can be a complicating factor in diabetes and listed along with a diabetes code. This code is restricted to males in ICD-10.

ENT (Otolaryngology)

There are codes listed in subsection "H90 Other disorders of the ear," that are listed followed by codes marked as approximate in ICD-9, for example:

H90.5 Unspecified sensorineural hearing loss
389.10 Sensorineural hearing loss, unspecified
389.11 Central hearing loss
389.16 Sensorineural hearing loss, asymmetrical

Since ICD-10 H90.5 is marked with three "equivalent" codes, it would appear that it is a combination of the three ICD-9 codes.

Surgery: General

There are a great number of Surgery Combination Codes. These are now more numerous due to the requirements of specificity and laterality. An example is represented by the following code for **gallbladder surgery**.

K80.61 Calculus of gallbladder and bile duct with cholecystitis, unspecified with obstruction

Codes for hemorrhoids in ICD-9 have become Combination Codes in ICD-10 because ICD-10 codes include hemorrhoids and the complications. The following are the new ICD-10 codes:

K64.0 First degree hemorrhoids
K64.1 Second degree hemorrhoids
K64.2 Third degree hemorrhoids
K64.3 Fourth degree hemorrhoids

Please note: The "degree" of the hemorrhoid is specified.
Other codes for hemorrhoids include the following:

K64.4 Residual hemorrhoid skin tags
K64.5 Perianal venous thrombosis: External hemorrhoids with thrombosis, perianal hematoma, thrombosed hemorrhoids, NOS
K64.8 Other hemorrhoids
K64.9 Unspecified hemorrhoids

Toxicology/Internal Medicine and General Medicine

"Poisoning by adverse effects of and underdosing of drugs, medicaments and biological substances (T36–T50):" codes in these subsections are all Combination

Codes. They include the substances taken as well as the intent. No additional external cause code is required for these codes. Codes for these categories are sequenced first, followed by the code(s) that specify the nature of the adverse effect, poisoning, or toxic effect. This sequencing instruction does not apply to underdosing codes (fifth or sixth character 6, for instance "T36.0X6 Underdosing of penicillins").

Nephrology and Cardiology

"I13.0 Hypertensive heart and chronic kidney disease with heart failure and stage 1 through stage 4 chronic kidney disease or unspecified chronic kidney disease:" this appears to be a multiple combination Combination Codes. There are five possible kidney disease codes, (N18-), which could occur with heart failure (I11-).

There Are Many Possible Combination Codes

Codes marked as "equivalent" appear through ICD-10. When these occur, extra care should be taken when using GEM tools to cross reference ICD-9 to ICD-10 codes. Even when there are no codes marked as "equivalent," there are many Combination Codes. Providers and coders must review codes applicable to their practice to determine which codes are Combination Codes.

It is recognized that making specific diagnosis may require specialist knowledge. To that end, ICD-10 generally has fourth- and fifth-position codes for "Other" and "Unspecified" codes. Patients can then be referred to appropriate specialists to determine what code(s) is appropriate.

Other Provider Requirements for ICD-10

The provider must be cognizant that ICD-10 requires active and knowledgeable documentation and communication of the patient's condition to billing and coding staff.

The current common practice of a provider simply checking a diagnosis code(s) and procedure code(s) on a charge ticket will no longer suffice. The level of detail and requirement to identify co-morbidities requires a much higher level of documentation and communication with billers and coders.

Seventh-Character Codes

The provider must be aware of the issues posed by seventh-character ICD-10 codes. A seventh character is an Encounter Status Indicator. This represents an aspect of the specific encounter that only the provider can identity and document. Not all ICD-10 codes have a seventh character, but when one exists it must be specified. Following are common examples.

A patient presents with a lumbar sprain. The ICD-10 code is: S33.8XXA, D, or S.

S33.8XXA Indicates that the patient is seen for an initial encounter. If a patient is being treated for the sprain, for example, physical therapy, the diagnosis code remains the same because the letter "A" also indicates active treatment if the patient is being treated.
S33.8XXD Indicates that a patient is being seen for a subsequent encounter. There is no longer active treatment.
S33.8XXS Specifies that the patient's condition is sequela, or produced after the acute phase of an illness, injury or disease. It may have occurred as a result of an earlier accident. There is no time limit as to when the sequelae can appear. It can appear early, as with a stroke, or can occur years later as in arthritis following an injury.

The use of the seventh-character code S can be very important in Worker's Compensation where it can represent a compensable consequence.

Only the provider knows which seventh character is appropriate. The practice must identify which diagnosis codes have seventh characters that are relevant to it.

Greater Level of Detail Required

When coding diagnosis for digits or other anatomic locations, the level of detail required has increased. Following are codes for "Non-displaced fracture of proximal phalanx of finger:"

S62.640 Non-displaced fracture of proximal phalanx of right index finger
S62.641 Non-displaced fracture of proximal phalanx of left index finger

There are separate codes for displaced fracture of proximal phalanx, non-displaced fracture of distal phalanx of right index finger, and so on.

ICD-10 provides a mechanism to code when you do not know the precise diagnosis. These are generally the codes ending in 8 or 9. In this case, the provider might consider "S62.648 Non-displaced fracture of proximal phalanx of specified finger with unspecified laterality."

External Cause of Morbidity Codes (Transport and Other)

Whenever a patient presents with an injury, it is important to document the circumstances of the injury.

If a patient was in a vehicular accident, the type of vehicle the patient was in and the type of the other vehicle should be documented, if possible. There are many specific codes for these, such as, "V34.5 Driver of three-wheeled motor vehicle injured in collision with heavy transport vehicle or bus in traffic accident."

Codes for accidents involving vehicles can be found in the Alphabetic Index to External Causes under "Accident, transport."

If a patient was injured in a transport accident not involving a motor vehicle, there are specific codes for these, for example, "Pedal cycle driver injured in collision with other pedal cycle in non-traffic accident V11.0." Here, seventh-character codes are involved:

V11.0XXA Initial encounter
V11.0XXD Subsequent encounter
V11.0XXS Sequela

Other examples of External Cause codes are codes to specify the Activity, Place of Occurrence, and External Cause Status (e.g., "Y92.030 Kitchen in apartment" as the place of occurrence of the external cause).

These codes and documentation can become very important in the event that you become involved in a Personal Injury or Worker's Compensation case.

Please note that ICD-9 V and E codes have been incorporated into the main body of ICD-10 and are no longer supplemental, nor optional.

Other External Causes of Morbidity Code Examples

When other causes are known, they should be documented with the appropriate ICD-10 codes. Providers should at least know that these exist. Some of these are as follows:

Blood alcohol level Y90.-
Body mass index Z68.1
Tobacco use Z72.0
Lack of physical exercise Z72.3
Inappropriate diet and eating habits Z72.4

It is important that your practice review ICD-10 to determine potential problem areas and add them to the cross reference enclosed for your use.

These new requirements may appear confusing and complicated. However, we are confident that once a practice becomes familiar with the requirements relevant to its practice, they will result in better documentation and become easier to use.

Note: The onus is on the provider to ensure complete and accurate coding.

Chapter 6

Chapter Six

ICD-10 Coding Guidelines for General and Family Practice (Specific Coding for Differential Diagnoses)

Family and general practices have the burden of having to deal with many types of conditions and diseases. Unfortunately, this has often resulted in the use of diagnosis codes that are nonspecific or vague, for example, "Abdominal pain, unspecified" and "Diabetes, unspecified," and many others which should be avoided whenever possible.

This chapter is designed to assist the health care provider to choose diagnosis codes on the basis of chief complaints such as chest pain, sore throat, vision problems, and so on. This chapter is therefore focused on those categories:

Head/Neck

Neck pain
Sore throat
Headache
Eye (vision) problems

Upper Extremity

Elbow pain
Shoulder pain

Chest

Chest pain
Heart disease
Cardiac arrhythmia
Common respiratory problems

Abdomen

Abdominal pain
Chronic kidney disease

Spine

Cervical pain
Thoracic pain
Lumbar pain

Pelvis

Rectal pain and bleeding
Testicular pain
Urinary tract infection
Prostatitis
Women's health

Lower Extremity

Knee pain

Generalized

General pain
Dermatitis and skin related
Diabetes
Hypertension
Obesity
Malnutrition
Hyperlipidemia
Neurology
Mental and behavioral disorders

These categories have been further grouped into major system categories.

ENT (ear, nose, and throat)
Respiratory
Cardiovascular
Gastrointestinal
Genitourinary
Musculoskeletal
Endocrine
Neuropsychiatry
Dermatology
Cancer (oncology)

Risk Adjustment Factors (RAF) are measures that reimburse providers based on the health condition of their patients. Health Maintenance Organizations (HMOs) already utilize RAF. Medicare and other payers may adopt RAF by 2020.

By adopting this methodology, payment is made based on expected differences in expected cost due to the medical condition of the patient. Since the medical condition of patients is based on their diagnosis, the diagnoses are given point values. The average point value for all of a doctor's patients will determine the amount a doctor is compensated. ICD-10 Combination Codes can have a significant impact on point values.

These codes are designated by "asterisk RAF" (*RAF), due to the importance of RAF. These should be reviewed and when applicable to specific patients, they should be noted in the medical record and Encounter Data reports.

The following are extracted from a Centers for Medicare and Medicaid Services (CMS) publication, *Office of Information Products and Data Analytics, Medicare & Medicaid Research Review 2013: Volume 3, Number 3*.

It is estimated that one in four Americans have at least two chronic conditions that require ongoing medical care. The burden of multiple (two or more) multiple chronic conditions (MCC) is even greater among Medicare patients. Over two-thirds of Medicare beneficiaries in traditional Medicare, also known as fee-for-service, have two or more chronic conditions. About one in seven (14%) have six or more. Among beneficiaries with three or more chronic conditions, one-third have hypertension and high cholesterol, along with diabetes and/or ischemic heart disease. *The co-occurrence of chronic conditions has far-reaching implications for treatment, coordination of care, and health care costs. The 14% of beneficiaries with six or more chronic conditions account for almost half of total Medicare spending.*

This makes clear why there is an emphasis on Combination Codes in ICD-10.

In the discussions that follows, *"*RAF" will indicate Combination Codes that may be relevant in RAF scoring and/or diagnosis codes that are considered to be RAF codes.*

The following sections, which specify "pain," focus on nontraumatic causes. When external factors are the cause of pain, these can generally be found in "Chapter 19 Injury, Poisoning and Certain Consequences of External Causes."

The following diagnoses are given in general descriptions commonly seen in family or general practice. The ICD-10 code given for that diagnosis is where you will find the more detailed information for properly coding that condition.

When a dash (-) appears after an ICD-10 code, it indicates that there are subcategories associated with the code.

The dash (-) convention is used throughout this chapter and the entire text of our book.

Head/Neck

Ear, Nose, and Throat (ENT)

Sore Throat

The Common Cold

The common cold, acute nasopharyngitis, J00 does not include:

Acute pharyngitis J02-
Chronic sore throat J31.2 or
Pain in throat R07.0 (sore throat)

Tonsillitis and Adenoiditis

Providers must be sure to differentiate between tonsillitis and adenoiditis. If both occur, there is a specific code for this.

J35.01 Chronic tonsillitis
J35.03 Chronic tonsillitis and adenoiditis
J03 Acute tonsillitis, not chronic
J03.00 Acute streptococcal
J03.01 Acute recurrent streptococcal
J03.80 Acute due to other specified organism
J03.81 Acute recurrent due to other specified organism
    Acute tonsillitis excludes sore throat. (See "J02.0 Pharyngitis.")
J35.8 Other chronic diseases of tonsils and adenoids

In ICD-10 there is the additional classification of "acute, recurrent." You must use your judgment to determine the time frame between episodes to qualify as "acute, recurrent."

Pharyngitis

J02.0 Streptococcal pharyngitis
J02.8 Acute pharyngitis due to other specified organisms—use additional code to specify the identify infection agent (B95–B97)
J02.9 Acute pharyngitis, unspecified
J31.1 Chronic nasopharyngitis
J31.2 Chronic pharyngitis

There are no "acute, recurrent" codes for pharyngitis.

The conditions pharyngitis, tonsillitis, sinusitis, and so on are all subcategories under "Acute upper respiratory infections" (J00–J06). When there is an inflammation that is not from an infection, use an additional code to identify the agent, if known.

Larynx, Trachea, and Epiglottis

There are no "acute, recurrent" codes here. Unspecified codes do not differentiate between the trachea and larynx, but rather use the term "supraglottitis."

Type	*Acute*	*Chronic*
Laryngitis	J04.0	J37.0
Laryngotracheitis	J04.2	J37.1
Tracheitis without obstruction	J04.10	N/A
Tracheitis with obstruction	J04.11	N/A
Supraglottitis without obstruction	J04.30	N/A
Supraglottitis with obstruction	J04.31	N/A

Vocal Cord and Larynx Codes

Type	*Code*
Laryngeal spasm	J38.5
Edema of larynx	J38.4
Nodules of vocal cords	J38.2
Polyp of vocal cord and larynx	J38.1
Stenosis (obstruction) of larynx	J38.6
Mass (neoplasm) benign of larynx	D14.1
Neoplasm of uncertain behavior of larynx	D38.0
(Other neoplasms types are found in the index of neoplasms)	
Paralysis, unspecified	J38.00
Paralysis, unilateral	J38.01
Paralysis, bilateral	J38.02

Headache

Headache, facial pain Not Otherwise Specified (NOS) R51
Excludes 1: Atypical facial pain (G50.1)
Migraine and other headache syndromes (G43–G44)
Trigeminal neuralgia (G50.0)
Dizziness and giddiness, light headaches, vertigo R42
Migraine G43
Migraine without aura, not intractable G43.00
With status migrainosus G43.001

Without status migrainosus G43.009
Migraine without aura, intractable G43.01-
With status migrainosus G43.011
Without status migrainosus G43.019
Migraine with aura, not intractable G43.1-
With status migrainosus G43.101
Without status migrainosus G43.110
Migraine without aura, intractable G43.10
With status migrainosus G43.111
Without status migrainosus G43.119
Tension-type headache
Tension-type, unspecified, intractable G44.201
not intractable G44.209
Headache attributed to rhinosinusitis J01
Cluster headache
Cluster headache syndrome,
Unspecific, intractable G44.001
not intractable G44.009

Eye (Vision) Problems

A common problem seen in family and general practice is called "pink eye." It is an inflammation of the conjunctiva (mucous membrane that covers the white of eye and inner surfaces of the eyelids). There are different types of "pink eye" as follows:

H10.021- Bacterial conjunctivitis
H10.01- Follicular conjunctivitis
B30- Viral conjunctivitis
H10.21 Irritant (toxic) conjunctivitis
H10.45 Other acute conjunctivitis
H40.113- Primary open-angle glaucoma
J11.31- Subconjunctival hemorrhage
H20.00 Iritis

Open-angle glaucoma is a condition that leads to progressive atrophy of the optic nerve in the presence of an open angle. It can lead to loss of vision and has been historically associated with elevated intra-ocular pressure.

H40.113- Primary open-angle glaucoma

For glaucoma diagnosis, there is a seventh character to designate the stage of glaucoma. We suggest the use of the seventh character, 4, which specifies "indeterminate stage," unless the provider knows the specific stage.

Iritis

H20.00 Unspecified acute and subacute iridocyclitis
Please note that if the patient is also diabetic, use ICD-10 code E13.39

Subconjunctival Hemorrhage (bleeding beneath the conjunctiva)

H11.31 Conjunctival hemorrhage, right eye
H11.32 Conjunctival hemorrhage, left eye
H11.33 Conjunctival hemorrhage, bilateral

Black Eye Syndrome (contusion of eyeball and orbital tissues—trauma)

S05.11 Contusion of eyeball and orbital tissues, right eye
S05.12 Contusion of eyeball and orbital tissues, left eye

Pterygium (a benign growth of the conjunctiva)

H11.0- Pterygium of eye

There are different forms of pterygium, such as amyloid, central, double, peripheral, recurrent, and unspecified.

Upper Extremity

Shoulder Pain

Shoulder pain can arise from a number of different conditions including the following:

Sprain of the acromioclavicular joint/ligament S43.5-

S codes are used when the cause is external or traumatic. If the cause is not specified as traumatic, a code from the musculoskeletal (M) section is appropriate. Please note the use of the placeholder X when seventh characters are required.

Please note: ICD-10 distinguishes between subluxations (S43.11-) and dislocations (S43.12 and S43.16) of the acromioclavicular joint.

Adhesive capsulitis of shoulder M75.0-

Rotator Cuff Injuries

Rotator cuff injury, traumatic S46.0-
Rotator cuff strain, traumatic S46.01-

Rotator cuff laceration of muscle(s)/tendon(s), traumatic S46.02-
Rotator cuff tear or rupture, not specified as traumatic M75.1-
Bicipital (long head) tendonitis or tear, traumatic S46.10-
Nontraumatic M75.2-
Deltoid muscle strain S46.81-
Subluxations and dislocations of shoulder joint are found in S43.1-.
Subluxation of shoulder joint, right S43.001-
Subluxation of shoulder joint, left S43.002-
Dislocation of shoulder joint, right S43.004-
Dislocation of shoulder joint, left S43.005-

Please note that ICD-10 distinguishes between shoulder subluxation and dislocation. Additional codes in the S43.0- subcategories specify specific shoulder areas, such as posterior versus anterior humerus.

Labrum cartilage tear S43.43-
Osteoarthritis
Primary osteoarthritis, shoulder M19.01-
Post traumatic arthritis, shoulder M19.11-
Secondary arthritis, shoulder M19.21-

Elbow Pain

The following are some of the conditions that can result in elbow pain.

Medial epicondylitis M77.0-
Lateral epicondylitis (tennis elbow) M77.1-
Olecranon bursitis ("smiles" elbow aka gamer's elbow) M70.2-
Lower tricep tendonitis, nontraumatic M65.82-
Injury of muscle, fascia and tendon of tricep, traumatic S46.3-

Chest

Chest Pain

Chest pain can be scary. It is not always due to a heart attack; there can be a variety of causes.

Chest Wall

Costochondritis M94.0 Inflammation of one or more costal (rib) cartilages
Muscle spasm M62.838 Other muscle spasm
Intercostal pain R07.82 Other chest pain
Trauma S20–S29 External cause (S codes)

External cause (S codes) requires that the record specifies laterality (right vs. left), type of injury such as contusion, blister, laceration, and so on. The provider record must also specify specific site, such as thoracic vertebra and if the encounter was for an initial or subsequent visit. It should be noted that these codes are separated by front wall of thorax (chest) versus back wall of thorax.

Cardiac

Angina I20- Angina pectoris—use additional code to specify tobacco exposure—see Respiratory Problems section for tobacco codes.
Myocardial infarction I21–I23- Classic heart attack.

The specific choice of codes can be very difficult. In the absence of specialist knowledge, it may be prudent to use "I21.3 ST Elevation (STEMI) myocardial infarction of unspecified site."

Coronary Artery Disease I25.11- Atherosclerotic heart disease of native coronary artery with angina pectoris

These are Combination Codes, thus they do not require the use of an additional code for angina pectoris.

I25.111 Atherosclerotic heart disease of native coronary artery with angina pectoris with documented spasm

Common Respiratory Problems

Lung Pain

R07.1 Chest pain on breathing, painful respiration
J18.1 Lobar pneumonia, unspecified organism
R09.1 Pleurisy
I26.99 Other pulmonary embolism and infarction
R07.8 Pleurodynia, sudden lancinating chest or abdominal pain
Please Note: F41.0 Anxiety Disorder (Chest Pain can also be the result of a panic attack)

The common cold, "J00 Acute nasopharyngitis," is probably one of the most frequently seen problems in family and general practice. Please note the "Excludes1" and "Excludes 2" notations—this code does not include acute pharyngitis (J02-), chronic sore throat (J31.2), or other common illnesses.

Please see the sections J02 and J03 for codes for tonsillitis and pharyngitis.

When a respiratory problem is documented in more than one site, and there is no specific code for that condition, it should be coded to the lower code, for example, "Bronchitis J40."

Bronchitis

An inflammation of the bronchial tubes with two main types: acute and chronic.

J40 Bronchitis not specified as acute or chronic
Additional codes are used to identify tobacco exposure or use.
J41.0 (*RAF) Simple chronic bronchitis (smoker's cough)
J41.1 Mucopurulent chronic bronchitis
J41.8 Mixed simple and mucopurulent chronic bronchitis
J42 Unspecified chronic bronchitis

Emphysema

J43.0 Unilateral pulmonary emphysema (Macleod's syndrome)
J43.1 Panlobular emphysema
J43.2 Centrilobular emphysema
J43.8 Other emphysema
J43.9 (*RAF) Emphysema, unspecified

COPD (Chronic obstructive pulmonary disease)

J96.10 (*RAF) Chronic respiratory failure
J44.0 COPD with acute lower respiratory infection—use additional code to identify the infection
J44.1 COPD with (acute) exacerbation—excludes J44.0
J44.9 (*RAF) COPD Chronic obstructive asthma

If long-term use of oxygen, use "Z99.81 (*RAF) Dependence on supplemental oxygen." Be sure to document pulmonary condition.

Sinusitis Codes

	Acute	*Acute Recurrent*	*Chronic*
Maxillary	J01.00	J01.01	J32.0
Frontal	J01.10	J01.11	J32.1
Ethmoidal	J01.20	J01.21	J32.2
Sphenoidal	J01.30	J01.31	J32.2
Pansinusitis	J01.40	J01.41	J32.4
Other	J01.80	J01.81	J32.8
Unspecified	J01.90	J01.91	J32.9

The choice between "acute" and "acute recurrent" is subject to provider judgment with respect to time frames between episodes.

Wheezing—excludes asthma (J45-) R06.2
Apnea R06.81
Hyperventilation R06.4
Snoring R06.83

Tobacco

When tobacco is a factor in any illness, ICD-10 requires the use of an additional code from the F or Z series to identify current use, history, or exposure.

Nicotine dependence, unspecified	F17.20-
Cigarettes	F17.21-
Chewing tobacco	F17.22
Other tobacco product (e.g., cigars)	F17.29
Tobacco use (problems related to lifestyle)	Z72.0
Exposure to environmental tobacco smoke, occupational	Z57.31
Exposure to environmental tobacco smoke (second-hand smoke exposure and passive smoking)	Z77.22
Personal history of nicotine dependence	Z87.891

Abdomen

Abdominal Pain

Abdominal Pain is a commonly used code. With the adoption of ICD-10, many practices have gotten into the habit of using nonspecific codes such as:

R10.84 Generalized abdominal pain
and/or
R10.9 Unspecified abdominal pain

Insurance Carrier edits may result in denials for R10.9, so R10.84 may be preferable.

Since, to date, there have been no strict coding edits or audits via record requests, many practices have not taken adequate steps to properly document and code records and claims.

Claims should specify abdominal quadrants, for example:

R10.811 Right Upper Quadrant—to check for gall bladder (K80-) and liver problems (Cirrhosis K74.6- and Hepatitis B18-B19, Chronic viral hepatitis C B18.2-, K73.9*, Chronic hepatitis B and C viruses, and certain drugs)
R10.813 Right Lower Quadrant—to check for appendicitis (K35-K38 and Colitis K52.3)
R10.812 Left Upper Quadrant—check for pancreatitis (K85-)
R10.814 Left Lower Quadrant—to check for irritable bowel syndrome (K58.0- and colitis K52.3)
R10.13 Epigastric pain—ulcer, gastritis, pre-ulcer (K25-)
R10.82- Rebound abdominal—pain may indicate peritonitis (K65-)
K31.84 (*RAF) Gastroparesis—improper stomach muscle movement
I71.4 (*RAF) Abdominal aortic aneurysm without rupture

When a dash (-) appears after an ICD-10 code, it indicates that there are subcategories associated with the code. As an example, R10.82- has the following subcategory codes:

R10.821 Right upper quadrant rebound abdominal tenderness
R10.822 Left upper quadrant rebound abdominal tenderness
R10.823 Right lower quadrant rebound abdominal tenderness
R10.824 Left lower quadrant rebound abdominal tenderness
R10.825 Periumbilic rebound abdominal tenderness
R10.826 Epigastric rebound abdominal tenderness
R10.827 Generalized rebound abdominal tenderness

It is important to specify quadrants and to differentiate between abdominal, rebound abdominal, and epigastric abdominal pain. "Generalized abdominal pain" may be used in appropriate certain conditions such as gastritis.

It is important that the provider document abdominal quadrants for coders and billers. When possible problems attributed to specific quadrants are **not** applicable, for example, no peritonitis (K65-) is associated with "rebound abdominal pain," the pain code itself (R10.82-) should still be used.

Irritable Bowel Syndrome (IBS)

IBS is manifested by bloating, abdominal cramping, constipation, and/or diarrhea. It is often associated with stress, anxiety, depression, or previous intestinal infection.

K58.9 IBS without diarrhea
K58.0 IBS with diarrhea
Fecal Impaction K56.41 (*RAF)
Colostomy Z93.3 (*RAF) Colostomy status
Ileostomy Z93.2 (*RAF) Ileostomy status

Gastrointestinal

K30 Indigestion (dyspepsia)
K21.0 Gastro-esophageal reflux with esophagitis
K21.9 Gastro-esophageal reflux without esophagitis
K20.8 Other esophagitis
K31.84 Gastroparesis

Dialysis Status

Dependence on renal dialysis Z99.2 (*RAF)
Patient noncompliance with renal dialysis Z91.15 (*RAF)

Other Risk Adjustment Factors

Other disorders from impaired renal tubular function:

Secondary hyperparathyroidism of renal origin N25.81 (*RAF)
Alcoholic liver disease K70.9 (*RAF)

Spine

Back Pain

Back pain is one of the most common medical problems. It affects almost everyone at some point in their life. Back pain can range from dull, constant aching to sharp, sudden pain.

Acute back pain comes on suddenly and lasts from a few days to a few weeks. Please see the separate chapter on Pain.

There are different types of back pain.

M51.36 Other intervertebral disc degeneration of lumbar or lumbosacral intervertebral disc
M53.87 Other specified dorsopathies, lumbosacral region (spinal disease)

Sciatica is pain in the back, hip, and outer side of the leg with the following ICD-10 codes:

M54.30 Sciatica, unspecified side
M54.31 Sciatica, right side
M54.32 Sciatic, left side

If sciatic pain is bilateral use both M54.31 and M54.32.

Lumbago is pain in the muscles and joints of the lower back.

M54.5 Low back pain (some consider lumbago to be an outdated term replaced by low back pain)

When a patient has both lumbago and sciatica, providers must use a Combination Code, for example:

M54.40 Lumbago with sciatica, unspecified side
M54.41 Lumbago with sciatica, right side
M54.42 Lumbago with sciatica, left side

When pain occurs in the thoracic spine use:

M54.6 Pain in thoracic spine

If the pain is due to an intervertebral disc disorder, use M51-.

Occipital neuralgia is a medical condition characterized by chronic pain in the upper neck, back of head, and behind the eyes. These areas correspond to the locations of the lesser and greater occipital nerves.

M54.81 Occipital neuralgia

For back pain due to trauma see S30–S39.

Subluxation

Subluxation can be defined as a misalignment of the vertebrae. Medicare covers only subluxation of the spine for chiropractors. However, subluxation can also be extra-spinal.

Subluxation complex (vertebral) of cervical region M99.11
Subluxation complex (vertebral) of lumbar region M99.13
Subluxation complex (vertebral) of lower extremity M99.16
Subluxation complex (vertebral) of upper extremity M99.17

Subluxation codes are a subset of "Biomechanical lesions, not elsewhere classified (M99-)." This category should not be used if the condition can be classified elsewhere.

Neck Pain

Any abnormalities of the muscles, ligaments, and bones or injury can cause neck pain and stiffness. Conditions that can cause neck pain may include the following:

Fibromyalgia M79.7
Spondylosis with myelopathy cervical M47.12

Spondylosis with radiculopathy, cervical region M47.22
Cervical disc disorder with radiculopathy M50.1-
Unspecified inflammatory spondylopathy, cervicothoracic M46.93
Spinal stenosis, cervical region M48.02
Strain of muscle, fascia and tendon at neck level S16.1-
Other specified injuries of other specified part of neck S19.89-

Pelvis

Rectal Pain and Bleeding

Rectal pain or discomfort is a fairly common problem and can result from different conditions including the following:

Fissure and fistula of anal and rectal regions K60-
Hemorrhage not elsewhere classified R58
Constipation K59.0-
Hemorrhoids and perianal venous thrombosis K64-
Pruritis ani (severe itching) L29.0
Internal hemorrhoids K64.8
External hemorrhoids K64.4

Urinary Tract Infection, Site Not Specified N39.0

When ICD-10 code N39.0 is used, providers should check to see if the documentation specifies a site such as kidney and/or urethra. When the kidney or urethra is specified, the following codes can be considered in lieu of N39.0.

N34.2 Other urethritis NOS—use additional code (B95–B97) to identify infectious agent
N34.1 Nonspecific urethritis

Excludes diseases with a predominantly sexual mode of transmission, such as "A56.01—Chlamydial cystitis and urethritis." **Currently, there is only one code for male and female: A56.01**.

N10 Acute tubule-interstitial nephritis
N11.9 Chronic tubule-interstitial nephritis, unspecified
N12 Tubulo-interstitial nephritis, not specified as chronic or acute
A54- Gonococcal (gonorrhea) infection
A56.00 Chlamydial infection of lower genitourinary tract, unspecified
A56.01 Chlamydial cystitis and urethritis
A56.09 Other chlamydial infection of lower genitourinary tract
A74.9 Chlamydial infection, unspecified

Please note that if any of the above codes are appropriate and the patient is diagnosed with diabetes, the code for diabetes could change from "E11.8 Type 2 diabetes without unspecified complications" to "E11.69 Type 2 diabetes with other specified complication." The claim form would then include E11.69 plus one of the N codes specified above: N34.1, N10, N11.9, or N12.

Prostatitis

Prostatitis refers to inflammation of the prostate gland. This is a very common problem for males age 40 and above. This condition may be indicative of the following:

Enlarged prostate without lower urinary tract symptoms N40.0
Enlarged prostate with lower urinary tract symptoms N40.1
Elevated prostate specific antigen (PSA) R97.2
Malignant neoplasm (cancer) of prostate C61
Nonspecific urethritis N34.1
Trichomonal cystitis and urethritis A59.03
Prostatodynyia (painful prostate) syndrome N42.81
Herpes viral infection of urogenital system unspecified A60.00
Malignant neoplasm of testis C62-

When a patient has a confirmed history of a malignant neoplasm of the prostate, the following should appear in the medical record:

Personal history of malignant neoplasm of prostate Z85.46

Testicular Pain

Testicle or testicular pain can occur in one or both testicles. It can be caused by problems within the testis itself or caused by problems that start in the groin, abdomen, or kidneys. There are a number of possible causes including the following:

Torsion of testis N44.0-
Hydrocele and spermatocele N43-
Varicose veins scrotal varices I86.1
Neoplasm of uncertain behavior of right testis D40.11
Neoplasm of uncertain behavior of left testis D40.12
Epididymitis (inflammation of testis) N45.1—use additional code to identify infectious agent (B95–B97), if known
Prostatodynia syndrome, chronic pelvic pain in men N42.81
Contusion of unspecified external genital organ, male S30.201- (trauma)

Vascular disorder (e.g., hematocele) of male genial organs N50.1
Gonococcal (gonorrhea) infection A54-

Lower Extremity

Knee Pain

Knee pain can be caused by sudden injury, by an overuse injury, or by an underlying condition such as arthritis. The following are some of the conditions that can result in knee pain:

Osteoarthritis of the knee M17-
Patellofemoral disorders M22.2-
Chrondromalacia patellae M22.4-
Patellar tendonitis M76.5-
Sprain of medial collateral ligament of knee S83.41-
Other spontaneous disruption of medial collateral ligament M23.63-
Sprain of lateral collateral ligament of knee S83.42-
Other spontaneous disruption of lateral collateral ligament M23.64-
Sprain of anterior cruciate ligament (left knee) S83.512-
Sprain of anterior cruciate ligament (right knee) S83.511-
Other spontaneous disruption of anterior cruciate ligament M23.61-
Sprain of posterior cruciate ligament (right knee) S83.521-
Sprain of posterior cruciate ligament (left knee) S83.522-
Sprain of cruciate ligament of knee S83.5-
Tear of meniscus, current injury S83.2-
Derangement of unspecified medial meniscus due to old tear or injury, right knee M23.203
Derangement of anterior horn of medial meniscus due to old tear or injury, right knee M23.211
Tear of articular cartilage of knee, current injury S83.3-
Internal derangement of knee M23-
Contusion of knee, right knee S80.01-
Sprain of other specified part of the knee S83.8-

Separate codes exist for other lateral and medial meniscus injuries such as bucket, peripheral, and complex tears.

ICD-10 distinguishes between current (S codes) and non-current (previous/old) injuries (M codes) for ligament and cartilage and certain other types of injuries. The codes require specific laterality and type of ligament and cartilage.

ICD-10 distinguishes between subluxation and dislocations, for example:

Other subluxation of right knee S83.191-
Other dislocation of right knee S83.194-

Generalized

Cardiovascular System

Hypertension, Heart Disease, and Chronic Kidney Disease

There are no longer separate codes for "malignant" versus "benign" hypertension. ICD-10 codes are distinguished by either being primary or associated with another disease process.

For primary hypertension use I10.

Hypertensive Crisis

In 2017, a new sub-category "I16 Hypertensive crisis" has been added. A "hypertensive crisis" is a severe increase in blood pressure that can lead to a stroke: a top number (systolic pressure) of 180 mm Hg or higher, and a bottom number (diastolic pressure) of 120 mm Hg or higher.

I16.0 Hypertensive urgency
I16.1 Hypertensive emergency
I16.9 Hypertensive crisis, unspecified

If a patient has hypertension, heart disease, and chronic kidney disease (CKD), then a code from I13.- should be used. These are Combination Codes that specify that a patient has all three conditions. If a patient with renal disease also has both renal failure and chronic kidney disease, an additional code for renal failure is required (N18.1–N18.6).

I13- (*RAF) Hypertensive heart and chronic kidney disease is a combination of I11- and I12-

Codes for I11-

Hypertensive heart disease with heart failure I11.0
Hypertensive heart disease without heart failure I11.9

Codes for I12-

Hypertensive chronic kidney disease I12.0—includes any conditions in "N18 CKD stages 1, 2, 3, 4, 5, end stage, and CKD unspecified" and "N26 Unspecified contracted kidney"]

I13.0 Hypertensive heart and chronic kidney disease with heart failure and stage 1 through stage 4 chronic kidney disease, or unspecified chronic kidney disease

I13.10 Hypertensive heart and chronic kidney disease without heart failure, with stage 1 through stage 4 chronic kidney disease or unspecified chronic kidney disease

I13.11 Hypertensive heart and chronic kidney disease without heart failure with stage 5 chronic kidney disease or end stage renal disease

I12 - Hypertensive chronic kidney disease includes any condition in N18 and N26
N18.1 Chronic kidney disease, Stage 1 (*RAF)
N18.2 Chronic kidney disease, Stage 2 (mild) (*RAF)
N18.3 Chronic kidney disease, Stage 3 (moderate) (*RAF)
N18.4 Chronic kidney disease, Stage 4 (severe) (*RAF)
N18.5 Chronic kidney disease, Stage 5 (*RAF)
N18.6 End stage, renal disease (*RAF)
N18.9 Chronic kidney disease, unspecified

N codes N18.1-N18.6 are considered RAF factors by HMOs. If a patient is also on dialysis, an additional code, "Z99.2* Dialysis status," should also be listed as an additional RAF factor. If a patient refuses dialysis (is non-compliant), use "Z91.15* Patient's noncompliance with dialysis" as an additional RAF factor.

Please note that you have the option to use "I50.9" and "N18.9" (unspecified). ICD-10 generally gives providers an option when specialty knowledge is not available at the time of an encounter.

When a patient presents with an episode of elevated blood pressure and no formal diagnosis of hypertension is made, or an elevated reading is deemed an isolated, incidental finding, the following might be used:

R03.0 Elevated blood pressure reading, without diagnosis of hypertension

In layman's terms, R03.0 is the appropriate code for "white coat hypertension."

Cardiac Arrhythmia

I49.3 Ventricular premature depolarization
I25.11 Atherosclerotic heart disease of native coronary artery with unstable angina pectoris—these are Combination Codes and are listed in Chapter 9 of ICD-10, Circulatory System
I49.8 Other specified cardiac arrhythmias
R00.0 Tachycardia, unspecified

When cardiac conditions are presented, diagnostic tests such as electrocardiograms and chest X-rays are generally covered by Medicare. The diagnostic conditions are specified in Medicare Local Coverage Determinations (LCDs), which are available at no charge via the Internet.

The current LCD for electrocardiograms is L34315.and for chest x-rays is L34317. LCDs not only provide coverage guidelines (e.g., covered diagnosis codes), but also discuss documentation requirements.

Cardiology RAF Factors

Angina I20.9 (*RAF)

Use an additional code for nicotine and/or tobacco use or exposure (see section on Common Respiratory Problems).

Heart Failure, unspecified I50.9 (*RAF)

If there is a relationship between hypertension and heart failure, use a code from subsection I.11, instead of from I50.0. (e.g., "I11.0 Hypertensive heart disease with heart failure").

Hypertension with CKD-V I13.10 (*RAF)

Codes in Category I13- are Combination Codes that include hypertension, heart disease, and chronic kidney disease.

Peripheral vascular disease, unspecified I73.9 (*RAF)
Atrial fibrillation, unspecified I48.91 (*RAF)
Long-term current use of anticoagulation therapy Z79.01 (*RAF)
Supraventricular tachycardia I47.1 (*RAF)
Cardiomyopathy, unspecified I42.9 (*RAF)
Other secondary pulmonary hypertension I27.2 (*RAF)
Atherosclerosis of aorta I70.0 (*RAF)—(Use an additional code(s) to indicate complications due to exposure to tobacco)
Aortic ectasia, unspecified site I77.819 (*RAF)
Unspecified atherosclerosis of native arteries of extremities, unspecified extremity I70.209-
Abdominal aortic aneurysm without rupture I71.4 (*RAF)
Chronic embolism and thrombosis, of deep veins of lower extremity I82.5

Neurology

Sequelae of cerebrovascular disease, I69-, are Combination Codes that describe a condition and specific anatomical site affected, for example:

Hemiplegia I69.35- (*RAF)
Monoplegia I69.04-
I69.041 Monoplegia of lower limb following nontraumatic subarachnoid hemorrhage affecting right dominant side
History of CVA Z86.7- Personal history of diseases of the circulatory system
Parkinson's disease G20 (*RAF)
Epilepsy, unspecified G40.90- (*RAF)
Polyneuropathy in diseases classified elsewhere G63 (*RAF)
(Code first the underlying disease such as amyloidosis or B12 deficiency.)
(If patient also has diabetes, please review diabetes Combination Codes.)

Neuro/Psychiatry

Mental and Behavioral Disorders

These codes are located in Chapter 5 (F01–F99). Due to the complexity and uncertainty surrounding these disorders, there is a *separate chapter on depression* in this book; please see it for a discussion.

Family and general practices see these disorders frequently enough that there are RAF codes.

The following are RAF codes:

Major depression—must document/code as mild, moderate, severe, partial, or full remission
F32.- (*RAF) Major depressive disorder, single episode
F33.- (*RAF) Major depressive disorder, recurrent

Lifetime Conditions Include

F20.- (*RAF) Schizophrenia
F31.- (*RAF) Bipolar disorder

Drug Dependence

Opioid dependence, uncomplicated F11.20 (*RAF)
Sedative, hypnotic or anxiolytic dependence, uncomplicated (such as benzodiazepine dependence) F13.20 (*RAF)

You should document unsuccessful efforts to cut down before using F11.20 and/or F13.20, or use code "Z79.899 Other long-term (current) drug therapy."

Dementia

Senile, unspecified dementia without behavioral disturbance F03.90 (*RAF)
Senile with depression, unspecified
Dementia with behavioral disturbance F03.90 (*RAF)
Alcoholic with dementia F10.27 (*RAF)—see K70.9 (*RAF) for alcoholic liver disease, unspecified
Alzheimer's disease, unspecified G30.9 (*RAF)
Dementia in other diseases F02.80 (*RAF)

Attention Deficit Disorder

Predominantly inattentive type F90.0
Predominantly hyperactive type F90.1
Combined inattentive and hyperactive F90.2
Other type F90.8

Other Disorders

Anxiety, unspecified F41.9
Panic attack F41.0
Obsessive-compulsive disorder F42
Anorexia R63.0—loss of appetite
Anorexia nervosa F50.00—unspecified
    F50.01—restricting type
    F50.02—binge eating
Bulimia nervosa F50.2
Alcohol dependence, uncomplicated F10.20 (*RAF)

Note: Please see the chapter on depression in this book.

Due to the sheer volume of problems confronting a family or general practice, the above is meant only as a reference to some of the common issues. It is not meant to be complete or encyclopedic.

General Pain

There is a *separate chapter on the subject of pain* because it is complex. The Appendix also contains a list of pain codes with descriptions.

Some common pain types for family and general practice include the following:

Joint pain	M25.5	Excludes limbs, feet, and hands. Specify joint and left or right, for example, knee pain
	M46.1 (*RAF)	Sacroilitis, inflammation of the sacroiliac joint
Limb pain	M79.6-	Specify limb, digit(s), left or right
Peripheral neuropathy G90.-		Disorders of the autonomic nervous system
	G90.01	Carotid sinus syndrome
	G90.09	Other idiopathic peripheral Autonomic neuropathy
Back spasms	M62.830	Muscle spasms of back
Calf spasm (charley horse)	M62.831	Muscle spasms of calf
Other muscle spasms	M62.838	Other muscle spasm

The pain chapter discusses acute versus chronic pain and other subjects such as chronic pain syndrome.

Diabetes

The 2017 code changes include 261 new diabetes codes, which more than doubles the number of ICD-10 diabetes codes. In addition, there is a new code in Chapter 18, Symptoms, Signs and Abnormal Findings.

R73.03 Prediabetes.

Almost all of the new diabetes codes in sections E08–E13 involve eye (vision) conditions. These are retinal conditions that an ophthalmologist should diagnose.

Some practices have gotten into the habit of not recognizing Combination Codes such as diabetes. Since diabetes is such a common condition, there has been a great use of:

E11.8 Type 2 diabetes without unspecified complication
E11.9 Type 2 diabetes without complications

One code that practices often overlook is:

E11.69 (*RAF) **Type 2 diabetes** with other specified complications

This code requires the use of an additional code(s) to identify the complication(s). Some very common complications are:

I10 Hypertension
E66.0-9 Obesity

If patients have other chronic conditions such as arthritis, these can be listed as a complicating condition.

E11.618 (*RAF) Diabetes with other diabetic arthropathy

Arthritis is a very common diagnosis for general and family practices. When a patient has both diabetes and arthritis, E11.618 can be used.

Examples of RAF Codes for Other Complications Associated with Diabetes

E11.51 (*RAF) Type 2 diabetes mellitus with diabetic peripheral angiopathy without gangrene
E11.622 (*RAF) Type 2 diabetes with other skin ulcer
E11.6- (*RAF) Type 2 diabetes mellitus with neurological complications.
E11.69 (*RAF) Type 2 diabetes with other specific complications

The important point is that practices recognize that most diabetes mellitus conditions occur in combination with other conditions and all diabetes mellitus codes are Combination Codes.

Obesity

Morbid obesity is considered to be a RAF condition and should be documented in the medical record and Encounter Data.

E66.01 (*RAF) Morbid (severe) obesity due to excess calories

When this condition occurs, providers must also code the body mass index (BMI). When the BMI is greater than or equal to 40, this is considered severe obesity. A BMI equal to or greater than 35 is considered severe when co-morbid conditions, such as diabetes mellitus, hypertension, hyperlipidemia, congestive heart failure, coronary artery disease, and/or degenerative joint disease exist.

Very high BMI ratings have separate Encounter Status (Z) codes that should be recorded when they occur.

Z68.41 (*RAF) adult, BMI 40–44.9
Z68.42 (*RAF) adult, BMI 45–49.9
Z68.43 (*RAF) adult, BMI 50–59.9

Other conditions associated with obesity include the following:

Overweight E66.3
Drug induced obesity E66.1
Other obesity E66.8
Type 2 diabetes mellitus with hyperglycemia E11.65
Pure hypercholesterolemia E78.0
Mixed hyperlipidemia 78.2
Other hyperlipidemia 78.4
Essential (primary) hypertension 10

Malnutrition

E44–E46 (*RAF) Protein calorie malnutrition
All codes within the above range are considered to be RAF factors.
R64 (*RAF) Cachexia, wasting syndrome—excludes abnormal weight loss (R63.4) and nutritional marasmus (E41)
R63.0 Anorexia—Excludes 1: Anorexia nervosa (F50.0-)

Hyperlipidemia

Hyperlipidemia is defined as abnormally high concentration of fats or lipids in the blood. When it is presumed that a patient is experiencing abnormally high levels of fats and/or cholesterol, but the actual levels are still undetermined, code E78.5 is more appropriate than the more specific codes in the E78- range.

E78.00 Pure hypercholesterolemia, unspecified
(This code is used when raised total cholesterol is present, exhibiting significantly high LDL, but HDL and triglycerides are at normal levels.)
E78.01 Familiar hypercholesterolemia

E78.1 Pure hyperglyceridemia
E78.2 Mixed hyperlipidemia
E78.3 Hyperchylomicronemia
E78.4 Other hyperlipidemia—familial combined hyperlipidemia

If a patient also has diabetes, use "E11.69 Type 2 diabetes with other specified complications" plus (together with) E78.4.

E78.5 Hyperlipidemia, unspecified –

When the actual levels are undetermined, for example, "hypertriglyceridemia, E78.5" is more appropriate than the more specific codes.

When a patient also has diabetes, use Combination Code "E11.65 Type 2 diabetes with hyperglycemia."

Dermatitis and Skin Related

Many providers have gotten into the habit of writing or indicating "dermatitis" on charge tickets without further specification and are using the following codes:

L30.8 Other specified dermatitis
and/or
L30.9 Dermatitis, unspecified

These two codes, L30.8 and L30.9, can be used to designate dermatitis due to a chronic disease.

There is no current code for dermatitis due to cancer. L 30.8 is a candidate for use here.

Having said that, providers should try to be more specific and utilize other categories such as:

L20- Atopic dermatitis
L21- Seborrheic dermatitis (dandruff)
L22 Diaper dermatitis
L23- Allergic contact dermatitis
L24- Irritant contact dermatitis
L25- Unspecified contact dermatitis
L27.0 Generalized skin eruptions due to drugs and medicaments taken internally (Dermatitis due to chronic illness—use additional code to identify specific code for adverse effect if known.)
B37.2 Candida infection of the skin and nails
B86 Scabies, sarcoptic itch
B35.9 Dermatophytosis, unspecified (ringworm NOS)
B35.3 Tinea pedis (athlete's foot)

B36.0 Tinea versicolor (pityriasis versicolor)
M35.00 Sicca (Sjogren's) syndrome
L40- Psoriasis
Psoriasis vulgaris L40.0
Generalized pustular psoriasis L40.1
Other psoriasis L40.8
(Please see category L40 for additional psoriasis types.)

Pressure ulcers are localized injury to the skin and/or underlying tissue. These are Combination Codes (L89-) and require the specific site, for example, elbow, and the stage. If the stage is not known, providers can use the "unstageable" designation, for example:

L89.319 Pressure ulcer of right buttock, unspecified stage

Non-pressure ulcers (L97-) are also Combination Codes requiring the site (e.g., thigh) and other data, such as fat layer exposed, necrosis of muscle, necrosis of bone, and breakdown of skin.

*Varicose Veins I83.- (*RAF)*, are enlarged and twisted veins on the leg. These are considered to be RAF codes.

Other Skin-Related Problems

R21 Rash and other nonspecific skin eruptions
D69.2 (*RAF) Senile purpura-rash of purple spots caused by internal bleeding
L97.5- Non-pressure chronic ulcer of other part of foot

If the patient also has diabetes, use the Combination Code "E11.621 Type 2 diabetes with foot ulcer." Use another code (L97.4–L97.5) to specify the site of the foot ulcer.

Constant use of "other" and "unspecified" dermatitis may result in a request for a review of records.

Oncology

Document and code ACTIVE treatment including hormones such as Lupron and Tamoxifen.

For secondary metastases, code by location:

C77.- to C80.- **Entire range are RAF factors**, for example,
C77.1 (*RAF) Secondary and unspecified malignant neoplasm of intrathoracic lymph nodes

For leukemia, do not code as "history of," but rather as "in remission," for example,

C91.- (*RAF) Acute lymphoid leukemia

For lymphoma, document as "in remission" for the first five years after treatment:

C83.- to C88.- (*RAF) Entire range are RAF factors
C83- Non-follicular lymphoma
C84- Mature T/NK cell lymphoma
C85- Other specified and other specified types of non-Hodgkin lymphoma
C86- Other specified types of T/NK cell lymphoma
C88- Malignant immunoproliferative diseases and certain other B-cell lymphomas

Use "history of" for all cancers Z85.00*-Z85.9". The entire range are RAF factors.

Active treatment for oncology should be documented, which can include hormone medications as follows:

S0187 Tamoxifen, citrate, oral 10 mg
Q0164 Prochlorperazine maleate 5 mg, oral, FDA approved prescription anti-emetic, for use as a complete therapeutic substitute for an IV anti-emetic at the time for chemotherapy treatment, not to exceed a 24 hour dosage
J1950 Injection, leuprolide acetate (for depot suspension), per 3.75 mg
J9217 Leuprolide acetate (for depot suspension), 7.5 mg
J9218 Leuprolide, per 1 mg

Use of these medications can result in adverse effects, for example:

T44.7X- Poisoning by, adverse effect of, and underdosing of beta-adrenoreceptor antagonists
T46.1X- Poisoning by, adverse effect of, and underdosing of calcium channel blockers
T46.3X- Poisoning by, adverse effect of, and underdosing of coronary vasodilators

Cancers are grouped in categories "C00–C96 Malignant Neoplasms." Subgroupings include:

C34.00 Lung cancer
C56.9 Ovarian cancer
C95.9 Leukemia, and so on (blood)
C25- Pancreatic cancer
C18- Colon (bowel)
C41- Bone and articular cartilage
C71- Malignant neoplasm of brain

When a patient is seen for chemotherapy, use the appropriate Encounter for Other Specific Health Care codes, for example, "Z51.11 Encounter for antineoplastic chemotherapy."

Women's Health

This is a very broad category, which is not meant to be encyclopedic, but rather to enumerate some of the common problems seen by family and general practitioners.

Pelvic Inflammatory Disease "N70–N77 Inflammatory Diseases of Female Pelvic Organs"

Female pelvic peritonitis, unspecified N73.5
Female pelvic peritoneal adhesions (post-infective) N73.6
Other specified female pelvic inflammatory disease N73.8
Female pelvic inflammatory disease, unspecified N73.9

Breast

Benign neoplasm of breast D24.1 right
D24.2 left
Breast pain, mastodynia N64.4
Breast cancer, malignant neoplasm C50-
(Specificity is required, e.g., nipple, areola, right, etc.)
Malignant neoplasm of central portion of breast, female C50.11-
Malignant neoplasm of upper-inner quadrant of breast, female C50.21-
Malignant neoplasm of upper-outer quadrant of breast, female C50.41-
Malignant neoplasm of lower-outer quadrant of breast, female C50.51-
Malignant neoplasm of lower-outer quadrant of breast, male C50.52-
Malignant neoplasm of overlapping sites of breast C50.8-
Fibro-cystic breast disease, diffuse cystic mastopathy, right N60.11
left N60.12

Vaginitis: Inflammation of vagina and vulva—use additional code to identify infection agent, for example, gardnerella vaginalis B96.89.

Acute vaginitis N76.0
Acute vulvitis N76.2

Uterine Fibroids

Submucous leiomyoma of uterus D25.0

Hematuria: Blood in Urine

Gross hematuria R31.0

Benign essential microscopic hematuria R31.1
Painful urination (dysuria) R30.0

Ovary

Follicular cyst of ovary N83.0
Other ovarian cyst N83.29

Cervix

Mild cervical dysplasia N87.0
Moderate cervical dysplasia N87.1

Menstrual

Premenstrual tension, dysmenorrhea N94.4
Excessive, frequent and irregular menstruation N92.-
Other specified conditions associated N94.89

Menopausal

Menopausal and female climacteric states N95.1

Osteoporosis

Age-related osteoporosis without current pathological fracture M81.0
Other osteoporosis without current pathological fracture M81.8

Edema

Localized edema R60.0-
Generalized edema R60.1
Palpitations: awareness of heart beat R00.2

Pap Smear

Other abnormal cytological findings on specimens, from cervix/uteri R87.618
Encounter for gynecological examination (general), (routine) without abnormal findings Z01.419
Encounter for gynecological examination (general), (routine) with abnormal findings Z01.411

Other Factors Influencing Health Status/Contact with Health Services:

Amputation Z89.9 (*RAF) Acquired absence of limb, Unspecified for specific limb or digits, please see section Z89-
Long-term oxygen Z99.81 (*RAF) Dependence on supplemental oxygen
Long-term use of insulin Z79.4* (*RAF) Long-term (current) use of insulin

Personal History of Other Diseases and Conditions:

Personal history of peptic ulcer disease Z87.11

Other Conditions

Hematology

There are three section "blocks" of anemia types in the ICD-10-CM book: Anemias D50–D64:

Nutritional deficiency D50–D53
Hemolytic D55–D59
Aplastic and other D60–D64

Some of the most common types include the following:

Sickle Cell Disease Type	*Without Crisis*	*With Crisis*
Hb-SS	D57.1	D57.00
Hb-C	D57.20	D57.21
Hb-SC	D57.20	D57.21
Hb-S/Hb-C	D57.20	D57.21

D50.9 Iron deficiency anemia (the most common type)
D51.- Vitamin B12 deficiency anemia
D63.1 Anemia in chronic kidney disease
D63.8 Anemia in other chronic disease, classified elsewhere

Sickle cell anemia has different codes depending on "crisis:"
The following are hematology codes, which have been designated as RAF factors:

Polycythemia vera D45 (*RAF) Blood cancer—Excludes 1: Familial polycythemia (D75.0)
Pancytopenia D61.810 (*RAF) Antineoplastic chemotherapy induced—a shortage of red and white cells and platelets
Thrombocytopenia, unspecified D69.6 (*RAF) Deficiency of platelets
Thrombocythemia D47.3 (*RAF) Presence of high platelet counts in the blood
Neutropenia D70.9 (*RAF) Abnormally low neutrophile (a type of white blood cell in the blood). This unspecified code might be subject to computer edits. An alternative is "D70.8 Other neutropenia"

Prosthetic Joint Pain

Initial encounter only T84.84XA (*RAF)
All subsequent encounters T84.84XD (*RAF)

The 2017 ICD-10 code changes involve 294 new T codes. Almost all of the new codes involve stents, grafts, and other devices. Due to the ongoing use of stents, implants, grafts, and other devices, these should be included in the patient record and complications, such as pain, should be documented.

Amputation Z89.- (*RAF) Acquired absence of limb
Long-term oxygen Z99.81 (*RAF) Dependence on supplemental oxygen
Long-term use of insulin Z79.4 (*RAF)

Chapter 7

Chapter Seven

Worker's Compensation, Personal Injury, and Drug or Chemical Induced Diabetes

Drug or chemical induced diabetes (E09-) is the logical starting point for any injury-related diagnosis for diabetes. For drug or chemical induced diabetes, we must code first the source.

Diabetes is classified by type and causation. For Worker's Compensation and Personal Injury, the ICD-10 Tabular List "Poisoning by, averse effects of and underdosing of drugs, medicaments and biological substances (T36–T50)" should be reviewed to determine if causation can be located within this category.

"T36- Poisoning by, adverse effect of and underdosing of systemic antibiotics" are all seven character codes. In addition, all codes listed in this category are Combination Codes. No additional external cause codes are required.

An example could be a patient who was exposed to anesthetics

T41.0X1A Poisoning by inhaled anesthetics accidental (unintentional)
E09.21 Drug or chemical induced diabetes mellitus with diabetic nephropathy

Do not assume "undetermined intent." Undetermined intent is used when documentation in the record shows that intent cannot be determined.

Assign as many codes as necessary to report all causal substances involved.

Please note that there are categories for food poisoning (T61–T62), and exposure to venom, tobacco, and nicotine.

All diabetes mellitus codes are Combination Codes. The enclosed flowcharts are separated into six major categories:

- Type 1 diabetes
- Type 2 diabetes
- Diabetes due to underlying causes

- Pregnancy-induced diabetes
- Drug or chemical induced diabetes
- Other specified diabetes—includes diabetes mellitus due to genetic defects of beta-cell function and genetic defects in insulin action

All types of diabetes present should be coded in any and all major categories.

Diabetes Mellitus Discussion

Coding for diabetes mellitus is greatly expanded. The American Diabetes Association released statistics, as of June 10, 2014, that among American seniors (age 65 or older), the percentage with diagnosed and undiagnosed diabetes was 25.9%. It also reported that 86 million Americans age 20 and older had pre-diabetes. Diabetes has become an epidemic and exacerbates injuries.

A new study from UCLA was summarized and published in the *Los Angeles Times* during March 2016. Some of the findings are as follows:

1. 55% of California adults have either diabetes or pre-diabetes.
2. 46% of the population has pre-diabetes.
3. Up to 70% of those with pre-diabetes develop diabetes in their lifetime.
4. About 90% of people with pre-diabetes are unaware of their condition and don't get treatment. There are no symptoms of pre-diabetes, which can only be detected through blood tests.

The study also says that the vast majority of diabetes cases are Type 2, which is preventable. People can stave off developing diabetes by adopting a healthier diet and increasing their physical activity. People with injuries, however, often can't do either due to physical or economic circumstances.

Medicare and commercial carriers have not been editing claims as required by the definition of Combination Code. You can now get a claim processed for an office visit which shows separate diagnoses codes for Type 2 diabetes without complications (E11.9) and Chronic kidney disease (N18.6). A review of the ICD-10 diabetes codes would reveal that, when these conditions occur together, a Combination Code such as "E11.22 Type 2 diabetes with diabetic chronic kidney disease" should be used. In addition, an additional code should be used to identify the stage of chronic kidney disease, for example, "N18.6 End stage renal disease." An additional code should also be used to identify dialysis status (Z99.2).

The Combination Codes for diabetes were selected because the World Health Organization considers them to be statistically significant. The codes also force the provider to look at diabetes as a combination of diagnosis and/or manifestations. If and when edits for Combination Codes are enforced, providers will be obliged to know them in order to correct and resubmit claims. This may also help providers to more comprehensively document medical records.

ICD-10 is the government's focal point to implement data analytics and cloud computing, which is the only way to organize and understand huge volumes of data. You cannot organize this data in the absence of electronic claim submission and analytics. Providers in the Worker's Compensation arena already provide more comprehensive and detailed documentation than others because of requirements for medical-legal claims. However, claims will have to reflect the medical record via ICD-10 codes.

It will be interesting, to say the least, how edits will be enforced.

All diabetes mellitus codes are Combination Codes. Diabetes mellitus codes are in sections E08–E13 of ICD-10. There are in excess of 200 possible choices. When a condition is described by a specific code, use that code. When there are many complications, as many codes as are within a particular category may be used. An example is:

E08.00 Diabetes mellitus due to underlying condition with hyperosmolarity without non-ketotic hyperglycemic-hyperosmolar coma (NKHHC)

OR

E08.31 Diabetes mellitus due to underlying condition with unspecific diabetic retinopathy with macular edema

If both of these conditions exist, then both codes should be used.

If the type of diabetes is not documented in the medical record, the default is E11.8 Type 2.

If the medical record indicates that the patient uses insulin, "Z79.4 Long-term (current) use of insulin" should be assigned to indicate that the patient uses insulin. Z79.4 should not be used if insulin is given temporarily to bring a Type 2 patient's blood sugar under control during an encounter.

For diabetes in pregnancy and gestational diabetes, see ICD-10 Section O24.-.

For complications due to insulin pump malfunction, see subcategory T85.6.

Codes under categories E08, E09, and E13 identify complications/manifestations associated with secondary diabetes mellitus. The sequencing of the secondary diabetes codes is based on the Tabular List instructions for the three categories.

For "E08 Diabetes mellitus due to underlying condition codes," you must first code the underlying condition, for example, cystic fibrosis (E84-).

For "E09 Drug or chemical induced diabetes mellitus," code first the drug or toxin (T36–T65), if applicable, and use an additional code, if applicable, for adverse effect (T36–T50).

"E13 Other specified diabetes mellitus" includes diabetes due to genetic defects of beta-cell function and other specified types of diabetes.

Please note that when the condition cannot be exactly specified, *it is still acceptable to use "unspecified" or "other specified" codes when those codes are the most appropriate at the time of evaluation*.

For example:

E11.8 Type 2 diabetes mellitus with unspecified complications
E11.9 Type 2 diabetes without complications, (which is approximately equivalent to ICD-9–250.00)

"Regarding E08.8 - unspecified complication" and "E08.9 - No complications": Use of these diabetic codes are probably a result of coding errors. Because all diabetic codes are combination codes. As an example, "Hypertension" is a complication, but is not listed per say. In this case, an alternative to ".8" or ".9" diabetes codes could be "E11.69 - Type 2 diabetes with other specified complications." (Such as "I10 - Hypertension").

Diabetes Mellitus in Pregnancy, Childbirth, and the Puerperium

Diabetes mellitus is a significant complicating factor in pregnancy. Pregnant women who are diabetic should be assigned a code from Category 024 followed by the appropriate diabetes codes from E08–E13.

Use of Flowcharts

There are six different categories of diabetes mellitus. They are:

E08	Diabetes due to underlying conditions
E09	Diabetes due to drugs or chemicals
E10	Type 1 diabetes
E11	Type 2 diabetes
E13	Other specified diabetes—includes diabetes mellitus due to genetic defects of beta-cell function and genetic defects in insulin action
O24	Diabetes mellitus in pregnancy, childbirth, and puerperium

You first need to determine which category of diabetes mellitus applies to your patient. (Please remember, you can have more than one category of diabetes mellitus. For example, Type 1 diabetes mellitus and diabetes mellitus in pregnancy.) Then, go to the corresponding flowchart for that diabetes mellitus category to determine all of the proper codes that must be documented.

Please note: If a patient is pregnant, her pregnancy-related diabetes diagnosis should be listed first before the other diabetes codes.

Section O24 Diabetes mellitus during pregnancy, childbirth, and the puerperium

This section is divided into six categories.

- Category O24.0 deals with pre-existing diabetes mellitus, Type 1, in pregnancy, childbirth, and the puerperium
- Category O24.1 deals with pre-existing diabetes mellitus, Type 2, in pregnancy, childbirth, and the puerperium

- Category O24.3 deals with unspecified pre-existing diabetes mellitus in pregnancy, childbirth, and the puerperium
- Category O24.4 deals with gestational diabetes mellitus
- Category O24.8 deals with other pre-existing diabetes mellitus in pregnancy, childbirth, and the puerperium
- Category O24.9 deals with unspecified diabetes mellitus in pregnancy, childbirth, and the puerperium

"Category O24.4 Gestational diabetes mellitus" only involves cases of diabetes mellitus that arose during pregnancy. When this code is used, no other category O24 code should be used in addition (i.e., you would not have any other codes such as O24.8 or O24.9, in addition to the O24.4 code).

Note: E codes would still apply, but are listed after the appropriate O24- code.

"Category O24.8 Other pre-existing diabetes mellitus in pregnancy, childbirth and the puerperium" involves cases where the diabetes (other than Type 1 or 2) was pre-existing and now the patient is pregnant, in childbirth, or puerperium. In these cases, the O24.8 code is listed first, then the appropriate code for the pre-existing diabetes is listed. If there is long-term current insulin use, then the code Z79.4 is added.

The first step is to choose between the following flowcharts for your patient's diabetes during pregnancy, childbirth, or puerperium.

- Pre-existing diabetes mellitus, Type 1, in pregnancy, childbirth, and puerperium
- Pre-existing diabetes mellitus, Type 2, in pregnancy, childbirth, and puerperium
- Unspecified pre-existing diabetes mellitus in pregnancy, childbirth, and puerperium
- Gestational diabetes mellitus in pregnancy
- Gestational diabetes mellitus in childbirth
- Gestational diabetes mellitus in puerperium
- Other pre-existing diabetes mellitus in pregnancy, childbirth, or puerperium
- Unspecified diabetes mellitus in pregnancy, childbirth, or puerperium

Once the correct flowchart is chosen, proceed through the steps of the appropriate flowchart.

An abnormal glucose tolerance in pregnancy is assigned a code from subcategory O99.81, "Abnormal glucose complicating pregnancy, childbirth, and the puerperium."

Diabetes Flowcharts

Please note: The 2017 ICD-10-CM book has added a seventh character to the diabetes codes to specify which eye(s) is involved.

A seventh character of 1 for right eye
A seventh character of 2 for left eye
A seventh character of 3 for bilateral eye
A seventh character of 9 for unspecified eye

Our flowcharts do not take it to this level of specificity. Therefore, the provider will have to determine the seventh-character code to use (Figure 7.1).

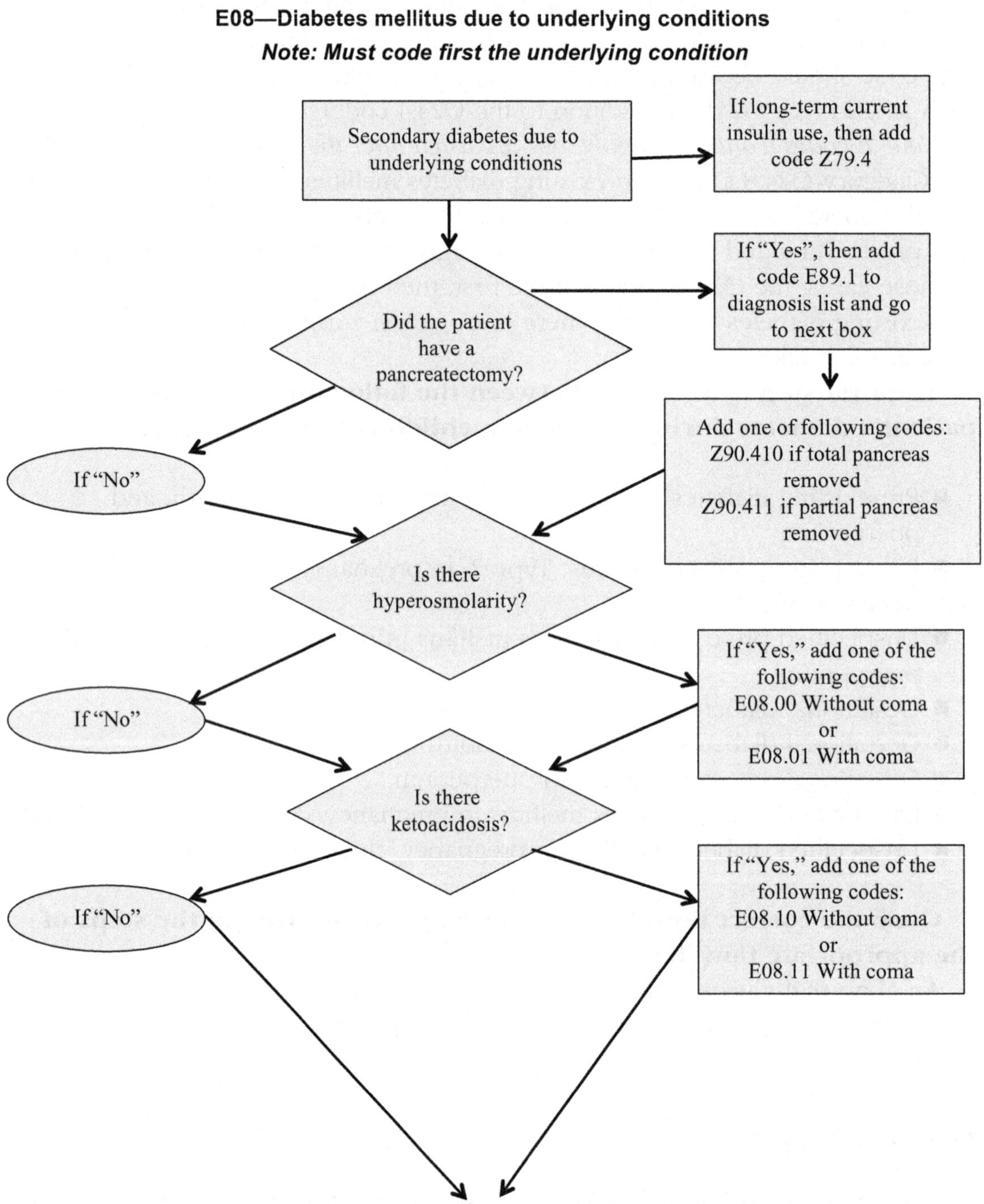

Figure 7.1

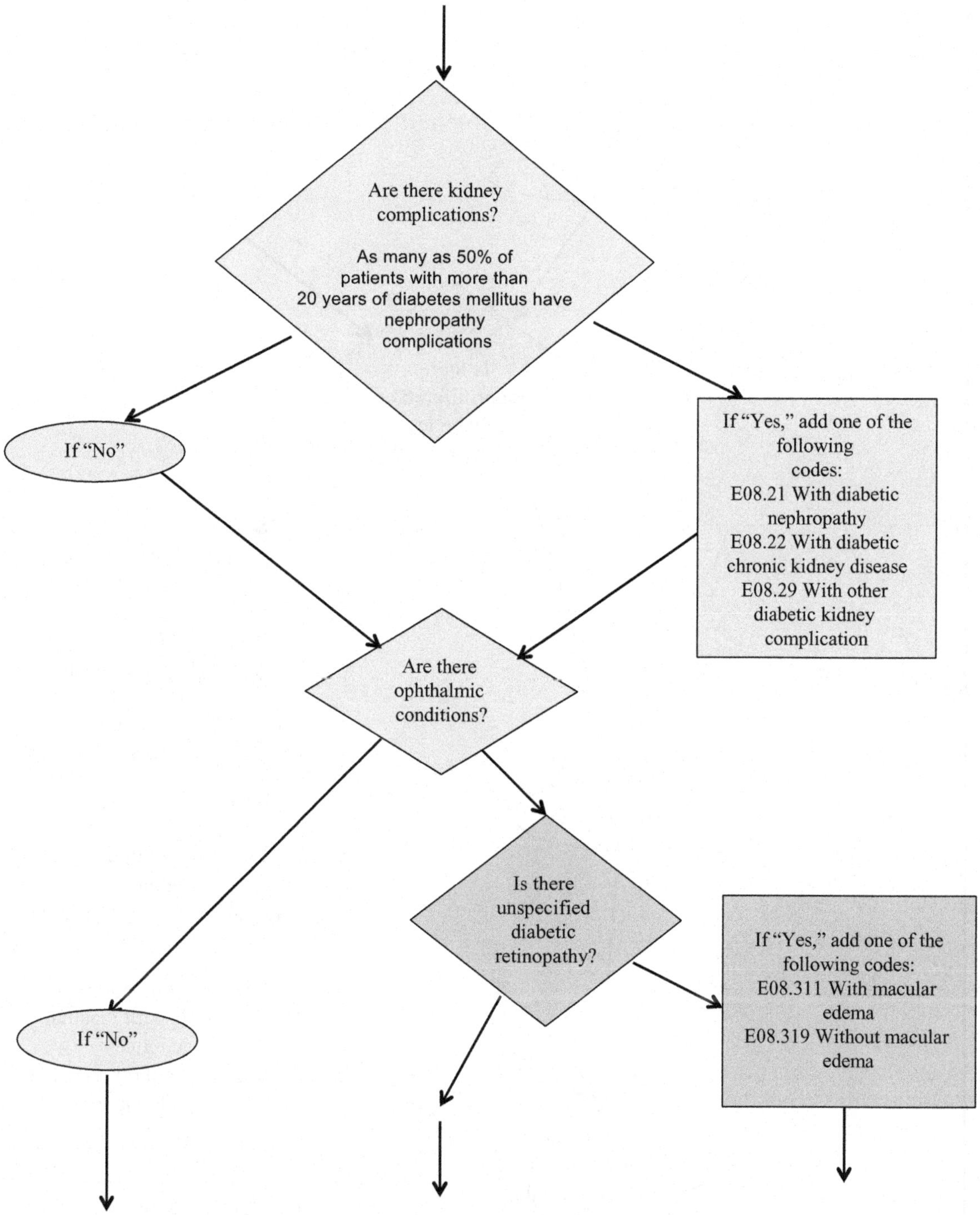

Figure 7.1 (Continued)

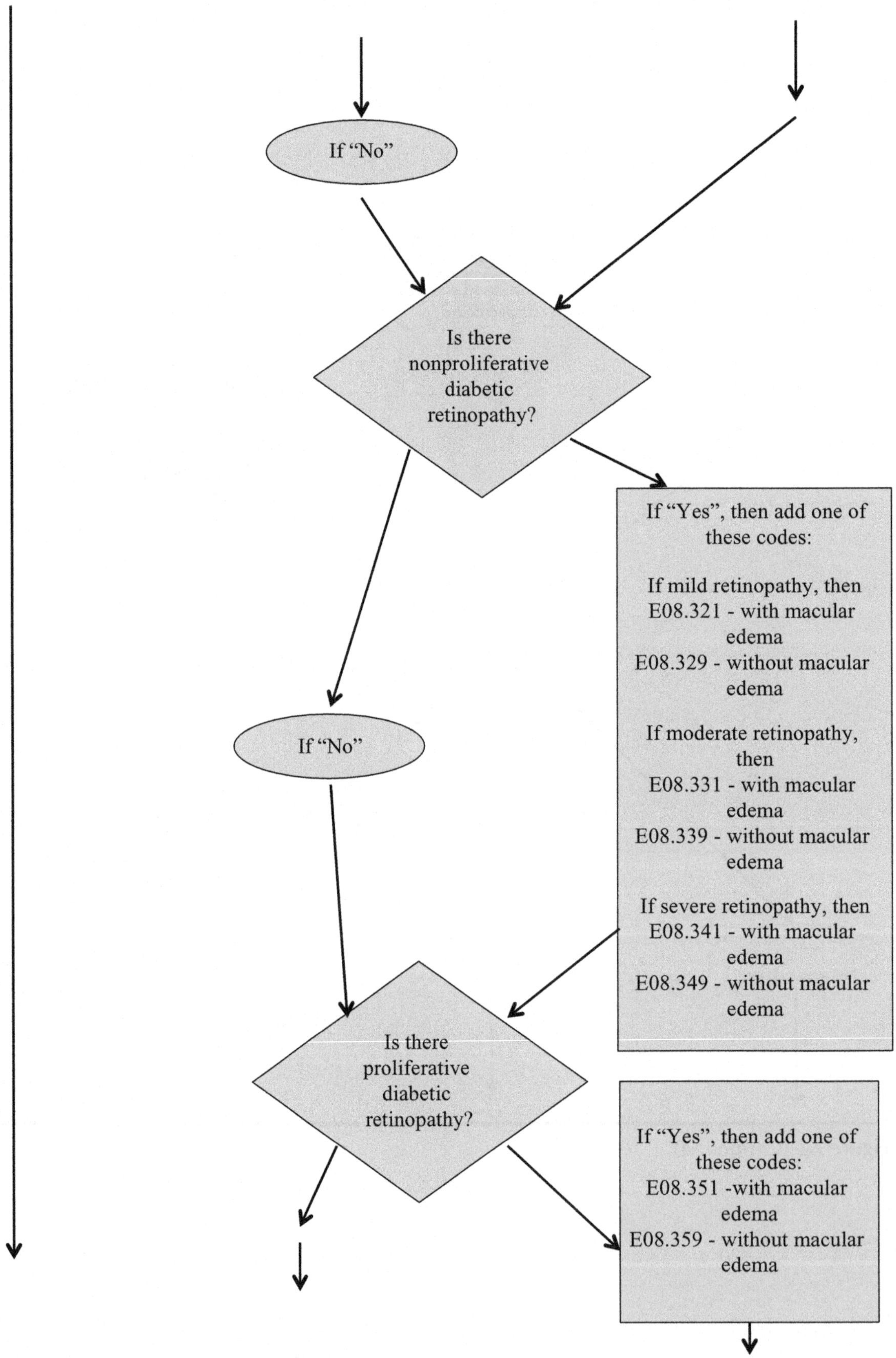
If "No"
Is there nonproliferative diabetic retinopathy?
If "Yes", then add one of these codes:
If mild retinopathy, then
E08.321 - with macular edema
E08.329 - without macular edema
If moderate retinopathy, then
E08.331 - with macular edema
E08.339 - without macular edema
If severe retinopathy, then
E08.341 - with macular edema
E08.349 - without macular edema
If "No"
Is there proliferative diabetic retinopathy?
If "Yes", then add one of these codes:
E08.351 -with macular edema
E08.359 - without macular edema

Figure 7.1

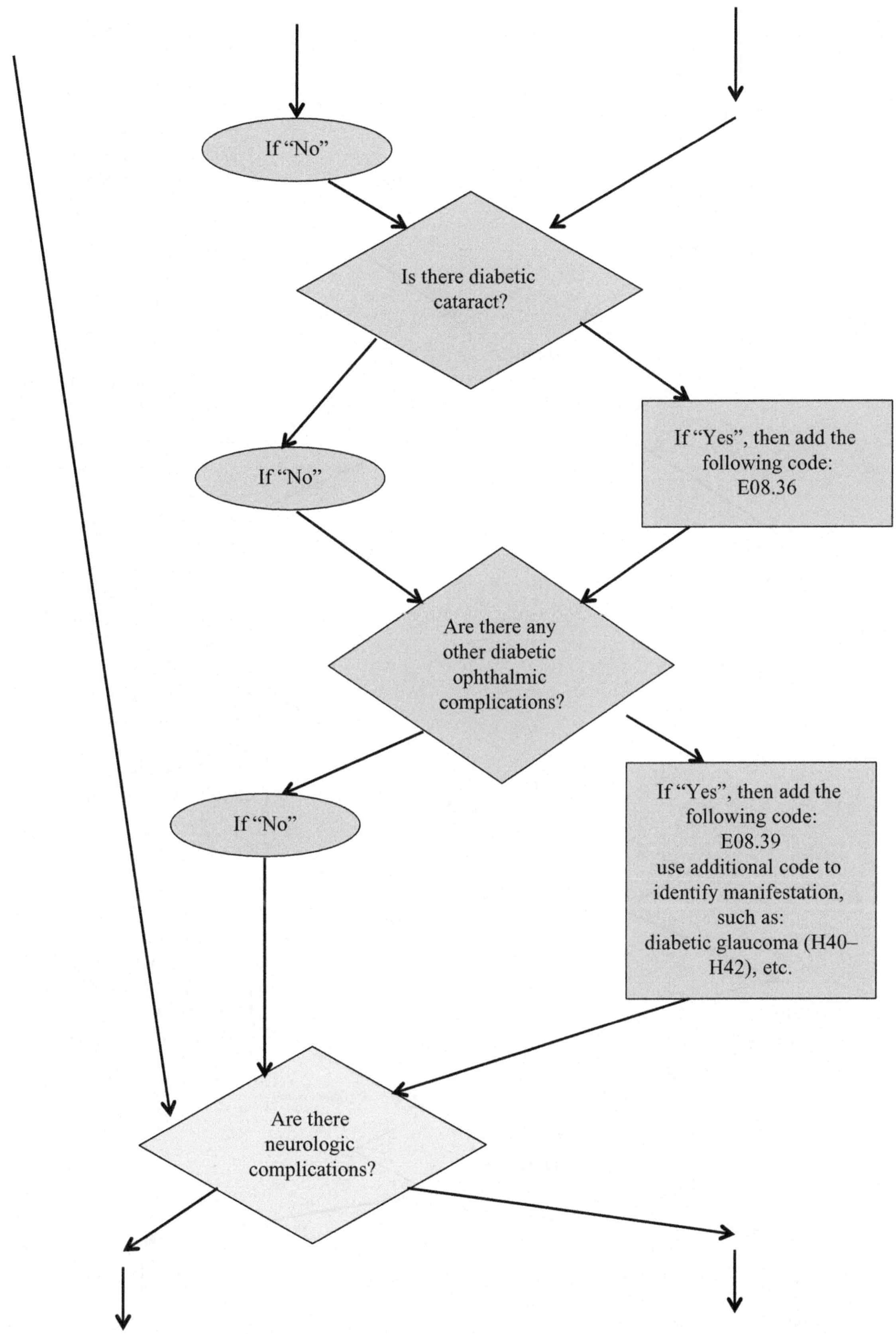

Figure 7.1 (Continued)

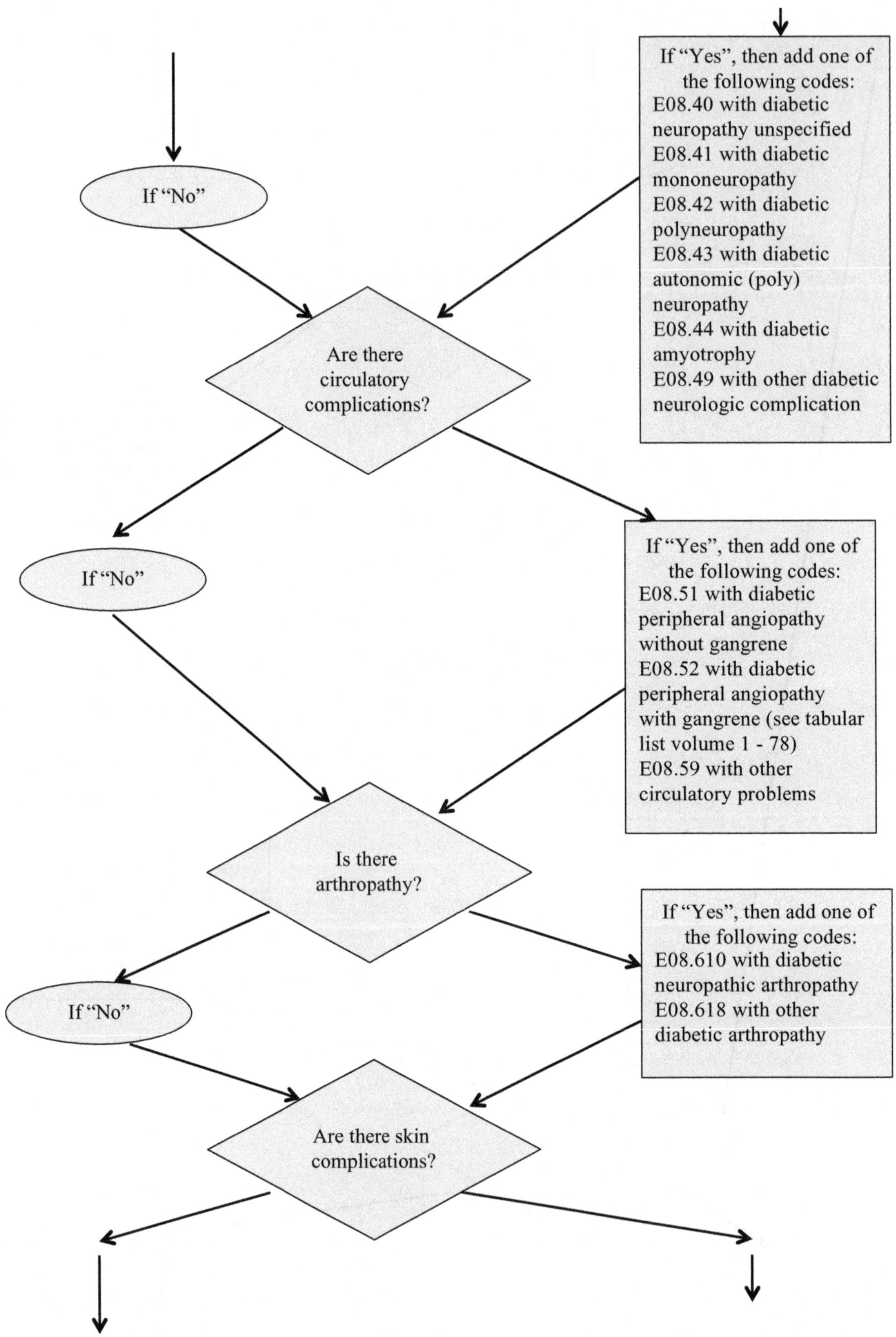
If "No"
If "Yes", then add one of the following codes:
E08.40 with diabetic neuropathy unspecified
E08.41 with diabetic mononeuropathy
E08.42 with diabetic polyneuropathy
E08.43 with diabetic autonomic (poly) neuropathy
E08.44 with diabetic amyotrophy
E08.49 with other diabetic neurologic complication
Are there circulatory complications?
If "No"
If "Yes", then add one of the following codes:
E08.51 with diabetic peripheral angiopathy without gangrene
E08.52 with diabetic peripheral angiopathy with gangrene (see tabular list volume 1 - 78)
E08.59 with other circulatory problems
Is there arthropathy?
If "No"
If "Yes", then add one of the following codes:
E08.610 with diabetic neuropathic arthropathy
E08.618 with other diabetic arthropathy
Are there skin complications?

Figure 7.1

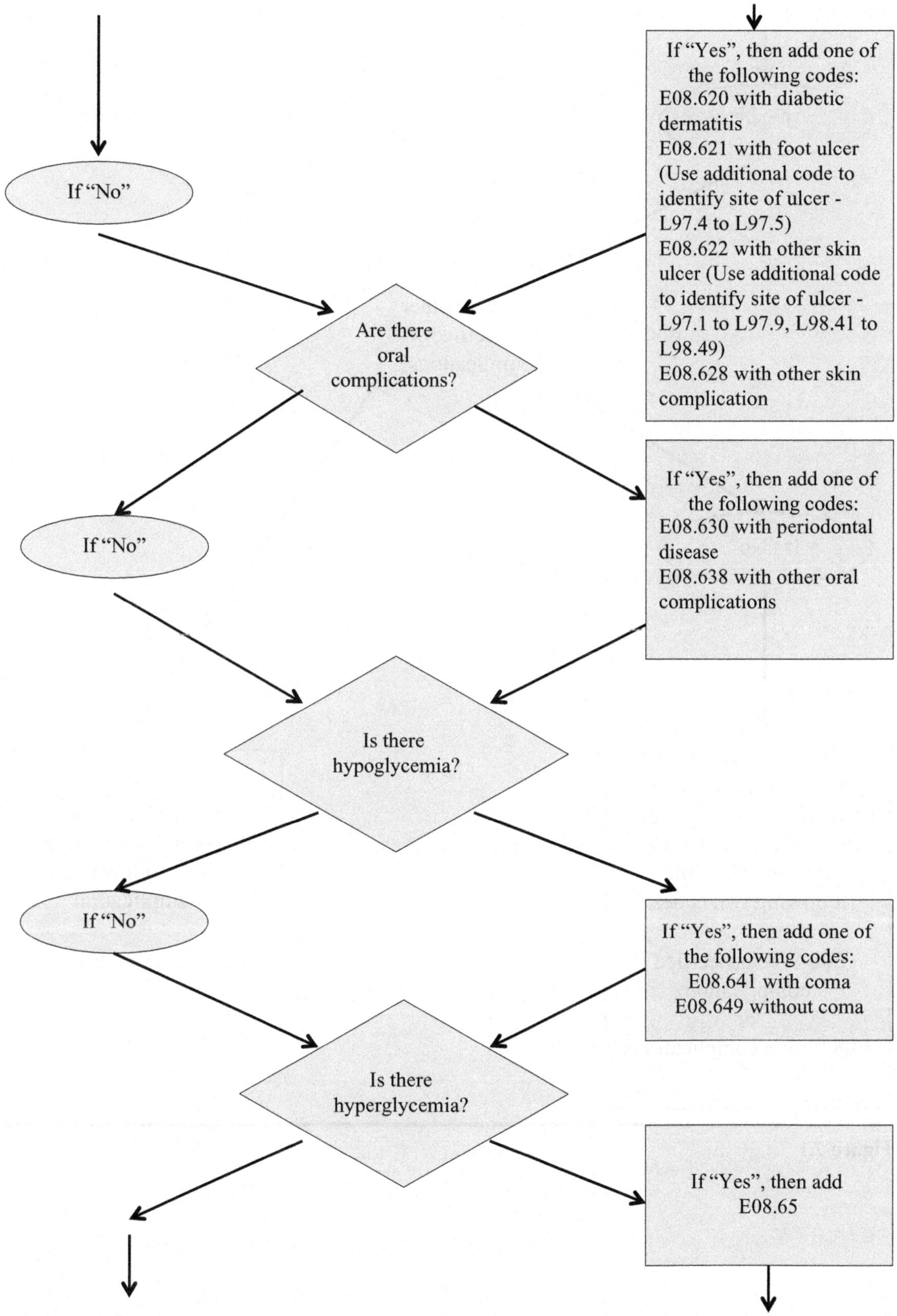

Figure 7.1 (Continued)

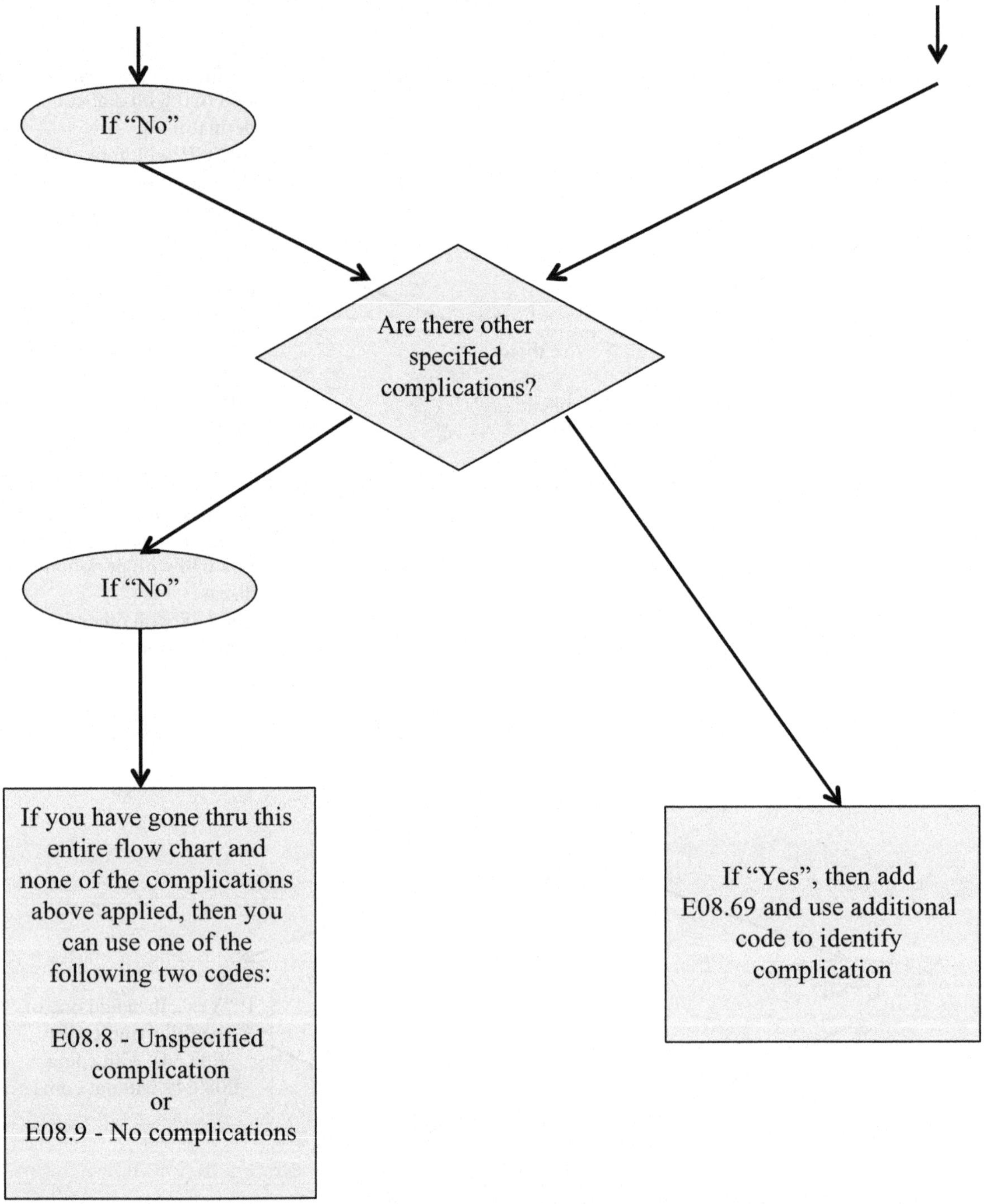
If "No"
Are there other specified complications?
If "No"
If you have gone thru this entire flow chart and none of the complications above applied, then you can use one of the following two codes:
E08.8 - Unspecified complication
or
E08.9 - No complications
If "Yes", then add E08.69 and use additional code to identify complication

Figure 7.1

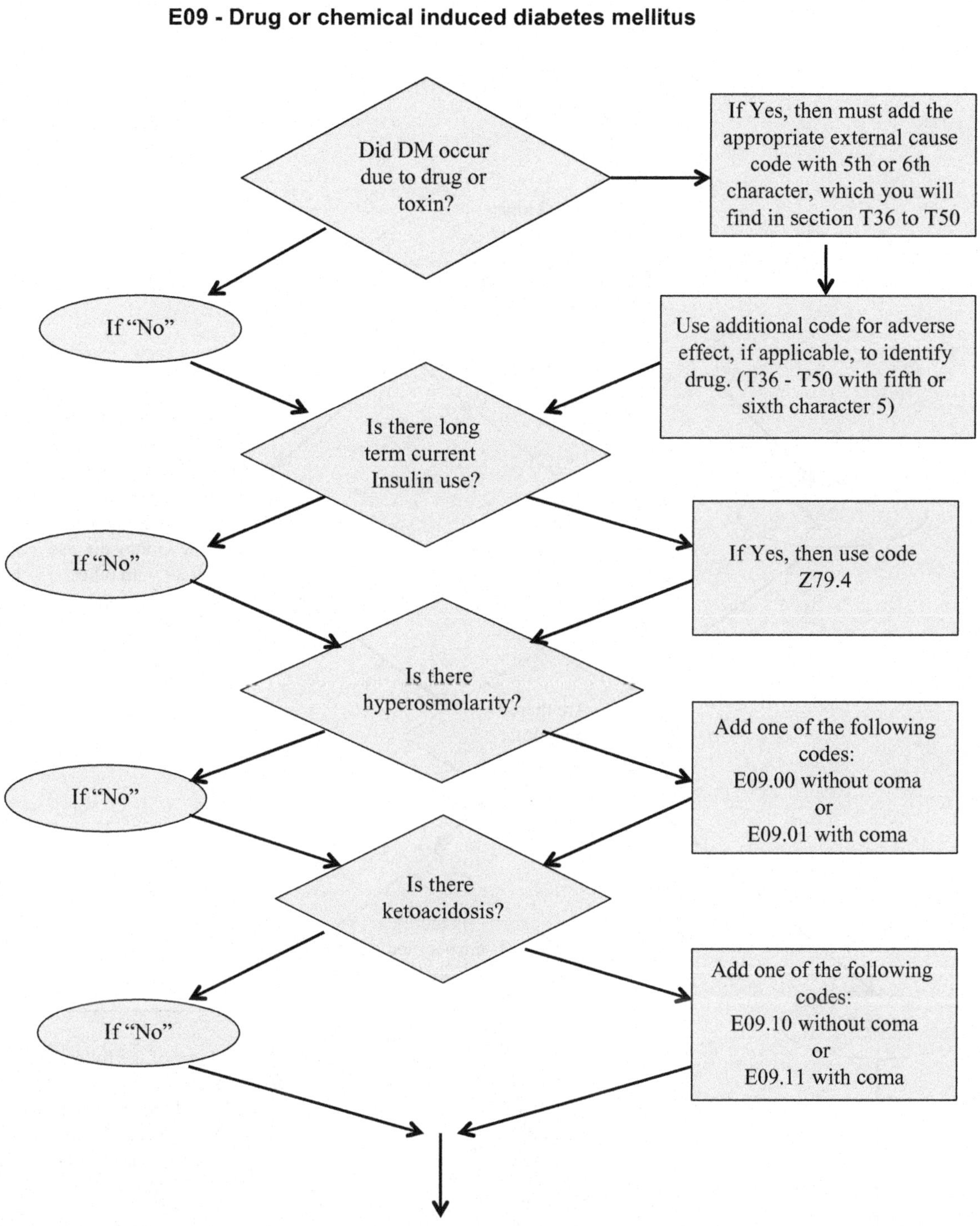

Figure 7.1 (Continued)

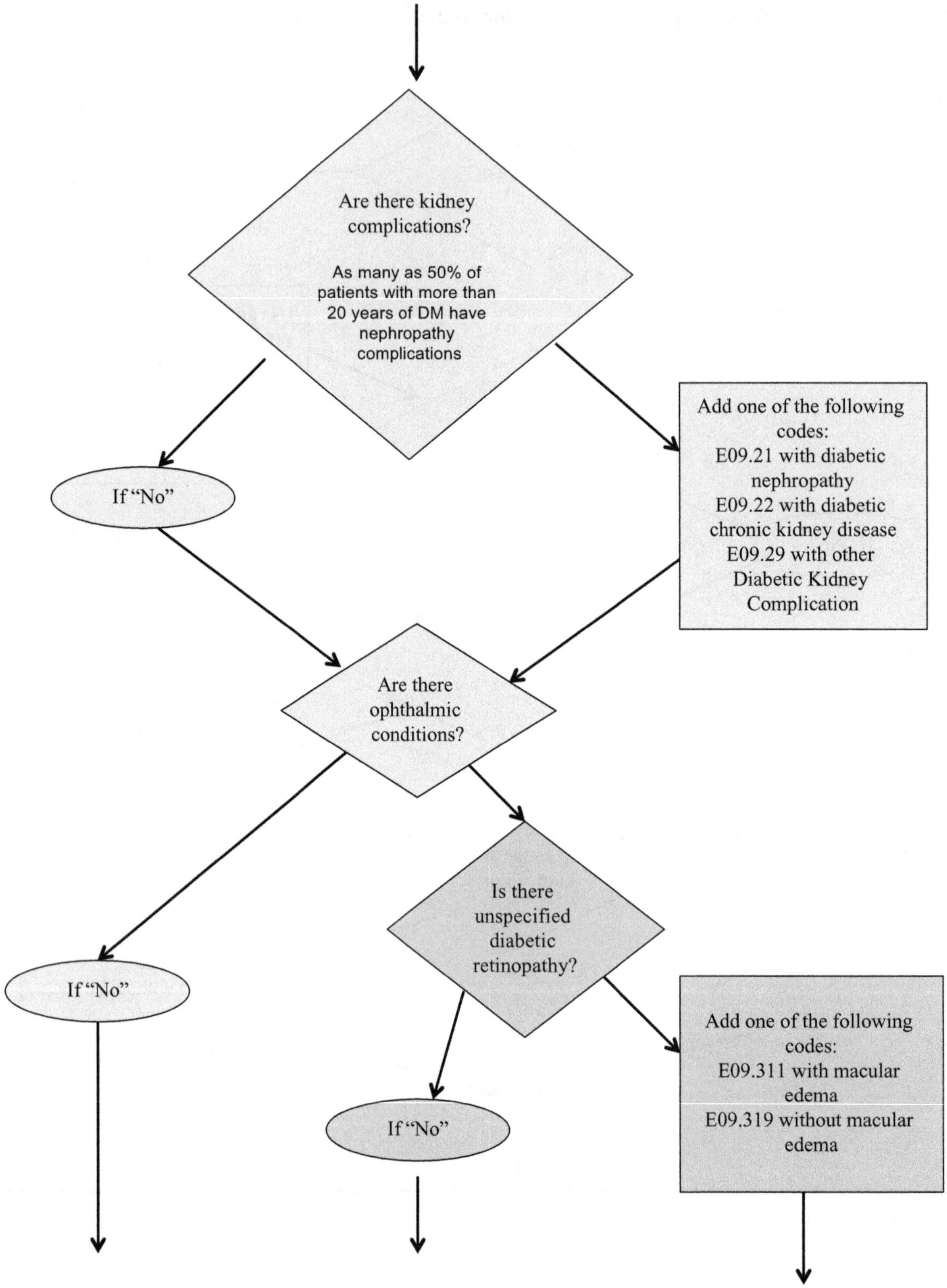
Are there kidney complications?
As many as 50% of patients with more than 20 years of DM have nephropathy complications
If "No"
Add one of the following codes:
E09.21 with diabetic nephropathy
E09.22 with diabetic chronic kidney disease
E09.29 with other Diabetic Kidney Complication
Are there ophthalmic conditions?
If "No"
Is there unspecified diabetic retinopathy?
If "No"
Add one of the following codes:
E09.311 with macular edema
E09.319 without macular edema

Figure 7.1

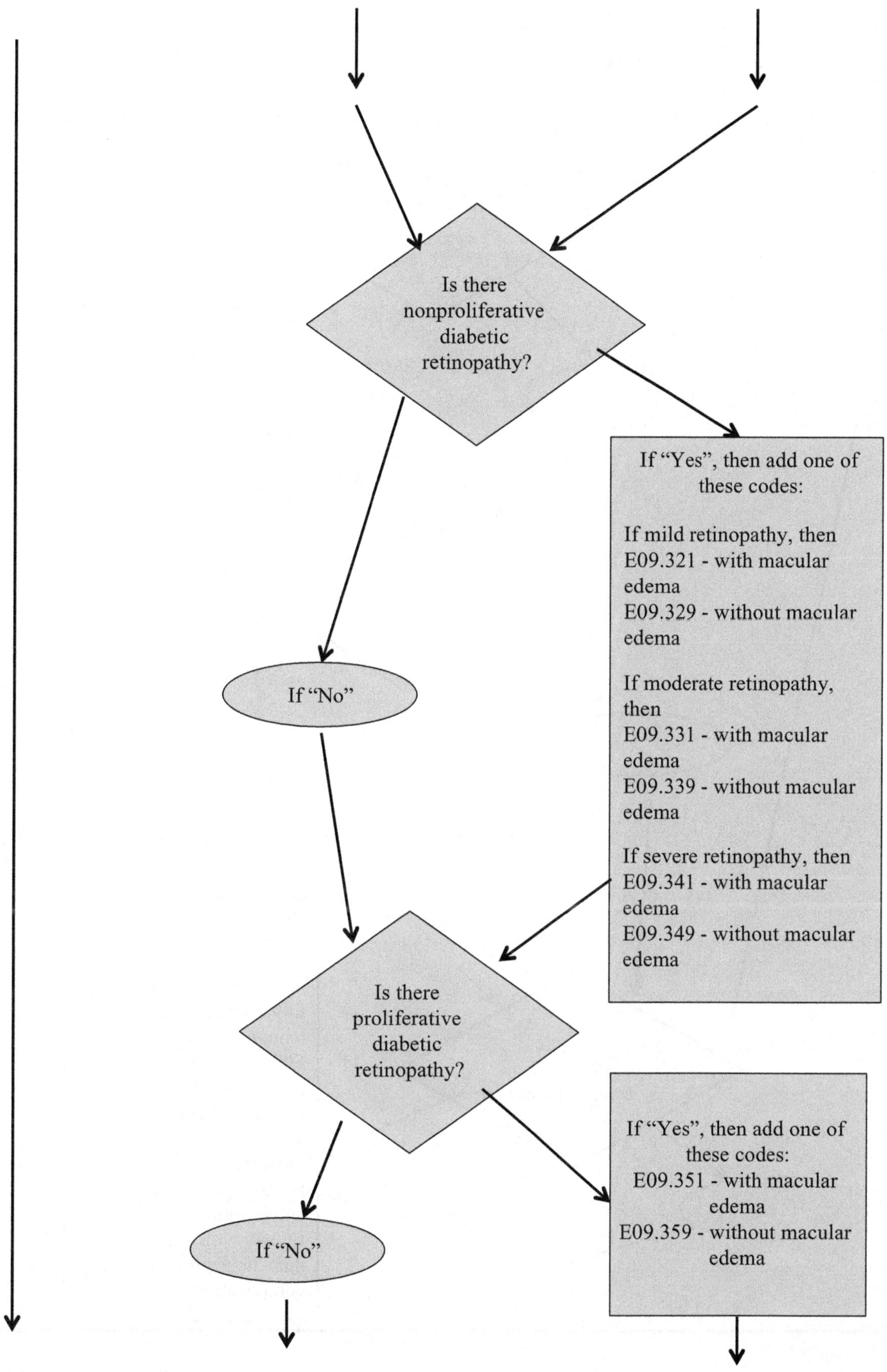

Figure 7.1 (Continued)

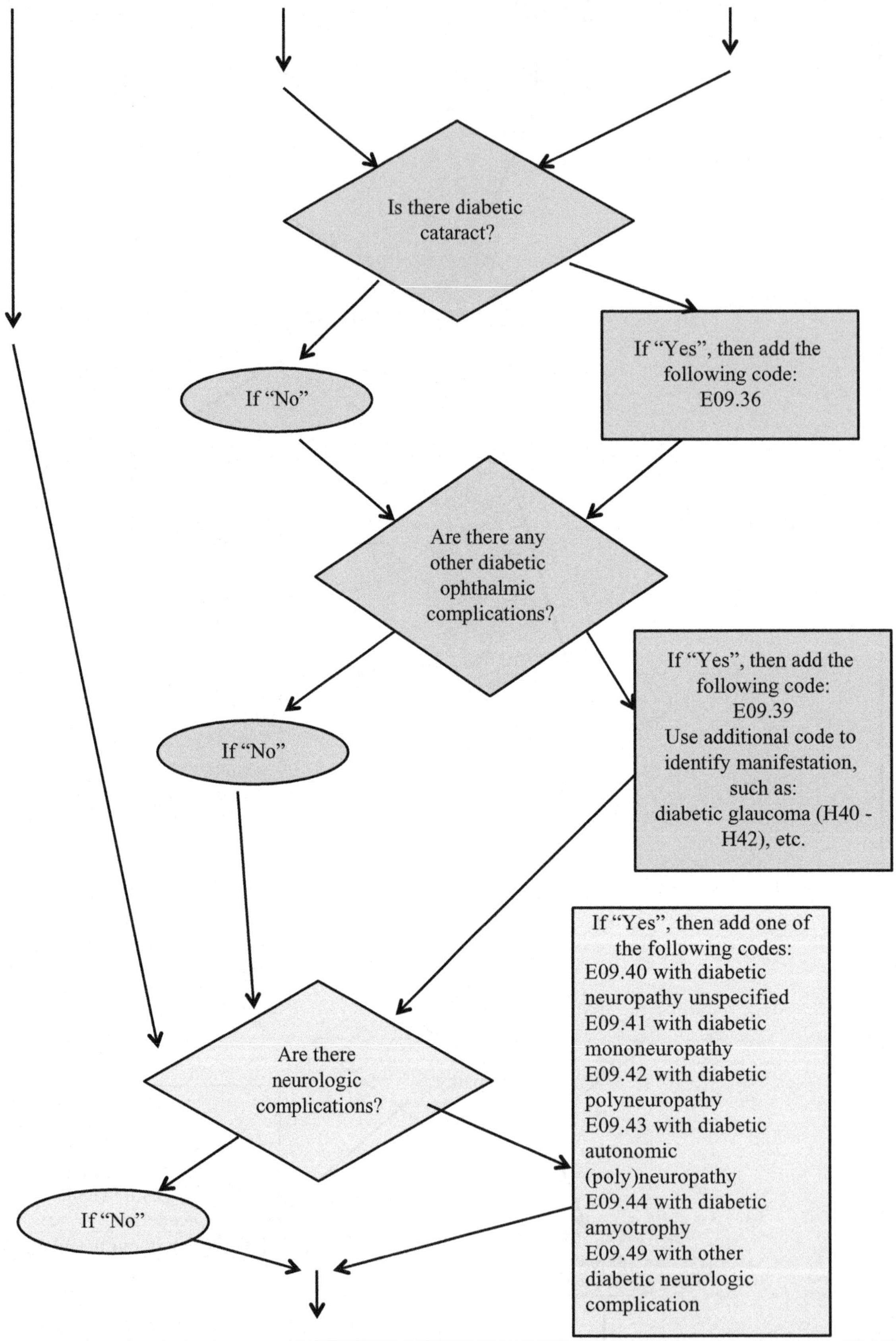
Is there diabetic cataract?
If "No"
If "Yes", then add the following code: E09.36
Are there any other diabetic ophthalmic complications?
If "No"
If "Yes", then add the following code: E09.39 Use additional code to identify manifestation, such as: diabetic glaucoma (H40 - H42), etc.
If "Yes", then add one of the following codes:
E09.40 with diabetic neuropathy unspecified
E09.41 with diabetic mononeuropathy
E09.42 with diabetic polyneuropathy
E09.43 with diabetic autonomic (poly)neuropathy
E09.44 with diabetic amyotrophy
E09.49 with other diabetic neurologic complication
Are there neurologic complications?
If "No"

Figure 7.1

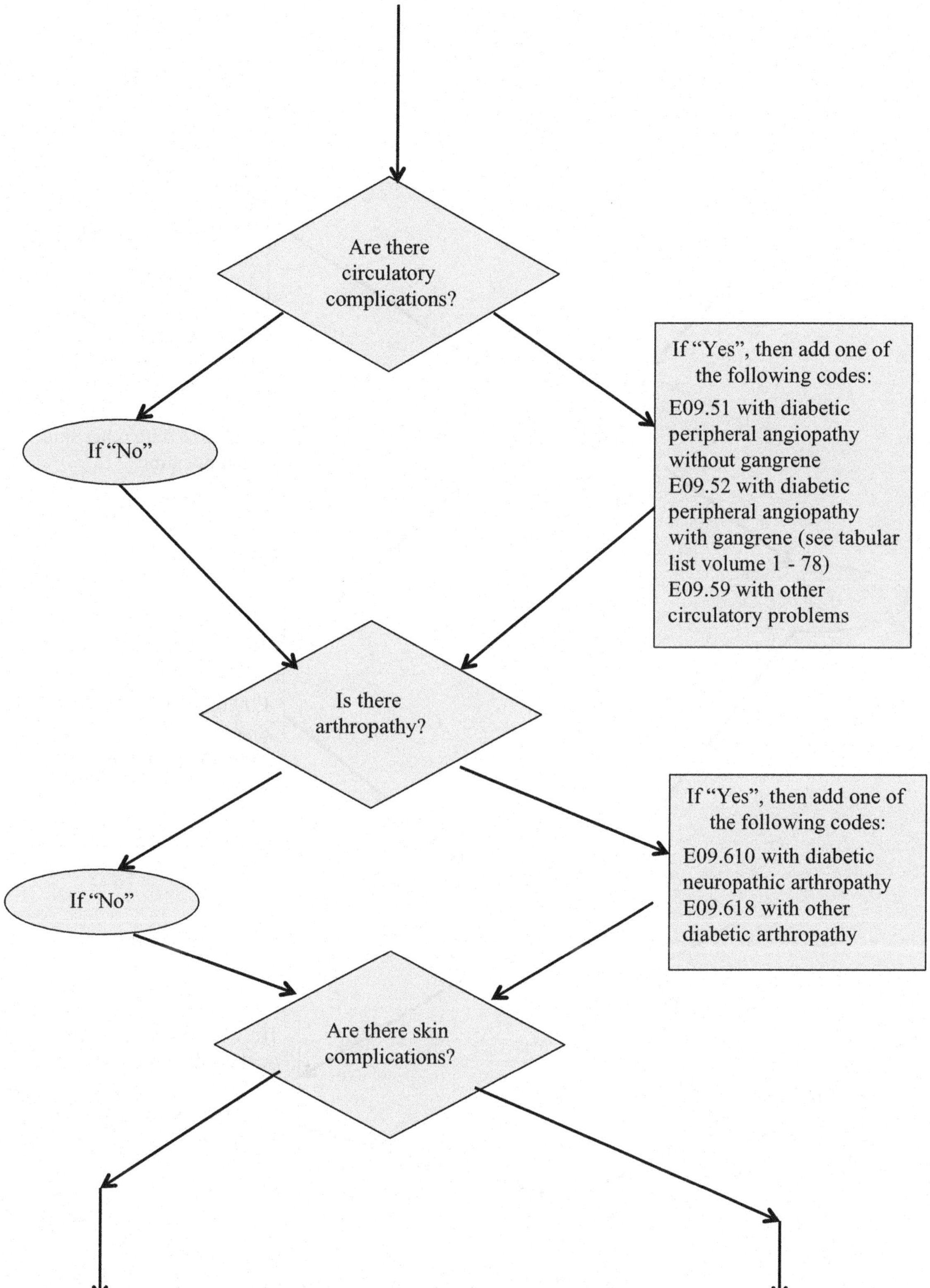

Figure 7.1 (Continued)

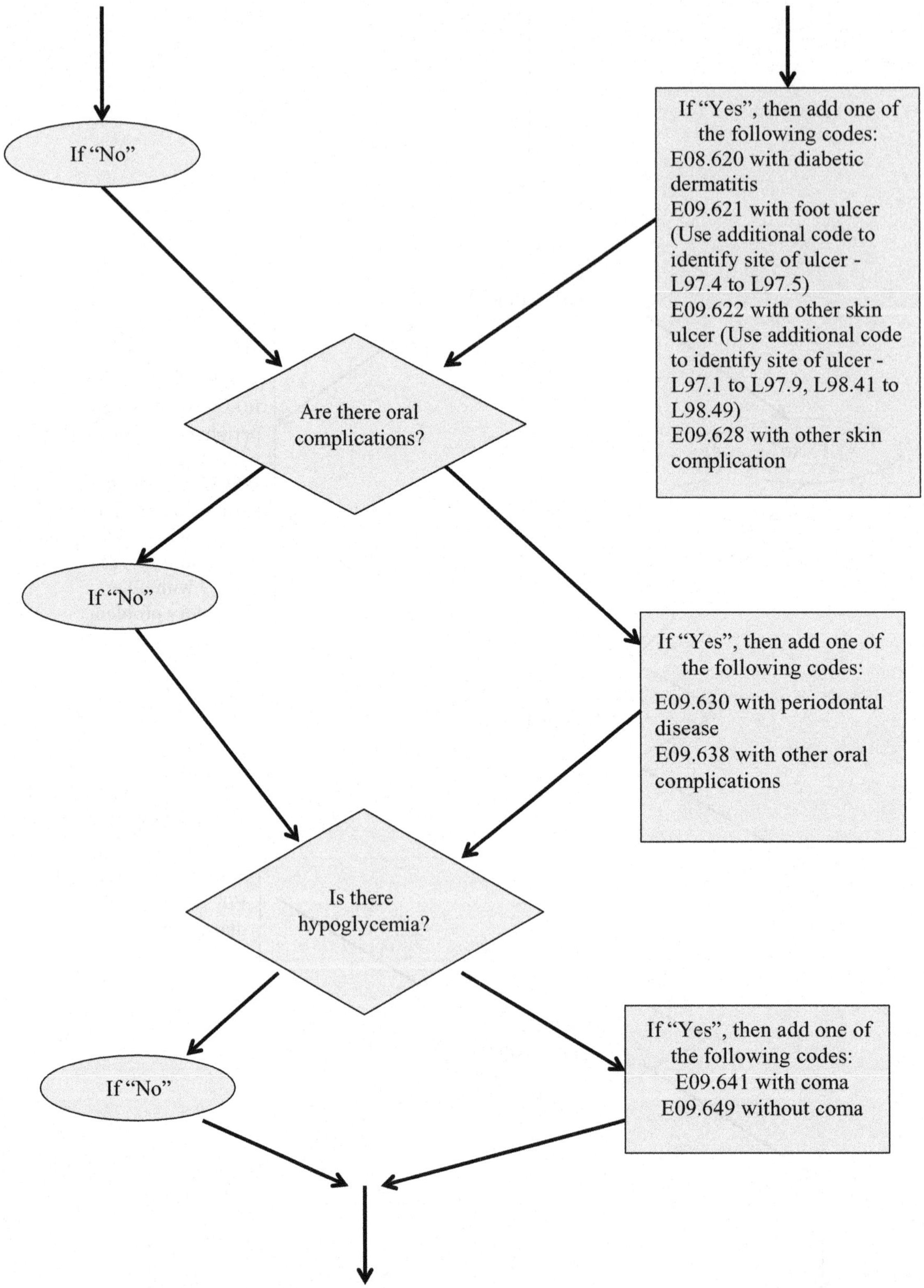

If "Yes", then add one of the following codes:
E08.620 with diabetic dermatitis
E09.621 with foot ulcer (Use additional code to identify site of ulcer - L97.4 to L97.5)
E09.622 with other skin ulcer (Use additional code to identify site of ulcer - L97.1 to L97.9, L98.41 to L98.49)
E09.628 with other skin complication
If "No"
Are there oral complications?
If "No"
If "Yes", then add one of the following codes:
E09.630 with periodontal disease
E09.638 with other oral complications
Is there hypoglycemia?
If "No"
If "Yes", then add one of the following codes:
E09.641 with coma
E09.649 without coma

Figure 7.1

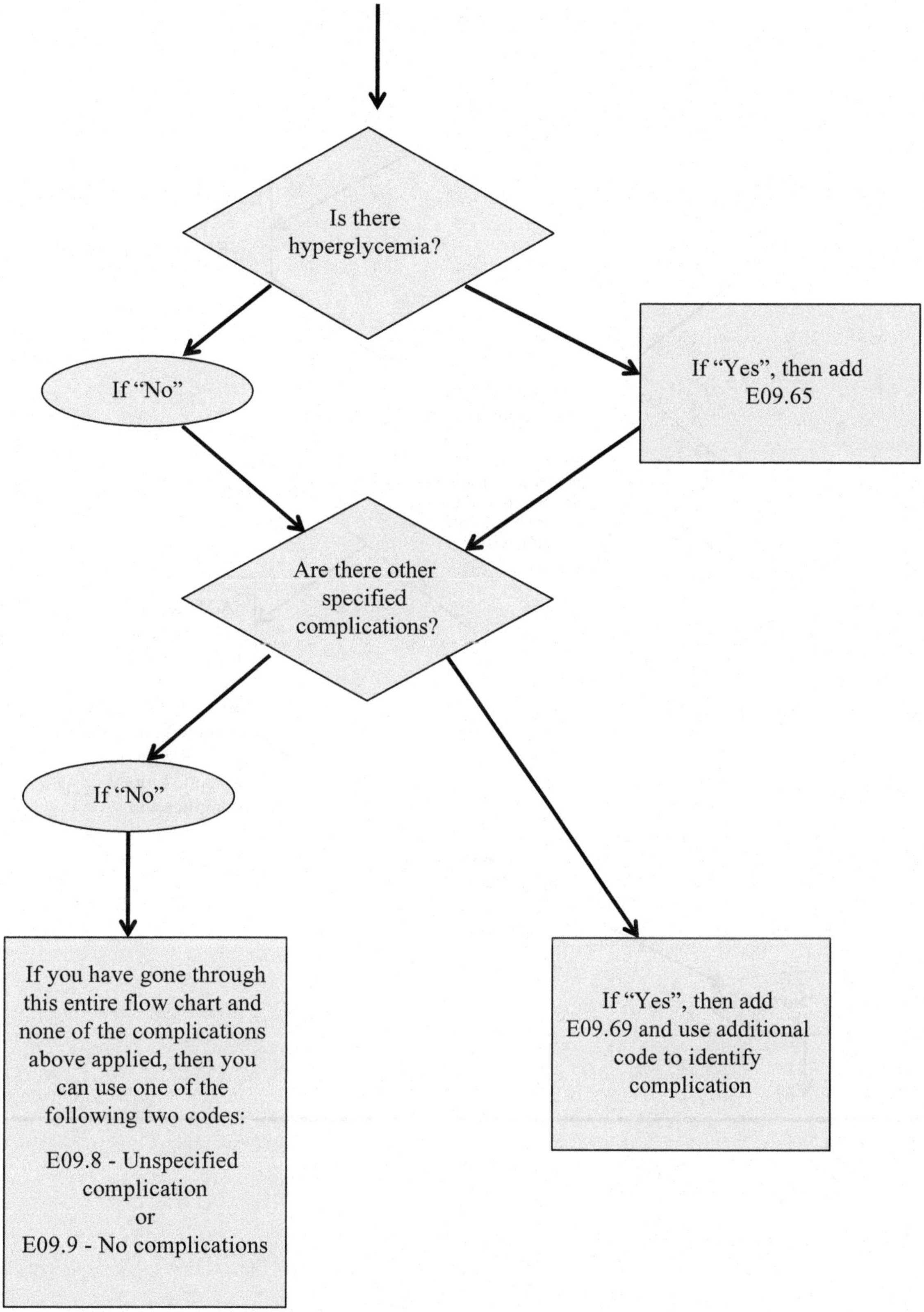

Figure 7.1 (Continued)

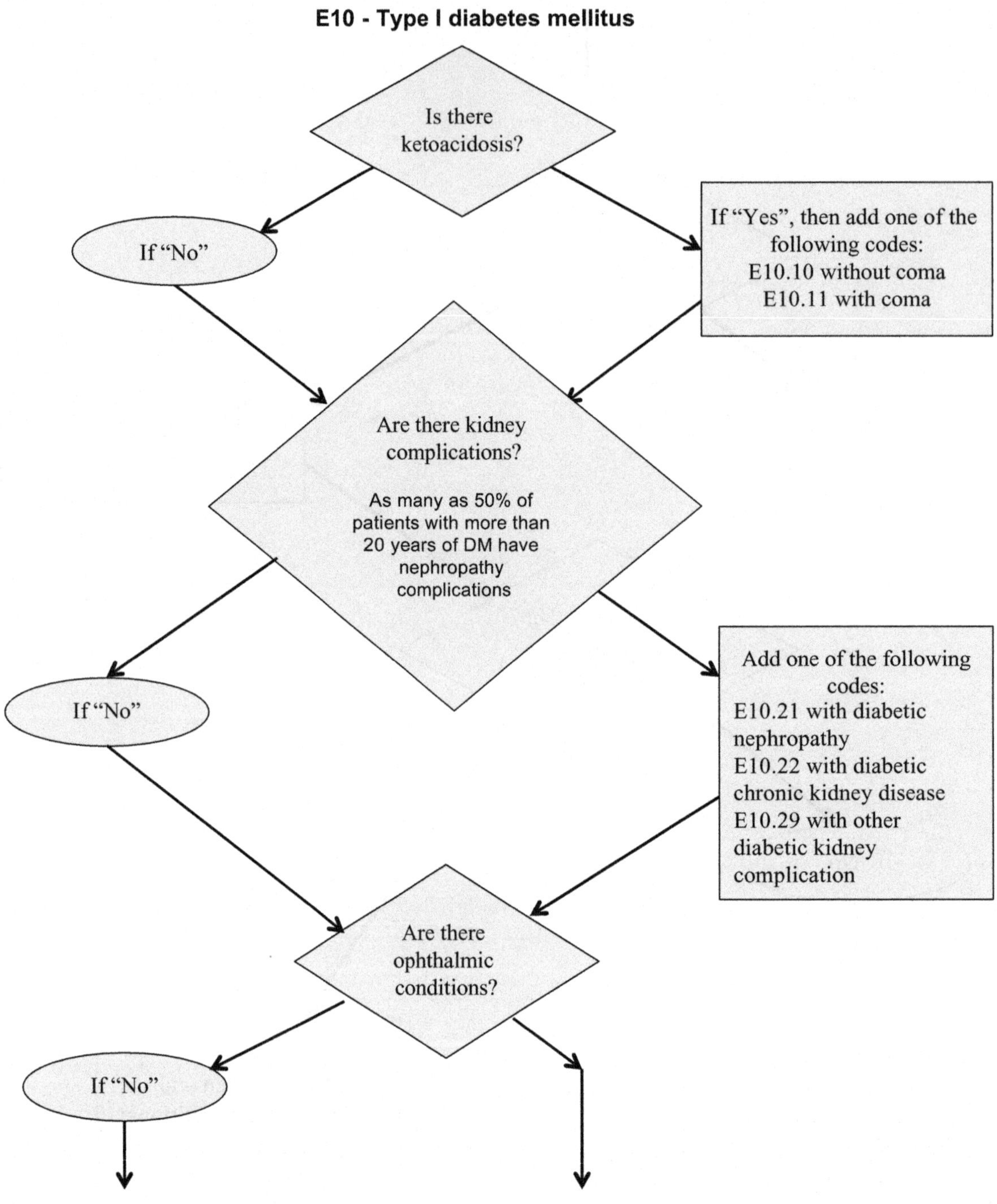
E10 - Type I diabetes mellitus
Is there ketoacidosis?
If "No"
If "Yes", then add one of the following codes:
E10.10 without coma
E10.11 with coma
Are there kidney complications?
As many as 50% of patients with more than 20 years of DM have nephropathy complications
If "No"
Add one of the following codes:
E10.21 with diabetic nephropathy
E10.22 with diabetic chronic kidney disease
E10.29 with other diabetic kidney complication
Are there ophthalmic conditions?
If "No"

Figure 7.1

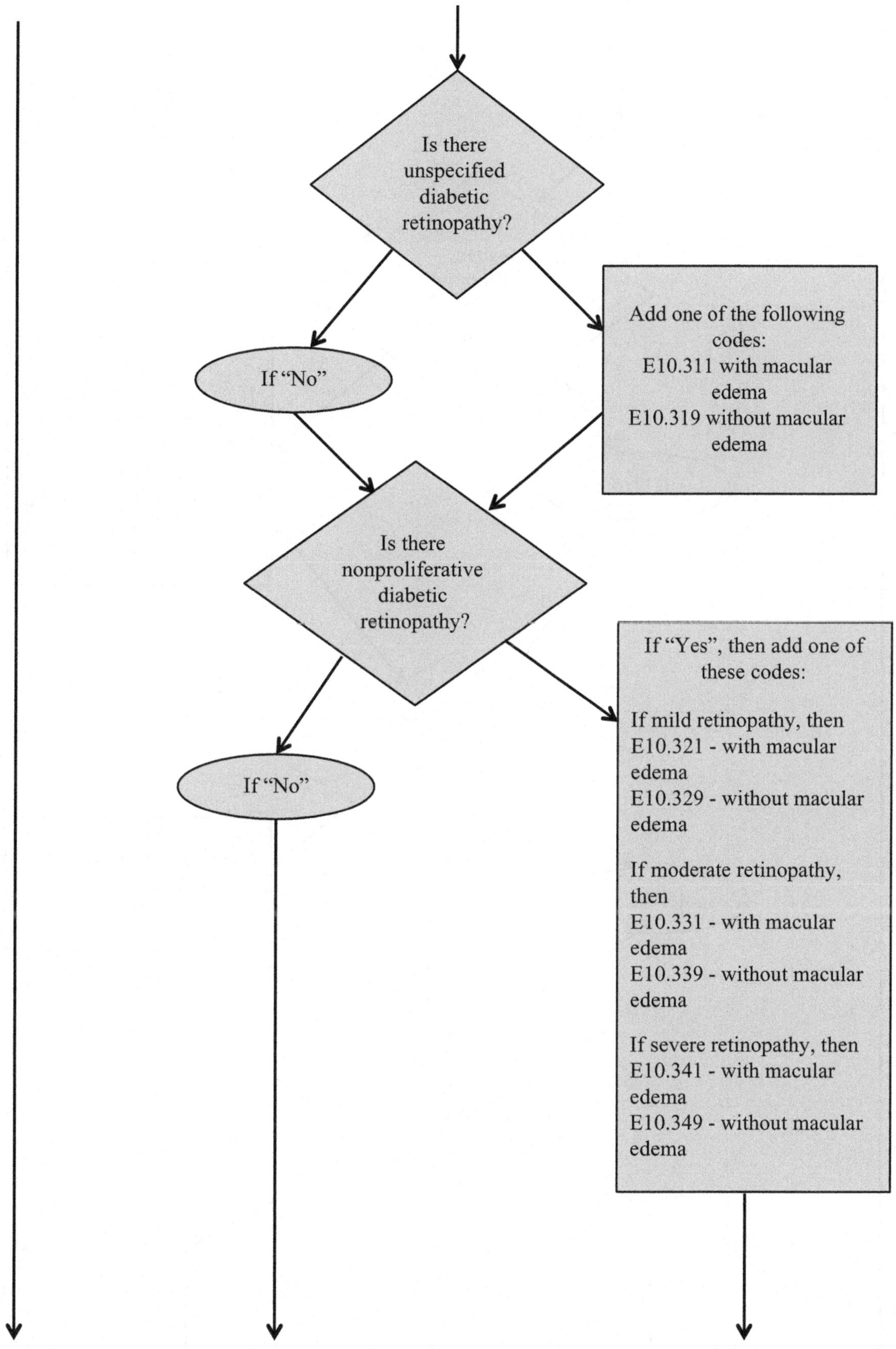

Figure 7.1 (Continued)

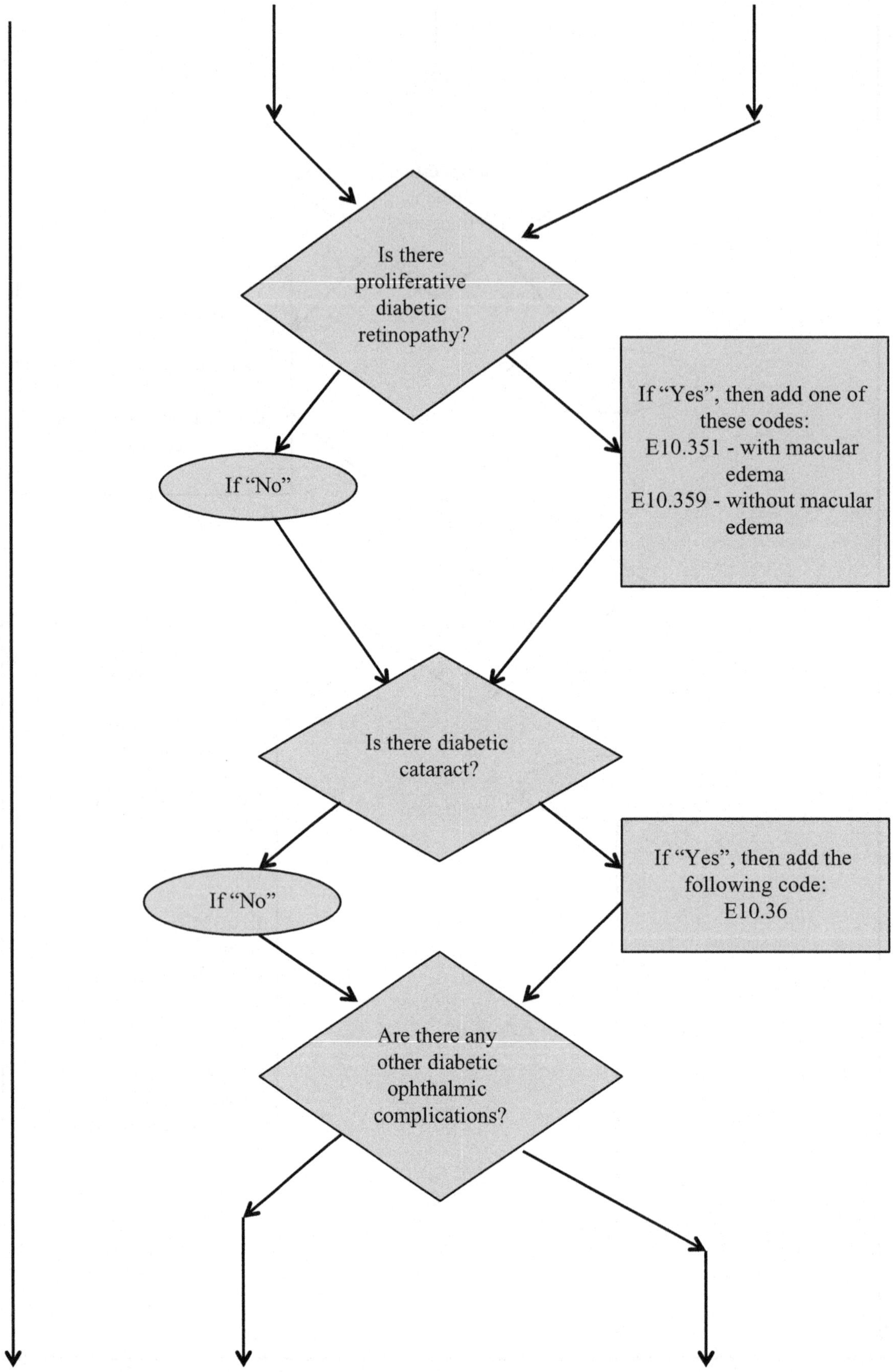

Is there proliferative diabetic retinopathy?
If "No"
If "Yes", then add one of these codes:
E10.351 - with macular edema
E10.359 - without macular edema
Is there diabetic cataract?
If "No"
If "Yes", then add the following code:
E10.36
Are there any other diabetic ophthalmic complications?

Figure 7.1

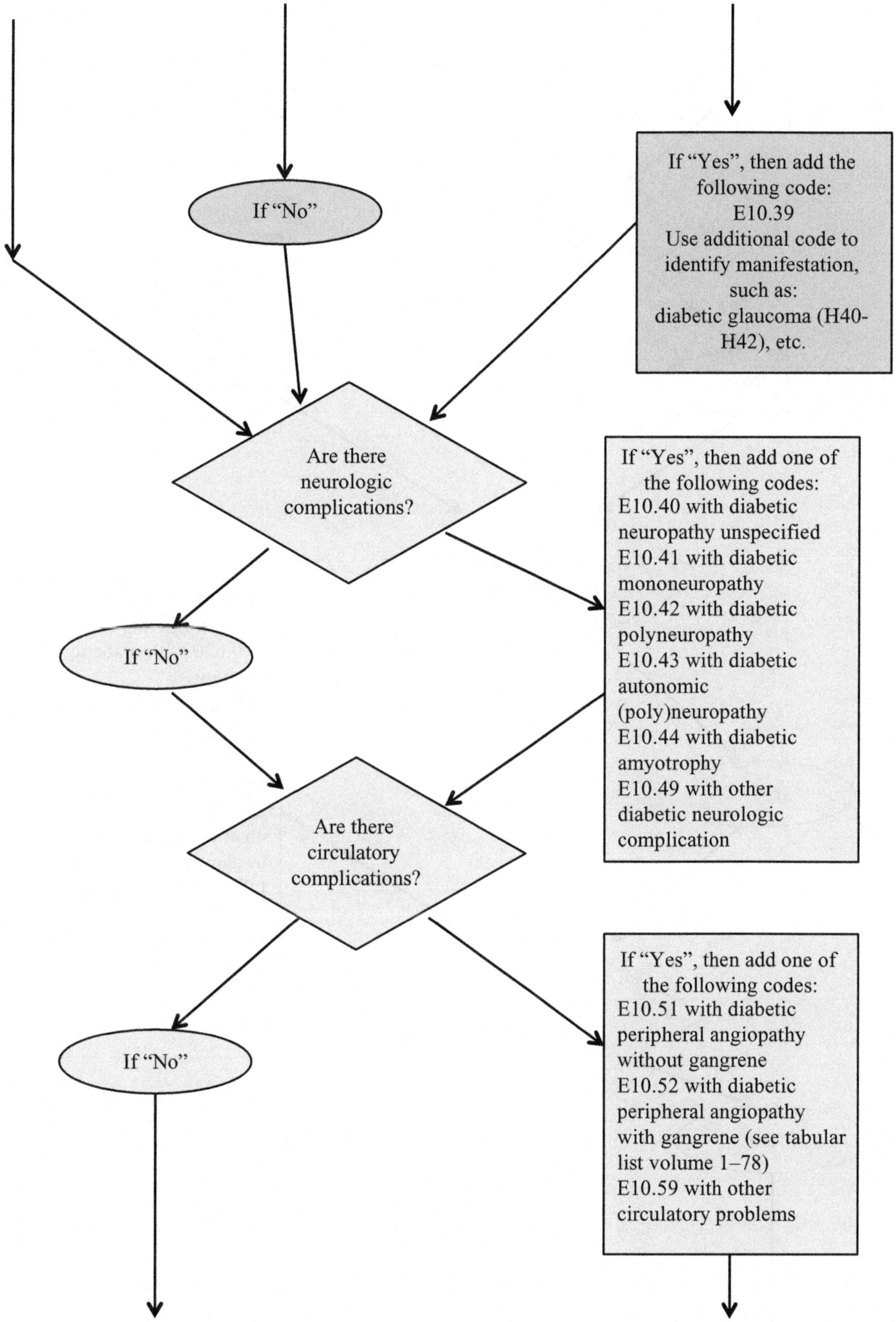

Figure 7.1 (Continued)

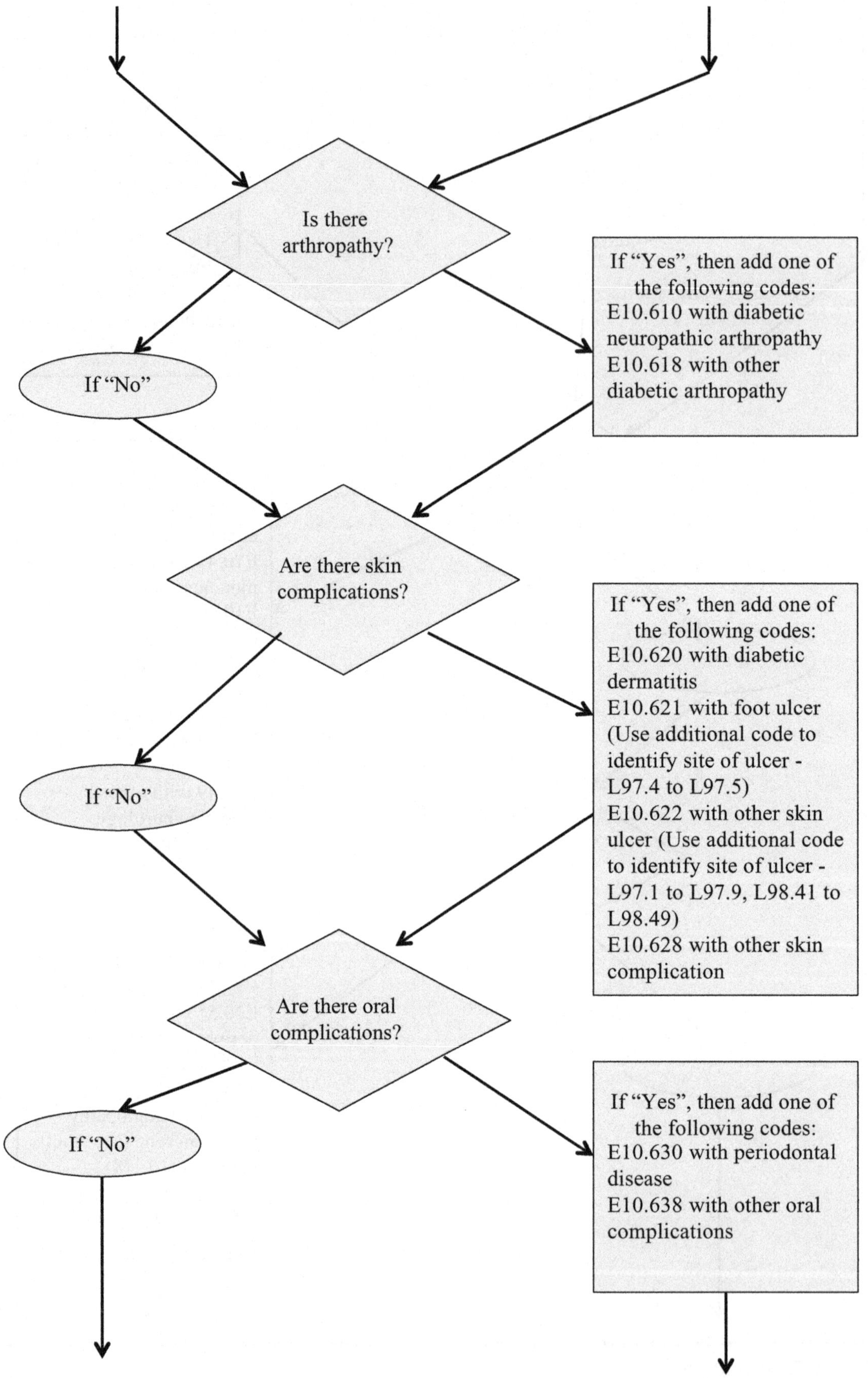
Is there arthropathy?
If "Yes", then add one of the following codes:
E10.610 with diabetic neuropathic arthropathy
E10.618 with other diabetic arthropathy
If "No"
Are there skin complications?
If "Yes", then add one of the following codes:
E10.620 with diabetic dermatitis
E10.621 with foot ulcer (Use additional code to identify site of ulcer - L97.4 to L97.5)
E10.622 with other skin ulcer (Use additional code to identify site of ulcer - L97.1 to L97.9, L98.41 to L98.49)
E10.628 with other skin complication
If "No"
Are there oral complications?
If "Yes", then add one of the following codes:
E10.630 with periodontal disease
E10.638 with other oral complications
If "No"

Figure 7.1

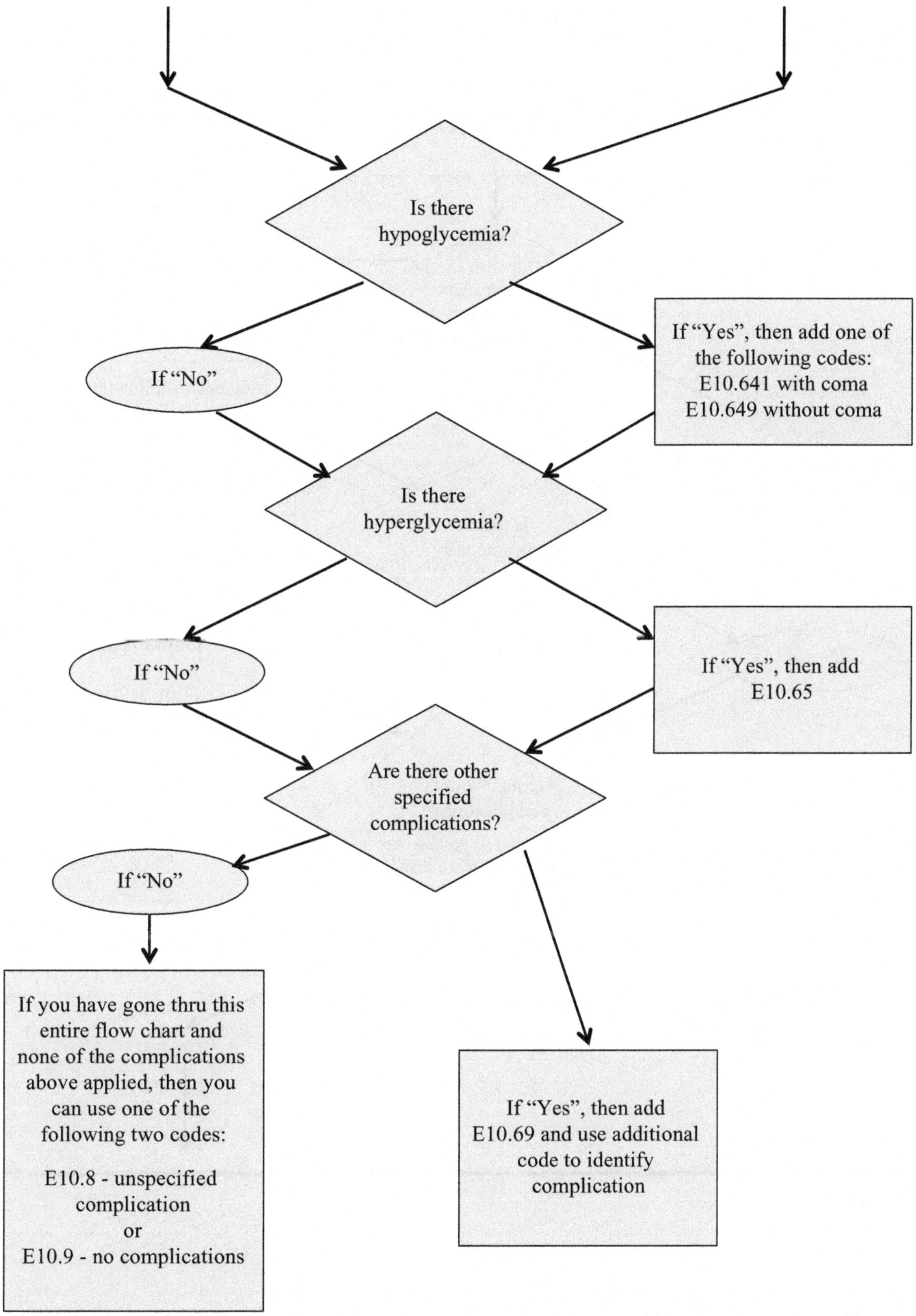

Figure 7.1 (Continued)

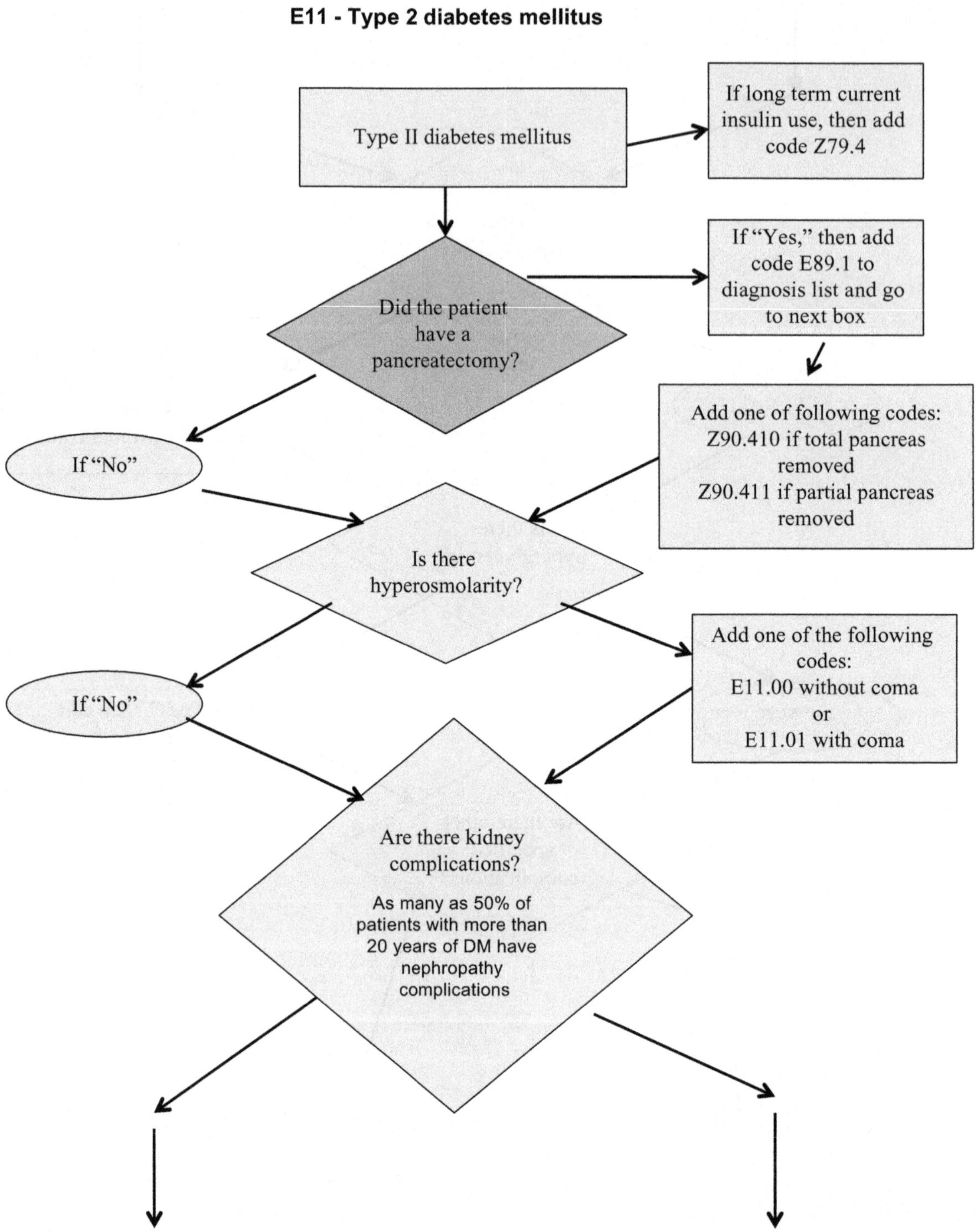
E11 - Type 2 diabetes mellitus
Type II diabetes mellitus
If long term current insulin use, then add code Z79.4
Did the patient have a pancreatectomy?
If "Yes," then add code E89.1 to diagnosis list and go to next box
Add one of following codes: Z90.410 if total pancreas removed Z90.411 if partial pancreas removed
If "No"
Is there hyperosmolarity?
Add one of the following codes: E11.00 without coma or E11.01 with coma
If "No"
Are there kidney complications?
As many as 50% of patients with more than 20 years of DM have nephropathy complications

Figure 7.1

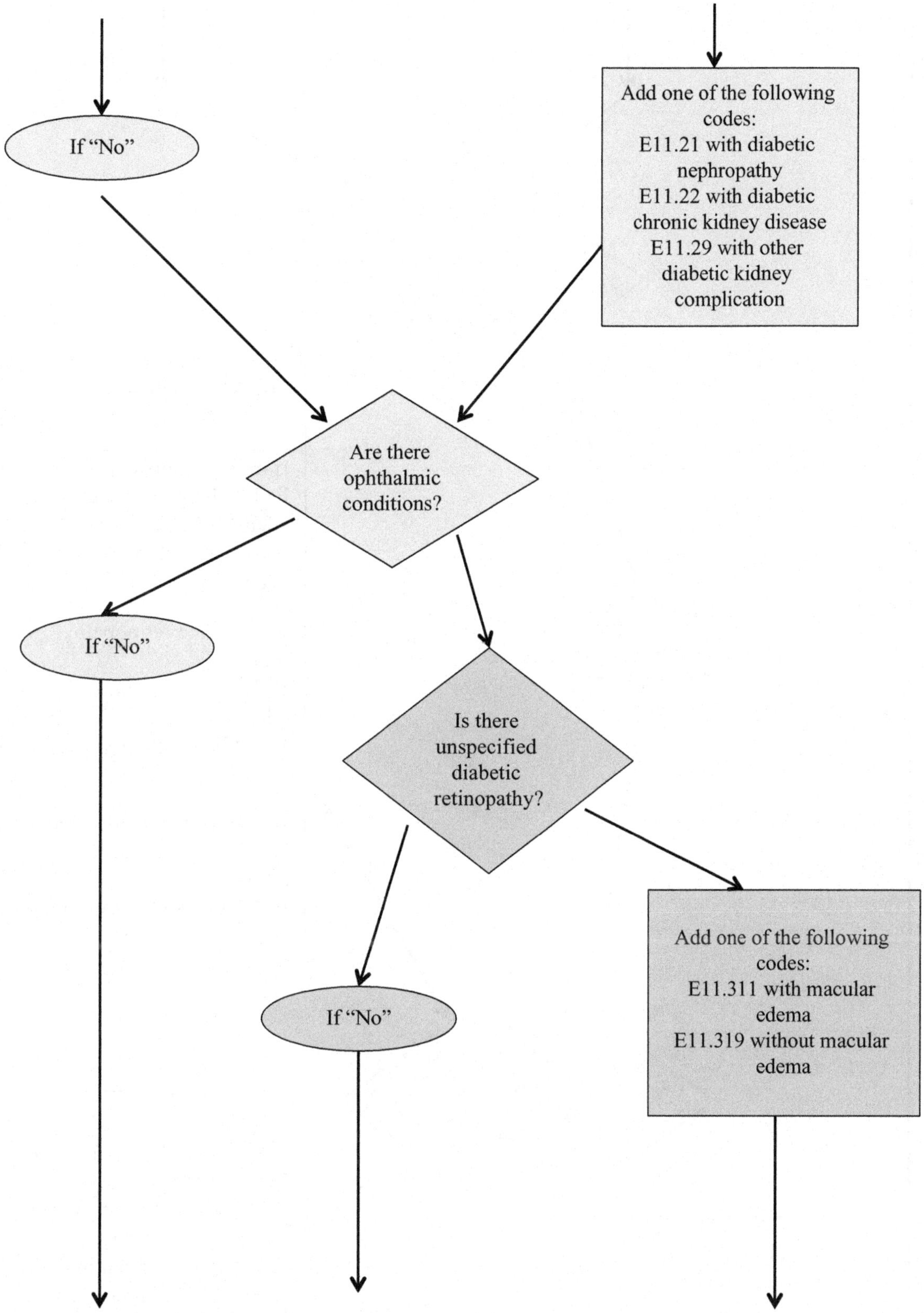

Figure 7.1 (Continued)

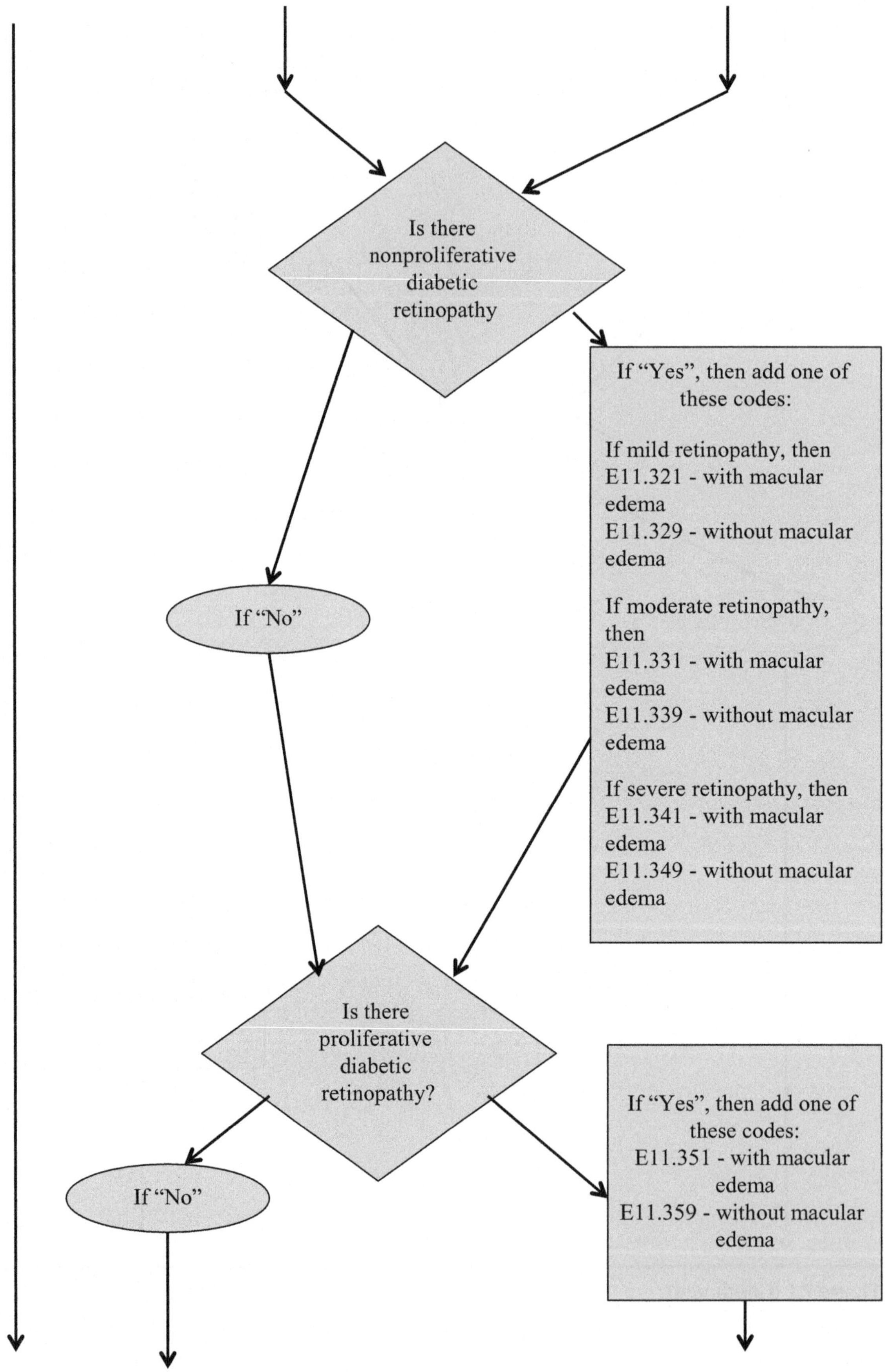

Is there nonproliferative diabetic retinopathy
If "Yes", then add one of these codes:
If mild retinopathy, then
E11.321 - with macular edema
E11.329 - without macular edema
If moderate retinopathy, then
E11.331 - with macular edema
E11.339 - without macular edema
If severe retinopathy, then
E11.341 - with macular edema
E11.349 - without macular edema
If "No"
Is there proliferative diabetic retinopathy?
If "No"
If "Yes", then add one of these codes:
E11.351 - with macular edema
E11.359 - without macular edema

Figure 7.1

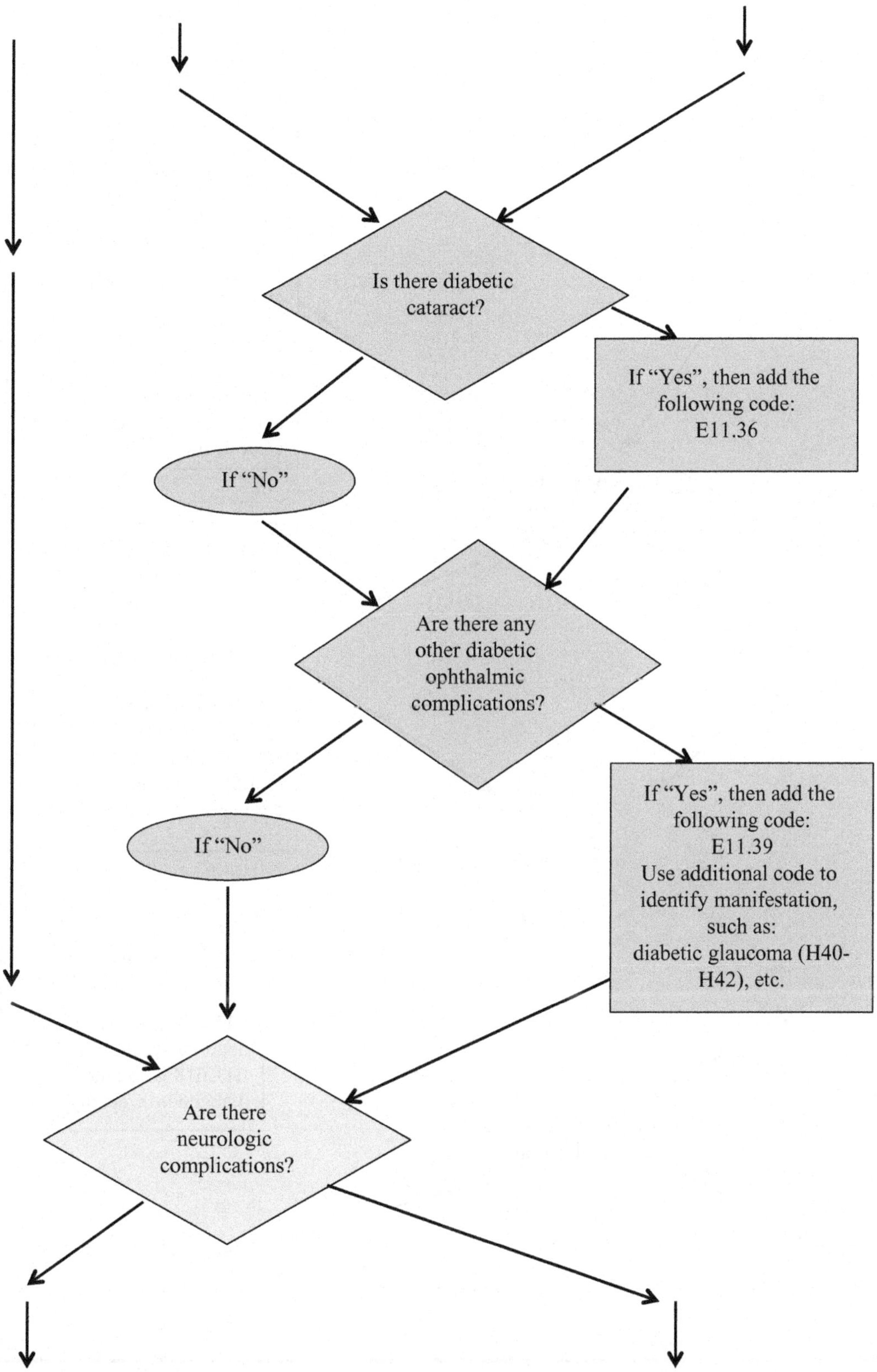

Figure 7.1 (Continued)

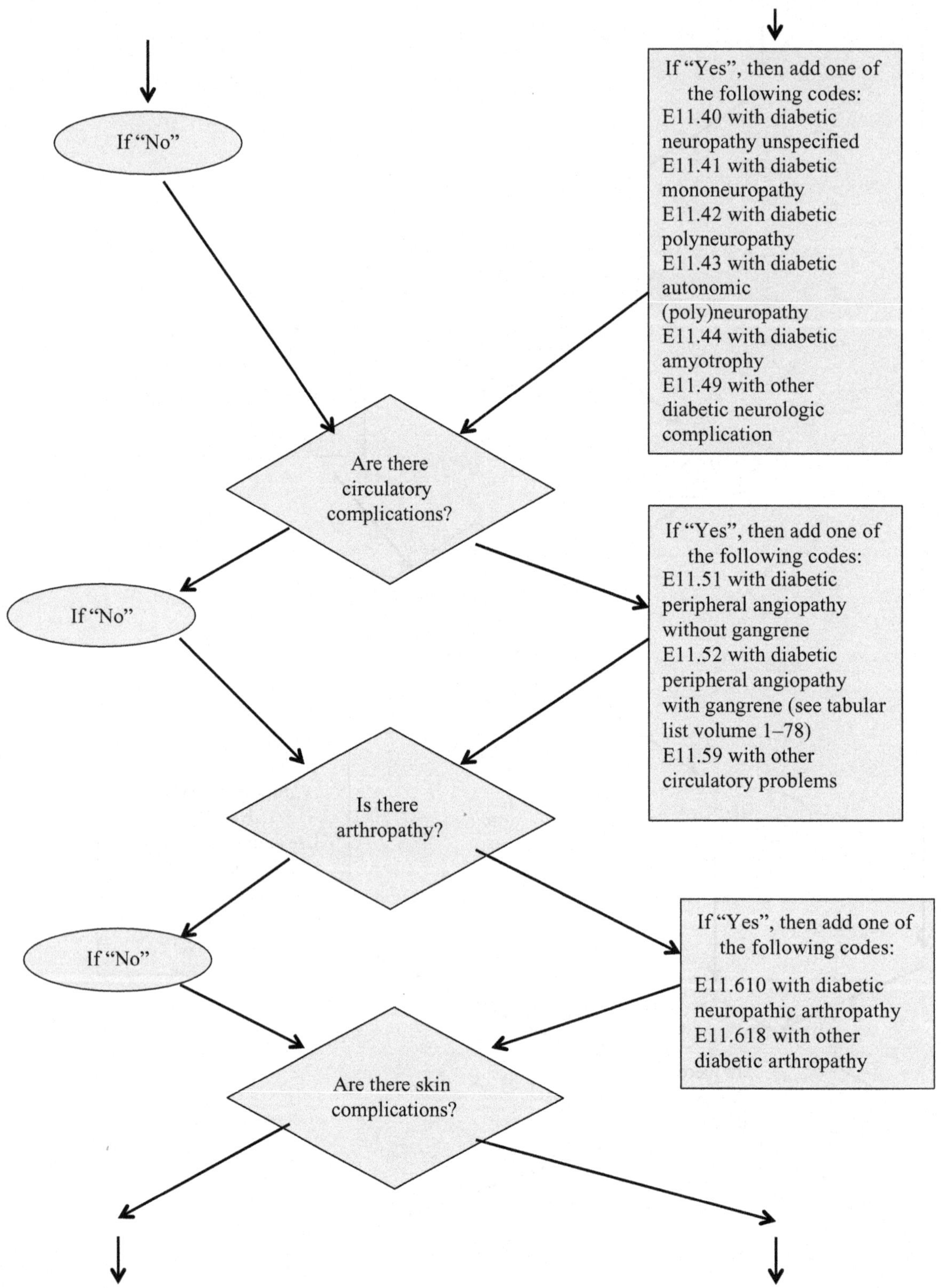
If "No"
If "Yes", then add one of the following codes:
E11.40 with diabetic neuropathy unspecified
E11.41 with diabetic mononeuropathy
E11.42 with diabetic polyneuropathy
E11.43 with diabetic autonomic (poly)neuropathy
E11.44 with diabetic amyotrophy
E11.49 with other diabetic neurologic complication
Are there circulatory complications?
If "No"
If "Yes", then add one of the following codes:
E11.51 with diabetic peripheral angiopathy without gangrene
E11.52 with diabetic peripheral angiopathy with gangrene (see tabular list volume 1–78)
E11.59 with other circulatory problems
Is there arthropathy?
If "No"
If "Yes", then add one of the following codes:
E11.610 with diabetic neuropathic arthropathy
E11.618 with other diabetic arthropathy
Are there skin complications?

Figure 7.1

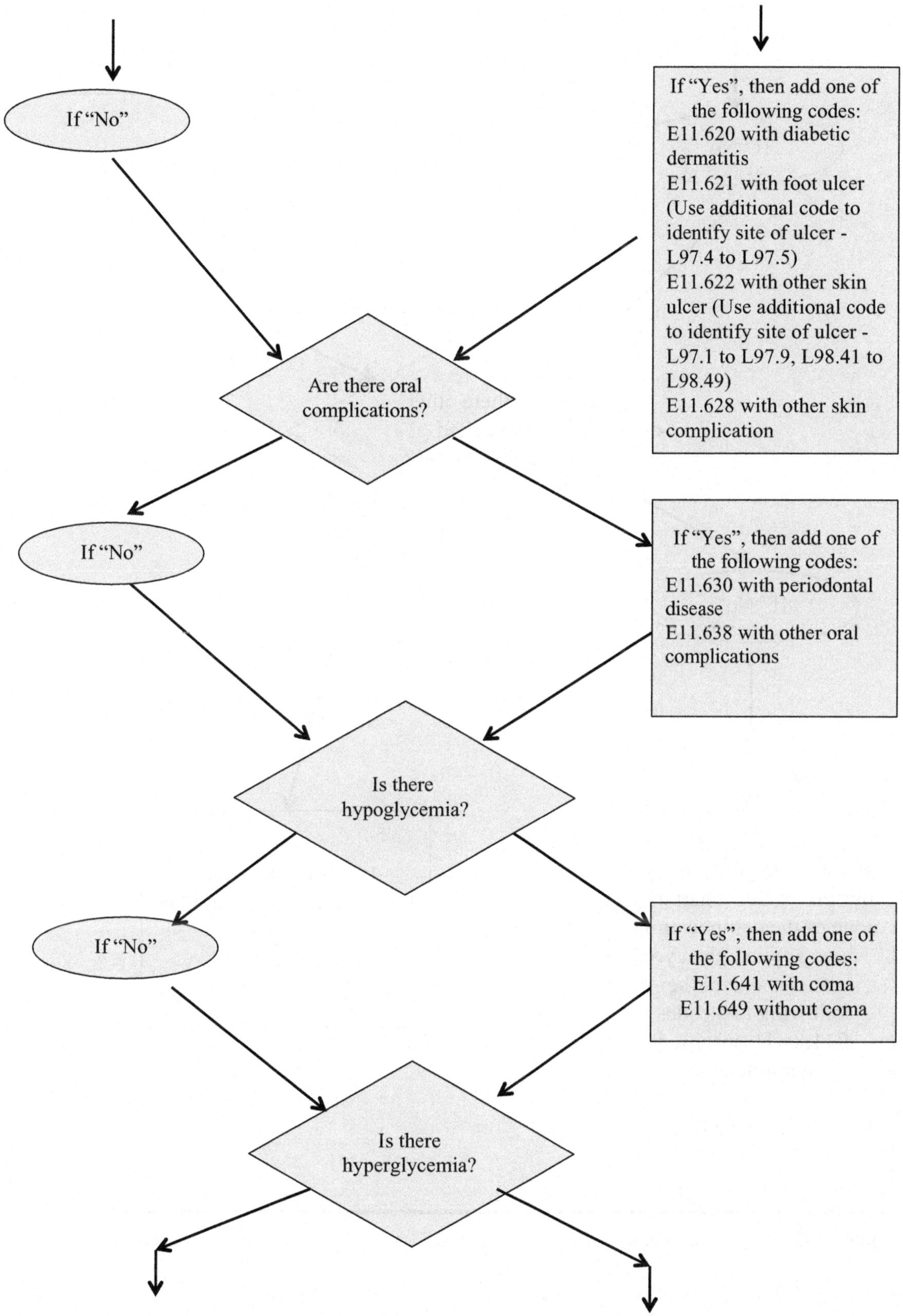

Figure 7.1 (Continued)

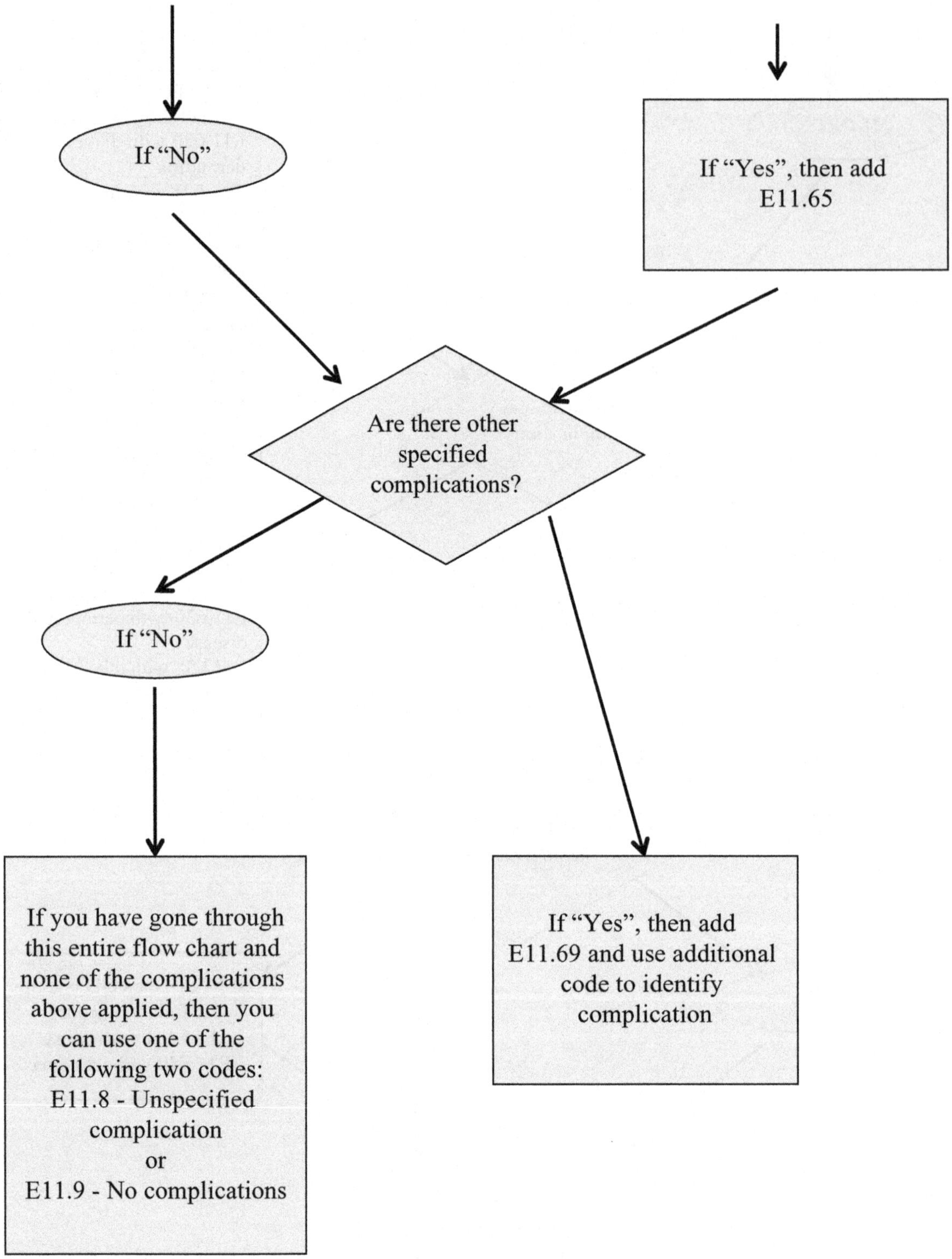
If "No"
If "Yes", then add E11.65
Are there other specified complications?
If "No"
If you have gone through this entire flow chart and none of the complications above applied, then you can use one of the following two codes: E11.8 - Unspecified complication or E11.9 - No complications
If "Yes", then add E11.69 and use additional code to identify complication

Figure 7.1

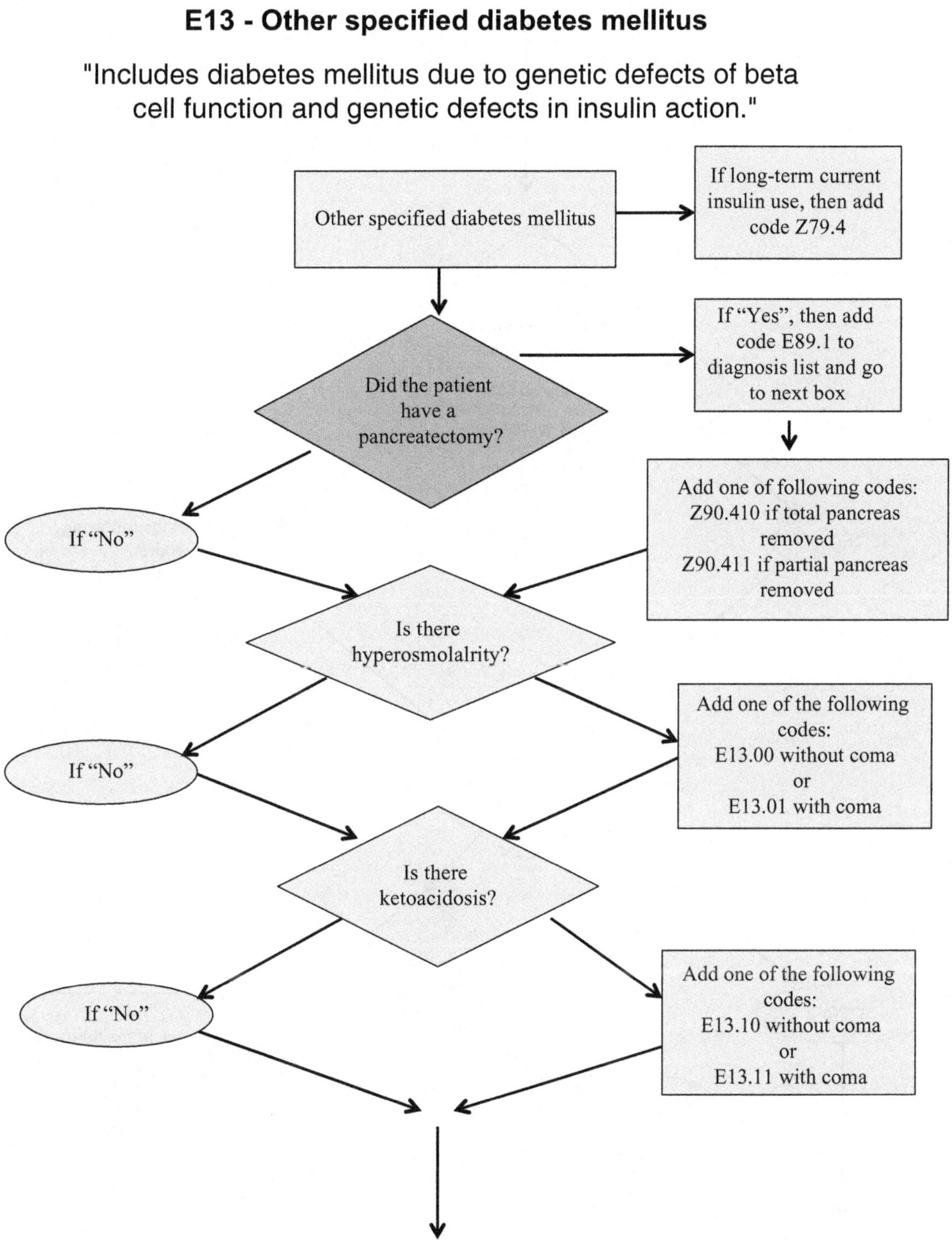

Figure 7.1 (Continued)

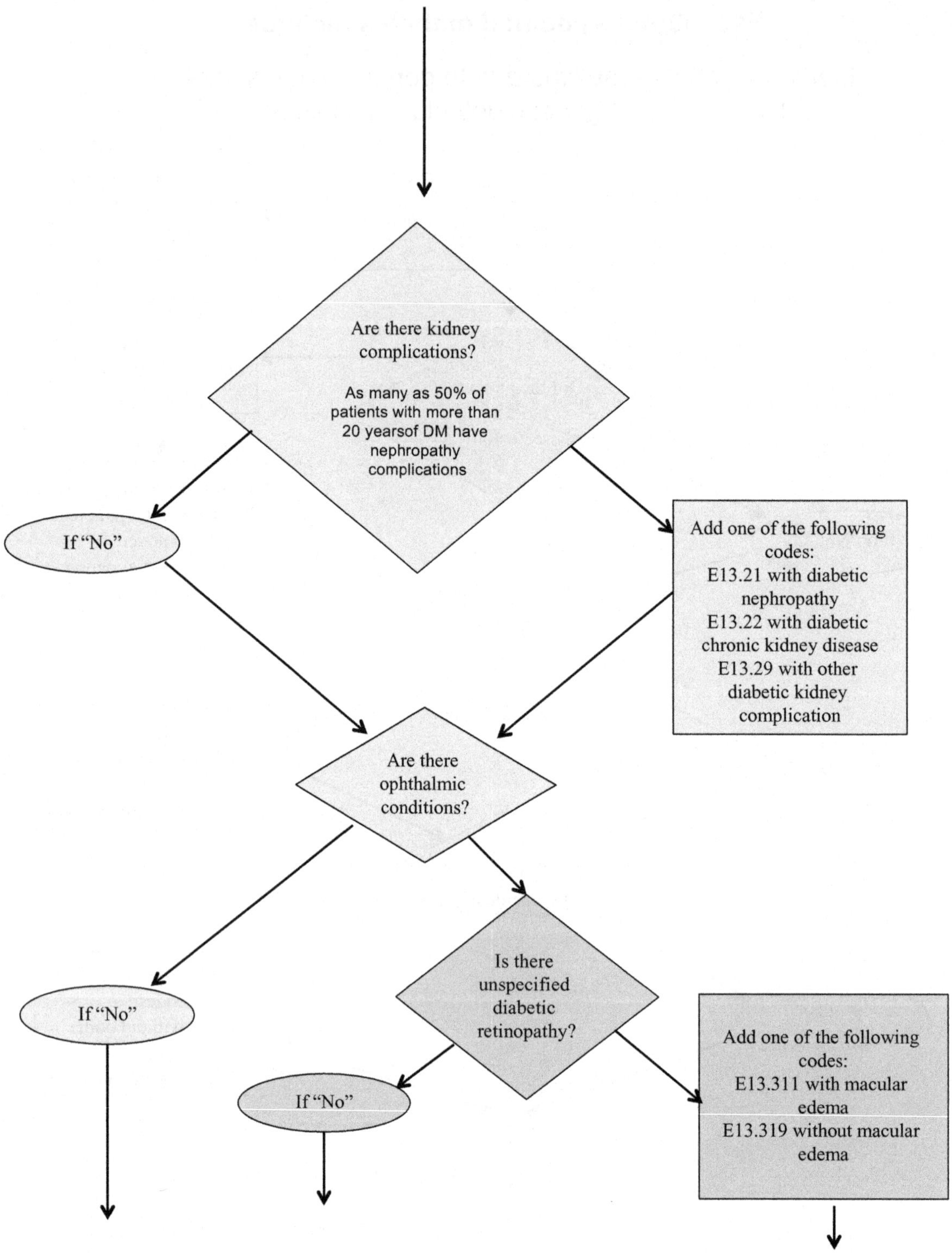
Are there kidney complications?
As many as 50% of patients with more than 20 yearsof DM have nephropathy complications
If "No"
Add one of the following codes:
E13.21 with diabetic nephropathy
E13.22 with diabetic chronic kidney disease
E13.29 with other diabetic kidney complication
Are there ophthalmic conditions?
If "No"
Is there unspecified diabetic retinopathy?
If "No"
Add one of the following codes:
E13.311 with macular edema
E13.319 without macular edema

Figure 7.1

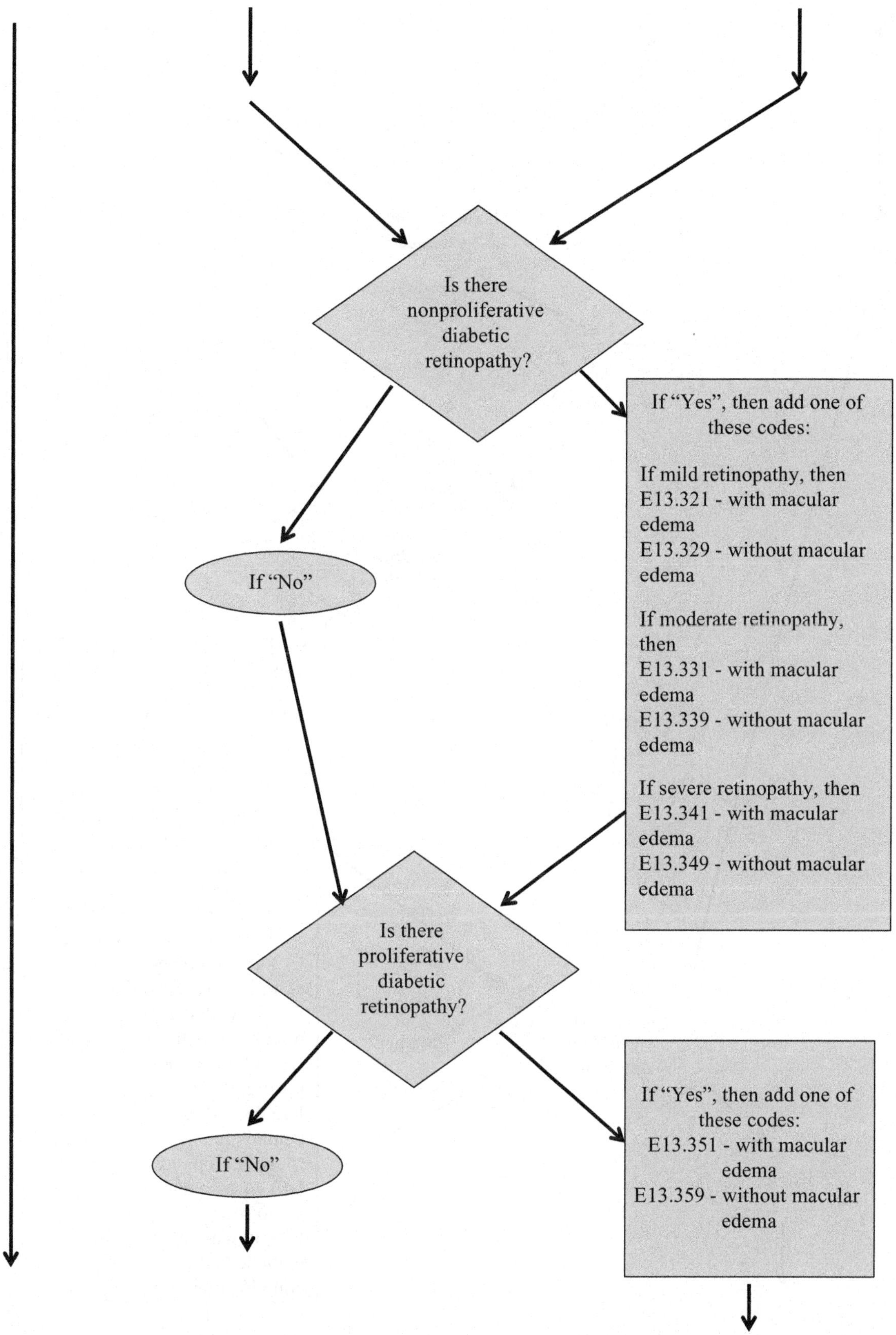

Figure 7.1 (Continued)

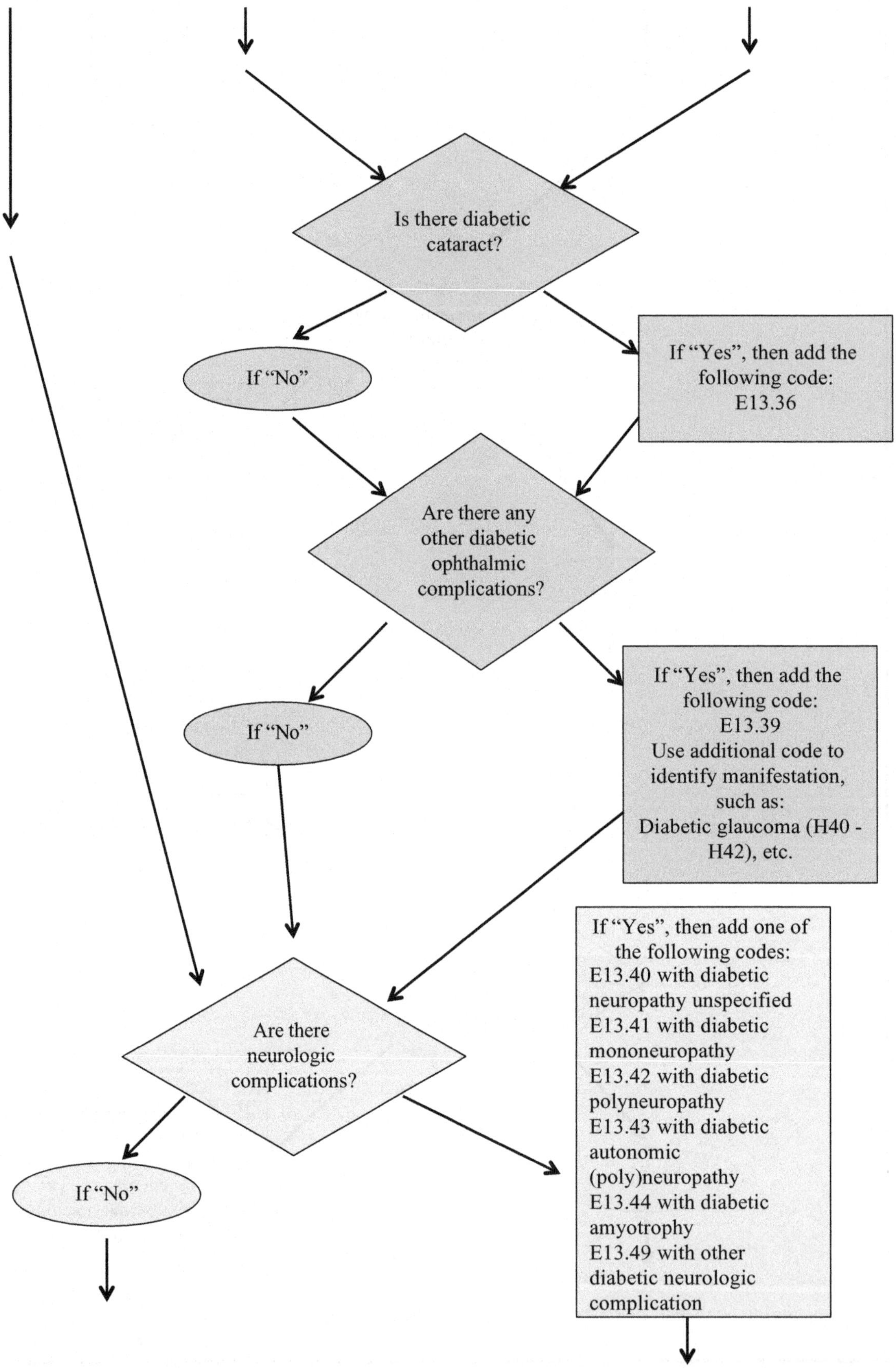
Is there diabetic cataract?
If "No"
If "Yes", then add the following code: E13.36
Are there any other diabetic ophthalmic complications?
If "No"
If "Yes", then add the following code: E13.39 Use additional code to identify manifestation, such as: Diabetic glaucoma (H40 - H42), etc.
Are there neurologic complications?
If "No"
If "Yes", then add one of the following codes:
E13.40 with diabetic neuropathy unspecified
E13.41 with diabetic mononeuropathy
E13.42 with diabetic polyneuropathy
E13.43 with diabetic autonomic (poly)neuropathy
E13.44 with diabetic amyotrophy
E13.49 with other diabetic neurologic complication

Figure 7.1

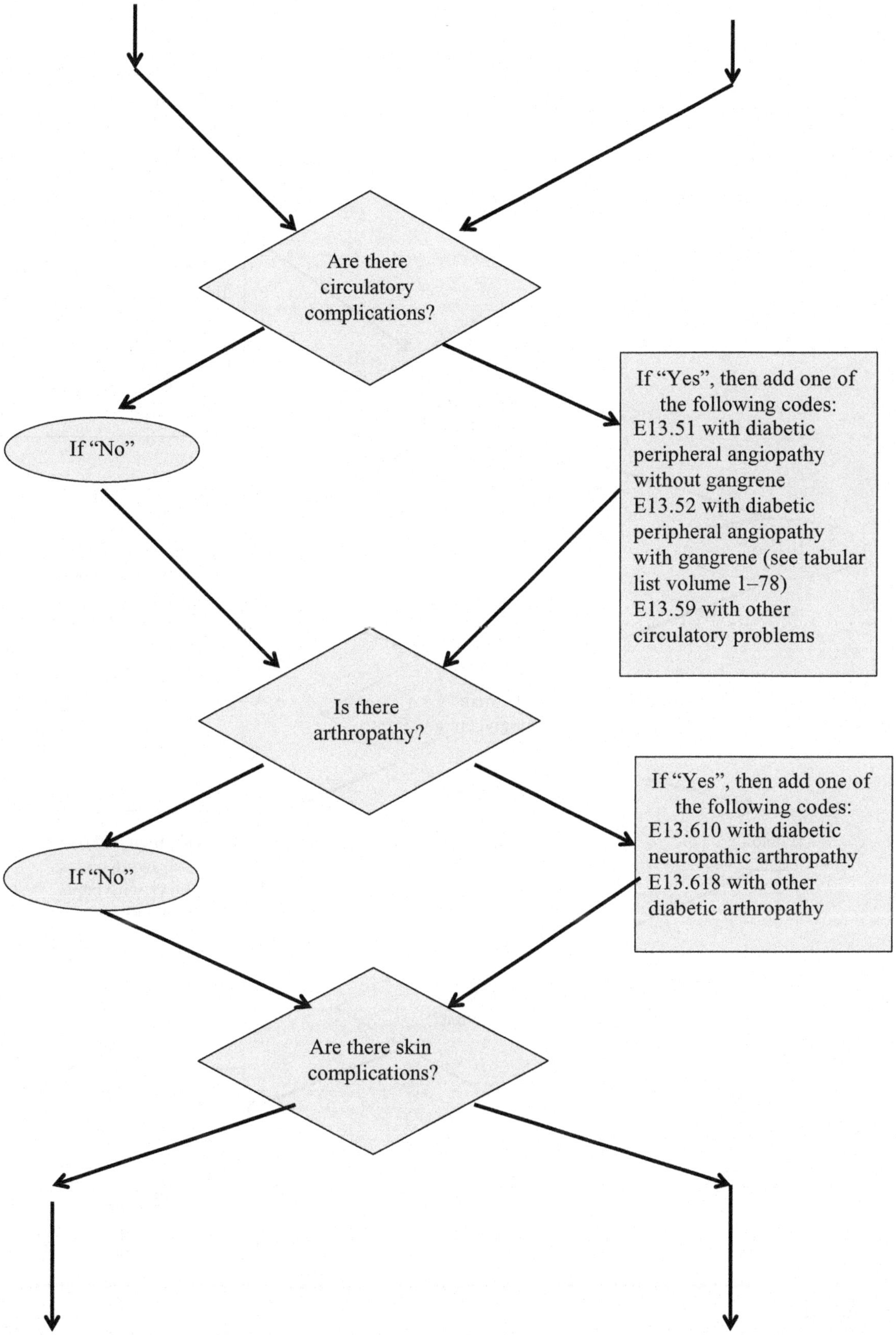

Figure 7.1 (Continued)

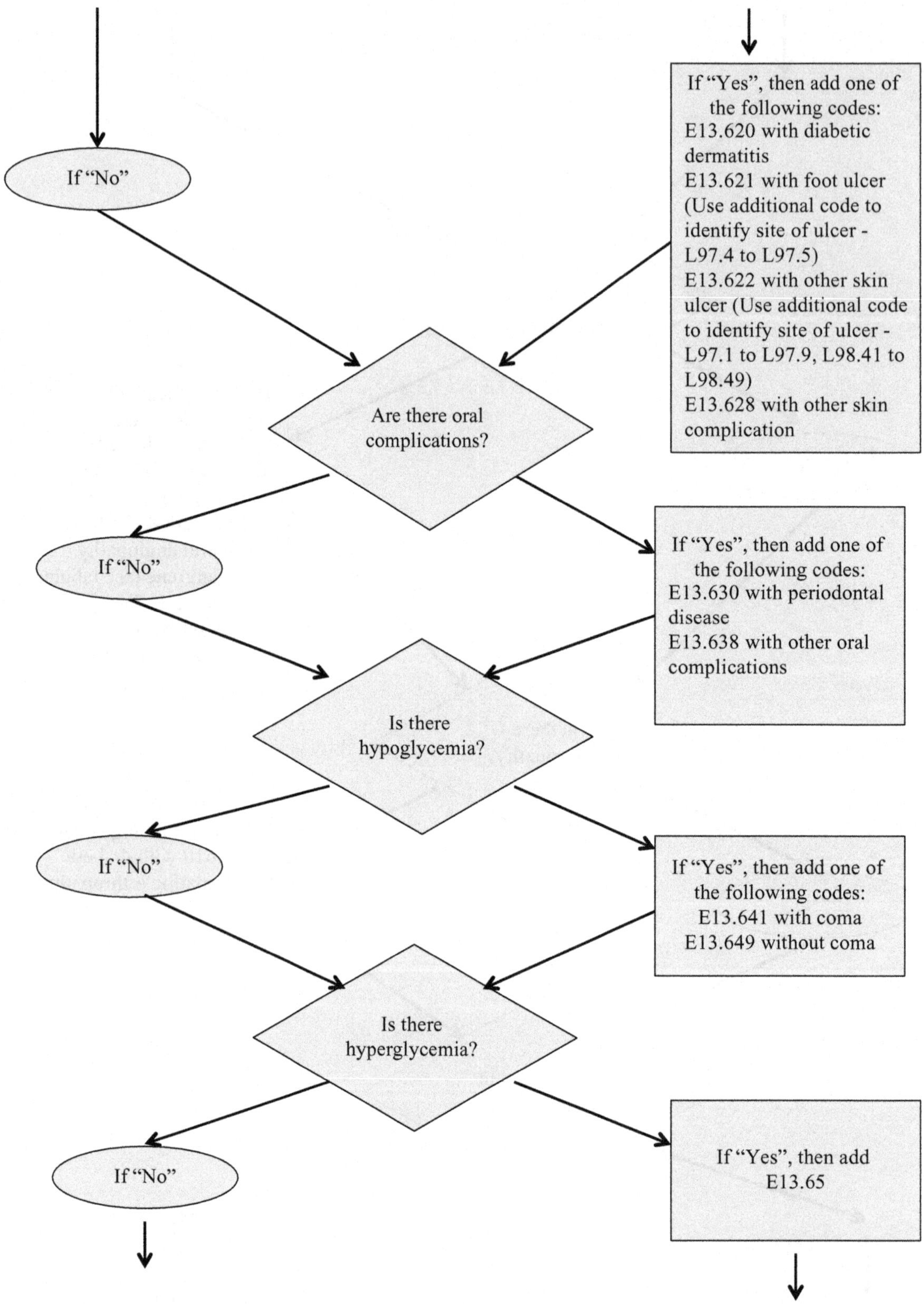
If "No"
If "Yes", then add one of the following codes:
E13.620 with diabetic dermatitis
E13.621 with foot ulcer (Use additional code to identify site of ulcer - L97.4 to L97.5)
E13.622 with other skin ulcer (Use additional code to identify site of ulcer - L97.1 to L97.9, L98.41 to L98.49)
E13.628 with other skin complication
Are there oral complications?
If "No"
If "Yes", then add one of the following codes:
E13.630 with periodontal disease
E13.638 with other oral complications
Is there hypoglycemia?
If "No"
If "Yes", then add one of the following codes:
E13.641 with coma
E13.649 without coma
Is there hyperglycemia?
If "No"
If "Yes", then add E13.65

Figure 7.1

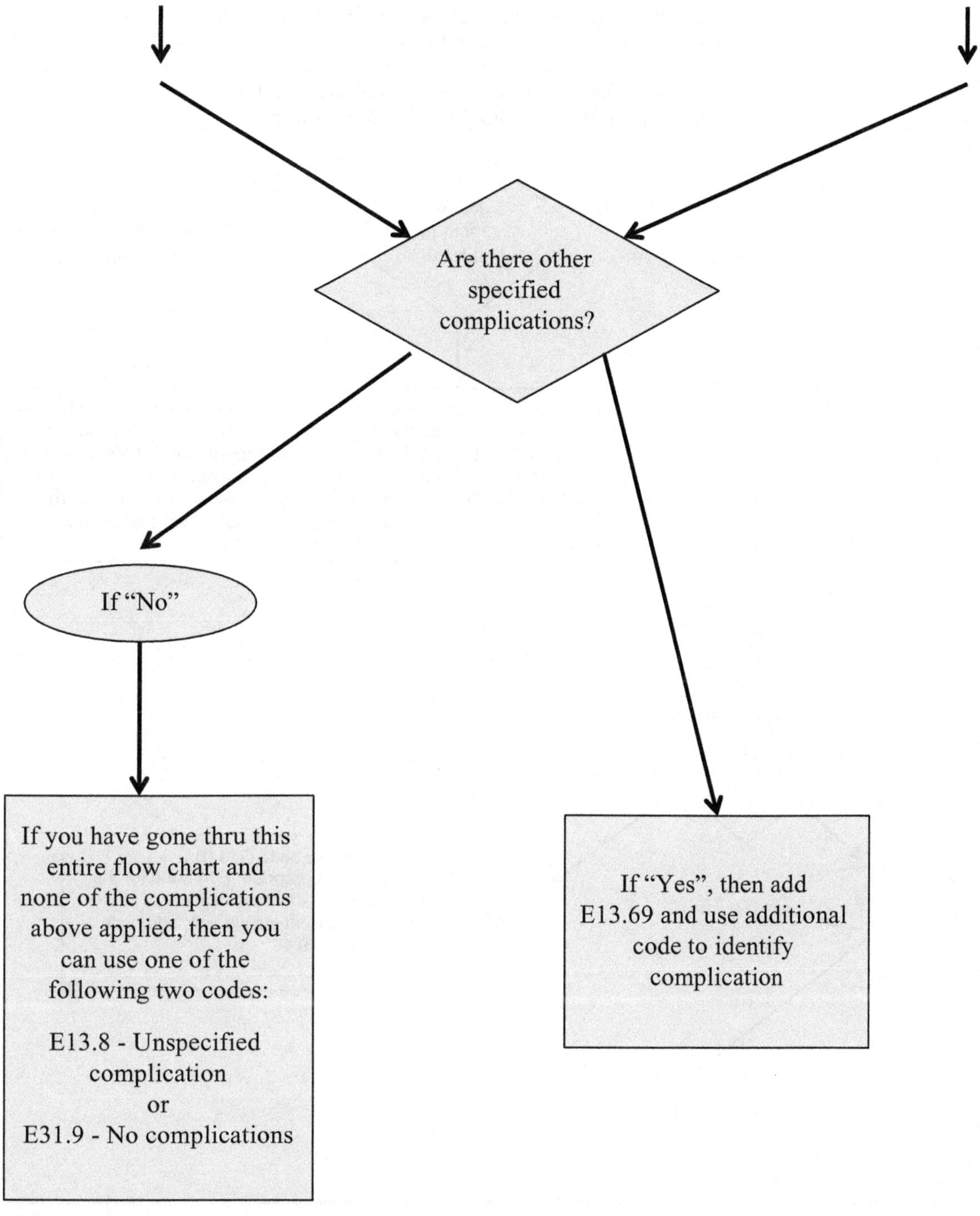

Figure 7.1 (Continued)

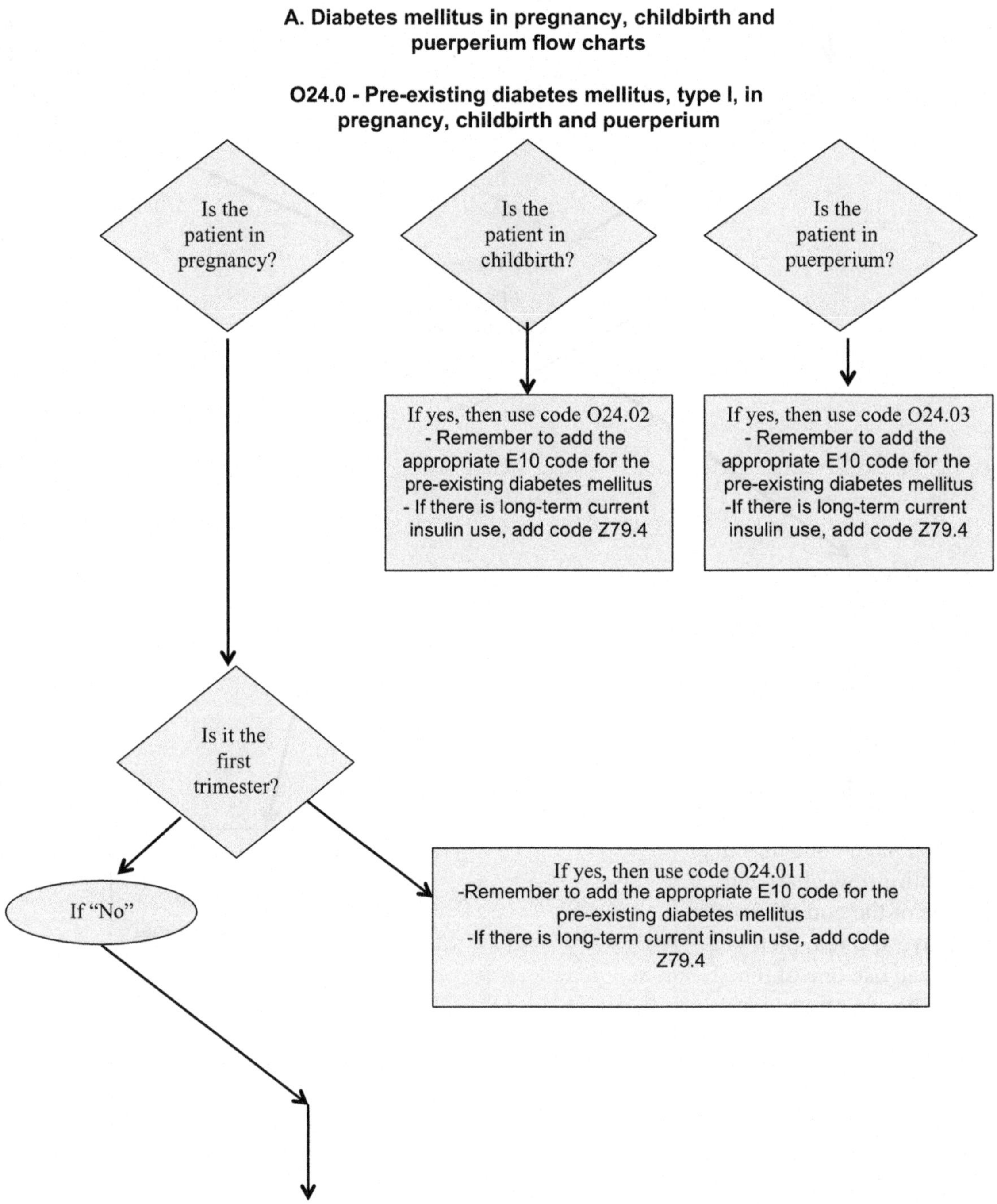
A. Diabetes mellitus in pregnancy, childbirth and puerperium flow charts
O24.0 - Pre-existing diabetes mellitus, type I, in pregnancy, childbirth and puerperium
Is the patient in pregnancy?
Is the patient in childbirth?
Is the patient in puerperium?
If yes, then use code O24.02 - Remember to add the appropriate E10 code for the pre-existing diabetes mellitus - If there is long-term current insulin use, add code Z79.4
If yes, then use code O24.03 - Remember to add the appropriate E10 code for the pre-existing diabetes mellitus -If there is long-term current insulin use, add code Z79.4
Is it the first trimester?
If "No"
If yes, then use code O24.011 -Remember to add the appropriate E10 code for the pre-existing diabetes mellitus -If there is long-term current insulin use, add code Z79.4

Figure 7.1

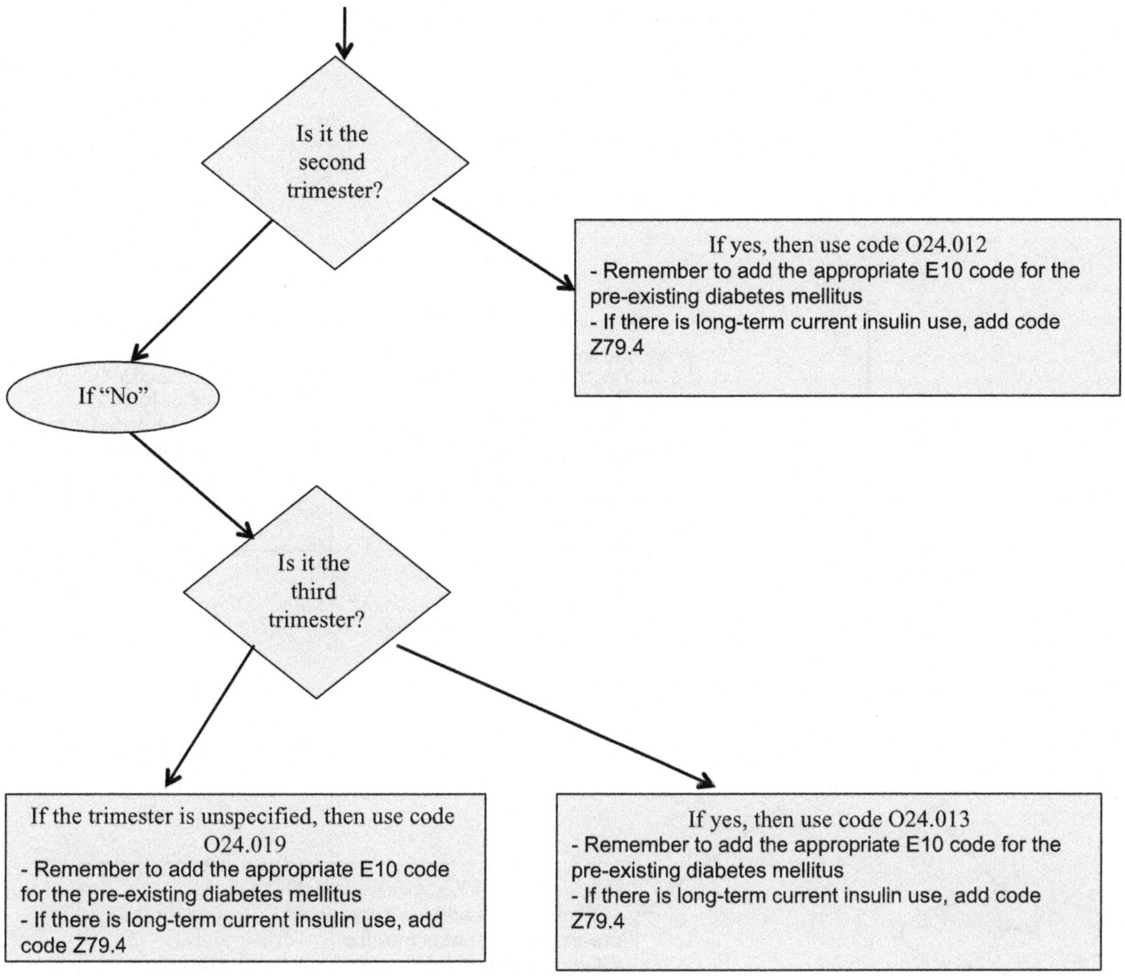

Figure 7.1 (Continued)

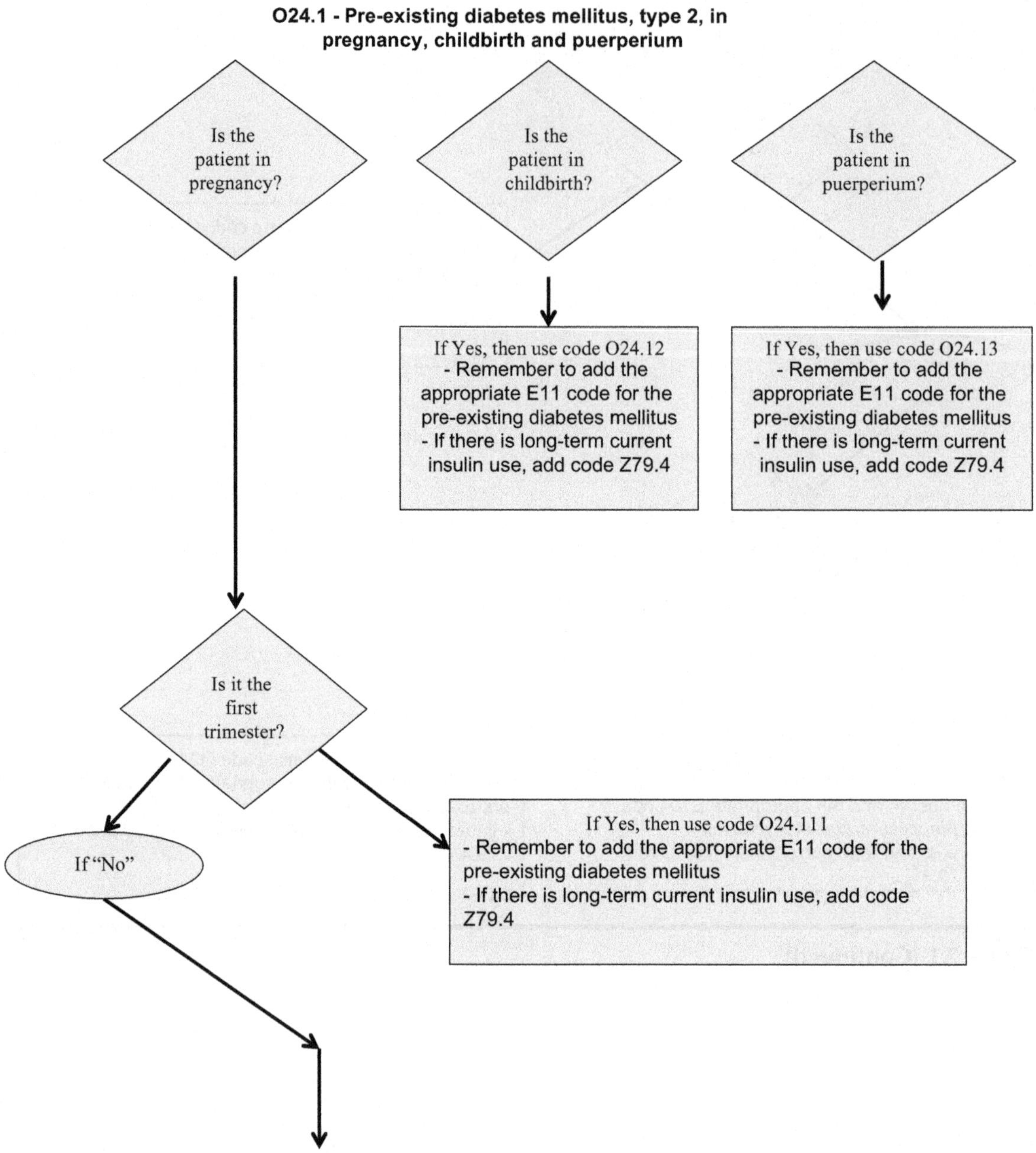
O24.1 - Pre-existing diabetes mellitus, type 2, in pregnancy, childbirth and puerperium
Is the patient in pregnancy?
Is the patient in childbirth?
Is the patient in puerperium?
If Yes, then use code O24.12
- Remember to add the appropriate E11 code for the pre-existing diabetes mellitus
- If there is long-term current insulin use, add code Z79.4
If Yes, then use code O24.13
- Remember to add the appropriate E11 code for the pre-existing diabetes mellitus
- If there is long-term current insulin use, add code Z79.4
Is it the first trimester?
If "No"
If Yes, then use code O24.111
- Remember to add the appropriate E11 code for the pre-existing diabetes mellitus
- If there is long-term current insulin use, add code Z79.4

Figure 7.1

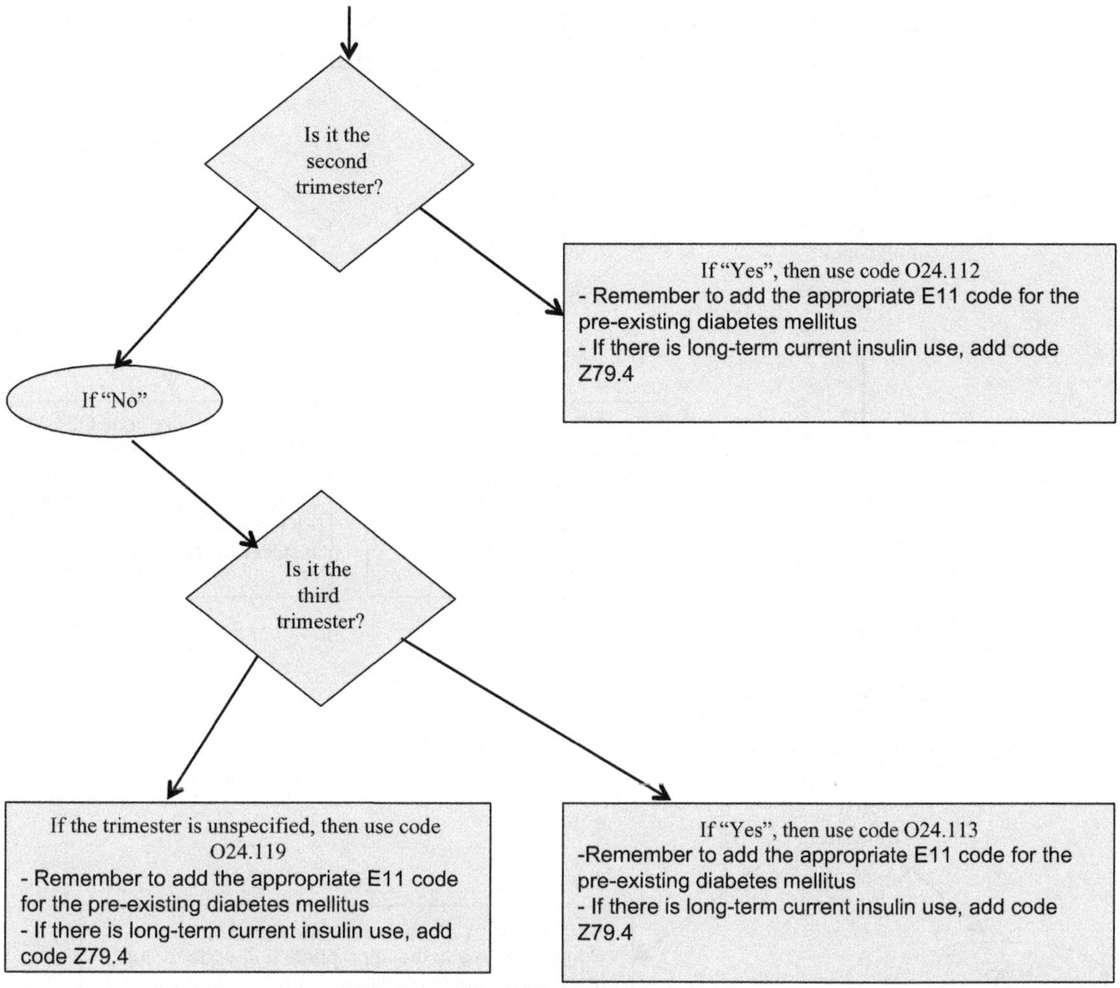

Figure 7.1 (Continued)

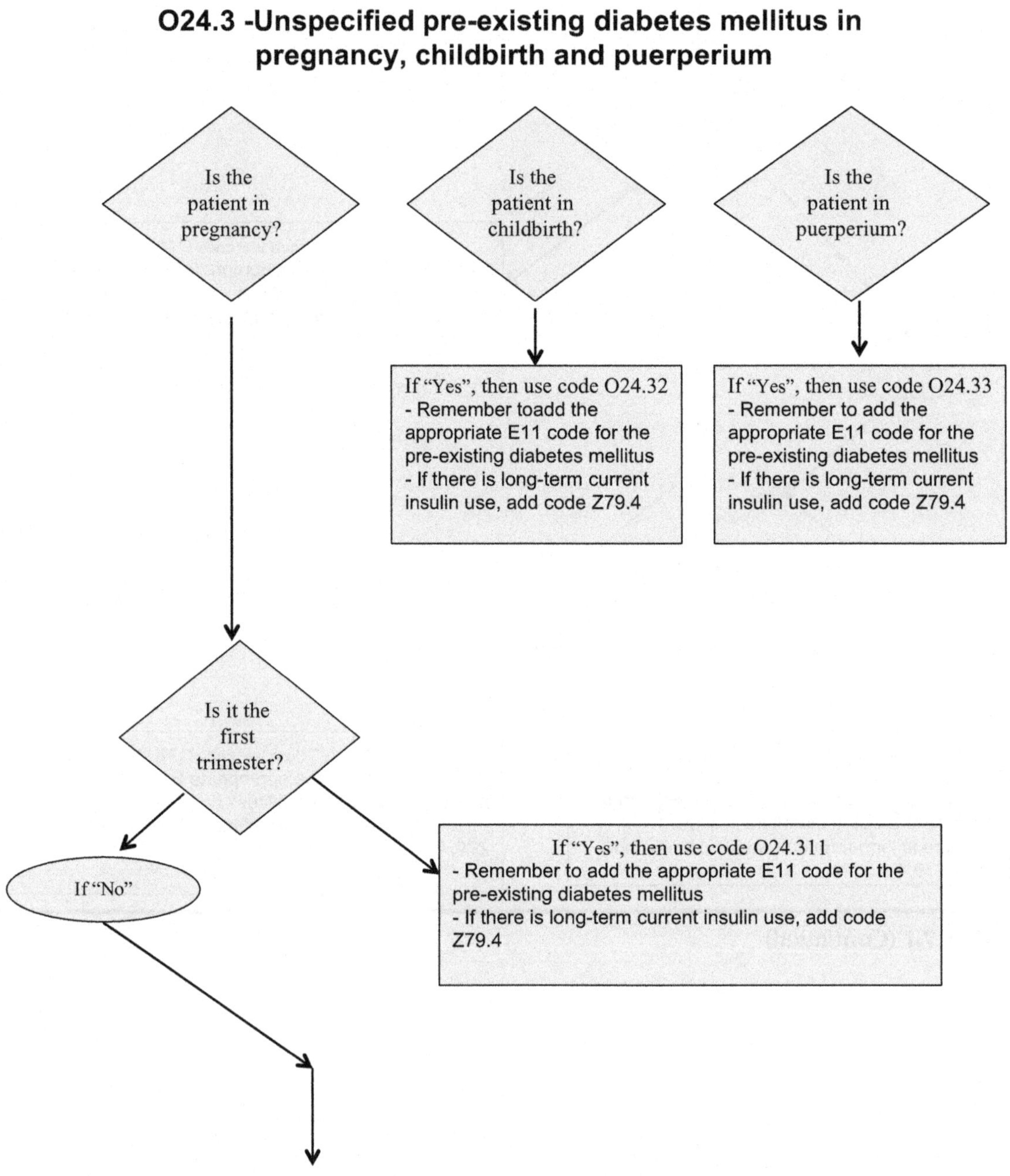
O24.3 -Unspecified pre-existing diabetes mellitus in pregnancy, childbirth and puerperium
Is the patient in pregnancy?
Is the patient in childbirth?
Is the patient in puerperium?
If "Yes", then use code O24.32
- Remember toadd the appropriate E11 code for the pre-existing diabetes mellitus
- If there is long-term current insulin use, add code Z79.4
If "Yes", then use code O24.33
- Remember to add the appropriate E11 code for the pre-existing diabetes mellitus
- If there is long-term current insulin use, add code Z79.4
Is it the first trimester?
If "No"
If "Yes", then use code O24.311
- Remember to add the appropriate E11 code for the pre-existing diabetes mellitus
- If there is long-term current insulin use, add code Z79.4

Figure 7.1

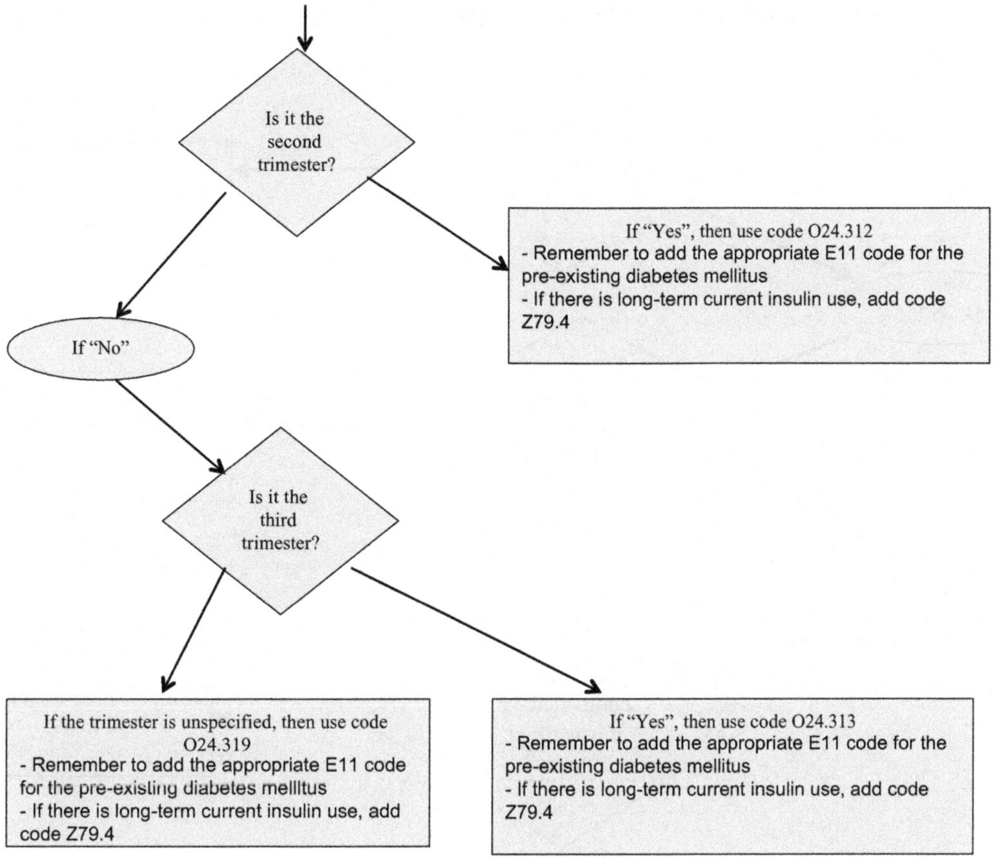

O24.41 - Gestational diabetes mellitus in pregnancy

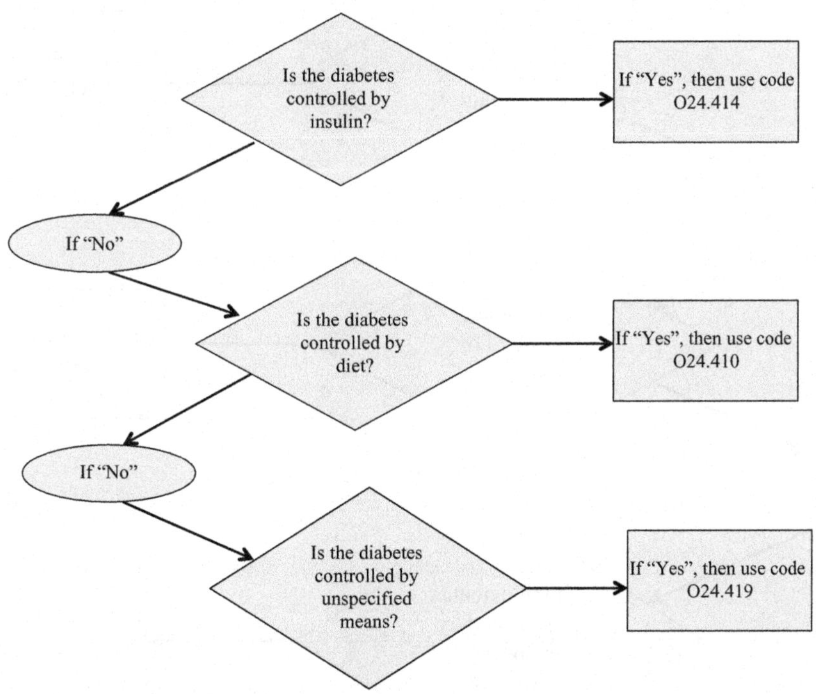

Figure 7.1 (Continued)

O24.43 - Gestational Diabetes Mellitus in Puerperium

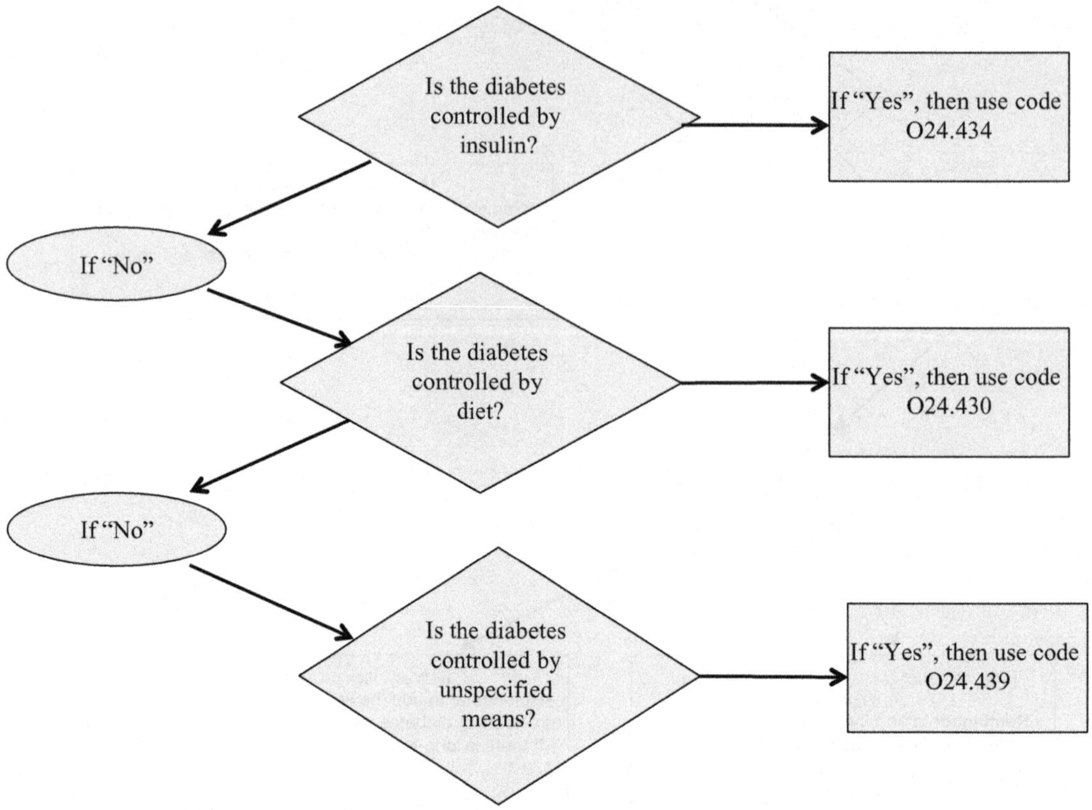

O24.43 - Gestational diabetes mellitus in puerperium

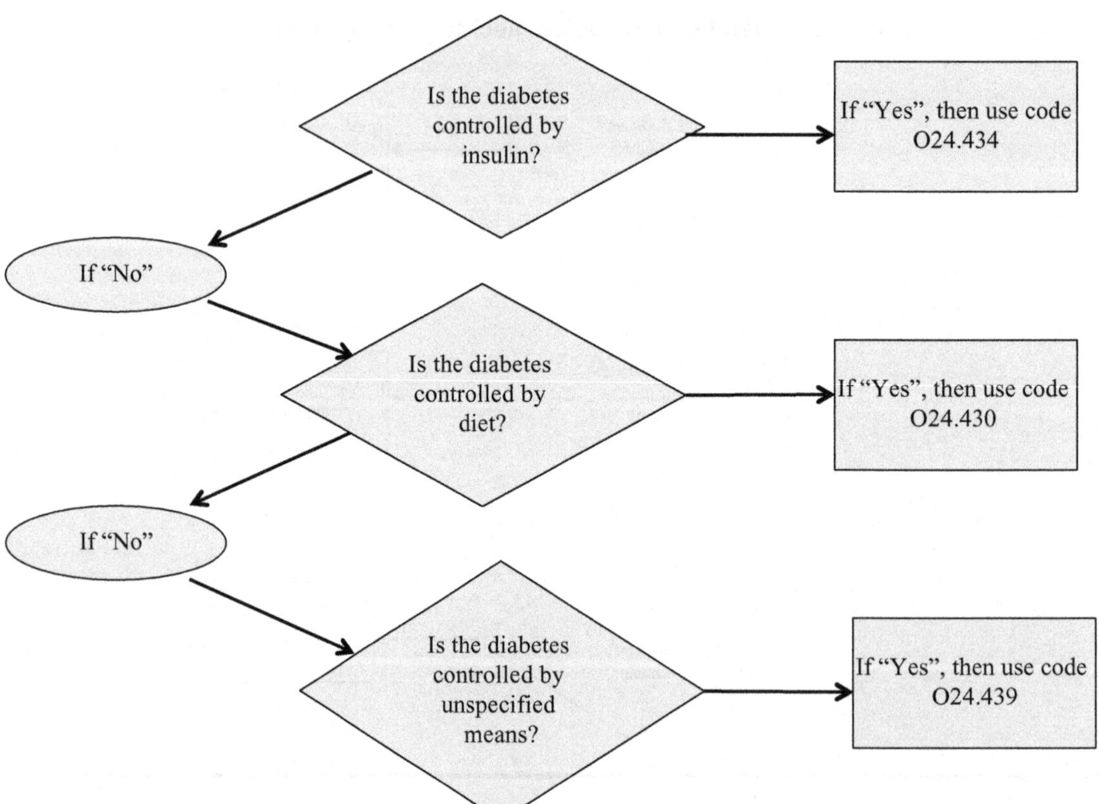

Figure 7.1

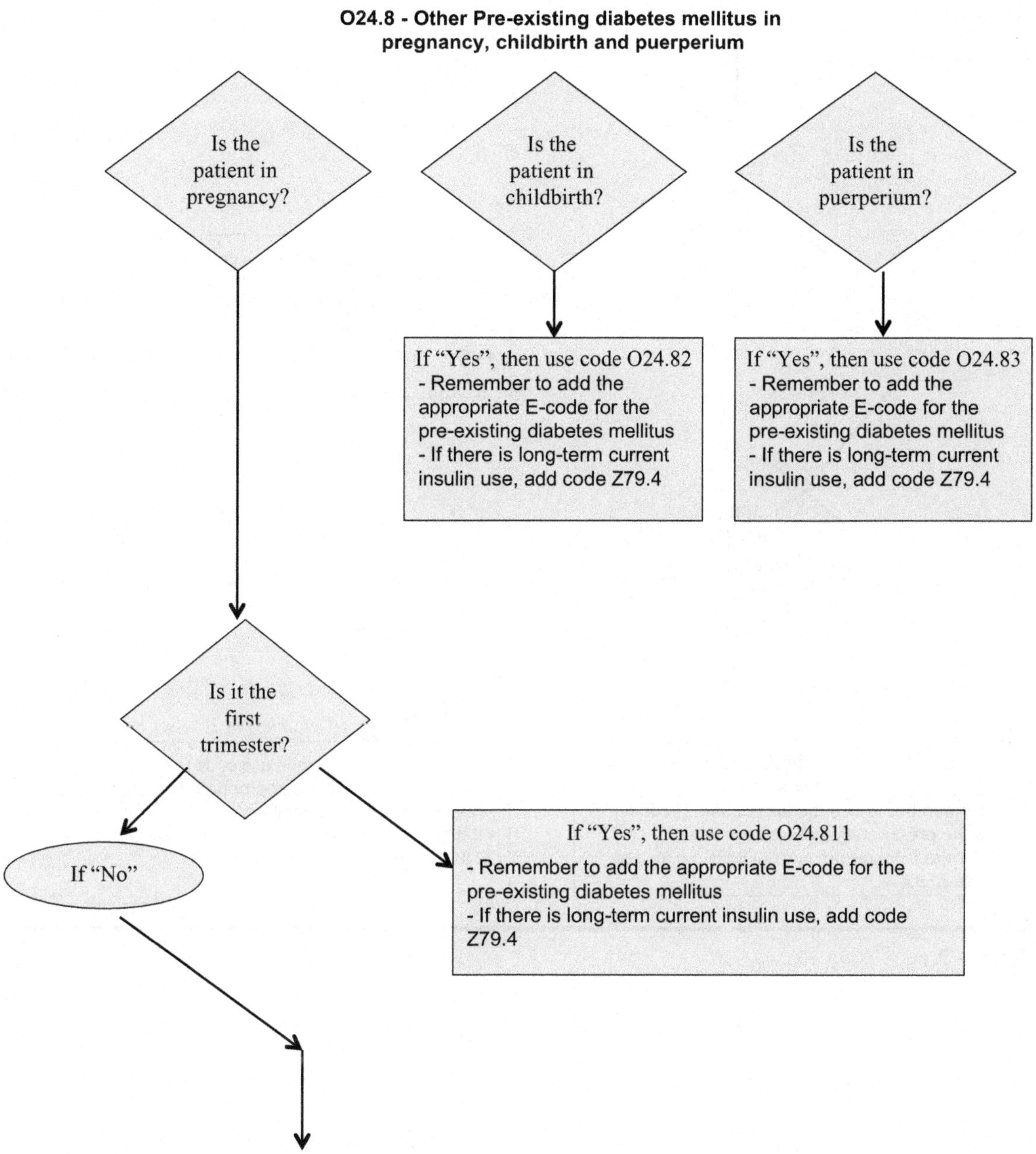

Figure 7.1 (Continued)

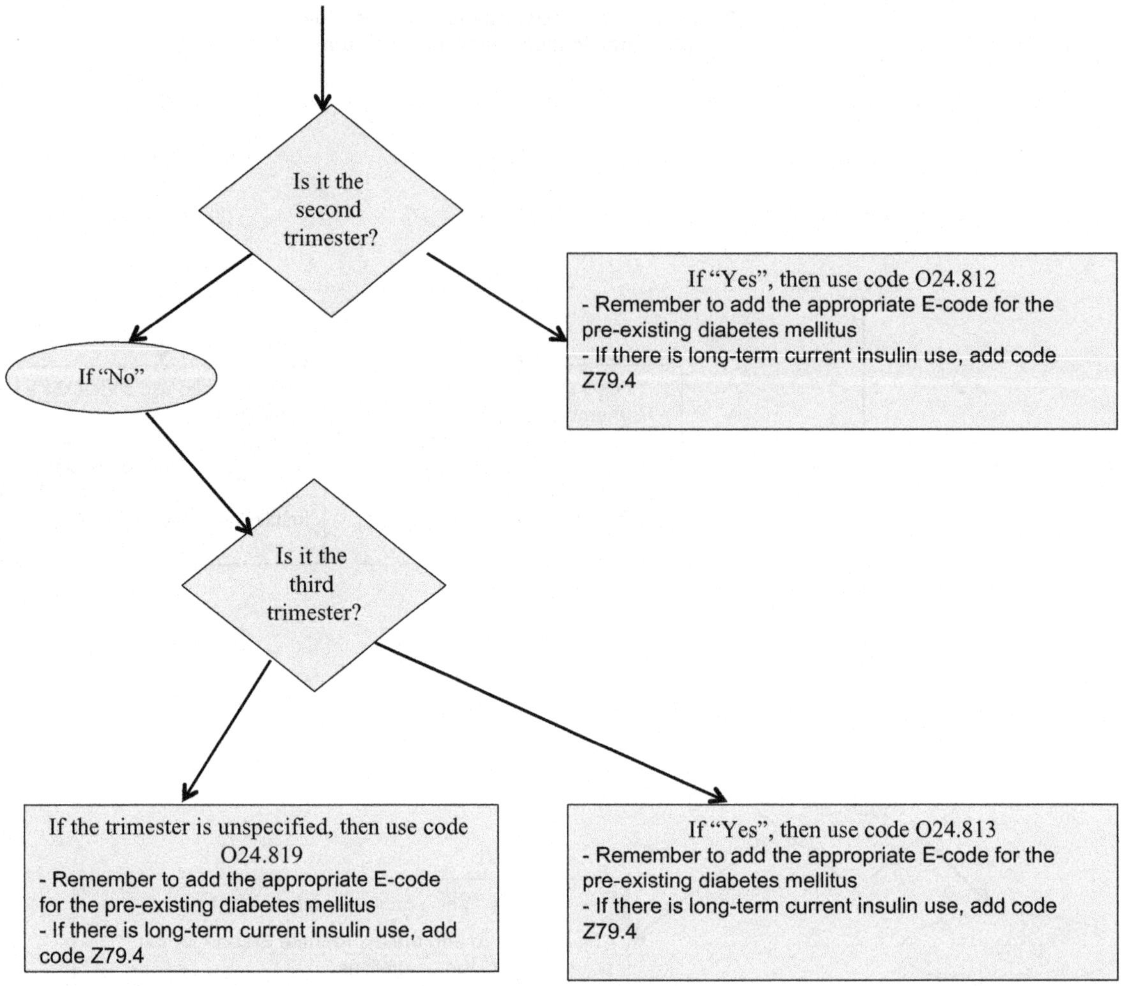
Is it the second trimester?
If "Yes", then use code O24.812
- Remember to add the appropriate E-code for the pre-existing diabetes mellitus
- If there is long-term current insulin use, add code Z79.4
If "No"
Is it the third trimester?
If the trimester is unspecified, then use code O24.819
- Remember to add the appropriate E-code for the pre-existing diabetes mellitus
- If there is long-term current insulin use, add code Z79.4
If "Yes", then use code O24.813
- Remember to add the appropriate E-code for the pre-existing diabetes mellitus
- If there is long-term current insulin use, add code Z79.4

Figure 7.1

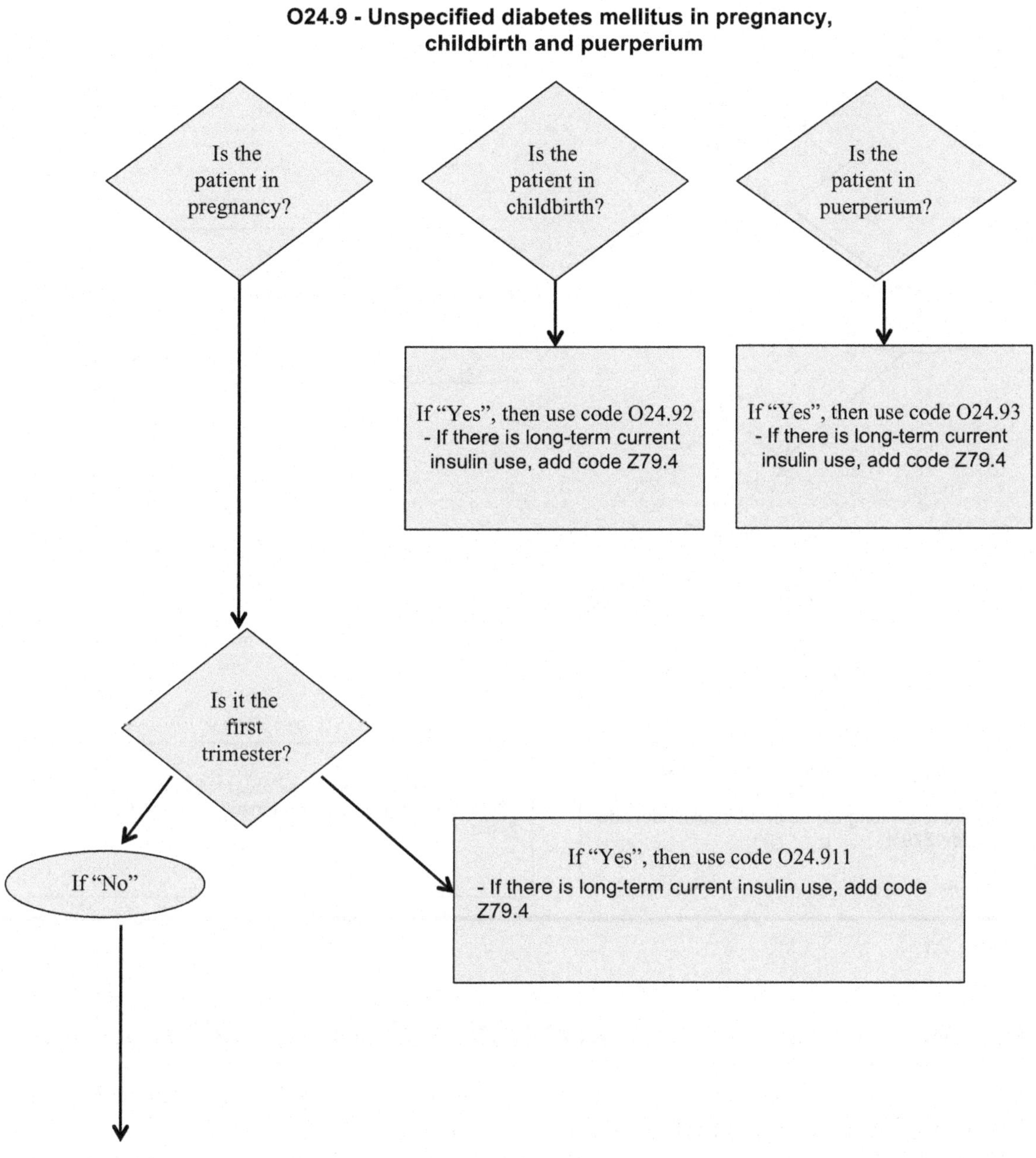

Figure 7.1 (Continued)

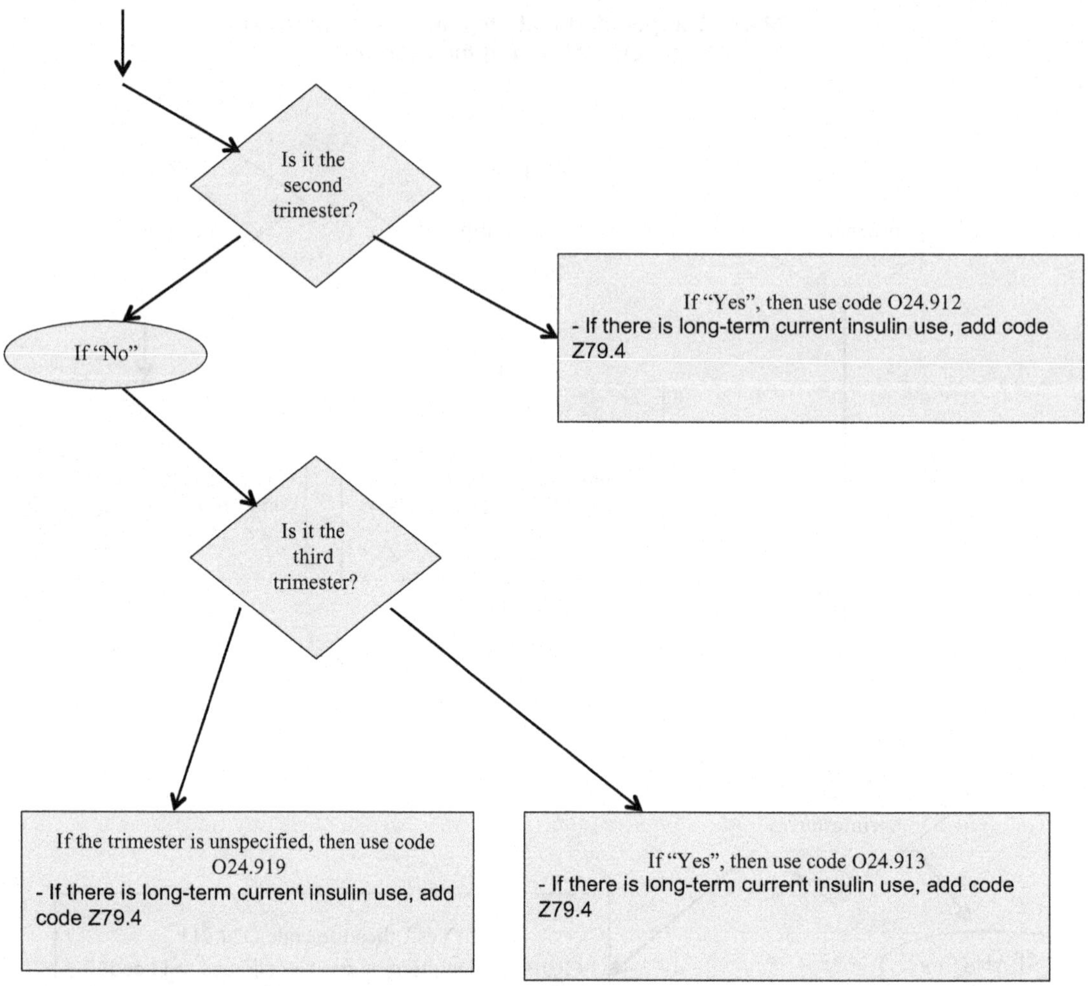

Figure 7.1

ICD-10-CM Draft Release Expert Edition: Diabetes Mellitus Section

Please note: The 2017 ICD-10-CM book has added a seventh character to the diabetes codes to specify which eye(s) is involved (Figure 7.2).

- A seventh character of 1 for right eye
- A seventh character of 2 for left eye
- A seventh character of 3 for bilateral eye
- A seventh character of 9 for unspecified eye

Tabular List ENDOCRINE, NUTRITIONAL AND METABOLIC E08 – E08.319

Endocrine, Nutritional and Metabolic E08 – E08.319

DIABETES MELLITUS (E08-E13)

Layman's: *Despite the use of the term "juvenile" when referring to type I diabetes, age is not the sole determining factor of whether a patient has type I or type II diabetes. Rather, the bodies of type I diabetics are unable to produce insulin on their own, whereas the bodies of type II diabetics cannot process insulin properly. Around 90-95% of Americans with diabetes have type II diabetes.*

ICD-10-CM Official Guidelines (Chapter 4)

a. ***Diabetes mellitus***

The diabetes mellitus codes are combination codes that include the type of diabetes mellitus, the body system affected, and the complications affecting that body system. As many codes within a particular category as are necessary to describe all of the complications of the disease may be used. They should be sequenced based on the reason for a particular encounter. Assign as many codes from categories E08 – E13 as needed to identify all of the associated conditions that the patient has.

1) ***Type of diabetes***

The age of a patient is not the sole determining factor, though most type 1 diabetics develop the condition before reaching puberty. For this reason type 1 diabetes mellitus is also referred to as juvenile diabetes.

2) ***Type of diabetes mellitus not documented***

If the type of diabetes mellitus is not documented in the medical record the default is E11.-, Type 2 diabetes mellitus.

3) ***Diabetes mellitus and the use of insulin***

If the documentation in a medical record does not indicate the type of diabetes but does indicate that the patient uses insulin, code E11, Type 2 diabetes mellitus, should be assigned. Code Z79.4, Long-term (current) use of insulin, should also be assigned to indicate that the patient uses insulin. Code Z79.4 should not be assigned if insulin is given temporarily to bring a type 2 patient's blood sugar under control during an encounter....

6) ***Secondary Diabetes Mellitus***

Codes under categories E08, Diabetes mellitus due to underlying condition, and E09, Drug or chemical induced diabetes mellitus, identify complications/manifestations associated with secondary diabetes mellitus, and E13, Other specified diabetes mellitus,. Secondary diabetes is always caused by another condition or event (e.g., cystic fibrosis, malignant neoplasm of pancreas, pancreatectomy, adverse effect of drug, or poisoning).

(a) *Secondary diabetes mellitus and the use of insulin*

For patients who routinely use insulin, code Z79.4, Long-term (current) use of insulin, should also be assigned. Code Z79.4 should not be assigned if insulin is given temporarily to bring a patient's blood sugar under control during an encounter.

(b) *Assigning and sequencing secondary diabetes codes and its causes*

The sequencing of the secondary diabetes codes in relationship to codes for the cause of the diabetes is based on the Tabular List instructions for categories E08 and E09, and E13.

(i) *Secondary diabetes mellitus due to pancreatectomy*

For postpancreatectomy diabetes mellitus (lack of insulin due to the surgical removal of all or part of the pancreas), assign code E89.1, Postprocedural hypoinsulinemia. Assign a code from category E13 and a code from subcategory Z90.41-, Acquired absence of pancreas, as additional codes.

(ii) *Secondary diabetes due to drugs*

Secondary diabetes may be caused by an adverse effect of correctly administered medications, poisoning or sequela of poisoning.

4th **E08 Diabetes mellitus due to underlying condition**

Code first the underlying condition, such as:
congenital rubella (P35.0)
Cushing's syndrome (E24.-)
cystic fibrosis (E84.-)
malignant neoplasm (C00-C96)
malnutrition (E40-E46)
pancreatitis and other diseases of the pancreas (K85-K86.-)

Use additional code to identify any insulin use (Z79.4)

Excludes1 *drug or chemical induced diabetes mellitus (E09.-)*
gestational diabetes (O24.4-)
neonatal diabetes mellitus (P70.2)
postpancreatectomy diabetes mellitus (E13.-)
postprocedural diabetes mellitus (E13.-)
secondary diabetes mellitus NEC (E13.-)
type 1 diabetes mellitus (E10.-)
type 2 diabetes mellitus (E11.-)

5th **E08.0 Diabetes mellitus due to underlying condition with hyperosmolarity**

E08.00 Diabetes mellitus due to underlying condition with hyperosmolarity without nonketotic hyperglycemic-hyperosmolar coma (NKHHC)

E08.01 Diabetes mellitus due to underlying condition with hyperosmolarity with coma

5th **E08.1 Diabetes mellitus due to underlying condition with ketoacidosis**

E08.10 Diabetes mellitus due to underlying condition with ketoacidosis without coma

E08.11 Diabetes mellitus due to underlying condition with ketoacidosis with coma

5th **E08.2 Diabetes mellitus due to underlying condition with kidney complications**

E08.21 Diabetes mellitus due to underlying condition with diabetic nephropathy

Diabetes mellitus due to underlying condition with intercapillary glomerulosclerosis
Diabetes mellitus due to underlying condition with intracapillary glomerulonephrosis
Diabetes mellitus due to underlying condition with Kimmelstiel-Wilson disease

E08.22 Diabetes mellitus due to underlying condition with diabetic chronic kidney disease

~~Diabetes mellitus due to underlying condition with chronic kidney disease due to conditions classified to .21 and .22~~

Use additional code to identify stage of chronic kidney disease (N18.1-N18.6)

E08.29 Diabetes mellitus due to underlying condition with other diabetic kidney complication

Renal tubular degeneration in diabetes mellitus due to underlying condition

5th **E08.3 Diabetes mellitus due to underlying condition with ophthalmic complications**

6th **E08.31 Diabetes mellitus due to underlying condition with unspecified diabetic retinopathy**

E08.311 Diabetes mellitus due to underlying condition with unspecified diabetic retinopathy with macular edema

E08.319 Diabetes mellitus due to underlying condition with unspecified diabetic retinopathy without macular edema

Unspecified Code Other Specified Code *Manifestation Code* | ICD-9-CM xWalks: ≈ (Approximate) = (Equivalent) + (Combo) – (Component)

2015 Draft ICD-10-CM Volume 1 - 77

Figure 7.2

6th **E08.32 Diabetes mellitus due to underlying condition with mild nonproliferative diabetic retinopathy**
Diabetes mellitus due to underlying condition with nonproliferative diabetic retinopathy NOS

E08.321 **Diabetes mellitus due to underlying condition with mild nonproliferative diabetic retinopathy with macular edema**

E08.329 **Diabetes mellitus due to underlying condition with mild nonproliferative diabetic retinopathy without macular edema**

6th **E08.33 Diabetes mellitus due to underlying condition with moderate nonproliferative diabetic retinopathy**

E08.331 **Diabetes mellitus due to underlying condition with moderate nonproliferative diabetic retinopathy with macular edema**

E08.339 **Diabetes mellitus due to underlying condition with moderate nonproliferative diabetic retinopathy without macular edema**

6th **E08.34 Diabetes mellitus due to underlying condition with severe nonproliferative diabetic retinopathy**

E08.341 **Diabetes mellitus due to underlying condition with severe nonproliferative diabetic retinopathy with macular edema**

E08.349 **Diabetes mellitus due to underlying condition with severe nonproliferative diabetic retinopathy without macular edema**

6th **E08.35 Diabetes mellitus due to underlying condition with proliferative diabetic retinopathy**

E08.351 **Diabetes mellitus due to underlying condition with proliferative diabetic retinopathy with macular edema**

E08.359 **Diabetes mellitus due to underlying condition with proliferative diabetic retinopathy without macular edema**

E08.36 **Diabetes mellitus due to underlying condition with diabetic cataract**

E08.39 **Diabetes mellitus due to underlying condition with other diabetic ophthalmic complication**
Use additional code to identify manifestation, such as:
diabetic glaucoma (H40-H42)

5th **E08.4 Diabetes mellitus due to underlying condition with neurological complications**

E08.40 **Diabetes mellitus due to underlying condition with diabetic neuropathy, unspecified**

E08.41 **Diabetes mellitus due to underlying condition with diabetic mononeuropathy**

E08.42 **Diabetes mellitus due to underlying condition with diabetic polyneuropathy**
Diabetes mellitus due to underlying condition with diabetic neuralgia

E08.43 **Diabetes mellitus due to underlying condition with diabetic autonomic (poly)neuropathy**
Diabetes mellitus due to underlying condition with diabetic gastroparesis

E08.44 **Diabetes mellitus due to underlying condition with diabetic amyotrophy**

E08.49 **Diabetes mellitus due to underlying condition with other diabetic neurological complication**

5th **E08.5 Diabetes mellitus due to underlying condition with circulatory complications**

E08.51 **Diabetes mellitus due to underlying condition with diabetic peripheral angiopathy without gangrene**

E08.52 **Diabetes mellitus due to underlying condition with diabetic peripheral angiopathy with gangrene**
+ 251.8 Other specified disorders of pancreatic internal secretion (443.89, 785.4)
+ 443.89 Other specified peripheral vascular disease (251.8, 785.4)
+ 785.4 Gangrene (251.8, 443.89)
Diabetes mellitus due to underlying condition with diabetic gangrene

E08.59 **Diabetes mellitus due to underlying condition with other circulatory complications**

5th **E08.6 Diabetes mellitus due to underlying condition with other specified complications**

6th **E08.61 Diabetes mellitus due to underlying condition with diabetic arthropathy**

E08.610 **Diabetes mellitus due to underlying condition with diabetic neuropathic arthropathy**
Diabetes mellitus due to underlying condition with Charcôt's joints

E08.618 **Diabetes mellitus due to underlying condition with other diabetic arthropathy**

6th **E08.62 Diabetes mellitus due to underlying condition with skin complications**

E08.620 **Diabetes mellitus due to underlying condition with diabetic dermatitis**
Diabetes mellitus due to underlying condition with diabetic necrobiosis lipoidica

E08.621 **Diabetes mellitus due to underlying condition with foot ulcer**
Use additional code to identify site of ulcer (L97.4-, L97.5-)

E08.622 **Diabetes mellitus due to underlying condition with other skin ulcer**
Use additional code to identify site of ulcer (L97.1-L97.9, L98.41-L98.49)

E08.628 **Diabetes mellitus due to underlying condition with other skin complications**

6th **E08.63 Diabetes mellitus due to underlying condition with oral complications**

E08.630 **Diabetes mellitus due to underlying condition with periodontal disease**

E08.638 **Diabetes mellitus due to underlying condition with other oral complications**

6th **E08.64 Diabetes mellitus due to underlying condition with hypoglycemia**

E08.641 **Diabetes mellitus due to underlying condition with hypoglycemia with coma**

E08.649 **Diabetes mellitus due to underlying condition with hypoglycemia without coma**

E08.65 **Diabetes mellitus due to underlying condition with hyperglycemia**

E08.69 **Diabetes mellitus due to underlying condition with other specified complication**
Use additional code to identify complication

E08.8 Diabetes mellitus due to underlying condition with unspecified complications

● New Code ▲ Revised Code | ♂ Male ♀ Female | N Newborn Age (0) P Pediatric Age (0-17) M Maternity Age (12-55) A Adult Age (15-124)

Figure 7.2

E08.9 **Diabetes mellitus due to underlying condition without complications**

4th E09 **Drug or chemical induced diabetes mellitus**

Code first poisoning due to drug or toxin, if applicable (T36-T65 with fifth or sixth character 1-4 or 6)

Use additional code for adverse effect, if applicable, to identify drug (T36-T50 with fifth or sixth character 5)

Use additional code to identify any insulin use (Z79.4)

Excludes1 *diabetes mellitus due to underlying condition (E08.-)*
gestational diabetes (O24.4-)
neonatal diabetes mellitus (P70.2)
postpancreatectomy diabetes mellitus (E13.-)
postprocedural diabetes mellitus (E13.-)
secondary diabetes mellitus NEC (E13.-)
type 1 diabetes mellitus (E10.-)
type 2 diabetes mellitus (E11.-)

5th E09.0 **Drug or chemical induced diabetes mellitus with hyperosmolarity**

E09.00 **Drug or chemical induced diabetes mellitus with hyperosmolarity without nonketotic hyperglycemic-hyperosmolar coma (NKHHC)**

E09.01 **Drug or chemical induced diabetes mellitus with hyperosmolarity with coma**

5th E09.1 **Drug or chemical induced diabetes mellitus with ketoacidosis**

E09.10 **Drug or chemical induced diabetes mellitus with ketoacidosis without coma**

E09.11 **Drug or chemical induced diabetes mellitus with ketoacidosis with coma**

5th E09.2 **Drug or chemical induced diabetes mellitus with kidney complications**

E09.21 **Drug or chemical induced diabetes mellitus with diabetic nephropathy**

Drug or chemical induced diabetes mellitus with intercapillary glomerulosclerosis
Drug or chemical induced diabetes mellitus with intracapillary glomerulonephrosis
Drug or chemical induced diabetes mellitus with Kimmelstiel-Wilson disease

E09.22 **Drug or chemical induced diabetes mellitus with diabetic chronic kidney disease**

~~Drug or chemical induced diabetes mellitus with chronic kidney disease due to conditions classified to .21 and .22~~

Use additional code to identify stage of chronic kidney disease (N18.1-N18.6)

E09.29 **Drug or chemical induced diabetes mellitus with other diabetic kidney complication**

Drug or chemical induced diabetes mellitus with renal tubular degeneration

5th E09.3 **Drug or chemical induced diabetes mellitus with ophthalmic complications**

6th E09.31 **Drug or chemical induced diabetes mellitus with unspecified diabetic retinopathy**

E09.311 **Drug or chemical induced diabetes mellitus with unspecified diabetic retinopathy with macular edema**

E09.319 **Drug or chemical induced diabetes mellitus with unspecified diabetic retinopathy without macular edema**

6th E09.32 **Drug or chemical induced diabetes mellitus with mild nonproliferative diabetic retinopathy**

Drug or chemical induced diabetes mellitus with nonproliferative diabetic retinopathy NOS

E09.321 **Drug or chemical induced diabetes mellitus with mild nonproliferative diabetic retinopathy with macular edema**

E09.329 **Drug or chemical induced diabetes mellitus with mild nonproliferative diabetic retinopathy without macular edema**

6th E09.33 **Drug or chemical induced diabetes mellitus with moderate nonproliferative diabetic retinopathy**

E09.331 **Drug or chemical induced diabetes mellitus with moderate nonproliferative diabetic retinopathy with macular edema**

E09.339 **Drug or chemical induced diabetes mellitus with moderate nonproliferative diabetic retinopathy without macular edema**

6th E09.34 **Drug or chemical induced diabetes mellitus with severe nonproliferative diabetic retinopathy**

E09.341 **Drug or chemical induced diabetes mellitus with severe nonproliferative diabetic retinopathy with macular edema**

E09.349 **Drug or chemical induced diabetes mellitus with severe nonproliferative diabetic retinopathy without macular edema**

6th E09.35 **Drug or chemical induced diabetes mellitus with proliferative diabetic retinopathy**

E09.351 **Drug or chemical induced diabetes mellitus with proliferative diabetic retinopathy with macular edema**

E09.359 **Drug or chemical induced diabetes mellitus with proliferative diabetic retinopathy without macular edema**

E09.36 **Drug or chemical induced diabetes mellitus with diabetic cataract**

E09.39 **Drug or chemical induced diabetes mellitus with other diabetic ophthalmic complication**

Use additional code to identify manifestation, such as:
diabetic glaucoma (H40-H42)

6th E09.4 **Drug or chemical induced diabetes mellitus with neurological complications**

E09.40 **Drug or chemical induced diabetes mellitus with neurological complications with diabetic neuropathy, unspecified**

E09.41 **Drug or chemical induced diabetes mellitus with neurological complications with diabetic mononeuropathy**

E09.42 **Drug or chemical induced diabetes mellitus with neurological complications with diabetic polyneuropathy**

Drug or chemical induced diabetes mellitus with diabetic neuralgia

E09.43 **Drug or chemical induced diabetes mellitus with neurological complications with diabetic autonomic (poly)neuropathy**

Drug or chemical induced diabetes mellitus with diabetic gastroparesis

Endocrine, Nutritional and Metabolic — E08.9 – E09.43

Figure 7.2 (Continued)

E09.44 **Drug or chemical induced diabetes mellitus with neurological complications with diabetic amyotrophy**

E09.49 **Drug or chemical induced diabetes mellitus with neurological complications with other diabetic neurological complication**

5th E09.5 **Drug or chemical induced diabetes mellitus with circulatory complications**

E09.51 **Drug or chemical induced diabetes mellitus with diabetic peripheral angiopathy without gangrene**

E09.52 **Drug or chemical induced diabetes mellitus with diabetic peripheral angiopathy with gangrene**

+ 249.70 Secondary diabetes mellitus with peripheral circulatory disorders, not stated as uncontrolled, or unspecified (443.89, 785.4)

+ 443.89 Other specified peripheral vascular disease (249.70, 785.4)

+ 785.4 Gangrene (249.70, 443.89)

Drug or chemical induced diabetes mellitus with diabetic gangrene

E09.59 **Drug or chemical induced diabetes mellitus with other circulatory complications**

5th E09.6 **Drug or chemical induced diabetes mellitus with other specified complications**

6th E09.61 **Drug or chemical induced diabetes mellitus with diabetic arthropathy**

E09.610 **Drug or chemical induced diabetes mellitus with diabetic neuropathic arthropathy**

Drug or chemical induced diabetes mellitus with Charcôt's joints

E09.618 **Drug or chemical induced diabetes mellitus with other diabetic arthropathy**

6th E09.62 **Drug or chemical induced diabetes mellitus with skin complications**

E09.620 **Drug or chemical induced diabetes mellitus with diabetic dermatitis**

Drug or chemical induced diabetes mellitus with diabetic necrobiosis lipoidica

E09.621 **Drug or chemical induced diabetes mellitus with foot ulcer**

Use additional code to identify site of ulcer (L97.4-, L97.5-)

E09.622 **Drug or chemical induced diabetes mellitus with other skin ulcer**

Use additional code to identify site of ulcer (L97.1-L97.9, L98.41-L98.49)

E09.628 **Drug or chemical induced diabetes mellitus with other skin complications**

6th E09.63 **Drug or chemical induced diabetes mellitus with oral complications**

E09.630 **Drug or chemical induced diabetes mellitus with periodontal disease**

E09.638 **Drug or chemical induced diabetes mellitus with other oral complications**

6th E09.64 **Drug or chemical induced diabetes mellitus with hypoglycemia**

E09.641 **Drug or chemical induced diabetes mellitus with hypoglycemia with coma**

E09.649 **Drug or chemical induced diabetes mellitus with hypoglycemia without coma**

E09.65 **Drug or chemical induced diabetes mellitus with hyperglycemia**

E09.69 **Drug or chemical induced diabetes mellitus with other specified complication**

Use additional code to identify complication

E09.8 **Drug or chemical induced diabetes mellitus with unspecified complications**

E09.9 **Drug or chemical induced diabetes mellitus without complications**

4th E10 **Type 1 diabetes mellitus**

Includes brittle diabetes (mellitus)
diabetes (mellitus) due to autoimmune process
diabetes (mellitus) due to immune mediated pancreatic islet beta-cell destruction
idiopathic diabetes (mellitus)
juvenile onset diabetes (mellitus)
ketosis-prone diabetes (mellitus)

Excludes1 *diabetes mellitus due to underlying condition (E08.-)*
drug or chemical induced diabetes mellitus (E09.-)
gestational diabetes (O24.4-)
hyperglycemia NOS (R73.9)
neonatal diabetes mellitus (P70.2)
postpancreatectomy diabetes mellitus (E13.-)
postprocedural diabetes mellitus (E13.-)
secondary diabetes mellitus NEC (E13.-)
type 2 diabetes mellitus (E11.-)

5th E10.1 **Type 1 diabetes mellitus with ketoacidosis**

E10.10 **Type 1 diabetes mellitus with ketoacidosis without coma**

E10.11 **Type 1 diabetes mellitus with ketoacidosis with coma**

5th E10.2 **Type 1 diabetes mellitus with kidney complications**

E10.21 **Type 1 diabetes mellitus with diabetic nephropathy**

Type 1 diabetes mellitus with intercapillary glomerulosclerosis
Type 1 diabetes mellitus with intracapillary glomerulonephrosis
Type 1 diabetes mellitus with Kimmelstiel-Wilson disease

E10.22 **Type 1 diabetes mellitus with diabetic chronic kidney disease**

~~Type 1 diabetes mellitus with chronic kidney disease due to conditions classified to .21 and .22~~

Use additional code to identify stage of chronic kidney disease (N18.1-N18.6)

E10.29 **Type 1 diabetes mellitus with other diabetic kidney complication**

Type 1 diabetes mellitus with renal tubular degeneration

5th E10.3 **Type 1 diabetes mellitus with ophthalmic complications**

6th E10.31 **Type 1 diabetes mellitus with unspecified diabetic retinopathy**

E10.311 **Type 1 diabetes mellitus with unspecified diabetic retinopathy with macular edema**

+ 250.51 Diabetes with ophthalmic manifestations, type I [juvenile type], not stated as uncontrolled (362.01, 362.07)

+ 362.01 Background diabetic retinopathy (250.51, 362.07)

+ 362.07 Diabetic macular edema (250.51, 362.01)

Figure 7.2

E10.319 **Type 1 diabetes mellitus with unspecified diabetic retinopathy without macular edema**
+ 250.51 Diabetes with ophthalmic manifestations, type I [juvenile type], not stated as uncontrolled (362.01)
+ 362.01 Background diabetic retinopathy (250.51)

6th E10.32 **Type 1 diabetes mellitus with mild nonproliferative diabetic retinopathy**
Type 1 diabetes mellitus with nonproliferative diabetic retinopathy NOS

E10.321 **Type 1 diabetes mellitus with mild nonproliferative diabetic retinopathy with macular edema**

E10.329 **Type 1 diabetes mellitus with mild nonproliferative diabetic retinopathy without macular edema**

6th E10.33 **Type 1 diabetes mellitus with moderate nonproliferative diabetic retinopathy**

E10.331 **Type 1 diabetes mellitus with moderate nonproliferative diabetic retinopathy with macular edema**

E10.339 **Type 1 diabetes mellitus with moderate nonproliferative diabetic retinopathy without macular edema**

6th E10.34 **Type 1 diabetes mellitus with severe nonproliferative diabetic retinopathy**

E10.341 **Type 1 diabetes mellitus with severe nonproliferative diabetic retinopathy with macular edema**

E10.349 **Type 1 diabetes mellitus with severe nonproliferative diabetic retinopathy without macular edema**

6th E10.35 **Type 1 diabetes mellitus with proliferative diabetic retinopathy**

E10.351 **Type 1 diabetes mellitus with proliferative diabetic retinopathy with macular edema**
+ 250.51 Diabetes with ophthalmic manifestations, type I [juvenile type], not stated as uncontrolled (362.02, 362.07)
+ 362.02 Proliferative diabetic retinopathy (250.51, 362.07)
+ 362.07 Diabetic macular edema (250.51, 362.02)

E10.359 **Type 1 diabetes mellitus with proliferative diabetic retinopathy without macular edema**
+ 250.51 Diabetes with ophthalmic manifestations, type I [juvenile type], not stated as uncontrolled (362.02)
+ 362.02 Proliferative diabetic retinopathy (250.51)

E10.36 **Type 1 diabetes mellitus with diabetic cataract**

E10.39 **Type 1 diabetes mellitus with other diabetic ophthalmic complication**
Use additional code to identify manifestation, such as:
diabetic glaucoma (H40-H42)

5th E10.4 **Type 1 diabetes mellitus with neurological complications**

E10.40 **Type 1 diabetes mellitus with diabetic neuropathy, unspecified**

E10.41 **Type 1 diabetes mellitus with diabetic mononeuropathy**

E10.42 **Type 1 diabetes mellitus with diabetic polyneuropathy**
Type 1 diabetes mellitus with diabetic neuralgia

E10.43 **Type 1 diabetes mellitus with diabetic autonomic (poly)neuropathy**
Type 1 diabetes mellitus with diabetic gastroparesis

E10.44 **Type 1 diabetes mellitus with diabetic amyotrophy**

E10.49 **Type 1 diabetes mellitus with other diabetic neurological complication**

5th E10.5 **Type 1 diabetes mellitus with circulatory complications**

E10.51 **Type 1 diabetes mellitus with diabetic peripheral angiopathy without gangrene**

E10.52 **Type 1 diabetes mellitus with diabetic peripheral angiopathy with gangrene**
Type 1 diabetes mellitus with diabetic gangrene

E10.59 **Type 1 diabetes mellitus with other circulatory complications**

5th E10.6 **Type 1 diabetes mellitus with other specified complications**

6th E10.61 **Type 1 diabetes mellitus with diabetic arthropathy**

E10.610 **Type 1 diabetes mellitus with diabetic neuropathic arthropathy**
Type 1 diabetes mellitus with Charcôt's joints

E10.618 **Type 1 diabetes mellitus with other diabetic arthropathy**

6th E10.62 **Type 1 diabetes mellitus with skin complications**

E10.620 **Type 1 diabetes mellitus with diabetic dermatitis**
Type 1 diabetes mellitus with diabetic necrobiosis lipoidica

E10.621 **Type 1 diabetes mellitus with foot ulcer**
Use additional code to identify site of ulcer (L97.4-, L97.5-)

E10.622 **Type 1 diabetes mellitus with other skin ulcer**
Use additional code to identify site of ulcer (L97.1-L97.9, L98.41-L98.49)

E10.628 **Type 1 diabetes mellitus with other skin complications**

6th E10.63 **Type 1 diabetes mellitus with oral complications**

E10.630 **Type 1 diabetes mellitus with periodontal disease**

E10.638 **Type 1 diabetes mellitus with other oral complications**

6th E10.64 **Type 1 diabetes mellitus with hypoglycemia**

E10.641 **Type 1 diabetes mellitus with hypoglycemia with coma**

E10.649 **Type 1 diabetes mellitus with hypoglycemia without coma**

E10.65 **Type 1 diabetes mellitus with hyperglycemia**

E10.69 **Type 1 diabetes mellitus with other specified complication**
Use additional code to identify complication

E10.8 **Type 1 diabetes mellitus with unspecified complications**

E10.9 **Type 1 diabetes mellitus without complications**
≈ 250.01 Diabetes mellitus without mention of complication, type I [juvenile type], not stated as uncontrolled

Unspecified Code | Other Specified Code | *Manifestation Code* | ICD-9-CM xWalks: ≈ (Approximate) = (Equivalent) + (Combo) ~ (Component)

Figure 7.2 (Continued)

4th **E11 Type 2 diabetes mellitus**

Includes diabetes (mellitus) due to insulin secretory defect
diabetes NOS
insulin resistant diabetes (mellitus)

Use additional code to identify any insulin use (Z79.4)

Excludes1 *diabetes mellitus due to underlying condition (E08.-)*
drug or chemical induced diabetes mellitus (E09.-)
gestational diabetes (O24.4-)
neonatal diabetes mellitus (P70.2)
postpancreatectomy diabetes mellitus (E13.-)
postprocedural diabetes mellitus (E13.-)
secondary diabetes mellitus NEC (E13.-)
type 1 diabetes mellitus (E10.-)

5th E11.0 **Type 2 diabetes mellitus with hyperosmolarity**

E11.00 **Type 2 diabetes mellitus with hyperosmolarity without nonketotic hyperglycemic-hyperosmolar coma (NKHHC)**

E11.01 **Type 2 diabetes mellitus with hyperosmolarity with coma**

5th E11.2 **Type 2 diabetes mellitus with kidney complications**

E11.21 **Type 2 diabetes mellitus with diabetic nephropathy**
Type 2 diabetes mellitus with intercapillary glomerulosclerosis
Type 2 diabetes mellitus with intracapillary glomerulonephrosis
Type 2 diabetes mellitus with Kimmelstiel-Wilson disease

E11.22 **Type 2 diabetes mellitus with diabetic chronic kidney disease**
~~Type 2 diabetes mellitus with chronic kidney disease due to conditions classified to .21 and .22~~
Use additional code to identify stage of chronic kidney disease (N18.1-N18.6)

E11.29 **Type 2 diabetes mellitus with other diabetic kidney complication**
Type 2 diabetes mellitus with renal tubular degeneration

5th E11.3 **Type 2 diabetes mellitus with ophthalmic complications**

6th E11.31 **Type 2 diabetes mellitus with unspecified diabetic retinopathy**

E11.311 **Type 2 diabetes mellitus with unspecified diabetic retinopathy with macular edema**
+ 250.50 Diabetes with ophthalmic manifestations, type II or unspecified type, not stated as uncontrolled (362.01, 362.07)
+ 362.01 Background diabetic retinopathy (250.50, 362.07)
+ 362.07 Diabetic macular edema (250.50, 362.01)

E11.319 **Type 2 diabetes mellitus with unspecified diabetic retinopathy without macular edema**
+ 250.50 Diabetes with ophthalmic manifestations, type II or unspecified type, not stated as uncontrolled (362.01, 362.07)
+ 362.01 Background diabetic retinopathy (250.50)

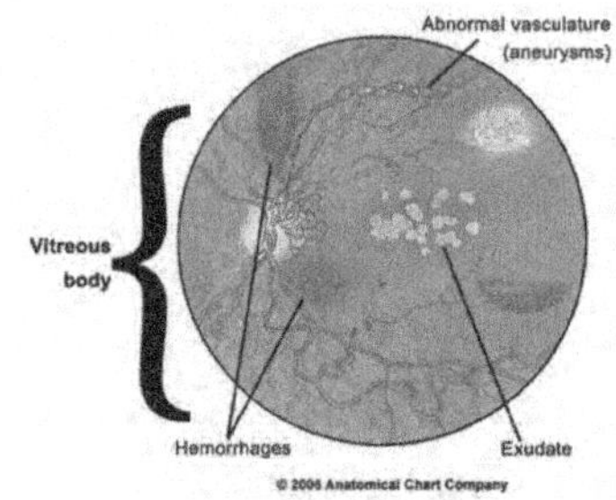

6th E11.32 **Type 2 diabetes mellitus with mild nonproliferative diabetic retinopathy**
Type 2 diabetes mellitus with nonproliferative diabetic retinopathy NOS

E11.321 **Type 2 diabetes mellitus with mild nonproliferative diabetic retinopathy with macular edema**

E11.329 **Type 2 diabetes mellitus with mild nonproliferative diabetic retinopathy without macular edema**

6th E11.33 **Type 2 diabetes mellitus with moderate nonproliferative diabetic retinopathy**

E11.331 **Type 2 diabetes mellitus with moderate nonproliferative diabetic retinopathy with macular edema**

E11.339 **Type 2 diabetes mellitus with moderate nonproliferative diabetic retinopathy without macular edema**

6th E11.34 **Type 2 diabetes mellitus with severe nonproliferative diabetic retinopathy**

E11.341 **Type 2 diabetes mellitus with severe nonproliferative diabetic retinopathy with macular edema**

E11.349 **Type 2 diabetes mellitus with severe nonproliferative diabetic retinopathy without macular edema**

6th E11.35 **Type 2 diabetes mellitus with proliferative diabetic retinopathy**

E11.351 **Type 2 diabetes mellitus with proliferative diabetic retinopathy with macular edema**
+ 250.50 Diabetes with ophthalmic manifestations, type II or unspecified type, not stated as uncontrolled (362.02, 362.07)
+ 362.02 Proliferative diabetic retinopathy (250.50, 362.07)
+ 362.07 Diabetic macular edema (250.50, 362.02)

E11.359 **Type 2 diabetes mellitus with proliferative diabetic retinopathy without macular edema**
+ 250.50 Diabetes with ophthalmic manifestations, type II or unspecified type, not stated as uncontrolled (362.02)
+ 362.02 Proliferative diabetic retinopathy (250.50)

E11.36 **Type 2 diabetes mellitus with diabetic cataract**

Figure 7.2

E11.39 Type 2 diabetes mellitus with other diabetic ophthalmic complication
Use additional code to identify manifestation, such as: diabetic glaucoma (H40-H42)

5th E11.4 **Type 2 diabetes mellitus with neurological complications**

E11.40 **Type 2 diabetes mellitus with diabetic neuropathy, unspecified**

E11.41 **Type 2 diabetes mellitus with diabetic mononeuropathy**

E11.42 **Type 2 diabetes mellitus with diabetic polyneuropathy**
Type 2 diabetes mellitus with diabetic neuralgia

E11.43 **Type 2 diabetes mellitus with diabetic autonomic (poly)neuropathy**
Type 2 diabetes mellitus with diabetic gastroparesis

E11.44 **Type 2 diabetes mellitus with diabetic amyotrophy**

E11.49 **Type 2 diabetes mellitus with other diabetic neurological complication**

5th E11.5 **Type 2 diabetes mellitus with circulatory complications**

E11.51 **Type 2 diabetes mellitus with diabetic peripheral angiopathy without gangrene**

E11.52 **Type 2 diabetes mellitus with diabetic peripheral angiopathy with gangrene**
Type 2 diabetes mellitus with diabetic gangrene

E11.59 **Type 2 diabetes mellitus with other circulatory complications**

5th E11.6 **Type 2 diabetes mellitus with other specified complications**

6th E11.61 **Type 2 diabetes mellitus with diabetic arthropathy**

E11.610 **Type 2 diabetes mellitus with diabetic neuropathic arthropathy**
Type 2 diabetes mellitus with Charcôt's joints

E11.618 **Type 2 diabetes mellitus with other diabetic arthropathy**

6th E11.62 **Type 2 diabetes mellitus with skin complications**

E11.620 **Type 2 diabetes mellitus with diabetic dermatitis**
Type 2 diabetes mellitus with diabetic necrobiosis lipoidica

E11.621 **Type 2 diabetes mellitus with foot ulcer**
Use additional code to identify site of ulcer (L97.4-, L97.5-)

E11.622 **Type 2 diabetes mellitus with other skin ulcer**
Use additional code to identify site of ulcer (L97.1-L97.9, L98.41-L98.49)

E11.628 **Type 2 diabetes mellitus with other skin complications**

6th E11.63 **Type 2 diabetes mellitus with oral complications**

E11.630 **Type 2 diabetes mellitus with periodontal disease**

E11.638 **Type 2 diabetes mellitus with other oral complications**

6th E11.64 **Type 2 diabetes mellitus with hypoglycemia**

E11.641 **Type 2 diabetes mellitus with hypoglycemia with coma**

E11.649 **Type 2 diabetes mellitus with hypoglycemia without coma**

E11.65 **Type 2 diabetes mellitus with hyperglycemia**

E11.69 **Type 2 diabetes mellitus with other specified complication**
Use additional code to identify complication

E11.8 **Type 2 diabetes mellitus with unspecified complications**

E11.9 **Type 2 diabetes mellitus without complications**
≈ 250.00 Diabetes mellitus without mention of complication, type II or unspecified type, not stated as uncontrolled

4th E13 **Other specified diabetes mellitus**

Includes diabetes mellitus due to genetic defects of beta-cell function
diabetes mellitus due to genetic defects in insulin action

Use additional code to identify any insulin use (Z79.4)

Excludes1 *diabetes (mellitus) due to autoimmune process (E10.-)*
diabetes (mellitus) due to immune mediated pancreatic islet beta-cell destruction (E10.-)
diabetes mellitus due to underlying condition (E08.-)
drug or chemical induced diabetes mellitus (E09.-)
gestational diabetes (O24.4-)
neonatal diabetes mellitus (P70.2)
postpancreatectomy diabetes mellitus (E13.-)
postprocedural diabetes mellitus (E13.-)
secondary diabetes mellitus NEC (E13.-)
type 2 diabetes mellitus (E11.-)

5th E13.0 **Other specified diabetes mellitus with hyperosmolarity**

E13.00 **Other specified diabetes mellitus with hyperosmolarity without nonketotic hyperglycemic-hyperosmolar coma (NKHHC)**

E13.01 **Other specified diabetes mellitus with hyperosmolarity with coma**

5th E13.1 **Other specified diabetes mellitus with ketoacidosis**

E13.10 **Other specified diabetes mellitus with ketoacidosis without coma**

E13.11 **Other specified diabetes mellitus with ketoacidosis with coma**

5th E13.2 **Other specified diabetes mellitus with kidney complications**

E13.21 **Other specified diabetes mellitus with diabetic nephropathy**
Other specified diabetes mellitus with intercapillary glomerulosclerosis
Other specified diabetes mellitus with intracapillary glomerulonephrosis
Other specified diabetes mellitus with Kimmelstiel-Wilson disease

E13.22 **Other specified diabetes mellitus with diabetic chronic kidney disease**
~~Other specified diabetes mellitus with chronic kidney disease due to conditions classified to .21 and .22~~
Use additional code to identify stage of chronic kidney disease (N18.1-N18.6)

E13.29 **Other specified diabetes mellitus with other diabetic kidney complication**
Other specified diabetes mellitus with renal tubular degeneration

5th E13.3 **Other specified diabetes mellitus with ophthalmic complications**

6th E13.31 **Other specified diabetes mellitus with unspecified diabetic retinopathy**

E13.311 **Other specified diabetes mellitus with unspecified diabetic retinopathy with macular edema**
\+ 250.50 Diabetes with ophthalmic manifestations, type II or unspecified type, not stated as uncontrolled (362.01, 362.07)
\+ 362.01 Background diabetic retinopathy (250.50, 362.07)
\+ 362.07 Diabetic macular edema (250.50, 362.01)

Figure 7.2 (Continued)

Endocrine, Nutritional and Metabolic

E13.319 – E13.9

E13.319 – E13.9 **ENDOCRINE, NUTRITIONAL AND METABOLIC** Tabular List

E13.319 **Other specified diabetes mellitus with unspecified diabetic retinopathy without macular edema**
+ 250.50 Diabetes with ophthalmic manifestations, type II or unspecified type, not stated as uncontrolled (362.01)
+ 362.01 Background diabetic retinopathy (250.50)

6th E13.32 **Other specified diabetes mellitus with mild nonproliferative diabetic retinopathy**
Other specified diabetes mellitus with nonproliferative diabetic retinopathy NOS

E13.321 **Other specified diabetes mellitus with mild nonproliferative diabetic retinopathy with macular edema**

E13.329 **Other specified diabetes mellitus with mild nonproliferative diabetic retinopathy without macular edema**

6th E13.33 **Other specified diabetes mellitus with moderate nonproliferative diabetic retinopathy**

E13.331 **Other specified diabetes mellitus with moderate nonproliferative diabetic retinopathy with macular edema**

E13.339 **Other specified diabetes mellitus with moderate nonproliferative diabetic retinopathy without macular edema**

6th E13.34 **Other specified diabetes mellitus with severe nonproliferative diabetic retinopathy**

E13.341 **Other specified diabetes mellitus with severe nonproliferative diabetic retinopathy with macular edema**

E13.349 **Other specified diabetes mellitus with severe nonproliferative diabetic retinopathy without macular edema**

6th E13.35 **Other specified diabetes mellitus with proliferative diabetic retinopathy**

E13.351 **Other specified diabetes mellitus with proliferative diabetic retinopathy with macular edema**

E13.359 **Other specified diabetes mellitus with proliferative diabetic retinopathy without macular edema**

E13.36 **Other specified diabetes mellitus with diabetic cataract**

E13.39 **Other specified diabetes mellitus with other diabetic ophthalmic complication**
Use additional code to identify manifestation, such as: diabetic glaucoma (H40-H42)

5th E13.4 **Other specified diabetes mellitus with neurological complications**

E13.40 **Other specified diabetes mellitus with diabetic neuropathy, unspecified**

E13.41 **Other specified diabetes mellitus with diabetic mononeuropathy**

E13.42 **Other specified diabetes mellitus with diabetic polyneuropathy**
Other specified diabetes mellitus with diabetic neuralgia

E13.43 **Other specified diabetes mellitus with diabetic autonomic (poly)neuropathy**
Other specified diabetes mellitus with diabetic gastroparesis

E13.44 **Other specified diabetes mellitus with diabetic amyotrophy**

E13.49 **Other specified diabetes mellitus with other diabetic neurological complication**

5th E13.5 **Other specified diabetes mellitus with circulatory complications**

E13.51 **Other specified diabetes mellitus with diabetic peripheral angiopathy without gangrene**

E13.52 **Other specified diabetes mellitus with diabetic peripheral angiopathy with gangrene**
Other specified diabetes mellitus with diabetic gangrene

E13.59 **Other specified diabetes mellitus with other circulatory complications**

5th E13.6 **Other specified diabetes mellitus with other specified complications**

6th E13.61 **Other specified diabetes mellitus with diabetic arthropathy**

E13.610 **Other specified diabetes mellitus with diabetic neuropathic arthropathy**
Other specified diabetes mellitus with Charcôt's joints

E13.618 **Other specified diabetes mellitus with other diabetic arthropathy**

6th E13.62 **Other specified diabetes mellitus with skin complications**

E13.620 **Other specified diabetes mellitus with diabetic dermatitis**
Other specified diabetes mellitus with diabetic necrobiosis lipoidica

E13.621 **Other specified diabetes mellitus with foot ulcer**
Use additional code to identify site of ulcer (L97.4-, L97.5-)

E13.622 **Other specified diabetes mellitus with other skin ulcer**
Use additional code to identify site of ulcer (L97.1-L97.9, L98.41-L98.49)

E13.628 **Other specified diabetes mellitus with other skin complications**

6th E13.63 **Other specified diabetes mellitus with oral complications**

E13.630 **Other specified diabetes mellitus with periodontal disease**

E13.638 **Other specified diabetes mellitus with other oral complications**

6th E13.64 **Other specified diabetes mellitus with hypoglycemia**

E13.641 **Other specified diabetes mellitus with hypoglycemia with coma**

E13.649 **Other specified diabetes mellitus with hypoglycemia without coma**

E13.65 **Other specified diabetes mellitus with hyperglycemia**

E13.69 **Other specified diabetes mellitus with other specified complication**
Use additional code to identify complication

E13.8 **Other specified diabetes mellitus with unspecified complications**

E13.9 **Other specified diabetes mellitus without complications**
≈ 250.00 Diabetes mellitus without mention of complication, type II or unspecified type, not stated as uncontrolled

● New Code ▲ Revised Code | ♂ Male ♀ Female | N Newborn Age (0) P Pediatric Age (0-17) M Maternity Age (12-55) A Adult Age (15-124)

Volume 1 - 84 2015 Draft ICD-10-CM

Figure 7.2

O22.93 Venous complication in pregnancy, unspecified, third trimester M ♀

4th O23 Infections of genitourinary tract in pregnancy
Use additional code to identify organism (B95.-, B96.-)
Excludes2 *gonococcal infections complicating pregnancy, childbirth and the puerperium (O98.2)*
infections with a predominantly sexual mode of transmission NOS complicating pregnancy, childbirth andthe puerperium (O98.3)
syphilis complicating pregnancy, childbirth and the puerperium (O98.1)
tuberculosis of genitourinary system complicating pregnancy, childbirth and the puerperium (O98.0)
venereal disease NOS complicating pregnancy, childbirth and the puerperium (O98.3)

5th O23.0 Infections of kidney in pregnancy
Pyelonephritis in pregnancy
O23.00 Infections of kidney in pregnancy, unspecified trimester M ♀
O23.01 Infections of kidney in pregnancy, first trimester M ♀
O23.02 Infections of kidney in pregnancy, second trimester M ♀
O23.03 Infections of kidney in pregnancy, third trimester M ♀

5th O23.1 Infections of bladder in pregnancy
O23.10 Infections of bladder in pregnancy, unspecified trimester M ♀
O23.11 Infections of bladder in pregnancy, first trimester M ♀
O23.12 Infections of bladder in pregnancy, second trimester M ♀
O23.13 Infections of bladder in pregnancy, third trimester M ♀

5th O23.2 Infections of urethra in pregnancy
O23.20 Infections of urethra in pregnancy, unspecified trimester M ♀
O23.21 Infections of urethra in pregnancy, first trimester M ♀
O23.22 Infections of urethra in pregnancy, second trimester M ♀
O23.23 Infections of urethra in pregnancy, third trimester M ♀

5th O23.3 Infections of other parts of urinary tract in pregnancy
O23.30 Infections of other parts of urinary tract in pregnancy, unspecified trimester M ♀
O23.31 Infections of other parts of urinary tract in pregnancy, first trimester M ♀
O23.32 Infections of other parts of urinary tract in pregnancy, second trimester M ♀
O23.33 Infections of other parts of urinary tract in pregnancy, third trimester M ♀

5th O23.4 Unspecified infection of urinary tract in pregnancy
O23.40 Unspecified infection of urinary tract in pregnancy, unspecified trimester M ♀
O23.41 Unspecified infection of urinary tract in pregnancy, first trimester M ♀
O23.42 Unspecified infection of urinary tract in pregnancy, second trimester M ♀
O23.43 Unspecified infection of urinary tract in pregnancy, third trimester M ♀

5th O23.5 Infections of the genital tract in pregnancy
6th O23.51 Infection of cervix in pregnancy
O23.511 Infections of cervix in pregnancy, first trimester M ♀
O23.512 Infections of cervix in pregnancy, second trimester M ♀
O23.513 Infections of cervix in pregnancy, third trimester M ♀
O23.519 Infections of cervix in pregnancy, unspecified trimester M ♀

6th O23.52 Salpingo-oophoritis in pregnancy
Oophoritis in pregnancy
Salpingitis in pregnancy
O23.521 Salpingo-oophoritis in pregnancy, first trimester M ♀
O23.522 Salpingo-oophoritis in pregnancy, second trimester M ♀
O23.523 Salpingo-oophoritis in pregnancy, third trimester M ♀
O23.529 Salpingo-oophoritis in pregnancy, unspecified trimester M ♀

6th O23.59 Infection of other part of genital tract in pregnancy
O23.591 Infection of other part of genital tract in pregnancy, first trimester M ♀
O23.592 Infection of other part of genital tract in pregnancy, second trimester M ♀
O23.593 Infection of other part of genital tract in pregnancy, third trimester M ♀
O23.599 Infection of other part of genital tract in pregnancy, unspecified trimester M ♀

5th O23.9 Unspecified genitourinary tract infection in pregnancy
Genitourinary tract infection in pregnancy NOS
O23.90 Unspecified genitourinary tract infection in pregnancy, unspecified trimester M ♀
O23.91 Unspecified genitourinary tract infection in pregnancy, first trimester M ♀
O23.92 Unspecified genitourinary tract infection in pregnancy, second trimester M ♀
O23.93 Unspecified genitourinary tract infection in pregnancy, third trimester M ♀

ICD-10-CM Official Guidelines (Chapter 15)

g. ***Diabetes mellitus in pregnancy***
Diabetes mellitus is a significant complicating factor in pregnancy. Pregnant women who are diabetic should be assigned a code from category O24, Diabetes mellitus in pregnancy, childbirth, and the puerperium, first, followed by the appropriate diabetes code(s) (E08-E13) from Chapter 4.

h. ***Long term use of insulin***
Code Z79.4, Long-term (current) use of insulin, should also be assigned if the diabetes mellitus is being treated with insulin.

4th O24 Diabetes mellitus in pregnancy, childbirth, and the puerperium
5th O24.0 Pre-existing diabetes mellitus, type 1, in pregnancy, childbirth and the puerperium
Juvenile onset diabetes mellitus, in pregnancy, childbirth and the puerperium
Ketosis-prone diabetes mellitus in pregnancy, childbirth and the puerperium
Use additional code from category E10 to further identify any manifestations
6th O24.01 Pre-existing diabetes mellitus, type 1, in pregnancy
O24.011 Pre-existing diabetes mellitus, type 1, in pregnancy, first trimester M ♀
O24.012 Pre-existing diabetes mellitus, type 1, in pregnancy, second trimester M ♀
O24.013 Pre-existing diabetes mellitus, type 1, in pregnancy, third trimester M ♀

Figure 7.2 (Continued)

O24.019 **Pre-existing diabetes mellitus, type 1, in pregnancy, unspecified trimester** M ♀

O24.02 **Pre-existing diabetes mellitus, type 1, in childbirth** M ♀

O24.03 **Pre-existing diabetes mellitus, type 1, in the puerperium** M ♀

5th **O24.1 Pre-existing diabetes mellitus, type 2, in pregnancy, childbirth and the puerperium**

Insulin-resistant diabetes mellitus in pregnancy, childbirth and the puerperium

Use additional code (for):

from category E11 to further identify any manifestations

long-term (current) use of insulin (Z79.4)

6th **O24.11 Pre-existing diabetes mellitus, type 2, in pregnancy**

O24.111 **Pre-existing diabetes mellitus, type 2, in pregnancy, first trimester** M ♀

O24.112 **Pre-existing diabetes mellitus, type 2, in pregnancy, second trimester** M ♀

O24.113 **Pre-existing diabetes mellitus, type 2, in pregnancy, third trimester** M ♀

O24.119 **Pre-existing diabetes mellitus, type 2, in pregnancy, unspecified trimester** M ♀

O24.12 **Pre-existing diabetes mellitus, type 2, in childbirth** M ♀

O24.13 **Pre-existing diabetes mellitus, type 2, in the puerperium** M ♀

5th **O24.3 Unspecified pre-existing diabetes mellitus in pregnancy, childbirth and the puerperium**

Use additional code (for):

from category E11 to further identify any manifestation

long-term (current) use of insulin (Z79.4)

6th **O24.31 Unspecified pre-existing diabetes mellitus in pregnancy**

O24.311 **Unspecified pre-existing diabetes mellitus in pregnancy, first trimester** M ♀

O24.312 **Unspecified pre-existing diabetes mellitus in pregnancy, second trimester** M ♀

O24.313 **Unspecified pre-existing diabetes mellitus in pregnancy, third trimester** M ♀

O24.319 **Unspecified pre-existing diabetes mellitus in pregnancy, unspecified trimester** M ♀

O24.32 **Unspecified pre-existing diabetes mellitus in childbirth** M ♀

O24.33 **Unspecified pre-existing diabetes mellitus in the puerperium** M ♀

ICD-10-CM Official Guidelines (Chapter 15)

i. Gestational (pregnancy induced) diabetes

Gestational (pregnancy induced) diabetes can occur during the second and third trimester of pregnancy in women who were not diabetic prior to pregnancy. Gestational diabetes can cause complications in the pregnancy similar to those of pre-existing diabetes mellitus. It also puts the woman at greater risk of developing diabetes after the pregnancy. Codes for gestational diabetes are in subcategory O24.4, Gestational diabetes mellitus. No other code from category O24, Diabetes mellitus in pregnancy, childbirth, and the puerperium, should be used with a code from O24.4

The codes under subcategory O24.4 include diet controlled and insulin controlled. If a patient with gestational diabetes is treated with both diet and insulin, only the code for insulin-controlled is required. Code Z79.4, Long-term (current) use of insulin, should not be assigned with codes from subcategory O24.4.

An abnormal glucose tolerance in pregnancy is assigned a code from subcategory O99.81, Abnormal glucose complicating pregnancy, childbirth, and the puerperium.

5th **O24.4 Gestational diabetes mellitus**

Diabetes mellitus arising in pregnancy

Gestational diabetes mellitus NOS

6th **O24.41 Gestational diabetes mellitus in pregnancy**

O24.410 **Gestational diabetes mellitus in pregnancy, diet controlled** M ♀

O24.414 **Gestational diabetes mellitus in pregnancy, insulin controlled** M ♀

O24.419 **Gestational diabetes mellitus in pregnancy, unspecified control** M ♀

6th **O24.42 Gestational diabetes mellitus in childbirth**

O24.420 **Gestational diabetes mellitus in childbirth, diet controlled** M ♀

O24.424 **Gestational diabetes mellitus in childbirth, insulin controlled** M ♀

O24.429 **Gestational diabetes mellitus in childbirth, unspecified control** M ♀

6th **O24.43 Gestational diabetes mellitus in the puerperium**

O24.430 **Gestational diabetes mellitus in the puerperium, diet controlled** M ♀

O24.434 **Gestational diabetes mellitus in the puerperium, insulin controlled** M ♀

O24.439 **Gestational diabetes mellitus in the puerperium, unspecified control** M ♀

5th **O24.8 Other pre-existing diabetes mellitus in pregnancy, childbirth, and the puerperium**

Use additional code (for):

from categories E08, E09 and E13 to further identify any manifestation

long-term (current) use of insulin (Z79.4)

6th **O24.81 Other pre-existing diabetes mellitus in pregnancy**

O24.811 **Other pre-existing diabetes mellitus in pregnancy, first trimester** M ♀

O24.812 **Other pre-existing diabetes mellitus in pregnancy, second trimester** M ♀

O24.813 **Other pre-existing diabetes mellitus in pregnancy, third trimester** M ♀

O24.819 **Other pre-existing diabetes mellitus in pregnancy, unspecified trimester** M ♀

O24.82 **Other pre-existing diabetes mellitus in childbirth** M ♀

O24.83 **Other pre-existing diabetes mellitus in the puerperium** M ♀

5th **O24.9 Unspecified diabetes mellitus in pregnancy, childbirth and the puerperium**

Use additional code for long-term (current) use of insulin (Z79.4)

6th **O24.91 Unspecified diabetes mellitus in pregnancy**

O24.911 **Unspecified diabetes mellitus in pregnancy, first trimester** M ♀

O24.912 **Unspecified diabetes mellitus in pregnancy, second trimester** M ♀

O24.913 **Unspecified diabetes mellitus in pregnancy, third trimester** M ♀

O24.919 **Unspecified diabetes mellitus in pregnancy, unspecified trimester** M ♀

O24.92 **Unspecified diabetes mellitus in childbirth** M ♀

O24.93 **Unspecified diabetes mellitus in the puerperium** M ♀

Unspecified Code | Other Specified Code | *Manifestation Code* | ICD-9-CM xWalks: ≈ (Approximate) = (Equivalent) + (Combo) ~ (Component)

Figure 7.2

Chapter 8

Chapter Eight

Worker's Compensation and Personal Injury Billing Guide

Worker's Compensation and Personal Injury claims by their very nature focus on External Cause coding. External causes are found in Chapter 19 of ICD-10 under the heading Injury, Poisoning and Certain Other Consequences of External Causes (S00–T88).

General Equivalency Mapping (GEM) tools can cause a great deal of confusion and result in errors unless doctors, billers, and coders can independently research ICD-10 for correct codes. An example is carpal tunnel syndrome. In ICD-9, carpal tunnel syndrome is found as code "354.00 Carpal tunnel syndrome, unspecified side." Using a GEM tool, I was directed to G56. Reviewing this code in ICD-10, I was directed to sub-codes such as "G56.1 Carpal tunnel syndrome, right upper limb."

Since this involves either Worker's Compensation or Personal Injury, it may imply the need of an External Cause code, which G56.1 is not. There are a few S codes that could be used, such as "S64.1 Injury to Median nerve." A larger discussion of this is included in this book. If the patient has carpal tunnel syndrome as a result of an external cause, such as a fall, this code is the more appropriate.

It is up to the doctor to determine the exact diagnosis code to use. We are merely giving examples. The doctor may actually conclude that the injury is at the elbow.

Code Extensions for External Cause Code

Most categories in Chapter 19 have a seventh-character requirement for each applicable code. Most categories have three seventh-character values (with the exception of fractures): A, D, and S.

Seventh character A, initial encounter, is used when the patient is receiving active treatment for the condition.

Seventh character D, subsequent encounter, is used for encounters after the patient has received active treatment. An example is for follow-up visits following treatment of the injury or condition.

Seventh character S, sequela, is used for complications or conditions that arise as a direct result of a condition such as scar formation after a burn. When using the seventh character S, it is necessary to use both the injury code that precipitated the sequela itself, and the specific sequela code. The S is added only to the injury code, not the sequela code. The seventh character S identifies the injury responsible for the sequela. The specific type of sequela (e.g., scar) is listed first, followed by the injury code.

For example:

L90.5 Scar conditions *(as a result of the burn)*
T22.139S Burn of first degree of unspecified upper arm
X15.0 Contact with hot stove (kitchen)

Please be aware, A, D, and S codes can be used on the same patient all at the same time. For example, the patient has two injuries, with one no longer under active care, and the other injury still being treated in active care.

Coding Injuries

When coding injuries, assign separate codes for each injury, unless a Combination Code is provided. The code for the most serious injury, as determined by the provider, and the focus of treatment, is sequenced first.

For example, a patient fell off a ladder and fractured his right wrist, contused his right elbow, and cut his right hand, with fracture being the most severe. You would use the following codes in the listed order:

1. S62.330A Displaced fracture of neck of second metacarpal bone, right hand
2. S50.01 Contusion of right elbow
3. S61.411 Laceration without foreign body of right hand

Providers must identify Combination Codes that are relevant to their practices. An example of a non-injury Combination Code is Lumbago with Sciatica. When these occur simultaneously, a Combination Code "M54.4 Lumbago with Sciatica" is required. Coding "Lumbago M54.5" and "Sciatica M54.3" on the same claim will probably result in claim denial.

All diabetes mellitus codes are now Combination Codes. When treating a patient who has diabetes resulting from a drug or chemical exposure, you must be aware to use the correct code(s). You always have to know that if the patient has another form of diabetes, the other type(s) may be relevant to evaluating the patient's condition.

Coding of Traumatic Fractures

Fractures of specified sites are coded individually by site in accordance with provisions within categories and the level of detail furnished by the medical record. When a specific type of fracture occurs, and type is known, it should be specified, for example, Colles' fracture, Smith's fracture, or Barton's fracture of the radius.

Injury Coding Can Be a Big Challenge

It is important to note that there are major differences between ICD-9 and ICD-10 beyond the sheer volume of codes, as follows:

1. There are no direct ICD-9 counterparts for S codes because External Cause codes were "E supplemental" and not required.
2. There are S codes for which there are no ICD-9 counterparts. As an example, there are now codes for subluxation and dislocation at the vertebral level (S13). There were no such codes at the vertebral level in ICD-9.
3. ICD-10 codes often specify laterality, for example "left" versus "right," or specific type such as "Galeazzi fracture."
4. There are codes for strains versus sprains, for example, "S76.81 Strain of other specified muscles, fascia and tendons at thigh level" versus "S83.9 Sprain of unspecified site of knee." The important point is that sprains and strains are now distinguished from each other. In ICD-9, they were not separated.

Place of Occurrence and Activity Codes

ICD-10 provides for much greater data on injuries. Chapter 20 External Causes of Morbidity (V00–Y99) permits the classification of environmental events and circumstances as the cause of injury and other adverse effects. When a code from this section is applicable, it should be used secondary to a code from another chapter indicating the nature of the condition. Most often, the condition will be classifiable to Chapter 19 codes.

An example could be: A patient fell from a motorcycle and cut his hand.

S61.419A Open wound of right hand
Y99.410 Specified street or highway as the place of occurrence
V20.000A Motorcycle driver injured in collision with pedestrian or animal in a non-traffic accident

This indicates that not only did the patient cut his right hand, but where and how it happened. It also specifies that the patient is under active treatment for the open wound. (The CPT procedure code(s) gives the treatment rendered.)

Due to the potential legal issues involved, the medical record should contain detail on injuries and the provider must be aware that circumstance and places of occurrence are now required elements for claims. The greater emphasis on electronic claims submission can cause greater complication for claims missing data such as S codes.

Encounter Codes

Chapter 21 contains codes for "Factors Influencing Health Status and Contact with Health Services (Z00–Z99)." Z codes represent reasons for encounters. A corresponding procedure code must accompany a Z code if a procedure is performed. For Worker's Compensation and Personal Injury, the block "Z00–Z13 Persons encountering health services for examinations" is relevant.

Z04.1 Encounter for examination and observation following transport accident
Z04.2 Encounter for examination and observation following work accident
Z04.3 Encounter for examination and observation following other accident

An encounter specifies the reason(s) a patient was seen. The actual service rendered is given by the CPT code, for example, office visit. There can be multiple encounter codes and multiple procedure codes depending on the circumstances.

As an example, a patient is seen for examination and observation following a transport accident. The Encounter code is Z04.1, which specifies why the patient was seen. During the encounter, the provider may determine that the patient has an open wound on his right hand. The provider then does a simple closure procedure to stop the bleeding. The Diagnosis code for the wound is S61.411A. The A is used because this is the initial encounter for the wound.

A new patient is seen for observation following an accident:

CPT 99203-25 Office visit
ICD-10 Code Z04.1 Encounter for examination and observation following transport accident

The provider provides a simple repair of a superficial wound:

(CPT 12001) Simple repair of superficial wound
S61.411A Laceration without foreign body of right hand

The modifier "-25" is used to indicate that another service beyond evaluation and management (E&M) was provided.

Place of Occurrence, Activity, and Encounter codes should all appear on Workers Compensation and Personal Injury claims.

Using the Crosswalk

Enclosed in the Appendix is a crosswalk of certain ICD-9 to ICD-10 Diagnosis codes. It is intended only as a general guide to assist in identifying ICD-10 codes. The Crosswalk is in ICD-9 sequence, so the user can look for an ICD-9 code to assist in finding the appropriate ICD-10 code. Since many ICD-10 codes, for example, S or External Cause codes, have no ICD-9 counterpart, that column is left blank for those codes.

Please note: The following example cases are based on real medical reports and associated claim forms. Errors in documentation and claim forms are pointed out to demonstrate the need for complete and accurate documentation and coding.

Personal Injury Example Case 1

Please note: We have abbreviated the history and documentation, as it is only for demonstrative purposes. An actual Personal Injury or Worker's Compensation report would have much greater detail and documentation.

Patient: Patron at a restaurant slipped on wet floor, landing on back and hit elbows against floor.

Diagnosis per report narrative: lumbar strain and right carpal tunnel syndrome.

Incomplete Diagnosis on original Claim Form: 847.2 Lumbar sprain/strain.

Corrected Inclusive ICD-10 Billing

Z04.3 Encounter for examination and observation following other accident
S33.5XXA Sprain of ligaments of lumbar spine, subsequent encounter
S39.012A Strain of muscle, fascia, tendon of lower back
S64.11XA Injury of median nerve at wrist and hand level of right arm

Please note: A codes are used here as the patient is in active treatment.

There was no diagnosis for carpal tunnel syndrome on the claim form, but the report clearly states the presence of carpal tunnel syndrome. Prior medical records were not specific or clear on the presence of other injuries.

You should add additional External Causes of Morbidity codes that classify external causes of accidental injury, as well:

W01.0XXA Fall on same level from slipping, tripping and stumbling without subsequent striking of object

As we look at the claim form, there were the additional codes of S23.3XXA and S33.9XXA on the CMS-1500 form that were not in the report. In the following table, these codes were converted to ICD-10 from the ICD-9 codes on the claim forms. This is a perfect example of the documentation not matching the billing. This could create major issues with reimbursement with the new ICD-10 coding system.

CPT	*ICD10 Diagnosis*
99213-25 Office Visit	Z04.3
	W01.0XXA
72070 X-ray spine; thoracic	S23.3XXA
72114 X-ray spine, lumbrosacral; minimum of six views	S33.5XXA
72170 X-ray pelvis	S33.9XXA

Claim Billing

Z04 Encounter for examination and observation for other reasons. This category is used when a patient without a diagnosis is suspected of having an abnormal condition, without signs or symptoms, which requires study, but after examination and observation is ruled out. This category is also used for administrative and legal observation status. The medicolegal or final report and progress reports meet the criteria for this category.

There are three remaining categories to determine. They are

Category 4 Place of Occurrence (Y92.511 Restaurant or cafe as place of occurrence)
Category 5 Activity (Y93.89 Activity, other specified)
Category 6 External Cause Status (Y99.8 Other external cause status)

See Figure 8.1 for completed claim form.

Worker's Compensation Example Case 2

Please note: Although this example has been taken from an actual Worker's Compensation report, we have abbreviated the history and documentation, as it is only for demonstrative purposes. An actual Worker's Compensation or Personal Injury report would have much greater detail and documentation.

Patient: Worker in a convalescent hospital as a certified nurse assistant. He was asked to lift a patient from his bed onto a wheel chair. The patient struck him and caused him to fall, sitting down into the wheel chair.

ICD-9 Diagnosis on original Claim Form:

847.0 Neck sprain
847.2 Lumbar sprain

Diagnosis per report narrative and past medical records:

PERSONAL INJURY EXAMPLE CASE 1

HEALTH INSURANCE CLAIM FORM

APPROVED BY NATIONAL UNIFORM CLAIM COMMITIEE (NUCC) 02/12

PICA PICA

CARRIER

1. MEDICARE (Medicare#) MEDICAID (Medicaid#) TRICARE (ID#/DoD#) CHAMPVA (Member ID#) GROUP HEALTH PLAN (ID#) FECA BLK LUNG (ID#) OTHER (ID#)
1a. INSURED'S I.D. NUMBER (For Program in Item 1)

2. PATIENT'S NAME (Last Name, First Name, Middle Initial)
Personal Injury Example Case 1
3. PATIENT'S BIRTH DATE MM DD YY SEX M F
4. INSURED'S NAME (Last Name, First Name, Middle Initial)

5. PATIENT'S ADDRESS (No., Street)
6. PATIENT RELATIONSHIP TO INSURED Self Spouse Child Other
7. INSURED'S ADDRESS (No., Street)

CITY STATE
8. RESERVED FOR NUCC USE
CITY STATE

ZIP CODE TELEPHONE (Include Area Code) ( )
ZIP CODE TELEPHONE (Include Area Code) ( )

9. OTHER INSURED'S NAME (Last Name, First Name, Middle Initial)
10. IS PATIENT'S CONDITION RELATED TO:
11. INSURED'S POLICY GROUP OR FECA NUMBER

a. OTHER INSURED'S POLICY OR GROUP NUMBER
a. EMPLOYMENT? (Current or Previous) YES NO
a. INSURED'S DATE OF BIRTH MM DD YY SEX M F

b. RESERVED FOR NUCC USE
b. AUTO ACCIDENT? YES NO PLACE (State)
b. OTHER CLAIM ID (Designated by NUCC)

c. RESERVED FOR NUCC USE
c. OTHER ACCIDENT? YES NO
c. INSURANCE PLAN NAME OR PROGRAM NAME

d. INSURANCE PLAN NAME OR PROGRAM NAME
10d. CLAIM CODES (Designated by NUCC)
d. IS THERE ANOTHER HEALTH BENEFIT PLAN? YES NO *If yes, complete items 9, 9a, and 9d.*

READ BACK OF FORM BEFORE COMPLETING & SIGNING THIS FORM.

12. PATIENT'S OR AUTHORIZED PERSON'S SIGNATURE I authorize the release of any medical or other information necessary to process this claim. I also request payment of government benefits either to myself or to the party who accepts assignment below.

SIGNED DATE

13. INSURED'S OR AUTHORIZED PERSON'S SIGNATURE I authorize payment of medical benefits to the undersigned physician or supplier for services described below.

SIGNED

PATIENT AND INSURED INFORMATION

14. DATE OF CURRENT ILLNESS, INJURY, or PREGNANCY (LMP) MM DD YY QUAL.
15. OTHER DATE QUAL. MM DD YY
16. DATES PATIENT UNABLE TO WORK IN CURRENT OCCUPATION FROM MM DD YY TO MM DD YY

17. NAME OF REFERRING PROVIDER OR OTHER SOURCE 17a. 17b. NPI
18. HOSPITALIZATION DATES RELATED TO CURRENT SERVICES FROM MM DD YY TO MM DD YY

19. ADDITIONAL CLAIM INFORMATION (Designated by NUCC)
20. OUTSIDE LAB? YES NO $ CHARGES

21. DIAGNOSIS OR NATURE OF ILLNESS OR INJURY Relate A-L to service line below (24E) ICD Ind.

A. Z04.3	B. S33.5XXA	C. S39.012A	D. S64.11XA
E. S23.3XXA	F. S33.9XXA	G. W01.0XXA	H. Y92.511
I. Y93.89	J. Y99.8	K.	L.

22. RESUBMISSION CODE ORIGINAL REF. NO.
23. PRIOR AUTHORIZATION NUMBER

	24. A. DATE(S) OF SERVICE From MM DD YY To MM DD YY	B. PLACE OF SERVICE	C. EMG	D. PROCEDURES, SERVICES, OR SUPPLIES (Explain Unusual Circumstances) CPT/HCPCS	MODIFIER	E. DIAGNOSIS POINTER	F. $ CHARGES	G. DAYS OR UNITS	H. EPSDT Family plan	I. ID. QUAL.	J. RENDERING PROVIDER ID. #
1				99213	25	A - J				NPI	
2				72070		E				NPI	
3				72114		B				NPI	
4				72170		F				NPI	
5										NPI	
6										NPI	

PHYSICIAN OR SUPPLIER INFORMATION

25. FEDERAL TAX I.D. NUMBER SSN EIN
26. PATIENT'S ACCOUNT NO.
27. ACCEPT ASSIGNMENT? (For govt. claims, see back) YES NO
28. TOTAL CHARGE
29. AMOUNT PAID $
30. Rsvd for NUCC Use

31. SIGNATURE OF PHYSICIAN OR SUPPLIER INCLUDING DEGREES OR CREDENTIALS (I certify that the statements on the reverse apply to this bill and are made a part thereof.)
32. SERVICE FACILITY LOCATION INFORMATION
33. BILLING PROVIDER INFO & PH# ( )

SIGNED DATE
a. NPI b.
a. NPI b.

NUCC Instruction Manual available at: www.nucc.org *PLEASE PRINT OR TYPE* APPROVED OMB-0938-1197 FORM 1500 (02-12)

Figure 8.1

Cervical spine injury with multi-level disc protrusions and subluxations at C3/C4, C4/C5 and C5/C6 on MRI and Lumbar spine injury with multilevel disc protrusions on MRI. The narrative specifies specific vertebral levels and states there were impaired neck motion and disc protrusions and annular tears.

Based on the diagnoses listed in the MRI reports, you find the following ICD-10 codes:

Z04.2 Encounter for examination and observation following a work accident
S33.0XXD Traumatic rupture of intervertebral disc, lumbar region
S13.240D Subluxation C3/C4
S13.150D Subluxation C4/C5
S13.160D Subluxation C5/C6
S13.0XXD Traumatic rupture of intervertebral disc, cervical region

We use D as the seventh character to indicate that this was an evaluation/examination after the initial phase of treatment.

In the case of the disc protrusions, we use the S13.0 and S33.0 codes, even though they lack specificity in regard to level, rather than the M codes, because we want to indicate that this is caused by an injury.

Please note: S13.0 has "Excludes 1 for Rupture or displacement (non-traumatic) of intervertebral disc NOS (M50.-)." S33.0 has "Excludes 1: Rupture or displacement (non-traumatic) of intervertebral disc NOS" (M51.- with fifth character 6).

Additional External Causes of Morbidity codes that classify activity, environmental events, and circumstances, need to be added, as well:

Y92.230 Place of occurrence. Patient room in hospital as the place of occurrence of external cause
Y04.8XXD Assault by other bodily force

Please note that the report specifies that the patient was "hit." If the incident was an accident, one could use "W50.0 Accidental hit or strike by another person."

Activity Codes are codes that explain what the patient was doing at the time of injury.

Y93.F9 Activity, other care giving.
Y99.0 Civilian activity for income or pay.
Z04- Encounter for examination and observation for other reasons. This category is used when a patient without a diagnosis is suspected of having an abnormal condition, without signs or symptoms, which requires study, but after examination and observation is ruled out. This category is also used for administrative and legal observation status. The medicolegal report and progress reports above meets the later criteria for this category.

See Figure 8.2 for completed claim form.

Please note: As shown on the CMS Form 1500 for this example, most of the diagnosis blocks on the form have been filled in in the diagnosis section. Since the ICD-10 code set increases the number of diagnoses codes by over 700%,

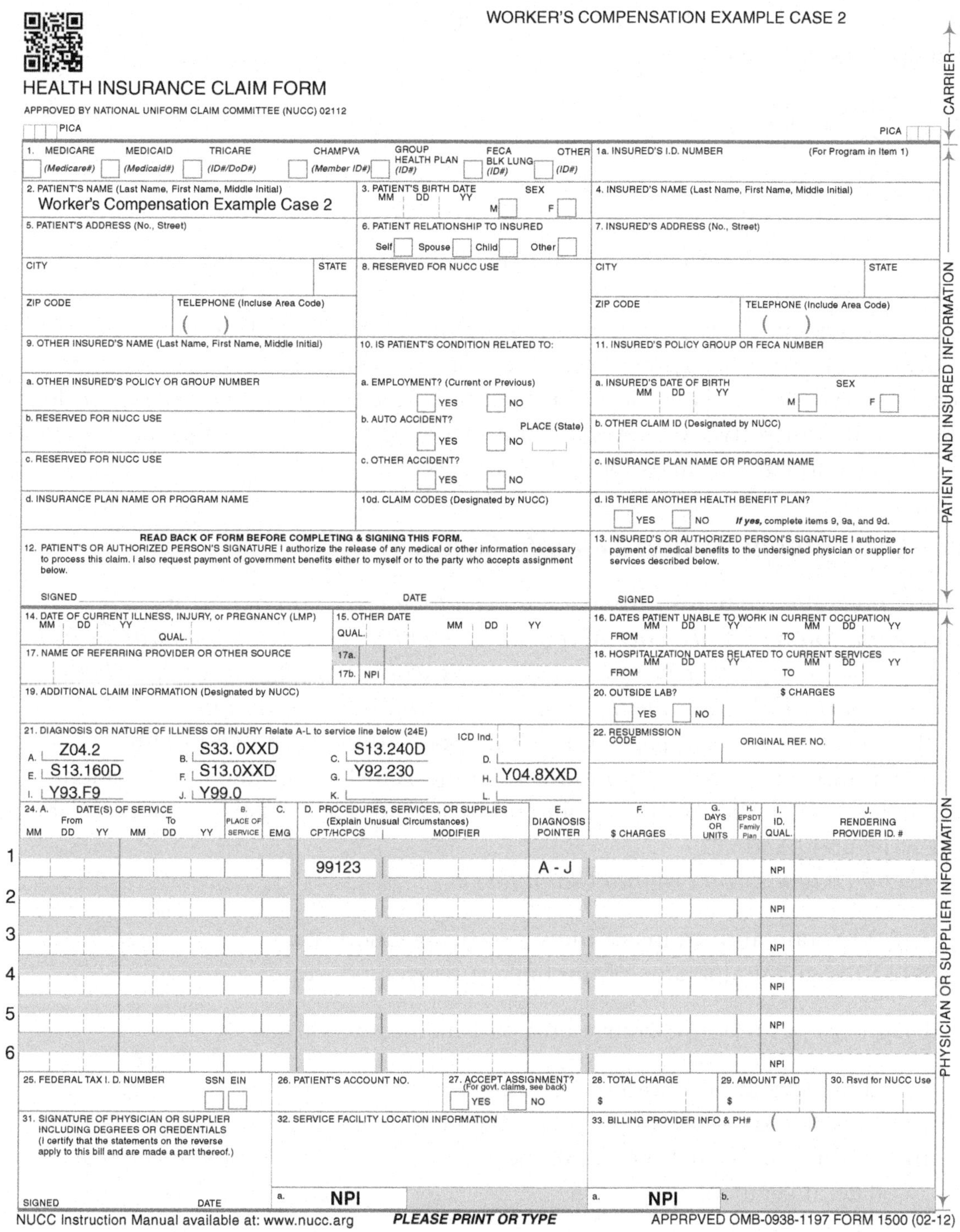
WORKER'S COMPENSATION EXAMPLE CASE 2

HEALTH INSURANCE CLAIM FORM

APPROVED BY NATIONAL UNIFORM CLAIM COMMITTEE (NUCC) 02112

PICA PICA

1. MEDICARE (Medicare#) MEDICAID (Medicaid#) TRICARE (ID#/DoD#) CHAMPVA (Member ID#) GROUP HEALTH PLAN (ID#) FECA BLK LUNG (ID#) OTHER (ID#)
1a. INSURED'S I.D. NUMBER (For Program in Item 1)

2. PATIENT'S NAME (Last Name, First Name, Middle Initial): Worker's Compensation Example Case 2
3. PATIENT'S BIRTH DATE MM DD YY SEX M F
4. INSURED'S NAME (Last Name, First Name, Middle Initial)
5. PATIENT'S ADDRESS (No., Street)
6. PATIENT RELATIONSHIP TO INSURED Self Spouse Child Other
7. INSURED'S ADDRESS (No., Street)
CITY STATE
8. RESERVED FOR NUCC USE
CITY STATE
ZIP CODE TELEPHONE (Incluse Area Code) ( )
ZIP CODE TELEPHONE (Include Area Code) ( )
9. OTHER INSURED'S NAME (Last Name, First Name, Middle Initial)
10. IS PATIENT'S CONDITION RELATED TO:
11. INSURED'S POLICY GROUP OR FECA NUMBER
a. OTHER INSURED'S POLICY OR GROUP NUMBER
a. EMPLOYMENT? (Current or Previous) YES NO
a. INSURED'S DATE OF BIRTH MM DD YY SEX M F
b. RESERVED FOR NUCC USE
b. AUTO ACCIDENT? YES NO PLACE (State)
b. OTHER CLAIM ID (Designated by NUCC)
c. RESERVED FOR NUCC USE
c. OTHER ACCIDENT? YES NO
c. INSURANCE PLAN NAME OR PROGRAM NAME
d. INSURANCE PLAN NAME OR PROGRAM NAME
10d. CLAIM CODES (Designated by NUCC)
d. IS THERE ANOTHER HEALTH BENEFIT PLAN? YES NO *If yes,* complete items 9, 9a, and 9d.

READ BACK OF FORM BEFORE COMPLETING & SIGNING THIS FORM.

12. PATIENT'S OR AUTHORIZED PERSON'S SIGNATURE I authorize the release of any medical or other information necessary to process this claim. I also request payment of government benefits either to myself or to the party who accepts assignment below.
SIGNED DATE

13. INSURED'S OR AUTHORIZED PERSON'S SIGNATURE I authorize payment of medical benefits to the undersigned physician or supplier for services described below.
SIGNED

14. DATE OF CURRENT ILLNESS, INJURY, or PREGNANCY (LMP) MM DD YY QUAL.
15. OTHER DATE QUAL. MM DD YY
16. DATES PATIENT UNABLE TO WORK IN CURRENT OCCUPATION FROM MM DD YY TO MM DD YY
17. NAME OF REFERRING PROVIDER OR OTHER SOURCE 17a. 17b. NPI
18. HOSPITALIZATION DATES RELATED TO CURRENT SERVICES FROM MM DD YY TO MM DD YY
19. ADDITIONAL CLAIM INFORMATION (Designated by NUCC)
20. OUTSIDE LAB? YES NO $ CHARGES
21. DIAGNOSIS OR NATURE OF ILLNESS OR INJURY Relate A-L to service line below (24E) ICD Ind.
A. Z04.2 B. S33. 0XXD C. S13.240D D.
E. S13.160D F. S13.0XXD G. Y92.230 H. Y04.8XXD
I. Y93.F9 J. Y99.0 K. L.
22. RESUBMISSION CODE ORIGINAL REF. NO.
23. PRIOR AUTHORIZATION NUMBER

	24. A. DATE(S) OF SERVICE From MM DD YY To MM DD YY	B. PLACE OF SERVICE	C. EMG	D. PROCEDURES, SERVICES, OR SUPPLIES (Explain Unusual Circumstances) CPT/HCPCS MODIFIER	E. DIAGNOSIS POINTER	F. $ CHARGES	G. DAYS OR UNITS	H. EPSDT Family Plan	I. ID. QUAL.	J. RENDERING PROVIDER ID. #
1				99123	A - J				NPI	
2									NPI	
3									NPI	
4									NPI	
5									NPI	
6									NPI	

25. FEDERAL TAX I. D. NUMBER SSN EIN
26. PATIENT'S ACCOUNT NO.
27. ACCEPT ASSIGNMENT? (For govt. claims, see back) YES NO
28. TOTAL CHARGE $
29. AMOUNT PAID $
30. Rsvd for NUCC Use
31. SIGNATURE OF PHYSICIAN OR SUPPLIER INCLUDING DEGREES OR CREDENTIALS (I certify that the statements on the reverse apply to this bill and are made a part thereof.)
SIGNED DATE
32. SERVICE FACILITY LOCATION INFORMATION a. NPI b.
33. BILLING PROVIDER INFO & PH# ( ) a. NPI b.

CARRIER — PATIENT AND INSURED INFORMATION — PHYSICIAN OR SUPPLIER INFORMATION

NUCC Instruction Manual available at: www.nucc.arg *PLEASE PRINT OR TYPE* APPRPVED OMB-0938-1197 FORM 1500 (02-12)

Figure 8.2

there will be occasions when there are not enough blocks on the form for all the diagnosis codes. When submitting electronic claims, this may not be an issue if your software allows you to enter as many codes as needed. In the case of hard-copy claims, you may have to submit multiple claim forms. If this occurs, the CPT convention is to use a "multiple modifiers" code (99) to be added to the basic procedure. In this case, all the diagnoses related to the office visit. An example could be as follows:

CPT Diagnosis Code(s)
99213325 A–D
992132599 E–H
992132599 I–J

In the foregoing example, the software only allows four diagnosis codes per line item. Since there are 10 diagnoses codes, we use 3 lines for the Evaluation and Management code (99213) to allow for presentation of all 10 diagnoses codes. If your software allows you to "point" to a different number of diagnoses codes, you must allow for the difference by indicating the number of codes allowed. If your software allows for only one diagnosis code per procedure, you would have to have 10 lines for 99213, and so on.

Worker's Compensation Example Case 3

Please note: Although this example has been taken from an actual Worker's Compensation report, we have abbreviated the history and documentation, as it is only for demonstrative purposes. An actual Worker's Compensation or Personal Injury report would have much greater detail and documentation.

Patient: Working as a dispatcher filling food orders, lifting and pulling a transportation cart loaded with food weighing 700–1000 pounds. The patient attempted to stop the cart from rolling down a ramp and sustained injury to his left wrist and hand.

ICD-9 Diagnosis on original Claim form:

842.00 Sprain and strains of the wrist, unspecified site
842.10 Sprain and strains of the hand, unspecified site

Diagnosis per report narrative and past medical records:

Left radial styloid non-union
Left wrist fracture—two reports specify Chauffeur's fracture
Impaired left wrist motion and tenderness of radio-carpal joint and radial collateral ligament

This is exactly why the doctor has to take the responsibility of understanding proper coding, especially with the increased complexity of ICD-10, as the codes used here are inadequate and could significantly affect the patient's care and case.

In our example, it was noted that Chauffeur's fracture was specified.

S52.512 Displaced fracture of left radial styloid process (Chauffeur's fracture)

In our example, one of the diagnoses is left radial styloid non-union. In this case, the patient was treated for the radial fracture, but a subsequent non-union occurred.

The non-union of the displaced fracture appears to be a sequela of the original fracture injury and therefore could be coded as:

S52.512K
S52.512S

Note: The use of K as a seventh character denotes "Subsequent encounter for closed fracture with non-union." Other seventh-character codes specific to fractures are listed at the end of this example.

The ICD-10-CM Draft Chapter 19 states:

> *"7th character "S", sequela, is for use for complications or conditions that arise as a direct result of a condition, such as scar formation after a burn. The scars are sequelae of the burn. When using 7th character "S," it is necessary to use both the injury code that precipitated the sequela and the code for the sequela itself. The "S" is added only to the injury code, not the sequela code. The 7th character "S" identifies the injury responsible for the sequela.* ***The specific type of sequela (e.g., scar) is sequenced first, followed by the injury code."*** (note: bolding of sentence by author)

Note: This sequela of the non-union of this fracture can be interpreted as compensable consequence of the original work injury. (This could vary, depending on which state's statutes apply.)

In regard to the sprain/strain diagnoses, we see in the report that there is no mention of wrist strain. In ICD-10, Strains and Sprains are separated out into separate codes, which was not the case in ICD-9. This gives providers more options: they can just diagnose this as a wrist sprain S63.-, or, if they feel a wrist strain was present as well, they can add the code S66.-.

S63.522D Subsequent encounter *(after initial treatment)* for sprain of radiocarpal joint of left wrist
S63.502D Subsequent encounter *(after initial treatment)* for unspecified sprain of left wrist

If the provider wanted to add a wrist strain diagnosis, the following could be added:

S66.912D Subsequent encounter *(after initial treatment)* for strain of unspecified muscle, fascia and tendon at wrist and hand level, left hand

The following codes could add clarity to the mechanism of injury and the purpose of the encounter. We recommend their inclusion as part of the Six-Category System.

Z04.2 Encounter for examination and observation following a work accident
V83.7 Person on outside of special industrial vehicle injured in nontraffic accident
Y92.59 Other trade areas as the place of service of the external cause
Y93.G1 Activity, food preparation, and clean up
Y99.0 Civilian activity done for income or pay

Seventh-Character Codes for Fracture

When billing for fractures, a seventh character is required. A fracture not indicated as open or closed should be coded to "closed." The open fracture designations are based on the Gustilo open fracture classification.

A. Initial encounter for closed fracture
B. Initial encounter for open fracture type I or II or open fracture NOS
C. Initial encounter for open fracture type IIIA, IIIB, or IIIC
D. Subsequent encounter for closed fracture with routine healing
E. Subsequent encounter for open fracture type I or II with routine healing
F. Subsequent encounter for open fracture type IIIA, IIIB, or IIIC with routine healing
G. Subsequent encounter for closed fracture with delayed healing
H. Subsequent encounter for open type fracture Type I or II with delayed healing
J. Subsequent encounter for open type fracture type IIIA, IIIB, or IIIC with delayed healing
K. Subsequent encounter for closed fracture with non-union
M. Subsequent encounter for open fracture type I or II with nonunion
N. Subsequent encounter for open type fracture type IIIA, IIIB or IIIC with non-union
P. Subsequent encounter for closed fracture with malunion
Q. Subsequent encounter for open fracture type I or II with malunion
R. Subsequent encounter for open type fracture type IIIA, IIIB, or III with malunion
S. Sequela

See Figure 8.3 for completed claim form.

Billing for Physical Therapy

Physical therapy billing can be very complicated when both Medicare and non-Medicare claims are billed. Let us assume we have two claims. One is for a Medicare patient and the other is for a private insurance patient. Claims can be

WORKER'S COMPENSATION EXAMPLE CASE 3

HEALTH INSURANCE CLAIM FORM

APPROVED BY NATIONAL UNIFORM CLAIM COMMITTEE (NUCC) 02/12

PICA | PICA

CARRIER

1. MEDICARE (Medicare#) | MEDICAID (Medicaid#) | TRICARE (ID#/DoD#) | CHAMPVA (Member ID#) | GROUP HEALTH PLAN (ID#) | FECA BLK LUNG (ID#) | OTHER (ID#)

1a. INSURED'S I.D. NUMBER (For Program in Item 1)

2. PATIENT'S NAME (Last Name, First Name, Middle Initial): Worker's Compensation Example Case 3

3. PATIENT'S BIRTH DATE MM DD YY — SEX M F

4. INSURED'S NAME (Last Name, First Name, Middle Initial)

5. PATIENT'S ADDRESS (No., Street)

6. PATIENT RELATIONSHIP TO INSURED: Self, Spouse, Child, Other

7. INSURED'S ADDRESS (No., Street)

CITY — STATE

8. RESERVED FOR NUCC USE

CITY — STATE

ZIP CODE — TELEPHONE (Incluse Area Code) ( )

ZIP CODE — TELEPHONE (Include Area Code) ( )

9. OTHER INSURED'S NAME (Last Name, First Name, Middle Initial)

10. IS PATIENT'S CONDITION RELATED TO:

11. INSURED'S POLICY GROUP OR FECA NUMBER

a. OTHER INSURED'S POLICY OR GROUP NUMBER

a. EMPLOYMENT? (Current or Previous) YES NO

a. INSURED'S DATE OF BIRTH MM DD YY — SEX M F

b. RESERVED FOR NUCC USE

b. AUTO ACCIDENT? YES NO — PLACE (State)

b. OTHER CLAIM ID (Designated by NUCC)

c. RESERVED FOR NUCC USE

c. OTHER ACCIDENT? YES NO

c. INSURANCE PLAN NAME OR PROGRAM NAME

d. INSURANCE PLAN NAME OR PROGRAM NAME

10d. CLAIM CODES (Designated by NUCC)

d. IS THERE ANOTHER HEALTH BENEFIT PLAN? YES NO *If yes, complete items 9, 9a, and 9d.*

READ BACK OF FORM BEFORE COMPLETING & SIGNING THIS FORM.

12. PATIENT'S OR AUTHORIZED PERSON'S SIGNATURE I authorize the release of any medical or other information necessary to process this claim. I also request payment of government benefits either to myself or to the party who accepts assignment below.

SIGNED — DATE

13. INSURED'S OR AUTHORIZED PERSON'S SIGNATURE I authorize payment of medical benefits to the undersigned physician or supplier for services described below.

SIGNED

PATIENT AND INSURED INFORMATION

14. DATE OF CURRENT ILLNESS, INJURY, or PREGNANCY (LMP) MM DD YY QUAL.

15. OTHER DATE QUAL. MM DD YY

16. DATES PATIENT UNABLE TO WORK IN CURRENT OCCUPATION FROM MM DD YY TO MM DD YY

17. NAME OF REFERRING PROVIDER OR OTHER SOURCE — 17a. — 17b. NPI

18. HOSPITALIZATION DATES RELATED TO CURRENT SERVICES FROM MM DD YY TO MM DD YY

19. ADDITIONAL CLAIM INFORMATION (Designated by NUCC)

20. OUTSIDE LAB? YES NO — $ CHARGES

21. DIAGNOSIS OR NATURE OF ILLNESS OR INJURY Relate A-L to service line below (24E) — ICD Ind.

A. Z04.2	B. S52.512K	C. S52.512S	D. S63.522D
E. S63.502D	F. S66.912D	G. V83.7	H. Y92.59
I. Y93.G1	J. Y99.0	K.	L.

22. RESUBMISSION CODE — ORIGINAL REF. NO.

23. PRIOR AUTHORIZATION NUMBER

	24. A. DATE(S) OF SERVICE From MM DD YY To MM DD YY	B. PLACE OF SERVICE	C. EMG	D. PROCEDURES, SERVICES, OR SUPPLIES (Explain Unusual Circumstances) CPT/HCPCS MODIFIER	E. DIAGNOSIS POINTER	F. $ CHARGES	G. DAYS OR UNITS	H. EPSDT Family Plan	I. ID. QUAL.	J. RENDERING PROVIDER ID. #
1				99213	A - J				NPI	
2									NPI	
3									NPI	
4									NPI	
5									NPI	
6									NPI	

PHYSICIAN OR SUPPLIER INFORMATION

25. FEDERAL TAX I. D. NUMBER SSN EIN

26. PATIENT'S ACCOUNT NO.

27. ACCEPT ASSIGNMENT? (For govt. claims, see back) YES NO

28. TOTAL CHARGE $

29. AMOUNT PAID $

30. Rsvd for NUCC Use

31. SIGNATURE OF PHYSICIAN OR SUPPLIER INCLUDING DEGREES OR CREDENTIALS (I certify that the statements on the reverse apply to this bill and are made a part thereof.)

SIGNED — DATE

32. SERVICE FACILITY LOCATION INFORMATION — a. NPI b.

33. BILLING PROVIDER INFO & PH# ( ) — a. NPI b.

NUCC Instruction Manual available at: www.nucc.org — ***PLEASE PRINT OR TYPE*** — APPROVED OMB-0938-1197 FORM 1500 (02-12)

Figure 8.3

even more complex for Worker's Compensation and Personal Injury claims, as shown in Example 3.

Example 1: Medicare patient who was playing golf and had a diagnosis of degeneration of a cervical disc. The ICD-9 code is 722.4. As shown in your crosswalk, the ICD-10 code is "M50.30 Other cervical disc degeneration, unspecified cervical region." The patient received three physical therapy procedures as follows:

G0283GP Electrical stimulation (unattended), to one or more areas for indication(s) other than wound care as part of a therapy plan of care
97016GP Application of a modality to one or more areas; vasopneumatic devices
97112GP Therapeutic neuromuscular reeducation of movement, balance, coordination, kinesthetic sense, posture, and/or proprioception for sitting and/or standing activities

Medicare requires the use of modifiers to identify the type of provider. "GN" indicates that services were delivered under an outpatient speech-language pathology plan of care. "GP" indicates that services were delivered under an outpatient therapy plan of care.

It should be noted that Medicare requires the use of the HCPCS code G0283 rather than CPT 97014.

Example 2: A private insurance patient who had an ICD-9 diagnosis of "846.0 Lumbrosacral (joint) (ligament) strain" was moving boxes at home and slipped but did not fall, which caused the strain. He received the same three treatments. The ICD-9 code 846.0 crosswalks to S33.8XXA, as shown in the Crosswalk.

G0283	Electrical stimulation (unattended), to one or more areas for indication(s) other than wound care as part of a therapy plan of care
97016	Application of a modality to one or more areas; vasopneumatic devices
97112	Therapeutic neuromuscular reeducation of movement, balance, coordination, kinesthetic sense, posture, and/or proprioception for sitting and/or standing activities

This claim was sent to Blue Cross. Interestingly, major carriers such as Blue Cross, Cigna, and United Health care also recognize and cover the HCPCS code G0283. Other carriers, such as Worker's Compensation, may not recognize this code.

The major difference between 97014 and G0283 is that the HCPCS code specifies that services are rendered under a plan of care.

Since this is not a Medicare claim, the procedure codes do not have the GP modifier.

In the second case (Example 2), the ICD-10 code is S33.8XXA. The seventh character A specifies that the patient is under active care. Since the diagnosis is for an S code, it is a code from Chapter 19 Injury, Poisoning and Certain other Consequences of External Causes. S codes require the use of a secondary code(s) from Chapter 20 to indicate cause of injury. In this case, we specified that the patient slipped but did not fall. A review of Chapter 20 shows that there is a code for "Other slipping, tripping and stumbling without falling W18.49XA." In this case, we now have two diagnoses codes for the procedures: S338.XXA and W18.49XA, which should appear on claims along with the CPT procedure codes.

It is important to recognize that if the patient in Example 2 was a Medicare patient, the GP modifier would be required.

In Example 3, let us assume that the patient was working as a driver of a pick-up truck who crashed into a loading dock and suffered subluxation of C1/C2 vertebrae. The loading dock was for a building still under construction.

Procedure

97014 Electrical stimulation (unattended).

Note: This code is used because some Worker's Compensation carriers do not recognize HCPCS codes such as G0283.

97016 Application of a modality to one or more areas; vasopneumatic devices

97112 Therapeutic neuromuscular reeducation of movement, balance, coordination, kinesthetic sense, posture, and/or proprioception for sitting and/or standing activities

Note: Medicare modifiers, for example, GP, are not used for non-Medicare patients.

If the patient is known to have suffered a subluxation at the level of C3 on C4 cervical vertebrae, such as through x-rays, then the following diagnosis code should be used: "S13.140A Subluxation of C3/C4 cervical vertebrae."

Please note that *there are no ICD-9 codes for subluxation or dislocation at the vertebral level.* These are new to ICD-10 and are another example of why simple GEM tools should not be relied upon.

A seventh character is required for this diagnosis code. The seventh character, A, specifies that the patient is under active treatment for this condition.

Since an S code is used, the following Activity and Place of Occurrence codes are required:

Y99.0 Civilian activity done for income or pay

Y92.61 Building (any) under construction as the place of occurrence

V57.3 Driver of pick-up truck or van injured in a collision with a fixed or stationary object in a non-traffic accident

Considering this is a Worker's Compensation injury and if you are billing for an evaluation and management service, such as an office visit, it may be advisable to include a Z code as justification for the E&M code separate billing:

Z04.2 Encounter for examination and observation following work accident

This identifies this injury as work related.

Please note: The modifier "-25" is used to indicate that another service beyond evaluation and management was provided.

As shown, it is important that providers get as much detail as possible when seeing a patient for injuries requiring the use of S codes.

Billing for Injections

Physicians often don't bill for services such as injections, because they don't know that the services are payable or do not know how to bill for them. Following are some of these services.

Trigger Point Injections CPT 20552 and 20553

These injections are used to treat pain. A review of many, many fee (charge) tickets in physician clinics show that these services often do not appear and are therefore not billed even though they are performed.

Documentation and diagnosis requirements appear in published Local Coverage Determinations (LCDs). For Southern California, these appear in LCD L28310. One of the listed ICD-9 codes is "720.1 Spinal enthesopathy." A review of the Crosswalk for this ICD-9 code shows that this code crosswalks to ICD-10 "M46.00 Spinal enthesopathy, site unspecified." However, there is a notation code # which specifies that you should look for "Note(s) for other information and possible problem areas."

The Note specifies that, when a specific site is known, you should use the code for that site which appears in the ICD-10 range M46.01–M46.09. As an example, if the site is the thoracic region, the ICD-10 code to use would be:

M46.04 Spinal enthesopathy, thoracic region

When the patient is a Workers' Compensation or Personal Injury patient and the pain is the result of an External Cause, then the use of an External Cause S code is required. An example is as follows:

S29.012A Strain of muscle, fascia and tendon of back wall of thorax

This is a seven-character code and the seventh character, A, indicates "Active treatment." For S codes, providers should also specify an Activity and a Place of Occurrence.

If there were one or two muscles, the CPT code is 20552. If there were three or more muscles, CPT 20553 is appropriate. Please note that medication is also billable. As an example, if Lidocaine were injected, you would also bill J2001 for up 10 mg. When multiples of 20 mg are used, you would increase the units billed, for example, 20 mg would be for two units.

Please note that if an evaluation and management service is also billed, a separate diagnosis code is required for the evaluation and management service and the evaluation and management code should have a "-25" modifier to denote that it is a separately billable service.

Trigger points are considered a minor surgical procedure and may entail a postoperative period.

Arthrocentesis

After administering a local anesthetic, the physician inserts a needle through the skin and into a joint or bursa. A fluid sample may be removed from the joint or a fluid may be injected for lavage or drug therapy. The needle is withdrawn and pressure is applied to stop any bleeding.

CPT	Description
20600	Arthrocentesis, aspiration, and/or injection; small joint or bursa (e.g., fingers, toes)
20605	Arthrocentesis, aspiration, and/or injection; intermediate joint or bursa (e.g., wrist, elbow or ankle, olecranon bursa)
20610	Arthrocentesis, aspiration, and/or injection; major joint or bursa (e.g., shoulder, knee, hip joint, subacromial bursa)

Again, this can be considered a minor surgical procedure with a post-operative period. An evaluation and management service billed on the same date requires a separate diagnosis(es) with a "-25" modifier. The medication is also separately billable using the appropriate HCPCS code(s).

There is no specific LCD on arthrocentesis. In this example, there was a claim that included both arthrocentesis and a therapeutic injection. The arthrocentesis was billed with an ICD-9 diagnosis code of "719.46 Pain in unspecified knee." This ICD-9 code crosswalks to ICD-10 code M25.569 which appears in our Crosswalk.

In the case of Worker's Compensation or Personal Injury patients, the appropriate External Cause S code should be used when treatment is for an externally caused injury. As an example: S40.011A Contusion of right shoulder

This is a seven-character code and the letter A indicates "active treatment." Again, the circumstances and place of occurrence should be documented.

Therapeutic, prophylactic, or diagnostic injection (specify substance or drug); subcutaneous or intramuscular

Providers are often reluctant to provide injectable medications because the Medicare allowance is very low. An example is "J1100 Injection, dexamethasone sodium phosphate, 1 mg" has a 2014 Medicare allowance of $0.58 and a payment after co-insurance of only $0.46.

In order to compensate providers, *Medicare will also cover the administration of the injection.*

CPT 96372 has an allowance of $27.19 per injection. Two injections for the same patient, on the same date, would then result in a payment of $43.43 after the 20% co-insurance.

When billing for injectable medications, the provider must use the appropriate HCPCS code. Injectable drugs are identified by specific codes starting with the letter J. As an example, J0696 identifies "Injection, ceftriaxone sodium, per 250 mg." The brand name for this medication is Rocephin. In our example, the amount provided is 1000 mg, so J0696 is billed with four units to properly identify that amount provided.

Some injections are subject to diagnosis code requirements. These are specified in published Local Coverage Determinations (LCDs). Darbepoetin Alfa and Epoetin Alfa have diagnosis requirements. In Southern California, LCD "L33525 Erythropoietin stimulating agents" specifies necessity and diagnosis requirements.

Certain injectable drugs, for example, Humira, are considered to be "self-administered" and are not paid. These are listed in the Self-Administered Drug Exclusion List R1.

However, when these are administered by a physician in the office, the Administration, CPT 96372 can be paid.

Worker's Compensation and Personal Injury providers can also bill for "CPT 96372, Administration of injections" using the appropriate ICD-10 codes.

The CPT notation specifies that 96372 does not include injections for allergen immunotherapy. For allergen immunotherapy, please see CPTs 95115-95117.

Billing for X-Rays

This is a hypothetical case of a patient who presents with pain in three fingers. In ICD-9, the alphabetic index for "pain, finger" shows as "729.5 Pain in unspecified limb." Based on the patient's complaint, it is decided to do an x-ray.

ICD-9	CPT
729.5	Pain in unspecified limb 73140 X-ray, finger, minimum of 2 views

The x-ray reveals that there are three fractured fingers. The fractures do not break the skin. The fractures are to the right index, right middle, and right ring fingers. Based on the x-ray results, you would change your coding as follows:

ICD-9	**ICD-10**
817.03 Multiple fracture of hand bones closed.	73140F6 right hand, second digit 73140F7 right hand, third digit and 73140F8 right hand, fourth digit *Coding tip:* ***Bill for three x-rays 73140F6, F7 and F8***

ICD-10

M79.641 Pain, finger in right hand. An x-ray is done and there are fractures. The diagnosis codes then change as follows:

S62.600A Fracture of unspecified phalanx of right index finger
S62.602A Fracture of unspecified phalanx of middle finger
S62.604A Fracture of unspecified phalanx of right ring finger

The notation at the beginning of Chapter 19 (S00–T88) states that traumatic fractures are coded using the appropriate seventh-character extension for initial encounters (A, B, and C), which include an initial encounter and evaluation. Also, fractures not indicated as open or closed should be coded as closed.

In the foregoing example, we do not know the exact site of the fracture, for example, proximal, medial, or distal phalanx, so we use codes for unspecified phalanx.

It should also be noted that Chapter 19 also specifies that a code from category M80 is not a traumatic fracture code, should be used for any patient with known osteoporosis who suffers a fracture, even if the patient had a minor fall or trauma, if that fall or trauma would not usually break a normal, healthy bone.

In our case, the patient should also be asked how the fracture occurred. Codes from Chapter 19 Injury, Poisoning and Certain other Consequences of External Causes state that a secondary code(s) from Chapter 20, External Causes of Morbidity should be used to indicate the cause of injury.

In our hypothetical example, the patient stated that he fell while roller-skating on in-line skates. We would then add an additional ICD-10 code: "V00.111A Fall from in-line roller skates."

If instead the patient stated that he was working as a motorcycle driver and hit a parked car, we would then add "V29.00XA Motorcycle driver injured in collision with unspecified motor vehicle in non-traffic accident."

You would also add ICD-10 Code "Y99.0 Civilian activity done for income or pay."

It is very important to record details when S codes are used, because you could become involved in a Personal Injury or Worker's Compensation case without knowing it.

In many radiology studies, the radiologist does not communicate with the patient. In these cases, radiologists may choose a diagnosis of degeneration. Since these codes (for degeneration) are now separated into Chapter 13 codes, "Diseases of the musculoskeletal system and connective tissue (M00-M99)," they can be easily detected versus S (External Cause) codes. M codes also include those for osteoporosis (M80.-).

Billing for Minor Surgical Procedures

Minor surgical procedures can often be performed in an office. They are considered minor because they do not require an ambulatory surgical center or hospital facility. When they are performed in an office environment, they often have a postoperative period. Since they are "minor," the postoperative period is short; often 10 days. Evaluation and management services not related to the surgery should be billed with a "-24" modifier and a diagnosis code unrelated to the surgical procedure. The following is an actual example of a minor surgical procedure performed in an office.

A patient presented with a cystic mass on a lower anterior abdominal wall. He wanted the mass removed. The provider performed a biopsy and then placed sutures to repair the biopsy site.

The following procedures were performed:

CPT	Description
9921325	Office visit level 3
J0696	Injection, ceftriaxone sodium 250 mg (Rocephin)
96372	Therapeutic, prophylactic, or diagnostic injection
10060	Incision and drainage of abscess or subcutaneous abscess, cyst, furuncle, or paronychia
12031	Repair, intermediate, wounds of scalp, axillae, trunk, and/or extremities

The following ICD-9 diagnosis codes were billed:

789.00	Abdominal pain unspecified
586	Renal failure, unspecified
250.00	Diabetes, without mention of complication
682.2	Other cellulitis and abscess of trunk

For ICD-10 the diagnosis codes would be changed as follows:

R10.30	Lower abdominal pain, unspecified
N19	Unspecified renal failure
E11.21	Type 2 diabetes with other diabetic kidney complication
L03.321	Acute lymphangitis of abdominal wall

All diabetes mellitus codes are now Combination Codes. "E11.21—Type2 diabetes with other kidney complication" was chosen because there is a diagnosis of renal failure. Since there was no documentation of Type 1 or Type 2, Type 2 is the default type for unspecified type of diabetes.

R10.30 was chosen for abdominal pain because it was documented that the pain was in the lower anterior wall. The quadrant was not specified, nor was there any documentation of periumbilical pain.

CPT 12031 is for "intermediate repair." Intermediate repair is used if layered closure of one or more of the deeper layers of subcutaneous tissue and superficial (non-muscle) fascia, in addition to the skin closure (sutures), is done. Since sutures were placed, CPT 12031 was billed. It should be noted that if more than 2.5 cm was repaired, then higher level codes, for example, 12032, 12034, and so on would be appropriate.

An office visit, 99213, was billed because the patient had a diagnosis of diabetes and renal failure, which were evaluated separate from the minor surgical procedure.

Worker's Compensation and Personal Injury Patients

If a patient presents with an abscess that was externally caused, the diagnostic coding should be modified to reflect the circumstances. As an example, suppose a patient has an abscess due to an infection resulting from a laceration, a possible diagnosis could be:

S31.120A Laceration of abdominal wall with foreign body, right upper quadrant, without penetration into peritoneal cavity
L02.211 Cutaneous abscess of abdominal wall

If a specimen is taken and sent to a laboratory to identify an infectious agent, and one is specified, this can be documented using ICD-10 codes for "Bacterial and viral infectious agents (B95–B97)." You might also wish to bill CPT 99000 - specimen handling.

Commonly Used Diagnosis Codes

Diagnosis codes commonly used in Worker's Compensation and Personal Injury are listed in the enclosed Crosswalk. The Crosswalk is in ICD-9 sequence and shows the ICD-10 code(s) that are the counterpart to ICD-9. Adjacent to the ICD-10 codes are notations about possible problem areas. Many of the ICD-10 codes have no ICD-9 counterparts. In many cases, there are many ICD-10 codes for a single ICD-9 code and vice versa. There are certain ICD-9 to ICD-10 crosswalks that require providers to closely review the codes, so that the correct ICD-10 code is used.

Certain conditions such as diabetes and abdominal pain require extra scrutiny. Diabetes mellitus was discussed previously in Chapter 4. Here, we will look at abdominal pain, carpal tunnel syndrome, and psychosocial issues a little closer.

Abdominal Pain: ICD-10 Category R10

Abdominal pain is a diagnosis that is frequently used, but can result in problems unless providers properly document it. In ICD-10, there is a distinction between abdominal pain and abdominal tenderness. You can still specify "unspecified," but there are choices for quadrant. For example, left upper and periumbilic versus epigastric versus generalized pain.

Again, there are still valid ICD-10 unspecified codes. For example:

R10.819 Abdominal tenderness, unspecified
R10.30 Lower abdominal pain, unspecified

Your practice should review and determine documentation requirements.

Carpal Tunnel Syndrome in Worker's Compensation and Personal Injury

A very common injury in Worker's Compensation and Personal Injury is carpal tunnel syndrome. Using ICD-9, one could find a single code under this title (354.0). In the beginning of the Billing Guide, we specified that using a GEM tool, you could be directed to ICD-10 code "G56.0 Carpal tunnel syndrome." For Worker's Compensation and Personal Injury, this could be considered inappropriate, since there was an External Cause.

Carpal tunnel syndrome can be defined as symptoms caused by compression of the median nerve. One possible ICD-10 code is "S64.1 Injury of the median nerve at the wrist."

Carpal tunnel syndrome is often accompanied by other injuries. Some possible associated diagnoses codes are

S63.511 Sprain of carpal joint of the right wrist
S63.512 Sprain of carpal joint of the left wrist
S64.00X Injury of the ulnar nerve at the wrist and hand level
S66.10X Injury of flexor tendons
S54.11X Injury of median nerve at forearm level, right arm
S44.11X Injury of median nerve at upper arm level, right arm

The provider must be aware that documentation should be as specific as possible in order to determine the correct diagnoses codes. It could be the case that there are multiple codes that are appropriate for carpal tunnel syndrome.

Carpal tunnel syndrome is not the only procedure that can have multiple possible diagnoses codes. When coding a procedure for the first time, it is important to investigate potential options.

Psychological Discussion

ICD-10 codes for psychological conditions are not S codes, because they don't have the physical manifestations of injuries such as fractures. These codes are in Chapter 5, "F01–F99 Mental and Behavioral Disorders." Category "F43 Reaction to severe stress, and adjustment disorders" can be a logical starting point to determine appropriate Worker's Compensation diagnoses codes.

Persons with Potential Health Hazards Related Socioeconomic and Psychosocial Circumstances: Z55-Z65

Z codes represent reasons for encounters. A corresponding procedure code, for example, office visit, must accompany a Z code.

Here are some examples of Z codes that represent reasons for encounters that might apply to Worker's Compensation:

Z56 Problems related to employment and unemployment
Z56.2 Threat of job loss

Z56.3 Stressful work schedule
Z56.4 Discord with boss and workmates
Z56.5 Uncongenial work environment
(See Z56 for a complete list)
Z57 Occupational exposure to risk factors
Z57.0 Occupational exposure to noise
Z57.7 Occupational exposure to vibration
(See Z57 for a complete list)

Encounter for Examination and Observation for other Reasons: Z04-

As previously stated, whenever you use a Z code that represents a reason for an encounter, you must include a corresponding procedure code (CPT code). Some examples of Z encounter codes are

Z04.6 Encounter for general psychiatric examination, requested by authority
Z04.2 Encounter for examination and observation following work accident
Z04.1 Encounter for examination and observation following transport accident
Z04.3 Encounter for examination and observation following other accident

Please note: You can have multiple Z codes for an encounter

Example: A person is working at a convenience store as a cashier and is robbed at gunpoint. His major complaint is anxiety.

Diagnosis: F43.0 Acute stress reaction and

Z65.4 Victim of crime and terrorism

The CPT code should be a psychiatric evaluation and management code, for example, "90791 Psychiatric evaluation."

Some of the relevant subcategories in Chapter 5, Mental and Behavior Disorders

There are many possible Psychosocial Diagnosis codes in ICD-10 that may be relevant in Worker's Compensation and Personal Injury. Some sections that may apply are

"Mental Disorders due to Known Psychological Conditions (F01–F09)"

"Anxiety, Dissociative, Stress-Related, Somatoform and Other Nonpsychotic Mental Disorders (F40–F48)"

"Behavioral Syndromes Associated with Physiological Disturbances and Physical Factors (F50–F59)," which include eating and sleep disorders

Also associated with significant psychosocial dysfunction is chronic pain.

"ICD-10–G89.4 Chronic pain syndrome" is used when pain is *associated with significant psychosocial dysfunction*. The category notation for G89 states that a code from this category should not be used if the underlying (definitive) diagnosis is known, unless the reason for the encounter is pain control/management and not management of the underlying condition.

Chapter 9

Chapter Nine

Cumulative Trauma

This is an important topic in Worker's Compensation. However, it is not clearly addressed by ICD-10. Rather, this must be coded using codes for "Injury, Poisoning and Certain Other Consequences of External Causes," as well as related codes.

Chapter 6 of the ICD-10-CM book lists "Diseases of the Nervous System" and includes codes G00–G99.

The notes at the very beginning of Chapter 6 of the ICD-10-CM book state "Excludes 2: Injury, poisoning and certain other consequences of external causes (S00–T88)."

Now, remember that "Excludes 2" means "not included here." In other words, the notes are saying that Chapter 6 G00–G99 does not include any diagnoses that were a result of an injury. This seems to make things very confusing, because conditions like carpal tunnel syndrome are part of Chapter 6.

In the United States, there has been a long-standing use of a carpal tunnel syndrome (CTS) diagnosis in the Worker's Compensation Industry. However, in order to have a Worker's Compensation claim, there must first be an injury. Yet, Chapter 6 just defined CTS as a Non-Injury condition.

CTS is defined as a painful condition of the hand and fingers caused by compression of a major nerve where it passes over the carpal bones through a passage at the front of the wrist, alongside the flexor tendons of the hand. It may be caused by repetitive movements over a long period, or by fluid retention, and is characterized by sensations of tingling, numbness, or burning.

This definition does seem to imply the possibility of CTS being caused by an injury, that is, an injury due to repetitive motion over a long period of time (cumulative trauma).

But, again, the ICD-10-CM appears to define it as a non-injury condition. Therefore, it is possible that Insurance carriers may deny Worker's Compensation claims that use the diagnosis code "G56.0 Carpal tunnel syndrome" because the coding implies that no injury took place.

It should be noted that "G56 Mononeuropathies of the upper limb" has an "Excludes 1: Current traumatic nerve disorder—see nerve injury by body region." This, again, implies that this is a Non-Injury code. But, even more importantly, it is stating that you cannot code both a G56 code and an S injury code of the median nerve at the same time. You must choose one or the other.

Therefore, a more appropriate code for Worker's Compensation cases may be "S64.1 Injury of median nerve at wrist and hand level."

Chapter 13 Diseases of the Musculoskeletal System and Connective Tissue (M00–M99) also has in its notes, "Excludes 2: Injury, poisoning and certain other consequences of external causes (S00–T88)." Therefore, all codes within Chapter 13 also imply Non-Injury.

To add to the confusion, in the discussion section of the Activity code (Y93) section of the ICD-10-CM book, it states that these Activity codes are appropriate for use for both acute injuries, such as those from Chapter 19, and *conditions that are due to the long-term, cumulative **effects** of an activity, such as those from Chapter 13.*

This seems to imply that Chapter 13 contains cumulative trauma, but they use the term "effects," and not "trauma." So, maybe they are referring more to normal wear and tear of living, for example, the effects of aging, and not something that would be considered trauma, or an injury

At the beginning the beginning of Chapter 13 (M00–M99), under ICD-10-CM Official Guidelines is the statement:

> ***b. Acute traumatic versus chronic or recurrent musculoskeletal conditions***
>
> *Many musculoskeletal conditions are a result of previous injury or trauma to a site, or are recurrent conditions. Bone, joint or muscle conditions that are the result of a healed injury are usually found in chapter 13. Recurrent bone, joint or muscle **conditions** are also usually found in chapter 13. **Any current, acute injury should be coded to the appropriate injury code from chapter 19**. Chronic or recurrent **conditions** should generally be coded with a code from chapter 13. If it is difficult to determine from the documentation in the record which code is best to describe a condition, query the provider.* (bolding is ours)

"Cumulative Trauma" in Worker's Compensation involves an "acute" and current condition that has evolved over a period of time.

Taking all of this into consideration, you should use the Chapter 19 (S00–T88) codes for all injury coding, including cumulative trauma conditions.

Another example of Cumulative Trauma:

A patient has developed black lung disease as a result of working in coal mines.

T57.8X1S Toxic effect of other specified inorganic substances, accidental (unintentional) Toxic effect of other specified inorganic substance NOS (here we might specify coal dust)

J60 Coal worker's pneumoconiosis

Please note that when codes from categories "T36–T65 Poisoning by adverse effects of and underdosing of drugs, medicaments and biological substances" are used, the T code(s) is sequenced first followed by the code(s) that specify the adverse effect. This sequencing instruction does not apply to underdosing codes (fifth or sixth character 6.)

It should be noted that codes from Sections T36 through T65 are further sub-categorized by "intent" such as

T57.8X2 intentional self-harm
T57.8X3 assault
T57.8X4 undetermined

The subcategories may be important in legal claims. If an employer knowingly allowed employees to be exposed to toxic substances, the T57.8X3 code could be used.

Compensable Consequences versus Cumulative Trauma

Please note, Compensable Consequences can be present in both Worker's Compensation and Personal Injury, where as Cumulative Trauma is a Worker's Compensation term.

Some providers may have trouble distinguishing between Compensable Consequences and Cumulative Trauma.

Compensable Consequences are not defined in the labor code, requiring the need for case law to establish a working definition. However, one definition is that a Compensable Consequence is not a new injury with a new date of injury, but the consequence of an industrial injury or the treatment for that injury.

Also, in a recent Noteworthy Panel Decision, *Bates versus Serologicals Corp*, CWC Lexis 194, Compensable Consequences doctrine was defined: "[W]here a subsequent injury is the direct and natural consequence of an original industrial injury, the subsequent injury is considered to relate back to the original injury and it generally is not treated as a new and independent injury."

Compensable Consequences can be health conditions that are either injuries, or non-injuries as categorized by ICD-10. One example of a health condition that has a non-injury code is diabetes. This can be a Compensable Consequence due to the original injury leading to patient inactivity and depression, thus resulting in poor eating habits and excessive weight gain, and eventually diabetes.

Please note: In the legal definition of Compensable Consequence, a Compensable Consequence is always considered to be an injury, even if it is a non-injury health condition, such as diabetes.

If the Compensable Consequence is an injury, then injury coding (S-T) should be used. However, there are exceptions when the Compensable Consequence is not an injury. Thus, compensable consequence codes in ICD-10 may be codes from Non-Injury sections of ICD-10 (e.g., not from Chapter 19). Therefore, it is important to document that they arose as a result of an injury.

However, in either case you should code in ICD-10 using sequela codes. By this we mean using the seventh-character code, S, to signify that the condition is a sequela of another condition (or, in other words, a Compensable Consequence).

For example:

A patient developed arthritis due to a metacarpal fracture of the right hand

M18.31 Unilateral post-traumatic osteoarthritis of first metacarpal joint, right hand

S62.201S Unspecified fracture of first metacarpal bone, right hand

Here, we are stating that the patient developed osteoarthritis due to the fracture. It should be noted that coding should be precise due to legal issues that may arise.

For example, it would be an error to use "M18.11 Unilateral primary osteoarthritis of first metacarpal joint, right hand," as it does not indicate that it is post-traumatic. The term post-traumatic in M18.31 is indicative of an external (work related) injury.

An example of a Compensable Consequence that uses an injury code could be as follows:

> A patient has a Worker's Compensation injury that involved a lumbar disc with nerve compression and a foot drop. Then, if the patient trips due to the foot drop and injures his wrist, you use an injury code (Chapter 19, S and T codes) for the new Compensable Consequence, for example, "S60.211A Contusion of right wrist." You would also need to follow this with the original injury code using a seventh character S to indicate that the wrist injury is a Compensable Consequence of the original injury.

Please note: If you have a Compensable Consequence as a result of a Worker's Compensation surgery, you'll find those injury codes in the T section.

At this time, we do not know how codes will be edited or interpreted by the courts. The important point is that the provider understands the codes and how they were utilized.

Chapter 10

Chapter Ten

Causation and Apportionment in Worker's Compensation and Personal Injury

In our introduction to Worker's Compensation and Personal Injury, we cautioned users about the dangers of using General Equivalency Mapping tools.

Causation

By including the external cause of morbidity codes in ICD-10 (where they were voluntary in ICD-9), the provider is given greater ability to express causation when coding.

In ICD-10, the W, V, Y, and Z codes of the Six-Category System should be used to give causation of the diagnosis. The Independent Medical Evaluator will need to determine the causation of the initial injury and the causation of any compensable consequences that are noted in the medical records for their specialty.

Apportionment

Apportionment in Worker's Compensation and Personal Injury is a way of determining out how much of your patients' permanent disability is due to their work injury and how much is due to other disabilities.

This is one of the advantages of ICD-10 coding. It gives you the flexibility to code your apportionment with injury coding and non-injury coding. You can indicate by your use of the Six-Category System that it is a Worker's Compensation or Personal Injury case. (There are no specific rules for apportionment in ICD-10, but this is an obvious topic that needs to be addressed with injury cases.)

For example, we could have an injured worker with lumbar sprain or strain and cervical disc myelopathy. Assuming all of these injuries are work related (externally caused), we can indicate this with the following diagnosis.

ICD-10
S13.0XXD Traumatic rupture of cervical intervertebral disc
S33.5XXD Sprain of ligaments of lumbar spine, subsequent encounter
S39.012D Strain of muscle, fascia, tendon of lower back

You also would include your other categories of coding form the Six-Category System to indicate a Worker's Compensation or Personal Injury.

Encounter Coding, one diagnosis not work related

In the event that a medical-legal evaluator concluded that the cervical disc pathology was not work related, the following option is available:

M50.0 Cervical disc disorder with myelopathy
S33.5XXD Sprain of ligaments of lumbar spine, subsequent encounter
S39.012D Strain of muscle, fascia, tendon of lower back

The M code is a five-character code that does not require a seventh character. The evaluator thus specifies the presence of cervical disc pathology, but not as work related.

Conversely, if an evaluator felt that only a portion of the cervical disc pathology was work related, and a portion was not work related, he or she has to determine how to code. Two possible options are as follows:

Please note: The ICD-10-CM states that you must "code to the most superior level of disorder."

Encounter Coding, one diagnosis partially work related

Option 1:
Still use the S code (S13.0XXD), but also include in the report that a certain percentage of that diagnosis is work related.
Option 2:
The doctor could put the S code and also use an M code. The M code indicates that the diagnosis is not due to external causes or injury. By including both codes, the doctor is stating that the injury is apportioned to two separate causes and would then have to put in the report the percentage that is apportioned to the work injury.

M50.0 Cervical disc disorder with myelopathy
S13.0XXD Traumatic rupture of cervical intervertebral disc

Encounter Coding, Not work related

In the event that an evaluator did not agree that injuries are work related, the alternative is to use non-injury codes as follows:

M54.5 Low back pain (lumbago) (Excludes 1 Low back strain)
M50.0 Cervical disc disorder with myelopathy

If the evaluator did not agree that an injury was work related, he or she should just bill the Health Condition codes. For example, you would not include Y99.0 code for civilian activity for income or pay.

Since S codes and non-external cause codes are separate, examiners can now express their opinion in the coding of their claims. Since this tool is now available, it is important that providers know about these and their potential uses.

Chapter 11

Chapter Eleven

Dilemma of the Independent Medical Evaluator (The Law of Unintended Consequences)

In this chapter, we will be referring to Independent Medical Evaluator (IME). Different terminology is used throughout the country. When using IME, we will be including all the different associated terms, Agreed Medical Evaluator, Qualified Medical Evaluator, and so on.

Obviously, one of the requirements for medical providers is that all claims must contain correct diagnostic codes. The issue that arises for Worker's Compensation and Personal Injury is that the coding is more complex and at risk of increased chance of error. This requirement will be a challenge for many providers, but for the IME, this could pose greater challenges. The IME cannot assume that the codes used by previous providers are correct, and the IME must ensure that the coding they use is accurate, as many aspects of the case depend on and are affected by the coding. Due to ICD-10 requiring extensive diagnostic decisions and highly specific code requirements, even the knowledgeable biller or coder will have difficulty determining the proper code to use. This puts the onus on the IME (and all providers). The challenges facing IMEs could be daunting unless the IME is knowledgeable about ICD-10.

If the IME bills sciatica and lumbago as two separate codes, rather than using the single combination code, *the claim may be rejected, either by the adjuster or via computer edits*. In other words, the claim may be denied not because the work up is wrong, but because it is a computerized edit that could deny the claim because the coding is wrong.

Errors in coding can have many consequences. For example, denied reimbursement, improper settlement determination, improper treatment, and so on.

Certain diagnoses that involve symptomatology do not have S or T codes, for example, sciatica and carpal tunnel syndrome. Thus, in Worker's Compensation, you may need to diagnose the actual cause of the symptoms, for example, "S34.21 Injury of nerve root of lumbar spine."

Another common problem is that providers often use "degenerative" diagnoses. In some cases, this could refer to codes that do not imply external cause or injury. For example, M codes. If an M code does not have a traumatic cause description, then it is advised that an S or T code be included to imply external cause or injury. Although M codes do not implicitly refer to injury causes, there are some exceptions where M codes state traumatic causes. These codes should be used when available. And, even in the case where the M code states traumatic cause, it is still advised that the S or T code that resulted in the degenerative sequela be included to tie it in to the Worker's Compensation or Personal Injury, for example, "M19.111 Post traumatic osteoarthritis, right shoulder," followed by "S43.004S Unspecified dislocation of right shoulder joint." It is important to be as detailed as possible.

For Worker's Compensation and Personal Injury cases, the provider must know that any use of External Cause codes (e.g., S and T codes) requires the use of Place of Occurrence and Activity codes (V, X, W, and Y codes). Z codes are used to indicate the reason for the encounter. For example:

1. *Worker's Compensation:* Y99.0 and Z04.2 to indicate administratively that this is a Worker's Compensation injury, plus any other V, X, W, or Y codes that apply to indicate how the injury occurred (e.g., slip and fall or lifting injury).
2. *Personal Injury:* Z04.1 or Z04.3 to indicate administratively that this is a Personal Injury, plus any other V, X, W, or Y codes that apply to indicate how the injury occurred (e.g., slip and fall or car accident).

Activity codes and Place of Occurrence codes help define the Worker's Compensation and Personal Injury status. These may be altered by future case rulings.

Overview for Independent Medical Evaluators

ICD-10 is designed to clarify, not complicate, services. However, the IME is ultimately responsible for ensuring the correct coding for the patient's case, and thus must be very knowledgeable of ICD-10 coding. The dilemma that IMEs face is that they cannot rely on other doctors coding the case correctly, which therefore could lead to unintended consequences for the patient.

The IME also has to stay up to date with any case rulings, and so on, which occur in regard to ICD-10, to ensure accurate coding. Also, the ICD-10 CM is a **draft**. We expect continually evolving ICD-10 protocols, especially in the Worker's Compensation and Personal Injury arena.

Some of the important things that an IME should know about ICD-10 are

- **IME has to know about combination codes, and S through Z codes.**
- **IME has to know that not all ICD-9 codes have a counterpart in ICD-10.**
- **IME has to know that the seventh character of ICD-10 is critical.**

Your claim can be denied if your coding is not correct.

It would be hard for an IME (or any physician) to state and defend a position when their own claims are denied due to invalid diagnosis codes, either by the adjuster **OR via computer edits**. *The implication may be not that your coding is incorrect, but that your diagnosis is incorrect.*

Chapter 12

Chapter Twelve

Multi-Specialty Discussions

In all the following cases, we would use the Six-Category Process, but, in the following discussions, we will only be interested in the Health Condition (Category 2 of the Six-Category Process).

Whiplash Injury Case

How a Provider Might Use ICD-10

Injuries to neck S10-S19

Pitfalls

- Be sure to use injury coding.
- Remember that sprains and strains are separated in ICD-10. So, you must use two codes, one for the ligamentous involvement, for example, "S13.4 Sprain of ligaments of cervical spine," and one for the musculotendinous involvement, for example, "S16.1 Strain of muscle, fascia and tendon at neck level."
- You can be led down the wrong path with GEM tools—see our following discussion for specifics.

Example

The patient in this case was a seat-belted driver involved in a motor vehicle accident in which the vehicle was rear-ended. The patient sustained injuries to the neck. The provider wrote a detailed history and performed a detailed physical examination of the musculoskeletal system.

The provider listed the following diagnoses:

1. Semi-chronic, symptomatic, post-traumatic injury of the cervical spine with musclotendino-ligamentous involvement, right and left posterior joint damage and suggestions of a slight intervertebral disc deformity, of unspecified level.

The provider made recommendations for medication, physical and chiropractic therapy, and also recommended an MRI study, which could result in recommendations for myofascial and trigger point injections and epidural blocks. Surgery could be considered if the patient does not get significant relief after all nonsurgical methods.

Based on the above, the following diagnoses codes may be considered for medical record and claim purposes:

S13.4XXA Sprain of ligaments of cervical spine
The code includes "Whiplash injury of the cervical spine"

Please note: The major code "S13 Dislocation and sprain of joints and ligaments at neck level" includes sprains, subluxation, and dislocation at the neck level.

S16.1XXA Strain of muscle, fascia and tendon at neck level

It should be noted that the provider recommended an MRI study. The results of the study could confirm or alter the diagnosis presented, thus categorize your diagnoses as "tentative awaiting MRI results."

If your MRI study comes back positive for traumatic rupture of the intervertebral cervical disc, then you would use:

S13.0XXA Traumatic rupture of the cervical intervertebral disc

When you look for Intervertebral Disc Injury in ICD-9, you will be led to Injury in the Alphabetic Index of Diseases, and then the subcategory of Intervertebral Disc. This points you to 959.19.

959.19 Other injury of other sites of trunk

Using a GEM tool on the Internet led us to S39.82XA: "S39.82 Other specified injuries of lower back." The GEM tool decided to add in the placeholder X and the seventh character of A to indicate active care.

So, we started with a cervical intervertebral disc injury of unspecified status, and we ended up with an "Other specified" injury of the lower back in active care status—not exactly what we were looking for.

The other ICD-9 code often used for Intervertebral Disc Injury would be "722.0 Displacement of cervical intervertebral disc without myelopathy." When we use a GEM tool to convert to an ICD-10 code, we are given "M50.20 other cervical disc displacement, unspecified." This is not an injury code and could lead to serious repercussions if used in a Worker's Compensation and Personal Injury case. Also, ICD-10 requires greater specificity, for example, "M50.21 other cervical disc displacement, high cervical region."

In addition to that, according to the ICD-10-CM book, M50–M54 has the following "Excludes 1," "Current injury—see injury of spine by body region."

Using the Alphabetic Index of Disease to find our code, we would find that we need to go to Rupture, then subcategory Traumatic, then Cervical.

In ICD-10, this process leads you to "S13.0 Traumatic rupture of cervical intervertebral disc." This is the correct code.

If we try the same process in the ICD-9-CM book, we end up being led to 722.0, which when entered into a GEM tool on the Internet, leads us to the incorrect code.

This is just more evidence that when using General Equivalence Mapping (GEM) tools, or your Electronic Medical Record (EMR), you must confirm that the code they are suggesting is the correct code by reading the descriptor.

Billing

X-rays taken in-house are separately billable.

Activities of Daily Living (ADL) (CPT 97353) is separately billable when a patient is instructed in self-care and home management activities. This can be billed in 15 minute increments so time spent should be documented in the medical record.

The major Evaluation and Management code 99245 should be billed with a "-25" modifier if procedures such as x-rays and/or ADL are billed.

Please note: Often times, injuries can lead to arthritic conditions years post-injury. In ICD-10 there are specific codes for post-traumatic osteoarthritis. When arthritis develops as a result of a prior traumatic injury, these codes can be used. For example,

M17.31 Unilateral post-traumatic osteoarthritis of right knee

These codes should be listed in conjunction with the original external cause code.

Depression: The Leading Cause of Disability Worldwide

Scientific American reprinted an article on mental health, originally published in the UK on May 17, 2016. The *Scientific American* article states the "[t]he World Health Organization calls Depression the leading cause of disability worldwide." The article goes on to quote Glyn Lewis, who studies psychiatric disorders at University College London, that no new treatments which are widely used have been developed since the 1970s, despite the fact that "this is the major public-health problem in the Western world and middle-income countries."

There are some indications that the perception of the problem is changing. For many years, patients who received treatment for depression or other disorders through group health insurance plans had higher out-of-pocket expenses than for other types of illness. The Mental Health Parity and Addiction Equity Act of 2008 was passed in the fall of that year to require group health insurance plans to have benefits for mental health and substance abuse disorders that are equivalent to the coverage provided for other types of medical problems. Beginning in 2010, the law requires that patients who are seen for depression symptoms can't be charged a higher co-pay or deductible than they would have for treatments such as flu shots. Group health plans that cover medical and surgical treatments by out-of-network providers must also cover mental health and substance abuse treatments by out-of-network providers. If a plan imposes annual or lifetime dollar limits on medical and surgical benefits, those same limits must apply to mental and substance abuse benefits.

It is important to note that group health plans for employers who have 50 or fewer employees are not subject to the new regulations. Insurance plans bought on the private market are also exempt.

The new law does not require health insurance plans to cover mental or substance abuse problems. However, 49 states and Washington, DC, mandate some form of mental health coverage. These requirements indicate a better appreciation of the need for mental and substance abuse coverage.

How a Provider Might Use ICD-10

F Section of Chapter 5

CODES

Since this is a major health problem, it is surprising that Chapter 5 Mental and Behavioral Disorders does not have a more extensive narrative at the beginning of the chapter. In addition to being relatively brief, there is not much guidance in ICD-10 on work-related depression.

In ICD-9 there is a single code, 296.3, for "Major depressive disorder, recurrent episode." In ICD-10 there are subcategories of recurrent depressive disorders as follows:

F33.0 Major depressive disorder, recurrent, mild
F33.1 Major depressive disorder, recurrent, moderate
F33.2 Major depressive disorder, recurrent, severe without psychotic features
F33.3 Major depressive disorder, recurrent with psychotic symptoms
F33.40 Major depressive disorder, recurrent, in remission, unspecified
F33.41 Major depressive disorder, recurrent, in partial remission
F33.42 Major depressive disorder, recurrent, in full remission
F33.8 Other recurrent depressive disorders
F33.9 Major depressive disorder, recurrent, unspecified Major depression NOS

Similar subcategories also occur in ICD-10 for single-episode disorders.

It is important that providers make a distinction between the levels of depressive disorder as mild, moderate, or severe, as well as specifying recurrent versus in remission. These distinctions did not occur in ICD-9.

PITFALLS

What is the difference between mild, moderate, and severe depression?

An accurate distinction would require the judgment of someone trained in this subject. A review of literature on the subject can give us some insight.

In general:

People with mild depression can get by without medication and find that their symptoms subside over time without treatment.

People with moderate depression have a higher probability that daily work and social activities are affected. They may experience less ability to concentrate, and problem solving is impaired.

People with severe depression cannot perform daily activities beyond the most rudimentary.

From a medical billing standpoint, Worker's Compensation laws generally require a specific or defined work place incident or environment such as trauma due to a specific injury or environmental factors, such as black lung disease due to an uncontrolled work place environment—unless it is a compensable consequence of the injury.

Example

The first edition of our book on Worker's Compensation and Personal Injury gave an example of a person who was working at a convenience store as a cashier who was robbed at gunpoint. A possible diagnosis is

F43.0 Acute stress reaction

Another possible health condition that may arise in this type of trauma listed above is depression. We may want to indicate that this is a result of the work-related trauma. One way to code this situation is as follows:

F33.2 Major depressive disorder, recurrent severe without psychotic features
T79.8XXS Other complications of trauma

In this second example, we specify that the major depressive disorder is sequela due to trauma.

It is not known how carriers will edit individual claims. In the second example, the T code indicates an External Cause of injury. Individual carriers may opt to require External Cause codes for Worker's Compensation and Personal Injury claims. S and T codes generally require seventh-character codes.

There are many different External Cause codes that could cause depression and/or anxiety. In a work place, employees could be shocked by being exposed to lightning (T75-), drowning or nonfatal submersion (T75.1), electrocution

(T75.4), motion sickness (T75.3), or other specified effects of external causes (T75.8-)

Depression has been diagnosed as a secondary psychological disorder and complication of post-traumatic stress disorder (PTSD). The ICD-10 definition of PTSD is a condition that may develop after "a stressful event or situation … of an exceptionally threatening catastrophic nature, which is likely to cause pervasive distress in almost anyone" (World Health Organization, 1992: p. 147). In ICD-10 PTSD can be found in codes for F43.1. These are separate from acute stress reaction (F43.0) and adjustment disorders (F32.2-) codes. When PTSD is indicated, it should be listed as a sequela to the PTSD event.

The most common cause of work place depression and/or anxiety would probably be the result of a specific physical injury (indicated by S codes) that resulted in depression (compensable consequence) due to job loss, economic problems, and/or loss of physical capabilities.

It should be noted that Z (Status) codes should not be used with a diagnosis code from one of the body system chapters, if the diagnosis code includes the information provided by the Status code. For example, "Z94.1 Heart transplant status", should not be used with "T86.2 Complications of heart transplant."

ICD-10 and Pain Coding

Please note that "Injury, poisoning, and certain other consequences of external causes (S00 T88)" are an "Excludes 2" for codes "G00–G99 Diseases of the Nervous System" (which include pain codes).

Pain is a complex subject and may be difficult to properly describe with the ICD-10 codes. ICD-10 addresses many types of pain. Some of these are as follows

1. *Acute pain*
2. *Chronic pain*
3. *Central pain syndrome*
4. *Chronic pain syndrome*

In addition, there are certain types of pain that don't appear to fall within any easy category.

How a Provider Might Use ICD-10

When looking for codes for pain conditions, you would look under one of three categories in the Alphabetic Index to Diseases:

1. Look under "pain": the Alphabetic Index of Diseases lists pain by anatomical site and cause, such as "pain from medical devices"
2. Look under the anatomical site in the Alphabetic Index of Diseases
3. Look under "Syndrome," "Condition," "Disorder," or "Disease," in the Alphabetic Index of Diseases

Please note: Some ICD-10 codes have pain inherently included in the diagnosis. For example,

Acute pain of a specific anatomical site can generally be found in ICD-10 by reviewing codes for an anatomical site. For example, abdominal pain—if you look up "abdominal" in the Alphabetic Index of Disease you will find "Acute R10.0." Under the Tabular List Volume 1, you find that R10.0 is "Acute abdomen" (severe abdominal pain). Please note: R10 to R19 is the section for "Symptoms and signs involving the digestive system and abdomen" in ICD-10.

The quickest way to identify common pain types is to review the Alphabetic Index for Pain. Once you get to the listing of "pain," you can identify many types of pain by anatomical site or pain type. However, it is important to note that many types of pain do not appear here. An example is causalgia, which can be a severe burning pain caused by injury to a peripheral nerve (e.g., G56.4-).

The important point is to be aware of the different classes of pain and where you may generally find the appropriate code(s).

Ill-Defined Pain

When pain is ill-defined, many ICD-10 pain diagnosis codes can be found in Chapter 18, Symptoms, Signs and Abnormal Clinical and Laboratory Findings, not Elsewhere Classified (R00–R99). Codes in this section are generally site specific. A common ill-defined pain is "Other abdominal pain R10.8-."

In an attempt to provide greater specificity, providers must now specify and document abdominal quadrants and differentiate between abdominal tenderness versus rebound abdominal tenderness, as well as differentiating between periumbilic and epigastric pain. One of the reasons ICD-10 has implemented this greater specificity is to gather data on the location of pain occurrence and associated conditions. For example, pain in the upper right area of the abdomen may indicate inflammation of the gall bladder (cholecystitis).

Some of these codes do not specify pain in their description, but pain is implied in descriptions such as "R29.0 Tetany."

Since coders and staff members may not know the meaning of specific terminology, it is important that medical diagnosticians specify the presence of pain and its anatomical location.

Another class of ill-defined pain is known as complex regional pain syndrome (CRPA) G90.50-.

Pain G89-

Since pain is complex, sometimes it is important that the codes be used in conjunction with codes from other chapters to provide more detail. Category G89 codes must be specified as:

Acute
Chronic
Post-thoracatomy
Post-procedural

OR
Neoplasm related

As stated in the ICD-10-CM book (Figures 12.1 through 12.3), codes from category G89 should not be assigned if the underlying (definitive) diagnosis is known, unless the reason for the encounter is pain control/management and not management of the underlying condition.

Codes from category G89 may be used with site-specific codes if the G code provides more information. The sequencing of category G89 codes with site-specific pain codes is dependent on the circumstances of the encounter. If encounter is for pain control or pain management, assign the code from category G89 followed by the code identifying the specific site of pain.

If the encounter is for other reasons except pain control or management, and a related definitive diagnosis has not been established, assign the code for the specific site of pain first, followed by the appropriate code from category G89.

M79.601 Pain in right arm
G89.18 Other acute post-procedural pain

In the foregoing case, we assume that the patient had a surgical procedure involving the right arm. If postoperative pain is associated with a specific post-operative complication, assign the appropriate code from Chapter 19, for example:

T82.847 Pain from cardiac prosthetic devices, implants and grafts
G89.18 Other acute post-procedural pain

In the second example, the G code is used to identify acute or chronic pain. Please note the sequencing here. If an encounter is for pain control or pain

ICD-10-CM Official Guidelines (Chapter 6)

b. Pain - Category G89

1) General coding information

Codes in category G89, Pain, not elsewhere classified, may be used in conjunction with codes from other categories and chapters to provide more detail about acute or chronic pain and neoplasm-related pain, unless otherwise indicated below.

If the pain is not specified as acute or chronic, post thoracotomy, postprocedural, or neoplasm-related, do not assign codes from category G89.

A code from category G89 should not be assigned if the underlying (definitive) diagnosis is known, unless the reason for the encounter is pain control/ management and not management of the underlying condition.

When an admission or encounter is for a procedure aimed at treating the underlying condition (e.g., spinal fusion, kyphoplasty), a code for the underlying condition (e.g., vertebral fracture, spinal stenosis) should be assigned as the principal diagnosis. No code from category G89 should be assigned.

(a) Category G89 Codes as Principal or First-Listed Diagnosis

Category G89 codes are acceptable as principal diagnosis or the first-listed code:

- *When pain control or pain management is the reason for the admission/encounter (e.g., a patient with*

Figure 12.1

displaced intervertebral disc, nerve impingement and severe back pain presents for injection of steroid into the spinal canal). The underlying cause of the pain should be reported as an additional diagnosis, if known.

- *When a patient is admitted for the insertion of a neurostimulator for pain control, assign the appropriate pain code as the principal or first-listed diagnosis. When an admission or encounter is for a procedure aimed at treating the underlying condition and a neurostimulator is inserted for pain control during the same admission/encounter, a code for the underlying condition should be assigned as the principal diagnosis and the appropriate pain code should be assigned as a secondary diagnosis.*

(b) Use of Category G89 Codes in Conjunction with Site Specific Pain Codes

(i) Assigning Category G89 and Site-Specific Pain Codes

Codes from category G89 may be used in conjunction with codes that identify the site of pain (including codes from chapter 18) if the category G89 code provides additional information. For example, if the code describes the site of the pain, but does not fully describe whether the pain is acute or chronic, then both codes should be assigned.

(ii) Sequencing of Category G89 Codes with Site-Specific Pain Codes

The sequencing of category G89 codes with site-specific pain codes (including chapter 18 codes), is dependent on the circumstances of the encounter/admission as follows:

If the encounter is for pain control or pain management, assign the code from category G89 followed by the code identifying the specific site of pain (e.g., encounter for pain management for acute neck pain from trauma is assigned code G89.11, Acute pain due to trauma, followed by code M54.2, Cervicalgia, to identify the site of pain).

If the encounter is for any other reason except pain control or pain management, and a related definitive diagnosis has not been established (confirmed) by the provider, assign the code for the specific site of pain first, followed by the appropriate code from category G89....

*3) **Postoperative Pain***

The provider's documentation should be used to guide the coding of postoperative pain, as well as Section III. Reporting Additional Diagnoses and Section IV. Diagnostic Coding and Reporting in the Outpatient Setting.

The default for post-thoracotomy and other postoperative pain not specified as acute or chronic is the code for the acute form.

Routine or expected postoperative pain immediately after surgery should not be coded.

(a) Postoperative pain not associated with specific postoperative complication

Postoperative pain not associated with a specific postoperative complication is assigned to the appropriate postoperative pain code in category G89.

(b) Postoperative pain associated with specific postoperative complication

Postoperative pain associated with a specific postoperative complication (such as painful wire sutures) is assigned to the appropriate code(s) found in Chapter 19, Injury, poisoning, and certain other consequences of external causes. If appropriate, use additional code(s) from category G89 to identify acute or chronic pain (G89.18 or G89.28).

4th **G89 Pain, not elsewhere classified**

Code also related psychological factors associated with pain (F45.42)

Excludes1 *generalized pain NOS (R52)*
pain disorders exclusively related to psychological factors (F45.41)
pain NOS (R52)

Excludes2 *atypical face pain (G50.1)*
headache syndromes (G44.-)
localized pain, unspecified type – code to pain by site, such as:
abdomen pain (R10.-)
back pain (M54.9)
breast pain (N64.4)
chest pain (R07.1-R07.9)
ear pain (H92.0-)
eye pain (H57.1)
headache (R51)
joint pain (M25.5-)
limb pain (M79.6-)
lumbar region pain (M54.5)
painful urination (R30.9)
pelvic and perineal pain (R10.2)
shoulder pain (M25.51-)
spine pain (M54.-)
throat pain (R07.0)
tongue pain (K14.6)
tooth pain (K08.8)
renal colic (N23)
migraines (G43.-)
myalgia (M79.1)
pain from prosthetic devices, implants, and grafts (T82.84, T83.84, T84.84, T85.84)
phantom limb syndrome with pain (G54.6)
vulvar vestibulitis (N94.810)
vulvodynia (N94.81-)

G89.0 Central pain syndrome
Déjérine Roussy syndrome
Myelopathic pain syndrome
Thalamic pain syndrome (hyperesthetic)

5th **G89.1 Acute pain, not elsewhere classified**

G89.11 Acute pain due to trauma

G89.12 Acute post-thoracotomy pain
Post-thoracotomy pain NOS

G89.18 Other acute postprocedural pain
Postoperative pain NOS
Postprocedural pain NOS

ICD-10-CM Official Guidelines (Chapter 6)

*4) **Chronic pain***

Chronic pain is classified to subcategory G89.2. There is no time frame defining when pain becomes chronic pain. The provider's documentation should be used to guide use of these codes.

5th **G89.2 Chronic pain, not elsewhere classified**

Excludes1 *causalgia, lower limb (G57.7-)*
causalgia, upper limb (G56.4-)
central pain syndrome (G89.0)
chronic pain syndrome (G89.4)
complex regional pain syndrome II, lower limb (G57.7-)
complex regional pain syndrome II, upper limb (G56.4-)
neoplasm related chronic pain (G89.3)
reflex sympathetic dystrophy (G90.5-)

G89.21 Chronic pain due to trauma

G89.22 Chronic post-thoracotomy pain

G89.28 Other chronic postprocedural pain
Other chronic postoperative pain

G89.29 Other chronic pain

Figure 12.2

ICD-10-CM Official Guidelines (Chapter 6)

5) Neoplasm Related Pain

Code G89.3 is assigned to pain documented as being related, associated or due to cancer, primary or secondary malignancy, or tumor. This code is assigned regardless of whether the pain is acute or chronic. This code may be assigned as the principal or first-listed code when the stated reason for the admission/encounter is documented as pain control/pain management. The underlying neoplasm should be reported as an additional diagnosis.

When the reason for the admission/encounter is management of the neoplasm and the pain associated with the neoplasm is also documented, code G89.3 may be assigned as an additional diagnosis. It is not necessary to assign an additional code for the site of the pain.

G89.3 Neoplasm related pain (acute) (chronic)

Cancer associated pain
Pain due to malignancy (primary) (secondary)
Tumor associated pain

ICD-10-CM Official Guidelines (Chapter 6)

6) Chronic pain syndrome

Central pain syndrome (G89.0) and chronic pain syndrome (G89.4) are different than the term "chronic pain," and therefore codes should only be used when the provider has specifically documented this condition.

G89.4 Chronic pain syndrome

Chronic pain associated with significant psychosocial dysfunction

Figure 12.3

management, the G code is coded first. Otherwise, the site-specific code is listed first, followed by the G code.

The default for post-thoracotomy and other postoperative pain is the acute form. Routine or expected postoperative pain immediately after surgery should not be coded.

When an admission or encounter is for a procedure aimed at treating the underlying condition (e.g., spinal fusion), a code for the underlying condition (e.g., vertebral fracture) should be assigned as the principal code. Codes from G89- may be used with codes that identify the site if they provide additional information. Pain that is a normal result of a procedure should not be coded.

Central Pain Syndrome versus Chronic Pain Syndrome in ICD-10

There are different definitions for chronic pain syndromes versus central pain syndromes.

Central pain syndrome is a neurological condition caused by damage to or dysfunction of the central nervous system. This can be caused by stroke, Parkinson's disease, tumors, epilepsy, brain or spinal cord trauma, or multiple sclerosis.

Chronic pain syndrome is a different type of chronic pain (neuropathic pain) with biochemical changes that are triggered in the body. This type of pain affects all aspects of life, including the formation of psychological problems that require both medical treatment and counseling.

ICD-10 does not appear to make a clear distinction. Both types of pain appear in Chapter 6 Diseases of the Nervous System (G00–G99).

ICD-10 specifies that "Central pain syndrome (G89.0)" and "Chronic pain syndrome (G89.4)" are different than the term "chronic pain" and therefore should only be used when the provider has specifically documented this condition.

Remember, there are other different categories of pain such as:

G89.21 Chronic pain due to trauma
G89.22 Chronic post-thoracotomy pain
G89.28 Other chronic post-procedural pain
G89.3 Neoplasm related pain (acute) (chronic), for example, cancer, tumor or malignancy
G89.4 Chronic pain syndrome

Code "G89.3 Neoplasm related (active) (chronic)" is assigned to pain documented as being related, associated, or due to cancer, primary or secondary malignancy, or tumor. This code is used regardless of whether the pain is acute or chronic.

Pain Associated with Disease

Certain diseases have pain associated with them. When these occur, the specific disease type should be listed. If they provide additional information, then specific pain codes can be listed, for example:

K51- Ulcerative colitis
R10.11 Right upper quadrant pain (abdomen)

Please see the Appendix for a listing of types of pain by name and/or causation.

Fever is a reaction to an infection. Since the exact infection is probably not known until laboratory results are received, providers often use the code for "unspecified" (e.g., "R50.9 Fever, unspecified").

The use of the "unspecified" code may be appropriate, but carriers may reject claims with "unspecified" diagnosis codes. An alternative may be as follows:

B97.89 Other viral agents as the cause of diseases, classified elsewhere
R50.81 Fever presenting with conditions classified elsewhere—code first underlying condition

It should be noted that some non-injury ICD-10 diagnoses codes include pain in their coding. For example, "M50 Cervical disc disorder" has the notation "includes cervicothoracic disc disorders with cervicalgia."

Please note: Injury codes do not have a notation of "pain" included. This is because it is assumed that pain is present with an acute injury and no pain code is necessary. However, if the acute condition was being treated for the purpose of pain management, then a pain code, such as G89, should be used.

Proper coding is a skill set that requires knowledge by the provider to give proper documentation and the biller/coder to produce a proper medical claim. Proper coding can be significant if the provider is asked for an evaluation of Disability Status.

Pain Management Case

The patient was seen by a pain management specialist as a result of a referral by the primary treating physician for a work-related industrial injury.

The patient had also been referred to a psychiatrist for a "psychological assessment of psychiatric damage reportedly suffered."

The report specifies ACOEM/AMA guidelines that "the central nervous system may be altered by chronic pain." It also states that perpetuation of pain has emotional, behavioral, and psychological components.

The referring physician diagnosed the patient with "Traumatic rupture of lumbar intervertebral disc and lumbar sprain/strain" as the primary (underlying) diagnoses. The patient presented with low back pain which is aggravated with "forward flexion, extension and rotation." The pain varies in intensity from moderate to severe. The report further states that the presenting problem has had a deleterious effect on the patient's emotional and functional capacity.

The report lists Behavioral Observations including a Mental Status Examination, Psycho-Diagnostic Testing with scores and ratings, Past Medical and Psychiatric History, and a Whole Person Impairment Rating.

The Pain Management report addresses low back, pain syndrome, sleep, and psychological factors. This appears to be appropriate since it is inclusive with a psychological report.

The report also specifies a need for future medical care and a statement of Causation and Apportionment. It is specified that the psychiatric injury is NOT a separate work stress injury, but is a derivative psychiatric injury arising from the emotional effects of physical injuries.

How a Provider Might Use ICD-10

ICD-10-CM Official Guidelines (Chapter 6)

b. Pain - Category G89

1) General coding information

Codes in category G89, Pain, not elsewhere classified, may be used in conjunction with codes from other categories and chapters to provide more detail about acute or chronic pain and neoplasm-related pain, unless otherwise indicated below.

If the pain is not specified as acute or chronic, post thoracotomy, postprocedural, or neoplasm-related, do not assign codes from category G89.

A code from category G89 should not be assigned if the underlying (definitive) diagnosis is known, unless the reason for the encounter is pain control/ management and not management of the underlying condition.

When an admission or encounter is for a procedure aimed at treating the underlying condition (e.g., spinal fusion, kyphoplasty), a code for the underlying condition (e.g., vertebral fracture, spinal stenosis) should be assigned as the principal diagnosis. No code from category G89 should be assigned.

Figure 12.4

ICD-10-CM Official Guidelines (Chapter 6)

6) Chronic pain syndrome

Central pain syndrome (G89.0) and chronic pain syndrome (G89.4) are different than the term "chronic pain," and therefore codes should only be used when the provider has specifically documented this condition.

Figure 12.5

"G89.4 Chronic pain syndrome," which is for pain associated with significant psychosocial dysfunction, and "G89.21 Chronic pain due to trauma" are possible diagnosis codes here (Figures 12.4 and 12.5).

Although the underlying diagnostic condition is known, the patient is being seen for the purpose of pain management. Therefore, a category G89 code appears appropriate. However, since it is specified that the condition arose as a result of a work-related activity, G89.21 would appear to be appropriate, as well as G89.4, because the patient has chronic pain associated with significant psychosocial dysfunction.

Diagnosis Coding

Here are the appropriate ICD-10 codes:

Please note: We will give the proper sequencing of the codes at the end of this section.

S33.0 Traumatic rupture of lumbar intervertebral disc

S33.5 Sprain of ligaments of lumbar spine

S39.012 Strain of muscle, fascia and tendon of lower back

The provider specifically states that the pain, sleep disturbance, and psychological condition were sequela to the physical injury.

G89.21 Chronic pain due to trauma

G89.4 Chronic pain syndrome (Chronic pain associated with significant psychosocial dysfunction)

G47.01 Insomnia due to a medical condition.

This code has a notation to code the associated medical condition as well, for example, S33.0, S33.5, S39.012.

F45.42 Pain disorder with related psychological factors

PITFALLS

The category notation for G89 states that a code from this category should not be used if the underlying (definitive) diagnosis is known unless the reason for the encounter is pain control/management and not management of the underlying condition.

As previously stated, this case addresses the lower back, pain syndrome, sleep, and psychological factors.

The primary (underlying) diagnoses are Traumatic Rupture of Lumbar Intervertebral Disc and Lumbar Sprain and Lumbar Strain. The proper codes are:

S33.0XXS Traumatic rupture of lumbar intervertebral disc

Please note: We use an S in the seventh character to indicate that G and F codes are sequelae of this condition.

S33.5XXD Sprain of other parts of lumbar spine and pelvis
S39.012D Strain of muscle, fascia and tendon of lower back

Please note: We use the seventh-character code D to indicate that these conditions are no longer being actively treated.

As previously discussed, the appropriate pain diagnoses codes are:

G89.21 Chronic pain due to trauma
G89.4 Chronic pain syndrome (Chronic pain associated with significant psychosocial dysfunction)

In regard to coding the difficulty in sleeping, category G47.0 is for insomnia.

G47.01 Insomnia due to a medical condition
Code also associated medical condition

If the sleep disorder is due to medication, then the above would not be the appropriate code, because it is an "Excludes 2" for sleep disorder due to medication. The appropriate code would be found in the F10–F19 sections, "Mental and behavioral disorders due to psychoactive substance use."

There is the following possible code:

F45.42 Pain disorder with related psychological factors

This code should be accompanied by associated acute or chronic pain (G89.-) per ICD10 notation under F45.42.

Encounter Status

Please note: In addition to the Encounter Status codes (Z codes) we have discussed previously for Worker's Compensation and Personal Injury in our Six-Category System, this case brings attention to other possible additional Encounter Status codes. There is no limit on the number of Encounter (reason) codes. The physician should be aware of these possible codes. Some possible codes are as follows:

Z04.6 Encounter for general psychiatric examination, requested by authority. This would probably be used for an independent examination requested by a court or other legal authority.

Z56.6 Other physical and mental strain related to work

Z72.820 Sleep deprivation

It is up to the provider to choose which and how many encounter codes are appropriate.

Billing for Services

The report specifies that 12 separate tests including Beck Depression, Pain Appraisal Inventory, and so on were administered. However, it did not specify who administered the tests or how they were administered.

If the psychologist provider administered the tests, "CPT 96101 Psychological testing including assessment of emotionality, intellectual abilities", and so on would be appropriate. This CPT is billed per hour of face-to-face time. If each test took 1 hour, then 12 units would be billed.

If the tests were administered by a technician, then CPT 96102 should be used. If the tests were administered by a computer, then CPT 96103 would be appropriate.

If there is a mix of administrator types, then separate CPT codes could be used with the appropriate corresponding units. These should be specified in the report narrative.

The report narrative specifies a number of diagnostic conditions but the claim form does not show them all. Some of the diagnostic conditions described include the following:

1. Depression and anxiety
2. Sleep disturbance
3. Chronic pain

Based on the report narrative, the following may appear on a claim form:
CPT

99455 Work-related or medical disability examination by other than the treating physician that includes
Completion of medical history commensurate with the patient's condition
Performance of an examination commensurate with the patient's condition
Formulation of a diagnosis, assessment of capabilities and stability, and
Calculation of impairment
Development of future medical treatment plan, and
Completion of necessary documentation/certificates and report

Code 99455-25 may be replaced by other codes according to state statutes and industry regulations. As an example, California has specific codes for medical-legal evaluations.

The modifier "-25" is included to indicate that this Evaluation and Management service is being billed in addition to other services such as psychological testing.

96101 Psychological testing … if administered by the provider or 96102 or 96103 (as appropriate).

Proper sequencing of ICD-10 Diagnostic Codes:

G89.21 Chronic pain due to trauma
G89.4 Chronic pain syndrome (Chronic pain associated with significant psychosocial dysfunction)
F45.42 Pain disorder with related psychological factors
G47.01 Insomnia due to a medical condition
S33.0XXS Traumatic rupture of lumbar intervertebral disc
S33.5XXD Sprain of ligaments of lumbar spine
S39.012D Strain of muscle, fascia and tendon of lower back

Adverse Effects of Medication

The patient sustained an injury to her low back during the course of her employment when she experienced a sudden popping sensation in her low back as she was lifting and bringing down a 30 pound box from overhead. The box dropped to the ground when she felt the popping sensation, and as she bent over to lift the box from the ground, she experienced a pulling sensation in her low back. Patient complains of low back pain and bilateral posterior leg pain.

The MRI studies showed lumbar spine multilevel disc bulges. The narrative specifies:

1. Posterior disc protrusion at L1-L2, 2 mm.
2. Posterior disc protrusion at L2-L3, 4 mm.
3. Posterior disc protrusion at L3-L4, 3 mm.
4. Posterior disc protrusion at L4-L5, 4–5 mm, as well as lateral stenosis bilaterally.
5. Posterior disc protrusion at L5-S1, 4–5 mm disc protrusion. The findings are consistent with annular tear.

Codes

S33.0 Traumatic rupture of lumbar intervertebral disc
S34.21 Injury to nerve root of lumbar spine

Patient was initially treated with physical therapy and medications.

The medications resulted in gastritis and the patient was referred to an internist for treatment of the gastritis. There was no notation by the doctor as to whether there was bleeding present with the gastritis. If a front-office person was given the responsibility to determine the correct ICD-10 code, they would have the following choices:

K29.70 Gastritis, unspecified without bleeding
K29.71 Gastritis, unspecified with bleeding

Pitfalls

The front-office staff should never assume the status of greater specificity. (They should not assume whether the patient was bleeding or not.) They must go back to the doctor to find out this information. Therefore, it is important that the doctor includes such details in the notes for the front-office staff. In this case, there was no bleeding.

How a Provider Might Use ICD-10

The patient was taking the following medication: Ultram. ICD-10 specifies that the drug giving rise to the adverse effect should be identified by the use of codes from categories T36–T50 with fifth or sixth characters. ICD-10 also specifies to use as many codes as necessary to describe completely all drugs, and medicinal or biological substances.

Drug Named	Generic Name	Adverse Effect Code
Ultram	Tramadol	T40.4X5 These are shown in the Table of Drugs (Figure 12.6)

Table of Drugs and Chemicals

INDEX TO POISONING AND EXTERNAL CAUSES OF ADVERSE EFFECTS OF DRUGS AND OTHER CHEMICAL SUBSTANCES

ICD-10-CM Official Guidelines (Chapter 19):

e. Adverse Effects, Poisoning, Underdosing and Toxic Effects

Codes in categories T36-T65 are combination codes that include the substances related to adverse effects, poisonings, toxic effects and underdosing, as well as the external cause. No additional external cause code is required for poisonings, toxic effects, adverse effects and underdosing codes.

A code from categories T36-T65 is sequenced first, followed by the code(s) that specify the nature of the adverse effect, poisoning, or toxic effect. Note: This sequencing instruction does not apply to underdosing codes (fifth or sixth character "6", for example T36.0x6-).

1) *Do not code directly from the Table of Drugs and Chemicals. Always refer back to the Tabular List.*
2) *Use as many codes as necessary to describe completely all drugs, medicinal or biological substances.*
3) *If the same code would describe the causative agent for more than one adverse reaction, poisoning, toxic effect or underdosing, assign the code only once.*
4) *If two or more drugs, medicinal or biological substances are reported, code each individually unless a combination code is listed in the Table of Drugs and Chemicals.*
5) *The occurrence of drug toxicity is classified in ICD-10-CM as follows:*

   a) Adverse Effect

   Assign the appropriate code for adverse effect (for example, T36.0x5-) when the drug was correctly prescribed and properly administered. Use additional code(s) for all manifestations of adverse effects. Examples of manifestations are tachycardia, delirium, gastrointestinal hemorrhaging, vomiting, hypokalemia, hepatitis, renal failure, or respiratory failure.

Figure 12.6

Codes in categories T36–T65 are Combination Codes that include substances that were taken, as well as the intent. (Please note that the Internet search engines can be helpful in determining generic nomenclature.) The ICD-10 code for gastritis is K29. Since the type of gastritis is not specified, and there is no report of bleeding, the doctor used "K29.7 Gastritis, unspecified without bleeding."

The instructions for these codes T36–T65 specifies that a code from category T36–T65 is sequenced first, followed by the code(s) that specify the nature of the adverse effect. Therefore, we could code as follows:

T40.4X5 Poisoning by, adverse effect of, other synthetic narcotic
K29.70 Gastritis, unspecified without bleeding

The specific drugs are found in the Table of Drugs and Chemicals in Volume 2. These are listed alphabetically by generic name. Each drug/chemical is listed with six columns:

Poisoning, accidental (unintentional) sixth character = 1
Poisoning, intentional (self-harm) sixth character = 2
Poisoning, assault sixth character = 3
Poisoning, undetermined sixth character = 4
Adverse effect sixth character = 5
Underdosing sixth character = 6

The instructional notations for the Table of Drugs and Chemicals specify that "adverse effect" includes when a drug was correctly prescribed and administered. You would choose the code under the appropriate heading for each drug or chemical involved (Figure 12.7).

Final Coding

So, the final proper coding for Category 2 (Health Condition) is:

T40.4X5 Adverse effect of other synthetic narcotics
K29.70 Gastritis, unspecified without bleeding
S33.0XXS Traumatic rupture of lumbar intervertebral disc
S34.21XS Injury to nerve root of lumbar spine

Orthopedic Examination with Emphasis on Apportionment and How ICD-10 Helps

This case involves a patient who had an industrial accident resulting in a medial meniscus tear of the right knee. The patient had a past history of a lateral meniscus tear of the right knee in May of 2001. The current orthopedist gave a whole person impairment of 13% and apportioned 60% of the disability to the work-related injury. The remaining 40% was apportioned to activities outside of work

Drug, chemical	Poisoning, Accidental (unintentional)	Poisoning, Intentional self-harm	Poisoning, Assault	Poisoning, Undetermined	Adverse effect	Underdosing
Topical action drug NEC	T49.91	T49.92	T49.93	T49.94	T49.95	T49.96
ear, nose or throat	T49.6X1	T49.6X2	T49.6X3	T49.6X4	T49.6X5	T49.6X6
eye	T49.5X1	T49.5X2	T49.5X3	T49.5X4	T49.5X5	T49.5X6
skin	T49.91	T49.92	T49.93	T49.94	T49.95	T49.96
specified NEC	T49.8X1	T49.8X2	T49.8X3	T49.8X4	T49.8X5	T49.8X6
Toquizine	T44.3X1	T44.3X2	T44.3X3	T44.3X4	T44.3X5	T44.3X6
Toremifene	T38.6X1	T38.6X2	T38.6X3	T38.6X4	T38.6X5	T38.6X6
Tosylchloramide sodium	T49.8X1	T49.8X2	T49.8X3	T49.8X4	T49.8X5	T49.8X6
Toxaphene (dust) (spray)	T60.1X1	T60.1X2	T60.1X3	T60.1X4	–	–
Toxin, diphtheria (Schick Test)	T50.8X1	T50.8X2	T50.8X3	T50.8X4	T50.8X5	T50.8X6
Toxoid						
combined	T50.A21	T50.A22	T50.A23	T50.A24	T50.A25	T50.A26
diphtheria	T50.A91	T50.A92	T50.A93	T50.A94	T50.A95	T50.A96
tetanus	T50.A91	T50.A92	T50.A93	T50.A94	T50.A95	T50.A96
Trace element NEC	T45.8X1	T45.8X2	T45.8X3	T45.8X4	T45.8X5	T45.8X6
Tractor fuel NEC	T52.0X1	T52.0X2	T52.0X3	T52.0X4	–	–
Tragacanth	T50.991	T50.992	T50.993	T50.994	T50.995	T50.996
Tramadol	T40.4X1	T40.4X2	T40.4X3	T40.4X4	T40.4X5	T40.4X6
Tramazoline	T48.5X1	T48.5X2	T48.5X3	T48.5X4	T48.5X5	T48.5X6
Tranexamic acid	T45.621	T45.622	T45.623	T45.624	T45.625	T45.626
Tranilast	T45.0X1	T45.0X2	T45.0X3	T45.0X4	T45.0X5	T45.0X6

Figure 12.7

(the previous non-work-related meniscus injury in 2001). This was due to evidence of lateral meniscal derangement of the anterior horn of the right knee.

Coding

The following ICD-10 diagnoses are possible and are based solely on this provider's documentation. The ultimate choice of diagnosis is up to the provider, but these are presented as possible choices. Since the report did not state the type of tear involved, the provider has the following choices:

S83.211 Bucket-handle tear of medial meniscus, current injury, right knee
S83.221 Peripheral tear of medial meniscus, current injury, right knee
S83.231 Complex tear of medial meniscus, current injury, right knee
S83.241 Other tear of medial meniscus, current injury, right knee

Let's assume the provider determined it was a bucket-handle tear for purposes of demonstration. Then our code would be:

S83.211 Bucket-handle tear of medial meniscus, current injury, right knee

For the derangement of the lateral meniscus, we have:

M23.241 Derangement of anterior horn of lateral meniscus due to old tear or injury, right knee

The provider also stated that, at the time of his work, the patient was a candidate for right-knee surgery. This tells us that the S83- codes were current because there was no surgery performed as of the date of the report.

The provider stated that there was a 40% apportionment due to activities outside of work.

How a Provider Might Use ICD-10

By using the M code for the residual of the old injury, we are indicating that this is not a current injury. Our report can indicate that this old injury was not work-related and assign the apportionment of 40% to this diagnosis.

The report can also state that the current injury (S83.211) is work-related and assign an apportionment of 60 percent to that diagnosis.

Pitfalls:

It is important to use S and T codes for current injuries and use M codes, when appropriate, for old injuries or non-work-related conditions.

Medical-Legal Sleep Disorder Evaluation

This is a case study taken from a report to assess "causes and consequences" of the patient's insomnia on an industrial basis.

As part of the employee's job, she drove to various offices, and served and obtained documents. She worked mostly on computers and her activities involved prolonged sitting, standing, lifting, and carrying, and repetitive use of her hands.

The patient stated that during the course of her usual and customary duties, she developed right carpal tunnel syndrome, which was treated with improvement. At some point, she developed a tingling sensation involving the left upper extremity with pain to her thumb and index finger. This progressed until she was unable to lift, drive, or type with her left hand. This caused her to have difficulty sleeping. She had a neurological evaluation, which showed left carpal tunnel syndrome, for which she had surgery. She continued to have pain in the left wrist and developed arthritis at that wrist. She also had a flare-up of symptoms in her right wrist and hand. She continues to be symptomatic and has been unable to return to work.

She complained of the following:

Pain and numbness in both hands
Difficulty sleeping

Sleep History

She stated that it takes about 90 minutes to fall asleep and she awakens repeatedly about every hour because of pain and numbness. She stated she gets only

3 to 4 hours of sleep per night. She feels sleepy during the day. She has lost weight, from 240 pounds to about 180 pounds.

How a Provider Might Use ICD-10

The sleep impairment codes are listed in the G Section of the ICD-10-CM book. The appropriate code was found and is listed as follows. Also, we code the injury codes and list them as a sequelae, using S as the seventh character.

Coding

Based on the above, the following may be appropriate for billing purposes:

G47.01 Insomnia due to medical condition (note: code also medical condition and insomnia as sequela / compensable consequence to the median nerve condition at the wrists)

S64.11XS Injury of median nerve at wrist and hand level of right arm

S64.12XS Injury of median nerve at wrist and hand level of left arm

Note: When there is no bilateral code and a condition is for both sides, both the left and right codes should be listed.

Pitfalls

In this case, the main pitfall is that the injury to the median nerve is typically referred to in the medical community as "carpal tunnel syndrome." In ICD-10, this implies "non-injury," so it's more definitive to use the appropriate S codes as demonstrated here.

Discussion

The provider saw the patient to evaluate sleep disorder and related daytime impairment and concluded that the patient had sleep impairment due to continuing pain because of her bilateral median nerve symptoms. The provider also stated that the patient had no sleep problem previously, so that the impairment is caused by "pain related insomnia."

There is room for provider discretion in how the codes are used. However, the foregoing presentation is made to show that the patient's sleep and pain disorders are due to work-related causes. Most external cause (S and/or T) codes have a seventh-character provision for sequela, or seventh character S to indicate that the condition was the cause of a related symptom or condition.

As the provider becomes more versed in the use of ICD-10, there will be more specificity and less uncertainty in coding.

ICD-10: Waiting for the Other Shoe to Drop

In the months leading up to October 2015, there were dire warnings that, when ICD-10 came into effect, there would be widespread claim denials causing economic disruption. One local bank even began offering emergency lines of credit to its medical clients to assist them to cope with anticipated disruptions of revenue caused by ICD-10.

In the beginning, there was mostly silence. Even though there appears to be a climate of concern, there have been no reports of widespread bankruptcies or cash flow interruptions. Even though it has been relatively soon and widespread, we expect problems to arise in the near future.

Medicare and insurance carriers were allowing providers a grace period before more strictly enforcing ICD-10 requirements. However, I believe that carriers couldn't strictly enforce ICD-10 requirements because they didn't have the knowledge or technical capabilities. This may have changed.

The change from a three- to five-digit numeric code set to a three- to seven-alpha-numeric code set was a huge undertaking from a software and IT standpoint. It would be unrealistic to expect that edits required by ICD-10 would be implemented initially because programmers would have had to be knowledgeable about ICD-10 rules, as well as the code structure.

Following are reasons why payers can't properly adjudicate claims using ICD-10 codes.

As stated previously, one of the new requirements for ICD-10 is the implementation of Combination Codes. A Combination Code is a single code used to classify two diagnoses, or a diagnosis with a secondary process (manifestation), or a diagnosis with an associated complication. When a Combination Code lacks necessary specificity in describing the manifestation or complication, an additional code should be used as a secondary code.

All diabetes mellitus codes are now combination codes. If a patient has Type 2 diabetes with kidney complications, the appropriate combination code should be used. If for example, a patient has diabetes and also end stage renal disease (ESRD), you should use the following codes.

E13.22 Other specified diabetes with diabetic chronic kidney disease—use additional code to identify the stage of chronic kidney disease

This requirement tells us to add the following code to identify the manifestation or complication. Therefore, we would add the following:

N18.6 End stage renal disease

There is also a notation here that, if the disease requires chronic dialysis, an additional code is needed to identify the dialysis status.

Z99.2 Dependence on renal dialysis

It is doubtful that programmers have had sufficient training to know these requirements, much less implement proper edits.

Suppose, in addition, that a provider only specified the following:

E11.9 Type 2 diabetes mellitus without complications

Let us also assume that, with a prior claim, ESRD (N18.6) was reported. Unless the software has data mining capability to link the previous ESRD diagnosis to the unspecified diabetes now reported, who would know about the error?

If a provider does not know the ICD-10 requirements and therefore does not comply, does that make the provider a criminal? Should these be reasons for non-payment? We think there will be court cases and a lengthy period of time required to sort through the many complexities.

For Worker's Compensation and Personal Injury cases, the complexity in coding increases dramatically due to the requirement that "external injury" codes require accompanying Place of Occurrence and Activity codes to specify how and where an injury occurred. An example would be a Worker's Compensation injury that resulted in a dislocated L1/L2 vertebra. The dislocation would be codes as:

S33.111A Dislocation of L1/L2 lumbar vertebra, initial encounter

Please note that there are no ICD-9 codes for dislocation or subluxation at the vertebral level. These were added in ICD-10. Would a provider even know these were added?

Suppose the following Activity and Place of Occurrence codes are used:

V80.21 Animal rider injured in collision with pedal cycle
Y92.192 Bathroom in other specified residential institution as the place of occurrence of the external cause

In order to edit this claim, the software must "know" that an External Cause (S) code requires a Place of Occurrence and an Activity code. It must also "know" when a combination does not make sense. It must have artificial intelligence capability.

The alternative is to have trained adjustors who can review claims.

It is inevitable that, at some point, there will be court cases involving unlikely combinations of injury, place, and activity.

ICD-10 will not go away. An important point to remember is that ICD-10 is a disease classification system that is superior to the earlier version. However, it is not designed for U.S. reimbursement purposes. We will learn to adapt to and use it not just because it is required but because it is also superior to the former code set.

Orthopedic Independent Medical Evaluation: Complicated by Staph Infection following Surgery

This complex case involved a review of records from 17 different providers. The patient developed a post-surgical staph infection. He was transported to a hospital where he remained hospitalized for five days. He was referred to an infectious disease specialist and was treated intravenously with antibiotics for 12 weeks and was followed-up by the specialist for one year.

The Independent Medical Evaluator (IME) provided the following diagnoses:

1. Residuals of musculoligamentous strain lumbosacral spine, lumbar disc extrusion at L3-4 with L3-4 laminectomy and discectomy
2. Post-operative L3-4 discitis and osteomyelitis with lumbar epidural abscess with coagulase negative *Staphylococcus aureus*. Status post-surgical decompression and debridement performed and postoperative intravenous antibiotic

According to the patient, he sustained disc damage secondary to his infection and as a result may need additional fusion surgery.

How a Provider Might Use ICD-10

In ICD-10-CM Volume 1 Chapter 1, you will find the section "B95-B97 Bacterial and viral infectious agents." The notes state that these codes are used as supplementary or additional codes to identify the infectious agent(s) in diseases classified elsewhere. In other words, you need to also include the proper code for the infection itself (e.g., extradural and subdural abscess).

Pitfalls

Using the incorrect area of infection would be the pitfall in this section, as would leaving out the code for the infectious agent. Also, in the descriptor it states to be aware that there are words, like "susceptible" and "resistant," that need to be identified by the provider.

Coding

G06.1 Intraspinal abscess and granuloma (Intraspinal epidural abscess)
B95.61 Methicillin susceptible *Staphylococcus aureus* infection as the cause of diseases classified elsewhere
M46.46 Discitis, unspecified lumbar region
M46.26 Osteomyelitis of vertebra, lumbar region
S33.0XXS Traumatic rupture of lumbar intervertebral disc (Status post-surgical decompression and debridement)

Orthopedic Independent Medical Evaluation Involving Surgical Coding

The patient worked as a laborer lifting heavy boxes filled with water pumps that would range from 50 to 70 pounds. He also placed the boxes into a taping machine and then lifted the boxes to place them on a pallet. During the course of this employment, the employee developed lumbar pain.

He sought examination and underwent x-rays and MRIs, and had a series of epidural injections to the low back. He then underwent a lumbar microdiscectomy. In the final stages of this case, an IME saw the patient.

The report discussed prior medical records, x-rays, MRIs, and the provider's own medical evaluation.

The provider specified that permanent disability to the lumbar spine is 100% secondary to the continuous traumatic work injury and stated the following two diagnoses:

1. Status post microdiscectomy at L5-S1 to cure or relieve the traumatic rupture of the L5-S1 disc.
2. Moderate hypertrophic degenerative facet joint disease at L3-4 with lateral recessed stenosis, moderate to severe hypertrophic degenerative facet joint disease at L4-5 with lateral recessed stenosis, and mild hypertrophic degenerative facet joint disease at L5-S1 bilaterally with right lateral recessed stenosis.

How a Provider Might Use ICD-10

The original diagnosis was the traumatic rupture of the L5-S1 disc, and therefore handled with the S33.0 code. The Status of post microdiscectomy at L5-S1 followed as a result.

Then, as a sequela and compensable consequence, we have hypertrophic degenerative facet joint disease at L5-S1

Pitfalls

Often, the provider wants to clarify that the patient is post-surgical, as this can have significant ramifications. There are codes in ICD-10 for "Intraoperative and post-procedural complications and disorders," for example, "M96.1 Postlaminectomy syndrome." However, these codes would not be appropriate for the purpose of simply stating that the patient has had a procedure done. There is no coding in ICD-10-CM to indicate that the patient has had a surgical procedure performed, and is therefore "post-surgical" or "post-procedure." Using a "post-procedural complication" code by mistake can be a common pitfall regarding surgical coding.

Coding

M99.73 Connective tissue and disc stenosis of intervertebral foramina of lumbar region (There is a notation that the M99 Classification should not be used if the condition can be classified elsewhere.)

S33.0XXS Traumatic rupture of lumbar intervertebral disc. (An S is placed as a seventh character to indicate that this diagnosis is the cause of the sequela above.)

Appendix: Additional Important Data

Medicare Coverage, Diagnosis Requirements, and Coding Edits

Medicare coverage requirements are important to all practices including those which specialize in Worker's Compensation and Personal Injury cases. Increasingly, major carriers such as Blue Cross follow Medicare guidelines. Simultaneously, more Worker's Compensation carrier claims are being processed by the major indemnity carriers.

Medicare publishes Local Coverage Determinations (LCDs) for many services such as lumbar epidural injections and total joint arthroplasty. In Southern California these are LCD L34125 and LCD L33494, respectively—each Medicare geographic region has its own LCDs. These publications provide a narrative on indications, procedure requirements, and diagnosis requirements. It is in the best interest of practices to obtain and study these for the services that they render. When services are rendered in accordance with Medicare requirements, LCD's can be used to justify and properly document services.

Correct Coding Initiative (CCI) Edits

In addition to coverage requirements, CMS has also developed a system of edits for services. Basically, this is a listing in CPT (Current Procedural Terminology) numeric sequence that shows all CPTs, which are included in the allowance for a specific CPT. An example is "CPT 63319 Lumbar epidural injection." "CPT 63319" is listed in the first column multiple times. Adjacent to each 63319 listed is a different CPT code, which is considered inclusive in the allowance for CPT 63319. When billing CPT 63319, you can determine that "Electrocardiogram CPT 93000" will not be paid separately if billed with 63119. You can also see that radiology procedure "Epidurography CPT 72775" is also not paid separately. However, if you review the CPT requirements, you will discover that it can be billed and paid separately if, when it is performed, images are documented and a formal radiological report is issued.

CCI Edits are available online at your Medicare intermediary website and should be reviewed as needed for your services. CPT codes for inclusive services should be reviewed, such as CPT 72275.

ICD-9 Diagnosis Codes Are No Longer Used in Current LCDs

If you have older copies of the LCDs with ICD-9 codes, you should replace them with current publications.

LCDs specify covered diagnosis codes and non-covered diagnosis codes. It is important to note that Medicare LCDs may not list External Cause Codes. When there was an external cause, you must find the appropriate 'S' and/or 'T' code.

Failure to use an External Cause (S) code is tantamount to stating that there was/is no external cause and could result in legal issues for Worker's Compensation and Personal Injury claims.

Until all Medicare LCDs are corrected to list ICD-10 codes, rather than current ICD-9 codes, there is the potential for ongoing disputes and misunderstanding. This is something that practices must anticipate, especially where External Cause codes are required.

Worker's Compensation and Medicare Set Asides

When a patient who is, or is soon to be, covered under Medicare also has a pending settlement for future medical or prescription drug benefits related to a work-related injury, illness, or disease, he can request that his Worker's Compensation lawyer set up a Worker's Compensation Medicare Set-aside Arrangement (WCMSA) in which to deposit these funds. Worker's Compensation claims can be resolved by settlements, judgments, or awards. This information applies only to settlements (Compromise and Release).

Currently, the Centers for Medicare and Medicaid Services (CMS) require that every Worker's Compensation and proposed Medicare Set-aside Arrangement must be submitted to CMS for approval whenever the settling claimant meets the following:

1. **The claimant is already a Medicare beneficiary and the total value of the settlement including indemnity exceeds $10,000**

OR

2. **The claimant is reasonably expected to become eligible for Medicare within 30 months of the settlement and the total value of the settlement including indemnity is more than $250,000**

In these cases, some part of the settlement including indemnity must be set aside to pay for future medicals until the requirements are satisfied and Medicare will again pay the claimant's medical expenses.

When a Medicare Set-aside trust or other arrangement has not yet been created and the settlement itself does not allocate a specific amount of the lump sum settlement to future medical expenses, the amount can be allocated and often negotiated with CMS. CMS must approve a Medicare Set-aside or other arrangement (Personal Injury) and the amount to fund the arrangement before the settlement is finalized. CMS must be involved in the settlement process as early on as possible.

Medicare has established a Benefits Coordination and Recovery Center (BCRC). It can be contacted at 855-798-2627. (TTY/TDD: 1-855-797-2627 for the hearing and speech impaired).

Settlements of Worker's Compensation claims are handled differently than a no-fault or liability insurance claim. As part of settling your Worker's Compensation claim, the patient must repay Medicare for any Medicare payments for Worker's Compensation claim-related services already received.

Worker's Compensation Settlements and Payments

There can be a delay between when a bill is filed for work-related illness or injury and when the State Worker's Compensation Insurance decides they should pay the bill. Medicare cannot pay for items or services that Worker's Compensation will pay for promptly (generally 120 days). However, if the Worker's Compensation Insurer denies payment for your medical bills, pending a review of your claim (generally 120 days or longer), Medicare may make a "conditional payment."

If the Worker's Compensation Insurance denies payment and if you give Medicare proof that the claim was denied, then Medicare will pay for the Medicare-covered items and services. If this occurs in your medical practice, you should contact Provider Relations in your Medicare intermediary organization.

Pain Codes

Listing of Types of Pain		Notes
ICD-10	*Description*	
M26.2-	Temporomandibular joint disorder	See R68.84 (Jaw pain)
R68.84	Jaw pain	Excludes 1 M26.62
R30.9	Micturition pain	Genitourinary
K82.9	Gallbladder pain	Unspecified disease of gallbladder
N23	Unspecified renal colic	Kidney pain
K62.89	Anal or rectal pain	Other specified disease of anus and rectum
G56.4	Causalgia of upper limb	Complex regional pain syndrome II of upper limb
R10.8-	Abdominal pain	See discussion of Pain
R29.0	Tetany	Carpopedal spasm—painful cramps of hands and feet
G56.0-	Carpal tunnel syndrome	There is no anatomical pain code for wrist; use M79.63- or M79.64 for forearm and/or hand/fingers
G44.2-	Tension-type headache	Specify intractable or not intractable
G44.3-	Headache, post traumatic	Specify intractable or not intractable
G43	Migraine headache	Specify with or without status migrainosus
G50.1-	Facial pain	Disorder of 5th cranial nerve
R52-	Pain, unspecified	Includes acute pain NOS; chronic pain, NOS; generalized pain NOS and pain NOS
R07.0	Throat pain	Excludes 1 myalgia
R07.1	Chest pain on breathing	Painful respiration
R07.2	Precordial pain	Brought on by exertion, not at rest
G54.6	Phantom limb syndrome with pain	Perception of sensations, including pain, in a limb that has been amputated
N94-	See specific codes for nomenclature	Pain and other conditions associated with female genital organs and menstrual cycle
R07.81	Pain in the pleural cavity	The sudden occurrence of lancinating chest pain or abdominal pain attacks
R07.82	Intercostal neuralgia pain	Disorder of the nerves running between the ribs caused by damage or loss of nerve function
R10.82-	Rebound abdominal pain	Refers to pain upon removal of pressure rather than application of pressure to the abdomen
M02.3-	Reiter syndrome	Reactive arthritis resulting from a bacterial infection that can cause pain, redness, and swelling
I20.9	Angina (chest pain)	Pressure, squeezing, burning or tightness in the chest, shoulders, arms, jaw, throat, or back
N64.4	Mastodynia	Breast pain or tenderness—any discomfort or pain in the chest

Listing of Types of Pain		Notes
R10.2	Pelvic and perineal pain	Male chronic pain or discomfort localized to the pelvis, perineum or genitalia lasting more than three months
N94.81	Vulvodynia	Chronic pain affecting the vulvar area without an identifiable cause
N94.1	Painful coitus (female)	Associated with genital organs and/or menstrual cycle
B53.12	Painful coitus (male)	Painful ejaculation
F52.6	Dyspareunia	Difficult or painful intercourse
G12.29	Psychogenic pain	Physical pain caused by mental, emotional or behavioral factors
G58.9	Mononeuropathy	A type of damage to a nerve outside the brain and spinal cord (peripheral neuropathy)
T70.3	Diver's pain	Caisson disease due to decompression sickness
M76-	Tendonitis	Inflammation of a tendon—see also enthesopathy
H05.03-	Periostitis	Inflammation of the membrane enveloping the orbit of the eye
A48.3	Toxic shock syndrome	Acute septicemia in women typically caused by bacterial infection. Use additional code to identify the organism, B95, B96
K08.9	Toothache	Other specified disorders of teeth and supporting structures, toothache NOS
K12-	Stomatitis of the mouth	Inflamed and sore mouth
H65.0-	Ear ache	Otitis media is a group of inflammatory diseases of the middle ear
T79.5XXS	Bywater's (or Crush) syndrome	Major shock and renal failure following a crushing injury to a skeletal muscle
I82-	Deep vein thrombosis	Pain or tenderness in one or both legs
S76.21-	Groin pull	Strain of abductor muscle, fascia, and tendon of thigh
A05-1	Food poisoning	Abdominal pain resulting
K52.9	Enteritis	Non-infective inflammation of the intestine
B02-	Shingles	Painful inflammation of nerve ganglia in the middle of the body
D75.81	Myelofibrosis	Bone marrow disorder causing pain or fullness below the ribs on the left (kidney) side
M10-	Gout	Pain areas in joints of ankle, foot, knee, or toe

M35.0-	Sicca (aka Sjogren's) syndrome	Eye pain combing dry eyes, dry mouth, and other connective tissue
K74.60	Cirrhosis (liver disease)	Chronic pain in abdomen due to liver disease
K83.0	Cholangitis	Abdominal pain due to an infection of the bile duct
K75.1	Pylephlebitis of portal vein	Intra-abdominal infection complication
K35-	Appendicitis	Mid-abdominal or lower-right abdominal severe pain
G50.0	Trigeminal neuralgia	Neuralgia involving one or more branches of the trigeminal nerves causing severe pain
M54.9	Back pain	Unspecified
N64.4	Breast pain	Unspecified
H92.0-	Ear pain	Ostalgia and effusion of ear
R07.81	Chest pain other	Pleurodynia, intercostal and unspecified
H57.1-	Eye pain	Ocular pain
R51	Headache	Facial pain, NOS
M25.5-	Joint pain	Excludes limbs, foot, and hands
M79.6-	Limb pain	Limb, hand, foot, fingers, and toes
M54.5-	Lumbar region	Low back pain please note lumbago with sciatica is a combination code M54.4-
R10-	Abdominal pain	Please see chapter on family and general practice coding
N23-	Renal colic	Unspecified
M54-	Spine pain	See lumbar region M54.5
K14.6	Tongue pain	Glossodynia—burning mouth syndrome
F45.41	Mental pain	Pain disorder exclusively related to psychological factors
M79.1	Myalgia	Pain in a muscle or group of muscle, e.g., throat pain

Discussion of ICD-10 Crosswalks

In order to effectively use ICD-10, the user must have an understanding of how to look up ICD-10 codes. With ICD-9, you could generally find codes using the Alphabetic Index, which lists a code or codes to review in the Tabular List. You can still do this with ICD-10, but the task is much more difficult, since there are often major differences between ICD-9 and ICD-10 codes.

In order to determine the correct ICD-10 codes, you must have a copy of the ICD-10-CM book. Copies are available from numerous vendors. We have included a DVD copy for your convenience.

A useful software tool is General Equivalency Mapping (GEM) software. There are free versions available on the Internet. Typically, you type in an ICD-9 code and hit "Enter" or "Submit." An ICD-10 code or codes will then appear. *Do NOT automatically use what appears as a cross reference(s).* GEM software typically lists a disclaimer that the results **cannot** be used in billing.

Remember, we stated earlier:

1. *Many ICD-9 codes do not have a one-to-one crosswalk. Many codes have multiple possible choices.*
2. *There are over 400 instances where a single ICD-9 code can map to more than 50 ICD-10 codes.**
3. *There are over 200 instances where a single ICD-9 code can map to more than 100 ICD-10 codes.**
4. *ICD-10 represents an over 700% increase in the number of codes in ICD-9.*
5. *Medical records do not contain the necessary information to properly choose the correct ICD-10 code(s).*

**Note: These statistics were published by the CMS, April 2013, in an article "General Equivalence Mapping Frequently Asked Questions."*

When you find a code or codes that may be an appropriate crosswalk, you must review the code(s) as listed in ICD-10. It is very important that you review the notations listed in the ICD-10-CM book. There are diagnoses that are specified as "Excludes." Codes that are excluded are listed. If your diagnosis is excluded, you should review the code listed to see if it is the appropriate one to use.

Crosswalk from ICD-9 to ICD-10 of Common Diagnosis Codes Used in Worker's Compensation and Personal Injury with Notes on Potential Problem Areas

Please note: These Crosswalks are not a GEM tool. They are designed specifically for "Injury Coding." They are to be used to get you from an ICD-9 to the proper category of ICD-10 coding, and not the specific complete code itself.

In the Crosswalk, the # sign means that there are notes in the Crosswalk Notations listing informational data and potential problem areas. S codes in the crosswalk have no ICD-9 counterparts.

Be aware that many 'M' Codes are not injury codes and are not appropriate for an external injury diagnosis. Some 'M' codes, although they indicate injury, they are referring to "older" injuries, and not current injuries as detailed throughout this book.

Crosswalk for Diagnosis Codes Used for Worker's Compensation and Personal Injury Cases

ICD9	Description	ICD10	Description	# see Crosswalk Notes
None	Strains	S16.1XXA	Strain of muscle, fascia and tendon at neck level, Initial encounter	#
		S16.1XXD	Subsequent encounter	
		S16.1XXS	Sequela	
	Laceration at neck level	S16.2XX7	These are 7 character codes	
	Laceration of muscle, fascia and tendon, neck	S16.2XX7		
	Other specified injury at neck level	S16.8XX7		
	Unspecified injury at neck level	S16.9XX7		
	Injuries of neck, crushing	S17.NX7	N = assigned digit	
	Thorax S20 - S29	S20.NX7	N = assigned digit	#
	Abdomen, lower back, lumbar spine, pelvis external genitals	S30-S39	Includes contusions, abrasions, blisters, open wounds, fractures, etc.	
None	S39- Other and unspecified injuries of abdomen, lower back, pelvis and external genitals	S39.01XA	Strain of muscle, fascia and tendon of abdomen, lower back and pelvis Initial, encounter	
		S39.01XD	Subsequent encounter	
		S39.01XS	Sequela	
None		S39.012A	Strain of muscle, fascia and tendon of lower back, Initial encounter	
		S39.012D	Subsequent encounter	
		S39.012S	Sequela	
None		S39.013A	Strain of muscle, fascia and tendon of pelvis, Initial encounter	

Crosswalk for Diagnosis Codes Used for Worker's Compensation and Personal Injury Cases

ICD9	Description	ICD10	Description	# see Crosswalk Notes
		S39.013D	Subsequent encounter	
		S39.013S	Sequela	
	Injuries to shoulder and upper arm	S40- S49	Excludes burns, corrosions, frostbite, and insect bites, venomous (T codes)	
None	ICD 10 Combination Codes including	M54.40	Lumbago with sciatica, unspecified side	
	ICD 9 code 724.2 lumbago and	M54.41	Lumbago with sciatica, right side	
	ICD 9 code 724.3 sciatica	M54.42	Lumbago with sciatica, left side	
None	Dislocation and sprain of joints and ligaments at neck level	S13-	Subluxation, dislocations and sprains use the following codes:	#
None	Subluxation of cervical vertebrae	S13.100A	Subluxation of unspecified cervical vertebrae, Initial encounter	
		S13.100D	Subsequent encounter	
	There are different ICD 10 codes for dislocation e.g. S131.101X	S13.100S	Sequela	
		S13.110A	Subluxation of C0/C1 cervical vertebrae, Initial encounter	
		S13.110D	Subsequent encounter	
		S13.110S	Sequela	
		S13.120A	Subluxation of C1/C2 cervical vertebrae, Initial encounter	
		S13.120D	Subsequent encounter	
		S13.120S	Sequela	
		S13.130 A	Subluxation of C2/C3 cervical vertebrae, Initial encounter	
		S13.130D	Subsequent encounter	
		S13.130S	Sequela	
		S13.140A	Subluxation of C3/C4 cervical vertebrae, Initial encounter	

	S13.140D	Subsequent encounter
	S13.140S	Sequela
	S13.150A	Subluxation of C4/C5 cervical vertebrae, Initial encounter
	S13.150D	Subsequent encounter
	S13.150S	Sequela
	S13.160A	Subluxation of C5/C6 cervical vertebrae, Initial encounter
	S13.160D	Subsequent encounter
	S13.160S	Sequela
	S13.170A	Subluxation of C6/C7 cervical vertebrae, Initial encounter
	S13.170D	Subsequent encounter
	S13.170S	Sequela
	S13.180A	Subluxation of C7/T1 cervical vertebrae, Initial encounter
	S13.180D	Subsequent encounter
	S13.180S	Sequela
Dislocation and sprains of joints and ligaments of thorax	S23-	These are all 7 character codes
Subluxation of thoracic vertebra	S23.110A	Subluxation of T1/T2 thoracic vertebra, Initial encounter
	S23.110D	Subsequent encounter
	S23.110S	Sequela
	S23.120A	Subluxation of T2/T3 thoracic vertebra, Initial encounter
	S23.120D	Subsequent encounter
	S23.120S	Sequela
	S23.122A	Subluxation of T3/T4 thoracic vertebra, Initial encounter

Crosswalk for Diagnosis Codes Used for Worker's Compensation and Personal Injury Cases

ICD9	Description	ICD10	Description	# see Crosswalk Notes
		S23.122D	Subsequent encounter	
		S23.122S	Sequela	
		S23.130A	Subluxation of T4/T5 thoracic vertebra, Initial encounter	
		S23.130D	Subsequent encounter	
		S23.130S	Sequela	
		S23.140A	Subluxation of T6/T7 thoracic vertebra, Initial encounter	
		S23.140D	Subsequent encounter	
		S23.140S	Sequela	
		S23.142A	Subluxation of T7/T8 thoracic vertebra, Initial encounter	
		S23.142D	Subsequent encounter	
		S23.142S	Sequela	
		S23.150A	Subluxation of T8/T9 thoracic vertebra, Initial encounter	
		S23.150D	Subsequent encounter	
		S23.150S	Sequela	
		S23.152A	Subluxation of T9/T10 thoracic vertebra,	
		S23.152D	Subsequent encounter	
		S23.152S	Sequela	
		S23.160A	Subluxation of T10/T11 thoracic vertebra, Initial encounter	
		S23.160D	Subsequent encounter	
		S23.160S	Sequela	
		S23.162A	Subluxation of T11/T12 thoracic vertebra, Initial encounter	
		S23.162D	Subsequent encounter	
		S23.162S	Sequela	

	S23.170A	Subluxation of T12/L1 thoracic vertebra,
	S23.170D	Subsequent encounter
	S23.170S	Sequela
Dislocation and sprain of joints and ligaments of lumbar spine and pelvis	S33-	These are all 7-character codes
Subluxation of lumbar vertebra	S33.110A	Subluxation of L1/L2 lumbar vertebra, Initial encounter
	S33.110D	Subsequent encounter
	S33.110S	Sequela
	S33.120A	Subluxation of L2/L3 lumbar vertebra, Initial encounter
	S33.120D	Subsequent encounter
	S33.120S	Sequela
	S33.130A	Subluxation of L3/L4 lumbar vertebra, Initial encounter
	S33.130D	Subsequent encounter
	S33.130S	Sequela
	S33.140A	Subluxation of L4/L5 lumbar vertebra, Initial encounter
	S33.140D	Subsequent encounter
	S33.140S	Sequela
Injury of lumbar and sacral spinal nerves at abdomen, lower back and pelvis level	S34-	These are all 7 character codes
Injury of blood vessels at abdomen, lower back and pelvis level	S35-	These are all 7 character codes
Injury of intra-abdominal organs	S36	These are all 7 character codes
Injury of urinary and pelvic organs	S37	These are all 7 character codes
Crushing injury and traumatic amputation of abdomen, lower back, pelvis and genitals	S38	These are all 7 character codes

Crosswalk for Diagnosis Codes Used for Worker's Compensation and Personal Injury Cases

ICD9	Description	ICD10	Description	# see Crosswalk Notes
	Other and unspecified injuries to abdomen, lower back, pelvis and external genitals	S39	These are all 7 character codes	
	Open wound of upper arm	S41	These are all 7 character codes	
	Fracture of shoulder and upper arm	S42	These are all 7 character codes	
	Subluxation and sprains of joints ligaments of shoulder girdle	S43	These are all 7 character codes	
	Injury of nerves at shoulder and upper arm level	S44	These are all 7 character codes	
	Injury of blood vessels at shoulder and upper arm	S45	These are all 7 character codes	
	Injury of muscle, fascia and tendon at shoulder and upper arm level	S46	These are all 7 character codes	
	Crushing injury of shoulder and upper arm	S47	These are all 7 character codes	
	Traumatic amputation of shoulder and upper arm	S48-	These are all 7 character codes	
	Other and unspecified injuries of shoulder and upper arm	S49	S49 and S49.1 are 7 character codes	
	Injuries to elbow and forearm	S50-S59	There are 6 and 7 character codes in this set	
	Injuries to wrist, hand and fingers	S60-S69	There are 6 and 7 character codes in this set	
	Superficial injuries to hip and thigh	S70-S79	There are 6 and 7 character codes in this set	
	Injuries to the knee and lower leg	S80- S89	There are 6 and 7 character codes in this set	
	Injuries to the ankle and foot	S90- S99	There are 6 and 7 character codes in this set	
307.81	Tension headache	G44.209	Tension-type headache, unspecified, not intractable	
339.20	Post-traumatic headache, unspecified	G44.309	Post-traumatic headache, unspecified, not intractable	
353.0	Brachial plexus lesions	G54.0	Brachial plexus disorders	
353.1	Lumbosacral plexus lesions	G54.1	Lumbosacral plexus disorders	

353.2	Cervical root lesions, not elsewhere classified	G54.2	Cervical root disorders, not elsewhere classified	
353.3	Thoracic root lesions, not elsewhere classified	G54.3	Thoracic root disorders, not elsewhere classified	
354.4	Lumbosacral root lesions, not elsewhere classified	G54.4	Lumbosacral root disorders, not elsewhere classified	
353.8	Other nerve root and plexus disorders	G54.8	Other nerve root and plexus disorders	
718.48	Contracture of joint of other specified sites	M24.50	Contracture, unspecified Joint	# see notes M codes vs. S codes
719.00	Effusion of joint site, unspecified	M25.40	Effusion, unspecified joint	
719.48	Pain in joint involving other specified sites	M25.50	Pain in unspecified joint	
720.1	Spinal enthesopathy	M46.00	Spinal enthesopathy, site unspecified	
721.0	Cervical spondylosis without myelopathy	M47.812	Spondylosis without myelopathy or radiculopathy, cervical region	
721.2	Thoracic spondylosis without myelopathy	M47.814	Spondylosis without myelopathy or radiculopathy, thoracic region	
721.3	Lumbosacral spondylosis without myelopathy	M47.817	Spondylosis without myelopathy or radiculopathy, lumbosacral region	
721.6	Ankylosing vertebral hyperostosis	M48.10	Ankylosing hyperostosis (Forestier), site unspecified	
721.7	Traumatic spondylopathy	M48.30	Traumatic spondylopathy, site unspecified	
721.90	Spondylosis of unspecified site without myelopathy	M47.819	Spondylosis without myelopathy or radiculopathy, site unspecified	
721.91	Spondylosis of unspecified site with myelopathy	M47.10	Other spondylosis with myelopathy, site unspecified	
722.0	Displacement of cervical intervertebral disc without myelopathy	M50.20	Other cervical disc displacement, unspecified cervical region	

Crosswalk for Diagnosis Codes Used for Worker's Compensation and Personal Injury Cases

ICD9	Description	ICD10	Description	# see Crosswalk Notes
722.10	Displacement of lumbar intervertebral disc without myelopathy	M51.26	Other intervertebral disc displacement, lumbar region	
		M51.27	Other intervertebral disc displacement, lumbosacral region	
722.11	Displacement of thoracic intervertebral disc without myelopathy	M51.24	Other intervertebral disc displacement, thoracic region	
		M51.25	Other intervertebral disc displacement, thoracolumbar region	
722.4	Degeneration of cervical intervertebral disc	M50.30	Other cervical disc degeneration, unspecified cervical region	
722.51	Degeneration of thoracic or thoracolumbar intervertebral disc	M51.34	Other intervertebral disc degeneration, thoracic region	
		M51.35	Other intervertebral disc degeneration, thoracolumbar region	
722.52	Degeneration of lumbar or lumbosacral intervertebral disc	M51.36	Other intervertebral disc degeneration, lumbar region	
		M51.37	Other intervertebral disc degeneration, lumbosacral region	
722.6	Degeneration of intervertebral disc site unspecified	M51.34	Other intervertebral disc degeneration, thoracic region	
		M51.35	Other intervertebral disc degeneration, thoracolumbar region	
		M51.36	Other intervertebral disc degeneration, lumbar region	
		M51.37	Other intervertebral disc degeneration, lumbosacral region	
722.81	Postlaminectomy syndrome of cervical region	M96.1	Postlaminectomy syndrome, not elsewhere classified	

722.82	Postlaminectomy syndrome of thoracic region	M96.1	Postlaminectomy syndrome, not elsewhere classified
722.83	Postlaminectomy syndrome of lumbar region	M96.1	Postlaminectomy syndrome, not elsewhere classified
722.91	Other and unspecified disc disorder of cervical region	M50.80	Other cervical disc disorders, unspecified cervical region
		M50.90	Cervical disc disorder, unspecified cervical region
722.92	Other and unspecified disc disorder of thoracic region	M46.45	Discitis, unspecified, thoracolumbar region
		M51.84	Other intervertebral disorders, thoracic region
		M51.85	Other intervertebral disorders, thoracolumbar region
722.93	Other and unspecified disc disorder of lumbar region	M46.47	Discitis, unspecified, lumbosacral region
		M51.86	Other intervertebral disc disorders, lumbar region
		M51.87	Other intervertebral disc disorders, lumbosacral region
723.0	Spinal stenosis in cervical region	M48.02	Spinal stenosis, cervical region
723.1	Cervicalgia	M54.2	Cervicalgia
723.2	Cervicocranial syndrome	M53.0	Cervicocranial syndrome
723.3	Cervicobrachial syndrome (diffuse)	M53.1	Cervicobrachial syndrome
723.4	Brachial neuritis or radiculitis, NOS	M54.12	Radiculopathy, cervical region
		M54.13	Radiculopathy, cervicothoracic region
723.5	Torticollis, unspecified	M43.6	Torticollis
724.01	Spinal stenosis of thoracic region	M48.04	Spinal stenosis, thoracic region
724.02	Spinal stenosis, lumbar region, without neurogenic claudication	M48.06	Spinal stenosis, lumbar region

Crosswalk for Diagnosis Codes Used for Worker's Compensation and Personal Injury Cases

ICD9	Description	ICD10	Description	# see Crosswalk Notes
724.03	Spinal stenosis, lumbar region, with neurogenic claudication	M48.06	Spinal stenosis, lumbar region	
724.1	Pain in thoracic spine	M54.6	Pain in thoracic spine	
724.2	Lumbago	M54.5	Low back pain	
			See Combination Code M 54.4	
724.3	Sciatica	M54.30	Sciatica, unspecified side	
		M54.31	Sciatica, right side	
		M54.32	Sciatica, left side	
			See Combination Code M54.4	
724.4	Thoracic or lumbosacral neuritis or radiculitis, unspecified	M54.14	Radiculopathy, thoracic region	
		M54.15	Radiculopathy, thoracolumbar region	
		M54.16	Radiculopathy, lumbar region	
		M54.17	Radiculopathy, lumbosacral region	
724.5	Backache, unspecified	M54.89	Other dorsalgia	
		M54.9	Dorsalgia, unspecified	
724.6	Disorders of sacrum	M43.27	Fusion of spine, lumbosacral region	
		M43.28	Fusion of spine, sacral and sacrococcygeal region	
		M53.2X7	Spinal instabilities, lumbosacral region	
		M53.3	Sacrococcygeal disorders, not elsewhere classified	
724.79	Other disorders of coccyx	M53.3	Sacrococcygeal disorders, not elsewhere classified	
724.8	Other symptoms referable to back	M54.08	Panniculitis affecting regions of neck and back, sacral and sacrococcygeal region	
726.10	Disorders of bursae and tendons in shoulder region, unspecified	M75.100	Unspecified rotator cuff tear or rupture of unspecified shoulder, not specified as traumatic	

		M75.101	Unspecified rotator cuff tear or rupture of right shoulder, not specified as traumatic	
		M75.102	Unspecified rotator cuff tear or rupture of left shoulder, not specified as traumatic	
726.2	Other affections of should region, not elsewhere classified	M75.50	Bursitis of unspecified shoulder	
		M75.51	Bursitis of right shoulder	
		M75.52	Bursitis of left shoulder	
726.60	Enthesopathy of knee, unspecified	M70.50	Other bursitis of knee, unspecified knee	
		M70.51	Other bursitis of knee, right knee	
		M70.52	Other bursitis of knee, left knee	
726.90	Enthesopathy of unspecified site	M77.9	Enthesopathy, unspecified	
729.1	Myalgia and myositis, unspecified	M60.9	Myositis, unspecified	
		M79.1	Myalgia	
		M79.7	Fibromyalgia	
729.4	Fasciitis, unspecified	M72.9	Fibroblastic disorder, unspecified	
738.4	Acquired spondylolisthesis	M43.00	Spondylolysis, site unspecified	
		M43.10	Spondylolisthesis, site unspecified	
739.0	Nonallopathic lesions of head region, not elsewhere classified	M99.00	Segmental and somatic dysfunction of head region	
739.1	Nonallopathic lesions of cervical region not elsewhere classified	M99.01	Segmental and somatic dysfunction of cervical region	
739.2	Nonallopathic lesions of thoracic region, not elsewhere classified	M99.02	Segmental and somatic dysfunction of thoracic region	#
739.3	Nonallopathic lesions of lumbar region, not elsewhere classified	M99.03	Segmental and somatic dysfunction of lumbar region	#
739.4	Nonallopathic lesions of sacral region, not elsewhere classified	M99.04	Segmental and somatic dysfunction of sacral region	#
739.5	Nonallopathic lesions of pelvic region, not elsewhere classified	M99.05	Segmental and somatic dysfunction of pelvic region	#

Crosswalk for Diagnosis Codes Used for Worker's Compensation and Personal Injury Cases

ICD9	Description	ICD10	Description	# see Crosswalk Notes
739.6	Nonallopathic lesions of lower extremities, not elsewhere classified	M99.06	Segmental and somatic dysfunction of lower extremity	
739.7	Nonallopathic lesions of upper extremities, not elsewhere classified	M99.07	Segmental and somatic dysfunction of upper extremity	
739.8	Nonallopathic lesions of rib cage, not elsewhere classified	M99.08	Segmental and somatic dysfunction of rib cage	
739.9	Nonallopathic lesions of abdomen and other sites, not elsewhere classified	M99.09	Segmental and somatic dysfunction of abdomen and other regions	
756.12	Spondylolisthesis, congenital	Q76.2	Congenital spondylolisthesis	#
784.0	Headache	G44.1	Vascular headache, not elsewhere specified	#
		R51	Headache	#
846.0	Lumbosacral (joint) (ligament) sprain	S33.8XXA	Sprain of other parts of lumbar spine and pelvis, Initial encounter	#
		S33.8XXD	Subsequent encounter	
		S33.8XXS	Sequela	
846.1	Sacroiliac (ligament) sprain	S33.6XXA	Sprain of sacroiliac joint, Initial encounter	#
		S33.6XXD	Subsequent encounter	
		S33.6XXS	Sequela	
846.2	Sacrospinatus (ligament) sprain	S33.8XXA	Sprain of other parts of lumbar spine and pelvis, Initial encounter	#
		S33.8XXD	Subsequent encounter	
		S33.8XXS	Sequela	
846.3	Sacrotuberous (ligament) sprain	S33.8XXA	Sprain of other parts of lumbar spine and pelvis, Initial encounter	#
		S33.8XXD	Subsequent encounter	
		S33.8XXS	Sequela	
846.8	Other specified sites of sacroiliac region sprain	S33.8XXA	Sprain of other parts of lumbar spine and pelvis, Initial encounter	#

		S33.8XXD	Subsequent encounter	
		S33.8XXS	Sequela	
847.0	Neck sprain	S13.4XXA	Sprain of ligaments of cervical spine, Initial encounter	#
		S13.4XXD	Subsequent encounter	
		S13.4XXS	Sequela	
		S13.8XXA	Sprain of joints and ligaments of other parts of neck, Initial encounter	
		S13.8XXD	Subsequent encounter	
		S13.8XXS	Sequela	
847.1	Thoracic sprain	S23.3XXA	Sprain of ligaments of thoracic spine, Initial encounter	#
		S23.3XXD	Subsequent encounter	
		S23.3XXS	Sequela	
		S23.8XXA	Sprain of other specified parts of thorax, Initial encounter	
		S23.8XXD	Subsequent encounter	
		S23.8XXS	Sequela	
847.2	Lumbar sprain	S33.5XXA	Sprain of ligaments of lumbar spine, Initial encounter	#
		S33.5XXD	Subsequent encounter	
		S33.5XXS	Sequela	
847.3	Sprain of sacrum	S33.8XXA	Sprain of other parts of lumbar spine and pelvis, Initial encounter	# #
		S33.8XXD	Subsequent encounter	
		S33.8XXS	Sequela	
847.4	Sprain of coccyx	S33.8XXA	ICD 9 codes 847.3 and 847.4 are combined in ICD 10	#
		S33.8XXD		
		S33.8XXS		

Crosswalk for Diagnosis Codes Used for Worker's Compensation and Personal Injury Cases

QUICK USEFUL LIST OF ICD-10 CODES FOR Worker's Compensation and Personal Injury

S codes require 7th character

M15 - M19	Includes post-traumatic osteoarthritis of various joints
S13.0	Traumatic rupture of cervical invertebral disc
S13.4	Sprain of ligaments of cervical spine (includes whiplash injury of cervical spine)
S13.8	Sprain of joints and ligaments of other parts of neck
S13.9	Sprain of joints and ligaments of unspecified parts of neck
S14.2	Injury of nerve root of cervical spine
S16.1	Strain of muscle, fascia and tendon at neck level
S23.0	Traumatic rupture of thoracic invertebral disc
S23.3	Sprain of ligaments of thoracic spine
S23.8	Sprain of other specified parts of thorax
S23.9	Sprain of unspecified parts of thorax
S24.2	Injury of nerve root of thoracic spine
S29.01	Strain of muscle and tendon of thorax (Use 6th category for specific location)
S33.0	Traumatic rupture of lumbar invertebral disc
S33.5	Sprain of ligaments of lumbar spine
S33.6	Sprain of sacroiliac joint
S33.8	Sprain of other parts of lumbar spine and pelvis
S33.9	Sprain of unspecified parts of lumbar spine and pelvis
S34.21	Injury of nerve root of lumbar spine
S34.22	Injury of nerve root of sacral spine
S39.01	Strain of muscle, fascia and tendon of abdomen, lower back and pelvis (Use 6th category for specific location)
S64.1	Injury of the median nerve at the wrist and hand level (Use 5th category for specific location)

Notes on Crosswalks and Possible Problem Areas

ICD 9	ICD 10	ICD 10 Description	Notation
None	S16.1XX7	Strain of muscle, fascia, and tendon at neck level	In ICD 9 strains were synonymous with sprains For S16.1XX7 the 7 indicates that a seventh character is needed
	S23.3-4	Sprain of thorax	Please read descriptions closely; there are separate coded for some sprains vs. strains
None	S39.0117	Strain of muscle, fascia, and tendon of abdomen, lower back and pelvis	We use the number 7 to indicate when a seventh character is needed. Place holders use the ICD-10 convention of X
None	S39.0127	Strain of muscle, fascia, and tendon of abdomen	S39.0127. The 7 indicates that a seventh character is needed
None	S390137	Strain of muscle, fascia, and tendon of pelvis	S390137. The 7 indicates that a seventh character is needed
	S13	Dislocation and sprain of joints and ligaments at neck level	There are now codes for sprains and dislocation at the vertebral level
307.81	G44.201	Tension-type headache, unspecified, intractable	Your documentation must specify which tension-type headache
	G44.209	Tension-type headache, unspecified, not intractable	
	G44.211	Episodic tension-type headache, intractable	
	G44.219	Episodic tension-type headache, not intractable	
	G44.221	Chronic tension-type headache, intractable	
	G44.229	Chronic tension-type headache, not intractable	
718.48	G24.50	Contracture, unspecified Joint	There are specific ICD-10 codes for shoulder elbow, wrist, hand, hip, knee, ankle, and foot: M24.511 through M24.576. When using these codes you must specify left or right
		M codes vs. S codes: When a condition is the result of an External Cause, use S codes. In most cases M codes imply that a condition was not the result of an external cause	

Notes on Crosswalks and Possible Problem Areas

ICD 9	ICD 10	ICD 10 Description	Notation
719.00	M25.40	Effusion, unspecified Joint	If a joint is known, i.e., shoulder, the specific joint code should be used. These are M25.- through M25.9
720.1	M46.00	Spinal enthesopathy, site unspecified	When a specific site is known, use the code for that site (M46.01 through M46.09)
721.6	M48.10	Ankylosing hyperostosis (Forestier's disease), site unspecified	When site is known, use the code for that site (M48.11 through M48.19)
721.7	M48.30	Traumatic spondylopathy, site unspecified	When the site is known, use the code for that site (M48.31 through M48.38)
722.6	M51.3X	M51.34 through M51.37	M51.36 and M51.37 are both related to ICD 9 code 722.52
722.81	M96.1	Post-laminectomy syndrome, not elsewhere classified	M96.1 replaces ICD 9 codes 722.80, 722.81, 722.82 and 722.83

723.5	M43.6	Torticollis	ICD-10 contains "Excludes certain diagnosis" such as congenital, which are also excluded in ICD-9. However, these exclusions are now specified as ICD-10 codes, i.e., congenital is now Q68.0 rather than ICD-9 754.1
724.2	M54.5	Low back pain (lumbago)	In ICD-10 M54.5 excludes low back strain (S39.012), lumbago due to intervertebral disc displacement (M51.2-), and lumbago with sciatica (M54.4)
724.3	M54.30X M54.31 M54.32	Sciatica in ICD 10 is three codes unspecified R and L Right side Left side use both M54.31 and M54.32 for bilateral	When it occurs on the right side, M54.31 should be used, The left side requires M54.32 and documentation has to reflect the side
756.12	Q76.2	Congenital spondylolisthesis	ICD-10 excludes spondylolisthesis (acquired) (M 43.1-) and spondylolisthesis (acquired) (M43.0-)
784.0	G44.1 R51	Vascular headache, not elsewhere specified	Use G44.1 for vascular headaches R51 Headache unspecified. R51 excludes atypical face pain (G50.1), migraine and other headache syndromes (G43-G44), and trigeminal neuralgia (G50.0)

Glossary

acquired cataracts: categorized primarily by their location in the lens, though mixed morphology is common

- **nuclear**: located in the interior of the lens; the most common type
- **cortical**: originate at the outer rim of the lens and radiate inward; common in diabetes
- **subcapsular**: located on the surface of the lens in the front (anterior) or rear (posterior)

adult: age range is 15–124 years inclusive
AHA: American Hospital Association
AHIMA: American Health Information Management Association
Alphabetic Index to Diseases: Volume 2. The Alphabetic Index is arranged by condition
AMI: Acute Myocardial Infarction
"and": when "and" is used in the ICD-10-CM book it represents "and/or"
asphyxia: cutting off of oxygen to the lungs by external sources, whereas hypoxemia (also called hypoxia or anoxia) is the same condition due to internal causes
asthma: common definitions for ICD-10-CM are:

- **mild intermittent:** daytime symptoms, less than or equal to two times a week; nighttime symptoms three to four times a month
- **mild persistent:** daytime symptoms, greater than or equal to two times a week, but not daily; nighttime symptoms less than or equal to two times a month
- **moderate persistent:** daytime symptoms, daily; nighttime symptoms greater or equal to once a week
- **severe persistent:** daytime symptoms, multiple times per day; nighttime symptoms, near nightly

BMI: body mass index
***Clostridium difficile*:** a bacteria naturally occurring in the colon that can run amok in patients taking antibiotics
CMS: Centers for Medicare and Medicaid Services
"code also" note: instructs providers that two codes may be required to fully describe a condition, but does not provide sequencing direction
Combination Code: a single code to classify:

- two diagnoses, or
- a diagnosis with an associated secondary process (manifestation)
- a diagnosis with an associated complication

COPD: chronic obstructive pulmonary disease
CVID: common variable immunodeficiency
default codes: the code listed next to a main term in the ICD-10-CM Alphabetic Index is referred to as a default code. The default code represents that condition that is most commonly associated with the main term, or is the unspecified code for the condition
dehydrated: deficient in intracellular water volume
DHHS: Department of Health and Human Services
earwax: only considered impacted if it is tightly packed and causes blockage of the ear canal, generally requiring instruments to remove. Because most payers reimburse at a higher rate for the removal of impacted cerumen (CPT code 69210) than they do for a low-level office visit, it is critical that the severity of impaction be documented when submitting claims for 69210
encounter: this term is used in all settings, including hospital admissions
Excludes 1: a "pure" excludes, meaning "not coded here"
Excludes 2: meaning "not included here"
hearing loss: the critical factors when making the determination on the appropriate hearing loss diagnoses are:

- nature of the impairment as structural (conductive-non cochlear) or functional (sensory-cochlear), neural (auditory nerve) or central (brain)
- laterality of the hearing loss
- in the case of conductive hearing loss, the site of the structural defect or damage

HIPAA: Health Insurance Portability and Accountability Act
HIV: Human Immunodeficiency Virus
hypovolemic: deficient in extracellular blood volume
ICD-10-CM: International Classification of Diseases, 10th Revision, Clinical Modification
keratoses: distinguished from warts in that they are not caused by a virus
laterality: some ICD-10 codes indicate laterality, specifying whether the condition occurs on the left, right, or bilaterally
lay descriptions: plain-English descriptions highlight critical differences between similar codes
malaise/debility: weakness or feebleness, but mainly associated with a declining state of overall health
manifestation code: describe the manifestation of an underlying disease, not the disease, and are backed by blue highlights
maternity: age range 12 to 55 years inclusive
Medicare age conflict edits: Medicare Outpatient Code Editor detects inconsistencies between a patient's age and any diagnosis on the patient's record, for example, a five-year-old patient with benign prostatic hypertrophy
Medicare sex conflict edits: Medicare Outpatient Code Editor detects inconsistencies between a patient's sex and any diagnosis or procedure on the patient's record, for example, a male patient with cervical cancer

migraine headaches: signs and symptoms include: prolonged unilateral focus, sensitivity to light and/or sound, nausea or vomiting, and aura
MRSA: methicillin resistant *Staphylococcus aureus*
MSSA: methicillin susceptible *Staphylococcus aureus*
NCHS: National Center for Health Statistics
NEC: not elsewhere classified
newborn: age of 0 years; a subset of diagnoses intended only for newborns and neonates
NOS: not otherwise specified
pediatric: age range 0 to 17 years inclusive
peripartum: the peripartum period is defined as the last month of pregnancy to five months postpartum
placeholder character: ICD-10 utilizes a placeholder character X, which is used as a placeholder at certain codes to allow for future expansion
POA: present on admission
postpartum: the postpartum period begins immediately after delivery and continues for six weeks following delivery
precordial pain: differs from unstable angina in that it is:

- often brought on by exertion rather than occurring at rest
- sharp, stabbing, and immediate, rather than "crushing" and increasing in severity
- often accompanied by a feeling of mental distress and anxiety

provider: a physician or any qualified healthcare practitioner who is legally accountable for establishing the patient's diagnosis
punctuation:

- **brackets:** used in the Tabular List to enclose synonyms, alternative wording, or explanatory phrases. Used in the Alphabetic Index to identify manifestation codes
- **parentheses:** used in both the Alphabetic Index and the Tabular list to enclose supplementary words that may be present or absent in the statement of a disease or procedure without affecting the code number to which it is assigned. The terms within the parentheses are referred to as "nonessential modifiers." The nonessential modifiers in the Alphabetic Index to Disease apply to sub-terms following a main term, except when a nonessential modifier and a subentry are mutually exclusive, in which case the subentry takes precedence

rosacea: most common in middle-aged women rather than teenagers, and believed to have a neurovascular cause, rather than hormonal
schizoaffective disorder: when a patient exhibits both psychotic symptoms of schizophrenia and the episodic nature of mood disorders

screening: the testing for disease or disease precursors in seemingly well individuals so that early detection and treatment can be provided for those who test positive for the disease
"secondary only" diagnosis edits: certain codes may not be used as first-listed (principal) codes, rather only as secondary codes. All codes (with the exception of manifestation codes) without a maroon flag can be used as either a first-listed or secondary code, depending on the circumstances of the encounter
"see": when following a main term in the Alphabetic Index indicates that another term should be referenced
"see also": when following a main term in the Alphabetic Index indicates that there is another main term that may also be referenced that may provide additional useful Alphabetic Index entries
sequela: the residual effect (condition produced) after the acute phase of an illness or injury has terminated
seventh characters: certain ICD-10 categories have applicable seventh characters that are required for all codes within the category, or as the notes in the Tabular List instruct

A: seventh character "A" indicates Initial Encounter and is used while the patient is receiving active treatment for the condition
D: seventh character "D" indicates Subsequent Encounter and is used for encounters after the patient has received active treatment of the condition and is receiving routine care for the condition during the healing or recovery phase
S: seventh character "S" indicates sequela and is used for complications or conditions that arise as a direct result of a condition, such as a scar formation after a burn

SIRS: systemic inflammatory response syndrome
Tabular List Volume 1: used to select your code
Tabular List bullet: denotes a new category, subcategory, or code
Tabular List delta: denotes a revised category, subcategory, or code
tachypnea: condition similar to hyperventilation, in that it is characterized by rapid breathing; however, tachypnea is characterized by rapid shallow breathing whereas hyperventilation manifests in rapid, deep breathing
UHDDS: Uniform Hospital Discharge Data Set
"unspecified" code: for use when the information in the medical record is insufficient to assign a more specific code
WHO: World Health Organization
"with": should be interpreted to mean "associated with" or "due to" when it appears in a code title, the Alphabetic Index, or an instructional note in the Tabular List

Definitions of Transport Vehicles

1. A transport accident is any accident involving a device designed primarily for, or used at the time primarily for, conveying persons or good from one place to another.
2. A public highway (trafficway) or street is the entire width between property lines (or other boundary lines) of land open to the public as a matter of right or custom for purposes of moving persons or property from one place to another. A roadway is that part of the public highway designed, improved and customarily used for vehicular traffic.
3. A traffic accident is any vehicle accident occurring on the public highway (i.e., originating on, terminating on, or involving a vehicle partially on the highway). A vehicle accident is assumed to have occurred on the public highway unless another place is specified, except in the case of accidents involving only off-road motor vehicles, which are classified as nontraffic accidents unless the contrary is stated.
4. A nontraffic accident is any vehicle accident that occurs entirely in any place other than a public highway.
5. A pedestrian is any person involved in an accident who was not at the time of the accident riding in or on a motor vehicle, railway train, streetcar or animal-drawn or other vehicle, or on a pedal cycle or animal. This includes, a person changing a tire or working on a parked car. It also includes the use of a pedestrian conveyance such as a baby carriage, ice skates, rollerskates, a skateboard, nonmotorized or motorized wheelchair, motorized mobility scooter, or nonmotorized scooter.
6. A driver is an occupant of a transport vehicle who is operating or intending to operate it.
7. A passenger is an occupant of a transport vehicle other than the driver, except a person traveling on the outside of the vehicle.
8. A person on the outside of the vehicle is any person being transported by a vehicle but not occupying the space normally reserved for the driver or passengers, or the space intended for the transport of property. This includes the body, bumper, fender, roof, running board, or step of a vehicle.
9. A pedal cycle is any land transport vehicle operated solely by nonmotorized pedals including a bicycle or tricycle.
10. A pedal cyclist is any person riding a pedal cycle or in a sidecar or trailer attached to a pedal cycle.
11. A motorcycle is a two-wheeled motor vehicle with one or two riding saddles and sometimes with a third wheel for the support of a sidecar. The sidecar is considered part of the motorcycle.
12. A motorcycle rider is any person riding a motorcycle or in a sidecar or trailer attached to the motorcycle.

13. A three-wheeled motor vehicle is a motored tricycle designed primarily for on-road use. This includes a motor-driven tricycle, a motorized rickshaw, or a three-wheeled motor car.
14. A car (automobile) is a four-wheeled motor vehicle designed primarily for carrying up to seven persons. A trailer being towed by the car is considered part of the car.
15. A pick-up truck or van is a four- or six-wheeled motor vehicle designed for carrying passengers as well as property or cargo weighing less than the local limit for classification as a heavy goods vehicle, and not requiring a special driver's license. This includes a minivan and a sport-utility vehicle (SUV).
16. A heavy transport vehicle is a motor vehicle designed primarily for carrying property, meeting local criteria for classification as a heavy goods vehicle in terms of weight, and requiring a special driver's license.
17. A bus (coach) is a motor vehicle designed or adapted primarily for carrying more than 10 passengers, and requiring a special driver's license.
18. A railway train or railway vehicle is any device, with or without freight or passenger cars coupled to it, designed for traffic on a railway track. This includes subterranean (subways) or elevated trains.
19. A streetcar is a device designed and used primarily for transporting passengers within a municipality, running on rails, usually subjcct to normal traffic control signals, and operated principally on a right-of-way that forms part of the roadway. This includes a tram or trolley that runs on rails. A trailer being towed by a streetcar is considered part of the streetcar.
20. A special vehicle mainly used on industrial premises is a motor vehicle designed primarily for use within the buildings and premises of industrial or commercial establishments. This includes battery-powered trucks, forklifts, coal-cars in a coal mine, logging cars, and trucks used in mines or quarries.
21. A special vehicle mainly used in agriculture is a motor vehicle designed specifically for use in farming and agriculture (horticulture), to work the land, tend and harvest crops, and transport materials on the farm. This includes harvesters, farm machinery, tractors, and trailers.
22. A special construction vehicle is a motor vehicle designed specifically for use on construction and demolition sites. This includes bulldozers, diggers, earth levelers, dump trucks, backhoes, front-end loaders, pavers, and mechanical shovels.
23. A special all-terrain vehicle is a motor vehicle of special design to enable it to negotiate over rough or soft terrain, snow, or sand. This includes snow mobiles, all-terrain vehicles (ATV), and dune buggies. It does not include passenger vehicle designed as sport-utility vehicles (SUV).
24. A watercraft is any device designed for transporting passengers or goods on water. This includes motor or sail boats, ships, and hovercrafts.
25. An aircraft is any device for transporting passengers or goods in the air. This includes hot-air balloons, gliders, helicopters, and airplanes.
26. A military vehicle is any motorized vehicle operating on a public roadway owned by the military and operated by a member of the military.

General Sample Fee Slip

Patient Name:		**Date:**
Note:	Insurance:	Today's Charges: $
		Payment: ❑check ❑cash ❑cc $
		Received by:

	Office visit	New	Est	
	Minimal		99211	
	Problem focused	99201	99212	
	Exp problem focused	99202	99213	
	Detailed	99203	99214	
	Comp (established pt)	99204	99215	
	Comp (new pt)	99205		
	Significant, sep serv	-25	-25	
	Annual Physical	**New**	**Est**	
	< 1 y	99381	99391	
	1-4 y	99382	99392	
	5-11 y	99383	99393	
	12-17 y	99384	99394	
	18-39 y	99385	99395	
	40-64 y	99386	99396	
	65 y +	99387	99397	

	Medicare preventive services		
	Annual Physical exam, initial	G0438	
	Annual Physical exam, subsq	G0439	
	Pap	Q0091	
	Pelvic & breast	G0101	
	Prostate/PSA	G0103	
	Tobacco counseling/3-10 min	G0436	
	Tobacco counseling/>10 min	G0437	
	Welcome to Medicare exam	G0402	
	ECG w/Welcome to Medicare	G0403	
	Flexible sigmoidoscopy	G0104	
	Hemoccult, immunoassay	G0328	
	Flu shot	G0008	
	Hep B shot	G0010	
	Pneumonia shot	G0009	
	Consultation/preop clearance		
	Expanded problem focused	99242	
	Detailed	99243	
	Comprehensive/mod complex	99244	
	Comprehensive/high complex	99245	
	Other services		
	After posted hours	99050	
	Evening/weekend appointment	99051	
	Home health certification	G0180	
	Home health recertification	G0179	
	Post-op follow-up	99024	
	Prolonged/30-74 min	99354	
	Special reports/forms	99080	
	Disability/Workers comp	99455	
	Trans care mgmt/mod complex	99495	
	Trans care mgmt/high complex	99496	
	Radiology		

Diagnosis
Instructions:

Physician signature
X

Office procedures		
Audiometry	92551	
Cerumen removal, per ear	69210	
ECG, w/interpretation	93000	
ECG, rhythm strip	93040	
Cardio Vasc. Stress Test	93015	
Nebulizer	94640	
Nebulizer demo	94664	
Spirometry	94010	
Spirometry, pre and post	94060	
Tympanometry	92567	
Vasectomy	55250	
Holter Monitor	93224	
Fracture care, cast/splint	29__	
Site: ________		
Other procedure		

Skin procedures		Units
Burn care, initial	16000	
Foreign body, skin, simple	10120	
Foreign body, skin, complex	10121	
I&D, abscess	10060	
I&D, hematoma/seroma	10140	
Laceration repair, simple	120__	
Site: ________ Size: _____		
Laceration repair, layered	120__	
Site: ________ Size: _____		
Lesion, biopsy, one	11100	
Lesion, biopsy, each add'l	11101	
Lesion, destruct., benign, 1-14	17110	
Lesion, destruct., premal., single	17000	
Lesion, destruct., premal., ea. add'l	17003	
Lesion, excision, benign	114__	
Site: ________ Size: _____		
Lesion, excision, malignant	116__	
Site: ________ Size: _____		
Lesion, paring/cutting, one	11055	
Lesion, paring/cutting, 2-4	11056	
Lesion, shave	113__	
Site: ________ Size: _____		
Nail removal, partial	11730	
Nail removal, w/matrix	11750	
Skin tag, 1-15	11200	

Medications		Units
Ampicillin, up to 500mg	J0290	
B-12, up to 1,000 mcg	J3420	
Adrenalin epinephrine inj, 0.1mg	J0171	
Kenalog, 10mg	J3301	
Lidocaine, IV, 10mg	J2001	
Methylprednisolone	J1030	
Methylprednisolone sodium	J2930	
Normal saline, 1000cc	J7030	
Phenergan, up to 50mg	J2550	
Progesterone, 1 mg	J1050	
Testosterone, 200mg	J1080	
Toradol, 15mg	J1885	
Flu vaccines		
Fluvirin	90673	

Notes

	Matrix	
	Medicare Only	
	Electric Stim other than wound- G0283GP	G0283
	Electric Stim Therapy- 97016GP	97016
	Neuromuscular Reeducation- 97112GP	97112
	Insurance and PI only	
	Vasopneumatic Dev Therapy	97016
	Electric Stim Therapy	97014
	Neuromuscular Reeducation	97112
	Laboratory	
	Venipuncture	36415
	Blood glucose monitoring device	82962
	CBC, w/ auto, differential	85025
	CBC, w/o auto	85027
	Cholesterol	82465
	Pregnancy, blood	84703
	Pregnancy, urine	81025
	Renal panel	80069
	Strep, rapid, antibody	86403
	Strep culture	87081
	Strep A, rapid, direct observation	87880
	TB Skin Test	86580
	UA, complete, non-automated	81000
	UA, w/o micro, non-automated	81002
	Other procedure/lab	

	Vaccines	
	DT, <7 y	90702
	DtaP, <7 y	90700
	Flu, preservative-free, 6-35 months	90655
	Flu, preservative-free, 3 y +	90656
	Flu, quadrivalent, live, intranasal	90672
	Flu, inactivated, subunit, adjuvanted, IM	90653
	Hep A, adult	90632
	Hep A, ped/adol, 2 dose	90633
	Hep B, adult	90746
	Hep B, adult, 2 dose	90739
	Hep B, ped/adol 3 dose	90744
	Hep B-Hib	90748
	Hib, 4 dose	90645
	HPV, bivalent	90650
	HPV, quadrivalent	90649
	IPV	90713
	MMR	90707
	Pneumonia	90732
	Pneumonia conjugate, <5 y	90669
	Tdap, 7 y +	90715
	Varicella	90716

	Immunizations & Injections		Units
	Imm admin, one	90471	
	Imm admin, each add'l	90472	
	Imm admin, intranasal, one	90473	
	Imm admin, intranasal, each add'l	90474	
	Injection, ther/proph/diag	96372	
	Injection, trigger point	20552	
	Injection, joint, small	20600	
	Injection, joint, intermediate	20605	
	Injection, joint, major	20610	

ICD-10-CM Introduction

(Includes guidelines and definitions)

After having read this book, you should go through and reread the introduction of the ICD-10-CM book. You will now have a much greater understanding of the concepts and will be able to interpret and incorporate the information in this section of the ICD-10-CM book to a much greater level.

We have included a copy of that introduction here:

The ICD-10-CM is continually being revised and updated. You can search the internet for the latest version.

Introduction

INTRODUCTION

This 2015 update of the *International Classification of Diseases, 10th revision, Clinical Modification* (*ICD-10-CM*) was published by the United States Government in recognition of its responsibility to promulgate this classification throughout the United States for morbidity coding. The *International Statistical Classification of Diseases and Related Health Problems, 10th Revision* (*ICD-10*), published by the World Health Organization (WHO), is the foundation of ICD-10-CM. ICD-10 continues to be the classification used in cause-of-death coding in the United States. The ICD-10-CM is comparable with the ICD-10.

ICD-10-CM is the United States' clinical modification of the World Health Organization's ICD-10. The term clinical is used to emphasize the modification's intent: to serve as a useful tool in the area of classification of morbidity data for indexing of medical records, medical care review, and ambulatory and other medical care programs, as well as for basic health statistics. To describe the clinical picture of the patient the codes must be more precise than those needed only for statistical groupings and trend analysis.

THE ICD-9-CM COORDINATION AND MAINTENANCE COMMITTEE

Annual modifications are made to the ICD-9-CM through the ICD-9-CM Coordination and Maintenance Committee (C&M). The Committee is made up of representatives from two Federal Government agencies, the National Center for Health Statistics and the Centers for Medicare & Medicaid Services. The Committee holds meetings twice a year which are open to the public. Modification proposals submitted to the Committee for consideration are presented at the meetings for public discussion. Those modification proposals which are approved are incorporated into the official government version of the *ICD-9-CM* and become effective for use the October 1 of the year following their presentation.

Currently, The Committee is managing both the updating of the code sets ICD-9-CM and ICD-10-CM. It is assumed that The Committee will be renamed "The ICD-10-CM Coordination and Maintenance Committee."

THE ICD-9-CM TO ICD-10-CM TRANSITION

On October 1, 2015, medical coding in U.S. health care settings will change from ICD-9 to ICD-10. The transition will require business and systems changes throughout the health care industry. Everyone who is covered by the Health Insurance Portability and Accountability Act (HIPAA) must make the transition, not just those who submit Medicare or Medicaid claims.

The National Uniform Claim Committee (NUCC) has approved a transition timeline for the new version 02/12 1500 Health Insurance Claim Form (1500 Form). In June 2013, the NUCC announced the approval of the updated 1500 Form that accommodates reporting needs for ICD-10.

Official timeline:

January 6, 2014: Payers begin receiving and processing paper claims submitted on the revised 1500 Form (version 02/12).

January 6-March 31, 2014: Dual use period during which payers continue to process paper claims submitted on the old 1500 Form (version 08/05).

April 1, 2014: Payers process paper claims submitted only on the revised 1500 Form (version 02/12).

On January 1, 2012, standards for electronic health transactions changed from Version 4010/4010A1 to Version 5010. Unlike Version 4010, Version 5010 accommodates the ICD-10 code structure. This change occurs before the ICD-10 implementation date to allow adequate testing and implementation time.

These compliance dates are firm (despite the ICD-10-CM reporting delay) and not subject to change. If you are not ready, your claims will not be paid. Preparing now can help you avoid potential reimbursement issues.

BASIC STEPS TO PREPARE FOR VERSION 5010/ICD-10

Begin preparing now for the ICD-10 transition to make sure you are ready by the October 1, 2015, compliance deadline. The following quick checklist will assist you with preliminary planning steps.

- Identify your current systems and work processes that use ICD-9 codes. This could include clinical documentation, encounter forms/superbills, practice management system, electronic health record system, contracts, and public health and quality reporting protocols. It is likely that wherever ICD-9 codes now appear, ICD-10 codes will take their place.
- Talk with your practice management system vendor about accommodations for both Version 5010 and ICD-10 codes. Contact your vendor and ask what updates they are planning to your practice management system for both Version 5010 and ICD-10, and when they expect to have it ready to install. Check your contract to see if upgrades are included as part of your agreement. If you are in the process of making a practice management or related system purchase, ask if it is Version 5010 and ICD-10 ready.
- Discuss implementation plans with all your clearinghouses, billing services, and payers to ensure a smooth transition. Be proactive, don't wait. Contact your payers, clearinghouse, billing service with whom you conduct business, ask about their plans for the Version 5010 and ICD-10 compliance, and when they will be ready to test their systems for both transitions.
- Talk with your payers about how ICD-10 implementation might affect your contracts. Because ICD-10 codes are much more specific than ICD-9 codes, payers may modify terms of contracts, payment schedules, or reimbursement.
- Identify potential changes to work flow and business processes. Consider changes to existing processes including clinical documentation, encounter forms, and quality and public health reporting.
- Assess staff training needs. Identify the staff in your office who code, or have a need to know the new codes. There are a wide variety of training opportunities and materials available through professional associations, online courses, webinars, and onsite training. If you have a small practice, think about teaming up with other local providers. You might be able, for example, to provide training for a staff person from one practice, who can in turn train staff members in other practices. Coding professionals recommend that training take place approximately 6 months prior to the October 1, 2015 compliance date.
- Budget for time and costs related to ICD-10 implementation, including expenses for system changes, resource materials, and training. Assess the costs of any necessary software updates, reprinting of superbills, training and related expenses.
- Conduct test transactions using Version 5010/ICD-10 codes with your payers and clearinghouses. Testing is critical. Allow yourself enough time to first test that your Version 5010 transactions, and subsequently, claims containing ICD-10 codes are being successfully transmitted and received by your payers, clearinghouses, etc.
- If your organization still files paper claims, be sure to begin to transition to the new 1500 Form in compliance with the timeline provided on the previous page.

CHARACTERISTICS OF ICD-10-CM

ICD-10-CM far exceeds its predecessors in the number of concepts and codes provided. The disease classification has been expanded to include health-related conditions and to provide greater specificity at the sixth digit level and with a seventh digit extension. The sixth and seventh characters are not optional; they are intended for use in recording the information documented in the clinical record.

GUIDANCE IN THE USE OF ICD-10-CM

To code accurately, it is necessary to have a working knowledge of medical terminology and to understand the characteristics, terminology, and conventions of the *ICD-10-CM*. Transforming verbal descriptions of diseases, injuries, conditions, and procedures into numerical designations (coding) is a complex activity and should not be undertaken without proper training.

Originally coding was accomplished to provide access to medical records by diagnoses and operations through retrieval for medical research, education, and administration. Medical codes today are utilized to facilitate payment of health services, to evaluate utilization patterns, and to study the appropriateness of health care costs. Coding provides the bases for epidemiological studies and research into the quality of health care.

Coding must be performed correctly and consistently to produce meaningful statistics to aid in the planning for the health needs of the Nation.

Basic Steps in Coding Diagnoses/Diseases

1. Always consult Volume 2, Alphabetic Index to ICD-10-CM first.

   Locate the main entry term. The Alphabetic Index is arranged by condition. Conditions may be expressed as nouns, adjectives, and eponyms. Some conditions have multiple entries under their synonyms. Select the appropriate code. The Alphabetic Index does not always provide the full code. A dash (-) at the end of an Alphabetic Index entry indicates that additional characters are required. Even if a dash is not included at the Alphabetic Index entry, it is necessary to refer to the Tabular List to verify that no 7th character is required.

2. Refer to Volume 1 of the *ICD-10-CM,* locating the selected code. Selection of the full code, including laterality and any applicable 7th character can only be done in the Tabular List.

   Be guided by any exclusion notes or other instructions that would direct the use of a different code from that selected in the Index for a particular diagnosis, condition, or disease.

3. Read and be guided by the conventions used in the Tabular List (Volume 1, *ICD-10-CM*).

CONVENTIONS USED IN THE ICD-10-CM

The ICD-10-CM Tabular List and Alphabetic Index both make use of certain abbreviations, punctuation, and other conventions which need to be clearly understood. The conventions on the following pages apply to both the Tabular and Alphabetic sections unless otherwise stated:

Abbreviations:

NEC Not elsewhere classifiable. The category number for the term including NEC is to be used only when the coder lacks the information necessary to code the term to a more specific category. e.g.,

Z62.890 Parent-child estrangement NEC

NOS Not otherwise specified. This abbreviation is the equivalent of "unspecified." e.g.,

C7A.095 Malignant carcinoid tumor of the midgut NOS

Punctuation:

[ ] Brackets are used in the Tabular List to enclose synonyms, alternative wording or explanatory phrases. e.g,

C88.4 Extranodal marginal zone B-cell lymphoma of mucosa-associated lymphoid tissue [MALT-lymphoma]

[ ] Italicized brackets are found only in the Alphabetic Index and signify the need to submit a manifestation code secondary to the principal diagnosis. e.g,

Amyloid heart (disease) E85.4 *[I43]*

( ) Parentheses are used in both the Alphabetic Index and Tabular List to enclose supplementary words that may be present or absent in the statement of a disease or procedure without affecting the code number to which it is assigned. The terms within the parentheses are referred to as nonessential modifiers. e.g.,

A18.6 Tuberculosis of (inner) (middle) ear

: Colons are used in the Tabular List after an incomplete term which needs one or more of the modifiers following the colon to make it assignable to a given category. e.g.,

M91.0 Juvenile osteochondrosis of pelvis
Osteochondrosis (juvenile) of:
acetabulum
iliac crest [Buchanan]
ischiopubic synchondrosis [van Neck]
symphysis pubis [Pierson]

2015 Draft ICD-10-CM

Other Conventions

When the term "and" is used in a narrative statement it represents and/or.

As in the ICD-9-CM, lists of inclusion terms are included under some codes. These terms are the conditions for which that code is to be used. The terms may be synonyms of the code title, or, in the case of "other specified" codes, the terms are a list of the various conditions assigned to that code. The inclusion terms are not necessarily exhaustive.

Instructional Notations:

Includes This note appears immediately under a three character code title to further define, or give examples of, the content of the category. e.g.,

4th **V06 Pedestrian injured in collision with other nonmotor vehicle**
Includes collision with animal-drawn vehicle, animal being ridden, nonpowered streetcar

Unlike ICD-9-CM, the ICD-10-CM has two types of excludes notes. Each type of note has a different definition for use but they are all similar in that they indicate that codes excluded from each other are independent of each other.

Excludes1 A type 1 Excludes note is a pure excludes. It means 'NOT CODED HERE!' An Excludes1 note indicates that the codeexcluded should never be used at the same time as the code above the Excludes1 note. An Excludes1 is used when twoconditions cannot occur together, such as a congenital form versus an acquired form of the same condition. e.g.,

4th **M88 Osteitis deformans [Paget's disease of bone]**
Excludes1 *osteitis deformans in neoplastic disease (M90.6)*

Excludes2 A type 2 excludes note represents 'Not included here'. An excludes2 note indicates that the condition excluded is not part ofthe condition it is excluded from but a patient may have both conditions at the same time. When an Excludes2 note appearsunder a code it is acceptable to use both the code and the excluded code together. e.g.,

5th **S60.2 Contusion of wrist and hand**
Excludes2 *contusion of fingers (S60.0-, S60.1-)*

Code First/Use Additional Code notes (etiology/manifestation paired codes):

Certain conditions have both an underlying etiology and multiple body system manifestations due to the underlying etiology.

For such conditions the ICD-10-CM has a coding convention that requires the underlying condition be sequenced firstfollowed by the manifestation. Wherever such a combination exists there is a 'use additional code' note at the etiology code, and a 'code first' note at the manifestation code. These instructional notes indicate the proper sequencing order of thecodes, etiology followed by manifestation. e.g.,

I09.81 Rheumatic heart failure
Use additional code to identify type of heart failure (I50.-)

In most cases the manifestation codes will have in the code title, 'in diseases classified elsewhere.' Codes with this title area component of the etiology/manifestation convention. The code title indicates that it is a manifestation code. 'In diseases classified elsewhere' codes are never permitted to be used as first listed or principal diagnosis codes. They must be used inconjunction with an underlying condition code and they must be listed following the underlying condition. e.g.,

D77 ***Other disorders of blood and blood-forming organs in diseases classified elsewhere***
Code first underlying disease, such as:
amyloidosis (E85-)
congenital early syphilis (A50.0)
echinococcosis (B67.0-B67.9)
malaria (B50.0-B54)
schistosomiasis [bilharziasis] (B65.0-B65.9)
vitamin C deficiency (E54)

Value-Added Conventions

Several additional conventions to facilitate correct coding selection have been included:

Update Conventions:

● In the Tabular List, a bullet denotes a new category, subcategory or code. In other sections, the bullet denotes a completely new line of text. e.g.,

● I26.02 Saddle embolus of pulmonary artery with acute cor pulmonale

▲ In the Tabular List, a delta denotes a revised category, subcategory or code. In other sections, the delta denotes a revised line of text. e.g.,

▲ 6th T20.56 Corrosion of first degree of forehead and cheek

Additional Character Specificity Needed:

In both the Tabular List, the following symbols alert the user to the need for a more specific code:

4th Denotes the need for 4th character specificity. e.g.,

4th M10 Gout

5th Denotes the need for 5th character specificity. e.g.,

5th T36.6 Poisoning by, adverse effect of and underdosing of rifampicins

6th Denotes the need for 6th character specificity. e.g.,

6th E10.61 Type 1 diabetes mellitus with diabetic arthropathy

7th Denotes the need for 7th character specificity. e.g.,

7th Y35.411 Legal intervention involving bayonet, law enforcement official injured

Medicare Sex Conflict Edits:

Medicare Outpatient Code Editor detects inconsistencies between a patient's sex and any diagnosis or procedure on the patient's record (e.g., a male patient with cervical cancer). MMHSI flags codes to which these edits apply using color-coded gender symbols:

♀ Female only diagnosis e.g.,

C58 Malignant neoplasm of placenta ♀

♂ Male only diagnosis e.g.,

N42.83 Cyst of prostate ♂

Red text In the Tabular List, some categories and subcategories have common 4th, 5th, 6th or 7th digits for all subsets. To save space, these common description suffixes are often printed once in red text at the beginning of that section, rather than repeated a number of times. Oftentimes, this red text begins with additional placeholder characters required guidance. Anytime e.g.,

7th 6th digit character "X" must be used for each code from subcategories S50.0 and S50.1.

The appropriate 7th character is to be added to each code from category S50

A initial encounter
D subsequent encounter
S sequela

Diagnosis Code-Specific Color Highlights:

Code Manifestation codes are backed by blue highlights and describe the manifestation of an underlying disease, not the disease. Do not use them as principal diagnoses. e.g.,

D63.0 *Anemia in neoplastic disease*

Code "Other specified" (NEC) codes are backed by green highlighting and are catch-all codes that represent specific disease entities for which no specific code exists. e.g.,

7th S72.091 Other fracture of head and neck of right femur

Code "Unspecified" (NOS) codes are backed by gold highlighting and should only be used when it is not possible to assign a more specific code as they can result in denied claims or requests for additional documentation. For those categories for which an unspecified code is not provided, the "other specified" code may represent both other and unspecified. e.g.,

T80.90 Unspecified complication following infusion and therapeutic injection

Secondary Only Diagnosis Edits:

Certain codes may not be used as first listed (principal) codes, rather only as secondary codes. All codes (with the exception of manifestation codes) without a maroon flag can be used as either a first listed or secondary code, depending on the circumstances of the encounter.

2 Secondary Diagnosis only. e.g.,

Z86.010 Personal history of colonic polyps 2

2015 Draft ICD-10-CM

Medicare Age Conflict Edits:

The Medicare Outpatient Code Editor detects inconsistencies between a patient's age and any diagnosis on the patient's record. For example, a five-year-old patient with benign prostatic hypertrophy. Affected codes are flagged using orange symbols:

N Newborn - Age of 0 years; a subset of diagnoses intended only for newborns and neonates. e.g.,

P25.1 Pneumothorax originating in the perinatal period N

P Pediatric - Age range is 0–17 years inclusive. e.g.,

C93.32 Juvenile myelomonocytic leukemia, in relapse P

M Maternity - Age range is 12–55 years inclusive. e.g.,

O47.9 False labor, unspecified M ♀

A Adult - Age range is 15–124 years inclusive. e.g.,

I23.7 Postinfarction angina A

ICD-10-CM to ICD-9-CM Crosswalks:

To facilitate the trasition from the ICD-9-CM code set to ICD-10-CM, the top 500 utilized ICD-9-CM diagnosis codes have been crosswalked to their ICD-10-CM "equivalents." Crosswalked ICD-9-CM diagnosis codes are shown beneath their ICD-10-CM "equivalents" in white text on a salmon-colored background.

Because not all relationships between ICD-10-CM codes and the codes they replace in ICD-9-CM are either exact or one-to-one, there are symbols that precede the ICD-9-CM codes listed that provide insight into the nature of these relationships:

≈ Approximate. The complete meaning of the ICD-9-CM code and that of the ICD-10-CM code are not considered equivalent, but rather the closest possible match(es) between ICD-9-CM and ICD-10-CM. e.g.,

R20.0 Anesthesia of skin

≈ 782.0 Disturbance of skin sensation

= Equivalent. The complete meaning of the ICD-9-CM code and ICD-10-CM code are considered equivalent and they translate only to each other (i.e., one-to-one exact match). e.g.,

R91 Abnormal findings on diagnostic imaging of lung

= 793.91 Nonspecific (abnormal) findings on radiological and other examination of lung field

+ Combination. The complete meaning of the ICD-10-CM code is best equated to a combination of ICD-9-CM codes. The parenthetical note following the description of each listed ICD-9-CM code provides the additional ICD-9-CM codes that, when combined with the ICD-9-CM code shown, best represents the complete meaning of the single ICD-10-CM code. e.g.,

E08.52 ***Diabetes mellitus due to underlying condition with diabetic peripheral angiopathy with gangrene***

+ 251.8 Other specified disorders of pancreatic internal secretion (443.89, 785.4)

+ 443.89 Other specified peripheral vascular disease (251.8, 785.4)

+ 785.4 Gangrene (251.8, 443.89)

− Component. Multiple ICD-10-CM codes must be reported to equate to the single ICD-9-CM code they are replacing. The parenthetical note following the description of each listed ICD-9-CM code provides the additional ICD-10-CM codes that, when combined with the ICD-10-CM code listed, best represents the complete meaning of the single ICD-9-CM code. e.g.,

E08.52 ***Diabetes mellitus due to underlying condition with diabetic peripheral angiopathy with gangrene***

+ 251.8 Other specified disorders of pancreatic internal secretion (443.89, 785.4)

+ 443.89 Other specified peripheral vascular disease (251.8, 785.4)

+ 785.4 Gangrene (251.8, 443.89)

Lay Descriptions:

Plain-English descriptions highlight critical differences between similar codes. e.g.,

E78.0 Pure hypercholesterolemia

Layman's: *Raised total cholesterol, exhibiting significantly high LDL, but HDL and triglycerides at normal levels.*

ICD-10-CM Official Guidelines for Coding and Reporting

The Centers for Medicare and Medicaid Services (CMS) and the National Center for Health Statistics (NCHS), two departments within the U.S. Federal Government's Department of Health and Human Services (DHHS) provide the following guidelines for coding and reporting using the International Classification of Diseases, 10th Revision, Clinical Modification (ICD-10-CM). These guidelines should be used as a companion document to the official version of the ICD-10CM as published on the NCHS website. The ICD-10-CM is a morbidity classification published by the United States for classifying diagnoses and reason for visits in all health care settings. The ICD-10-CM is based on the ICD-10, the statistical classification of disease published by the World Health Organization (WHO).

These guidelines have been approved by the four organizations that make up the Cooperating Parties for the ICD-10-CM: the American Hospital Association (AHA), the American Health Information Management Association (AHIMA), CMS, and NCHS.

These guidelines are a set of rules that have been developed to accompany and complement the official conventions and instructions provided within the ICD-10-CM itself. The instructions and conventions of the classification take precedence over guidelines. These guidelines are based on the coding and sequencing instructions in the Tabular List and Alphabetic Index of ICD-10-CM, but provide additional instruction. Adherence to these guidelines when assigning ICD-10-CM diagnosis codes is required under the Health Insurance Portability and Accountability Act (HIPAA). The diagnosis codes (Tabular List and Alphabetic Index) have been adopted under HIPAA for all healthcare settings. A joint effort between the healthcare provider and the coder is essential to achieve complete and accurate documentation, code assignment, and reporting of diagnoses and procedures. These guidelines have been developed to assist both the healthcare provider and the coder in identifying those diagnoses and procedures that are to be reported. The importance of consistent, complete documentation in the medical record cannot be overemphasized. Without such documentation accurate coding cannot be achieved. The entire record should be reviewed to determine the specific reason for the encounter and the conditions treated.

The term encounter is used for all settings, including hospital admissions. In the context of these guidelines, the term provider is used throughout the guidelines to mean physician or any qualified health care practitioner who is legally accountable for establishing the patient's diagnosis. Only this set of guidelines, approved by the Cooperating Parties, is official.

The guidelines are organized into sections. Section I includes the structure and conventions of the classification and general guidelines that apply to the entire classification, and chapter-specific guidelines that correspond to the chapters as they are arranged in the classification. Section II includes guidelines for selection of principal diagnosis for non-outpatient settings. Section III includes guidelines for reporting additional diagnoses in non-outpatient settings. Section IV is for outpatient coding and reporting. It is necessary to review all sections of the guidelines to fully understand all of the rules and instructions needed to code properly.

Section I. Conventions, general coding guidelines and chapter specific guidelines

The conventions, general guidelines and chapter-specific guidelines are applicable to all health care settings unless otherwise indicated. The conventions and instructions of the classification take precedence over guidelines.

A. Conventions for the ICD-10-CM

The conventions for the ICD-10-CM are the general rules for use of the classification independent of the guidelines. These conventions are incorporated within the Alphabetic Index and Tabular List of the ICD-10-CM as instructional notes.

1. **The Alphabetic Index and Tabular List**
The ICD-10-CM is divided into the Alphabetic Index, an alphabetical list of terms and their corresponding code, and the Tabular List, a structured list of codes divided into chapters based on body system or condition. The Alphabetic Index consists of the following parts: the Index of Diseases and Injury, the Index of External Causes of Injury, the Table of Neoplasms and the Table of Drugs and Chemicals.
See Section I.C2. General guidelines
See Section I.C.19. Adverse effects, poisoning, underdosing and toxic effects

2. **Format and Structure:**
The ICD-10-CM Tabular List contains categories, subcategories and codes. Characters for categories, subcategories and codes may be either a letter or a number. All categories are 3 characters. A three-character category that has no further subdivision is equivalent to a code. Subcategories are either 4 or 5 characters. Codes may be 3, 4, 5, 6 or 7 characters. That is, each level of subdivision after a category is a subcategory. The final level of subdivision is a code. Codes that have applicable 7th characters are still referred to as codes, not subcategories. A code that has an applicable 7th character is considered invalid without the 7th character.
The ICD-10-CM uses an indented format for ease in reference.

3. **Use of codes for reporting purposes**
For reporting purposes only codes are permissible, not categories or subcategories, and any applicable 7th character is required.

4. **Placeholder character**
The ICD-10-CM utilizes a placeholder character "X". The "X" is used as a placeholder at certain codes to allow for future expansion. An example of this is at the poisoning, adverse effect and underdosing codes, categories T36-T50.
Where a placeholder exists, the X must be used in order for the code to be considered a valid code.

5. **7th Characters**
Certain ICD-10-CM categories have applicable 7th characters. The applicable 7th character is required for all codes within the category, or as the notes in the Tabular List instruct. The 7th character must always be the 7th character in the data field. If a code that requires a 7th character is not 6 characters, a placeholder X must be used to fill in the empty characters.

6. **Abbreviations**

a. Alphabetic Index abbreviations

NEC "Not elsewhere classifiable" This abbreviation in the Alphabetic Index represents "other specified". When a specific code is not available for a condition, the Alphabetic Index directs the coder to the "other specified" code in the Tabular List.

NOS "Not otherwise specified" This abbreviation is the equivalent of unspecified.

b. Tabular List abbreviations

NEC "Not elsewhere classifiable" This abbreviation in the Tabular List represents "other specified". When a specific code is not available for a condition the Tabular List includes an NEC entry under a code to identify the code as the "other specified" code.

NOS "Not otherwise specified" This abbreviation is the equivalent of unspecified.

7. **Punctuation**

[ ] Brackets are used in the Tabular List to enclose synonyms, alternative wording or explanatory phrases. Brackets are used in the Alphabetic Index to identify manifestation codes.

( ) Parentheses are used in both the Alphabetic Index and Tabular List to enclose supplementary words that may be present or absent in the statement of a disease or procedure without affecting the code number to which it is assigned. The terms within the parentheses are referred to as nonessential modifiers. The nonessential modifiers in the Alphabetic Index to Diseases apply to subterms following a main term except when a nonessential modifier and a subentry are mutually exclusive, the subentry takes precedence. For example, in the ICD-10-CM Alphabetic Index under the main term Enteritis, "acute" is a nonessential modifier and "chronic" is a subentry. In this case, the nonessential modifier "acute" does not apply to the subentry "chronic".

: Colons are used in the Tabular List after an incomplete term which needs one or more of the modifiers following the colon to make it assignable to a given category.

8. **Use of "and"**
See Section I.A.14. Use of the term "And"

9. **Other and Unspecified codes**

a. "Other" codes
Codes titled "other" or "other specified" are for use when the information in the medical record provides detail for which a specific code does not exist. Alphabetic Index entries with NEC in the line designate "other" codes in the Tabular List. These Alphabetic Index entries represent specific disease entities for which no specific code exists so the term is included within an "other" code.

b. **"Unspecified" codes**
Codes titled "unspecified" are for use when the information in the medical record is insufficient to assign a more specific code. For those categories for which an unspecified code is not provided, the "other specified" code may represent both other and unspecified.
See Section I.B.18 Use of Signs/Symptom/ Unspecified Codes

10. **Includes Notes**
This note appears immediately under a three character code title to further define, or give examples of, the content of the category.

11. **Inclusion terms**
List of terms is included under some codes. These terms are the conditions for which that code is to be used. The terms may be synonyms of the code title, or, in the case of "other specified" codes, the terms are a list of the various conditions assigned to that code. The inclusion terms are not necessarily exhaustive. Additional terms found only in the Alphabetic Index may also be assigned to a code.

12. **Excludes Notes**
The ICD-10-CM has two types of excludes notes. Each type of note has a different definition for use but they are all similar in that they indicate that codes excluded from each other are independent of each other.
   a. Excludes1
   A type 1 Excludes note is a pure excludes note. It means "NOT CODED HERE!" An Excludes1 note indicates that the code excluded should never be used at the same time as the code above the Excludes1 note. An Excludes1 is used when two conditions cannot occur together, such as a congenital form versus an acquired form of the same condition.
   b. Excludes2
   A type 2 Excludes note represents "Not included here". An Excludes2 note indicates that the condition excluded is not part of the condition represented by the code, but a patient may have both conditions at the same time. When an Excludes2 note appears under a code, it is acceptable to use both the code and the excluded code together, when appropriate.

13. **Etiology/manifestation convention ("code first", "use additional code" and "in diseases classified elsewhere" notes)**
Certain conditions have both an underlying etiology and multiple body system manifestations due to the underlying etiology. For such conditions, the ICD-10-CM has a coding convention that requires the underlying condition be sequenced first followed by the manifestation. Wherever such a combination exists, there is a "use additional code" note at the etiology code, and a "code first" note at the manifestation code. These instructional notes indicate the proper sequencing order of the codes, etiology followed by manifestation.
In most cases the manifestation codes will have in the code title, "in diseases classified elsewhere." Codes with this title are a component of the etiology/ manifestation convention. The code title indicates that it is a manifestation code. "In diseases classified elsewhere" codes are never permitted to be used as first-listed or principal diagnosis codes. They must be used in conjunction with an underlying condition code and they must be listed following the underlying condition. See category F02, Dementia in other diseases classified elsewhere, for an example of this convention.
There are manifestation codes that do not have "in diseases classified elsewhere" in the title. For such codes, there is a "use additional code" note at the etiology code and a "code first" note at the manifestation code and the rules for sequencing apply.
In addition to the notes in the Tabular List, these conditions also have a specific Alphabetic Index entry structure. In the Alphabetic Index both conditions are listed together with the etiology code first followed by the manifestation codes in brackets. The code in brackets is always to be sequenced second.
An example of the etiology/manifestation convention is dementia in Parkinson's disease. In the Alphabetic Index, code G20 is listed first, followed by code F02.80 or F02.81 in brackets. Code G20 represents the underlying etiology, Parkinson's disease, and must be sequenced first, whereas codes F02.80 and F02.81 represent the manifestation of dementia in diseases classified elsewhere, with or without behavioral disturbance.
"Code first" and "Use additional code" notes are also used as sequencing rules in the classification for certain codes that are not part of an etiology/ manifestation combination.
See Section I.B.7. Multiple coding for a single condition.

14. **"And"**
The word "and" should be interpreted to mean either "and" or "or" when it appears in a title.
For example, cases of "tuberculosis of bones", "tuberculosis of joints" and "tuberculosis of bones and joints" are classified to subcategory A18.0, Tuberculosis of bones and joints.

15. **"With"**
The word "with" should be interpreted to mean "associated with" or "due to" when it appears in a code title, the Alphabetic Index, or an instructional note in the Tabular List.
The word "with" in the Alphabetic Index is sequenced immediately following the main term, not in alphabetical order.

16. **"See" and "See Also"**
The "see" instruction following a main term in the Alphabetic Index indicates that another term should be referenced. It is necessary to go to the main term referenced with the "see" note to locate the correct code.
A "see also" instruction following a main term in the Alphabetic Index instructs that there is another main term that may also be referenced that may provide additional Alphabetic Index entries that may be useful. It is not necessary to follow the "see also" note when the original main term provides the necessary code.

17. **"Code also note"**
A "code also" note instructs that two codes may be required to fully describe a condition, but this note does not provide sequencing direction.

18. **Default codes**
A code listed next to a main term in the ICD-10-CM Alphabetic Index is referred to as a default code. The default code represents that condition that is most commonly associated with the main term, or is the unspecified code for the condition. If a condition is documented in a medical record (for example, appendicitis) without any additional information, such as acute or chronic, the default code should be assigned.

19. **Syndromes**
Follow the Alphabetic Index guidance when coding syndromes. In the absence of Alphabetic Index guidance, assign codes for the documented manifestations of the syndrome.

B. General Coding Guidelines

1. **Locating a code in the ICD-10-CM**
To select a code in the classification that corresponds to a diagnosis or reason for visit documented in a medical record, first locate the term in the Alphabetic Index, and then verify the code in the Tabular List. Read and be guided by instructional notations that appear in both the Alphabetic Index and the Tabular List.
It is essential to use both the Alphabetic Index and Tabular List when locating and assigning a code. The Alphabetic Index does not always provide the full code. Selection of the full code, including laterality and any applicable 7th character can only be done in the Tabular List. A dash (-) at the end of an Alphabetic Index entry indicates that additional characters are required. Even if a dash is not included at the Alphabetic Index entry, it is necessary to refer to the Tabular List to verify that no 7th character is required.

2. **Level of Detail in Coding**
Diagnosis codes are to be used and reported at their highest number of characters available.
ICD-10-CM diagnosis codes are composed of codes with 3, 4, 5, 6 or 7 characters. Codes with three characters are included in ICD-10-CM as the heading of a category of codes that may be further subdivided by the use of fourth and/or fifth characters and/or sixth characters, which provide greater detail.
A three-character code is to be used only if it is not further subdivided. A code is invalid if it has not been coded to the full number of characters required for that code, including the 7th character, if applicable.

3. **Code or codes from A00.0 through T88.9, Z00-Z99.8**
The appropriate code or codes from A00.0 through T88.9, Z00-Z99.8 must be used to identify diagnoses, symptoms, conditions, problems, complaints or other reason(s) for the encounter/visit.

4. **Signs and symptoms**
Codes that describe symptoms and signs, as opposed to diagnoses, are acceptable for reporting purposes when a related

definitive diagnosis has not been established (confirmed) by the provider. Chapter 18 of ICD-10-CM, Symptoms, Signs, and Abnormal Clinical and Laboratory Findings, Not Elsewhere Classified (codes R00.0 -R99) contains many, but not all codes for symptoms.

See Section I.B.18 Use of Signs/Symptom/ Unspecified Codes

5. **Conditions that are an integral part of a disease process**

Signs and symptoms that are associated routinely with a disease process should not be assigned as additional codes, unless otherwise instructed by the classification.

6. **Conditions that are not an integral part of a disease process**

Additional signs and symptoms that may not be associated routinely with a disease process should be coded when present.

7. **Multiple coding for a single condition**

In addition to the etiology/manifestation convention that requires two codes to fully describe a single condition that affects multiple body systems, there are other single conditions that also require more than one code. "Use additional code" notes are found in the Tabular List at codes that are not part of an etiology/manifestation pair where a secondary code is useful to fully describe a condition. The sequencing rule is the same as the etiology/manifestation pair, "use additional code" indicates that a secondary code should be added.

For example, for bacterial infections that are not included in chapter 1, a secondary code from category B95, Streptococcus, Staphylococcus, and Enterococcus, as the cause of diseases classified elsewhere, or B96, Other bacterial agents as the cause of diseases classified elsewhere, may be required to identify the bacterial organism causing the infection. A "use additional code" note will normally be found at the infectious disease code, indicating a need for the organism code to be added as a secondary code.

"Code first" notes are also under certain codes that are not specifically manifestation codes but may be due to an underlying cause. When there is a "code first" note and an underlying condition is present, the underlying condition should be sequenced first.

"Code, if applicable, any causal condition first", notes indicate that this code may be assigned as a principal diagnosis when the causal condition is unknown or not applicable. If a causal condition is known, then the code for that condition should be sequenced as the principal or first-listed diagnosis.

Multiple codes may be needed for sequela, complication codes and obstetric codes to more fully describe a condition. See the specific guidelines for these conditions for further instruction.

8. **Acute and Chronic Conditions**

If the same condition is described as both acute (subacute) and chronic, and separate subentries exist in the Alphabetic Index at the same indentation level, code both and sequence the acute (subacute) code first.

9. **Combination Code**

A combination code is a single code used to classify:

- Two diagnoses, or
- A diagnosis with an associated secondary process (manifestation)
- A diagnosis with an associated complication

Combination codes are identified by referring to subterm entries in the Alphabetic Index and by reading the inclusion and exclusion notes in the Tabular List.

Assign only the combination code when that code fully identifies the diagnostic conditions involved or when the Alphabetic Index so directs. Multiple coding should not be used when the classification provides a combination code that clearly identifies all of the elements documented in the diagnosis. When the combination code lacks necessary specificity in describing the manifestation or complication, an additional code should be used as a secondary code.

10. **Sequela (Late Effects)**

A sequela is the residual effect (condition produced) after the acute phase of an illness or injury has terminated. There is no time limit on when a sequela code can be used. The residual may be apparent early, such as in cerebral infarction, or it may occur months or years later, such as that due to a previous injury. Coding of sequela generally requires two codes sequenced in the following order: The condition or nature of the sequela is sequenced first. The sequela code is sequenced second.

An exception to the above guidelines are those instances where the code for the sequela is followed by a manifestation code identified in the Tabular List and title, or the sequela code has been expanded (at the fourth, fifth or sixth character levels) to include the manifestation(s). The code for the acute phase of an illness or injury that led to the sequela is never used with a code for the late effect.

See Section I.C.9. Sequelae of cerebrovascular disease See Section I.C.15. Sequelae of complication of pregnancy, childbirth and the puerperium See Section I.C.19. Application of 7th characters for Chapter 19

11. **Impending or Threatened Condition**

Code any condition described at the time of discharge as "impending" or "threatened" as follows:

- If it did occur, code as confirmed diagnosis.
- If it did not occur, reference the Alphabetic Index to determine if the condition has a subentry term for "impending" or "threatened" and also reference main term entries for "Impending" and for "Threatened."
- If the subterms are listed, assign the given code.
- If the subterms are not listed, code the existing underlying condition(s) and not the condition described as impending or threatened.

12. **Reporting Same Diagnosis Code More than Once**

Each unique ICD-10-CM diagnosis code may be reported only once for an encounter. This applies to bilateral conditions when there are no distinct codes identifying laterality or two different conditions classified to the same ICD-10-CM diagnosis code.

13. **Laterality**

Some ICD-10-CM codes indicate laterality, specifying whether the condition occurs on the left, right or is bilateral. If no bilateral code is provided and the condition is bilateral, assign separate codes for both the left and right side. If the side is not identified in the medical record, assign the code for the unspecified side.

14. **Documentation for BMI, Non-Pressure Ulcers and Pressure Ulcer Stages**

For the Body Mass Index (BMI), depth of non-pressure chronic ulcers and pressure ulcer stage codes, code assignment may be based on medical record documentation from clinicians who are not the patient's provider (i.e., physician or other qualified healthcare practitioner legally accountable for establishing the patient's diagnosis), since this information is typically documented by other clinicians involved in the care of the patient (e.g., a dietitian often documents the BMI and nurses often documents the pressure ulcer stages). However, the associated diagnosis (such as overweight, obesity, or pressure ulcer) must be documented by the patient's provider. If there is conflicting medical record documentation, either from the same clinician or different clinicians, the patient's attending provider should be queried for clarification.

The BMI codes should only be reported as secondary diagnoses. As with all other secondary diagnosis codes, the BMI codes should only be assigned when they meet the definition of a reportable additional diagnosis (*see Section III, Reporting Additional Diagnoses*).

15. **Syndromes**

Follow the Alphabetic Index guidance when coding syndromes. In the absence of Alphabetic Index guidance, assign codes for the documented manifestations of the syndrome. Additional codes for manifestations that are not an integral part of the disease process may also be assigned when the condition does not have a unique code.

16. **Documentation of Complications of Care**

Code assignment is based on the provider's documentation of the relationship between the condition and the care or procedure. The guideline extends to any complications of care, regardless of the chapter the code is located in. It is important to note that not all conditions that occur during or following medical care or surgery are classified as complications. There must be a cause-and-effect relationship between the care provided and the condition, and an indication in the documentation that it is a complication. Query the provider for clarification, if the complication is not clearly documented.

17. **Borderline Diagnosis**

If the provider documents a "borderline" diagnosis at the time of discharge, the diagnosis is coded as confirmed, unless the

2015 Draft ICD-10-CM

classification provides a specific entry (e.g., borderline diabetes). If a borderline condition has a specific index entry in ICD-10-CM, it should be coded as such. Since borderline conditions are not uncertain diagnoses, no distinction is made between the care setting (inpatient versus outpatient). Whenever the documentation is unclear regarding a borderline condition, coders are encouraged to query for clarification.

18. Use of Sign/Symptom/Unspecified Codes

Sign/symptom and "unspecified" codes have acceptable, even necessary, uses. While specific diagnosis codes should be reported when they are supported by the available medical record documentation and clinical knowledge of the patient's health condition, there are instances when signs/symptoms or unspecified codes are the best choices for accurately reflecting the healthcare encounter. Each healthcare encounter should be coded to the level of certainty known for that encounter.

If a definitive diagnosis has not been established by the end of the encounter, it is appropriate to report codes for sign(s) and/or symptom(s) in lieu of a definitive diagnosis. When sufficient clinical information isn't known or available about a particular health condition to assign a more specific code, it is acceptable to report the appropriate "unspecified" code (e.g., a diagnosis of pneumonia has been determined, but not the specific type). Unspecified codes should be reported when they are the codes that most accurately reflects what is known about the patient's condition at the time of that particular encounter. It would be inappropriate to select a specific code that is not supported by the medical record documentation or conduct medically unnecessary diagnostic testing in order to determine a more specific code.

C. Chapter-Specific Coding Guidelines

In addition to general coding guidelines, there are guidelines for specific diagnoses and/or conditions in the classification. Unless otherwise indicated, these guidelines apply to all health care settings. Please refer to Section II for guidelines on the selection of principal diagnosis.

1. Chapter 1: Certain Infectious and Parasitic Diseases (A00-B99)

a. Human Immunodeficiency Virus (HIV) Infections

1) Code only confirmed cases

Code only confirmed cases of HIV infection/illness. This is an exception to the hospital inpatient guideline Section II, H.

In this context, "confirmation" does not require documentation of positive serology or culture for HIV; the provider's diagnostic statement that the patient is HIV positive, or has an HIV-related illness is sufficient.

2) Selection and sequencing of HIV codes

(a) Patient admitted for HIV-related condition

If a patient is admitted for an HIV-related condition, the principal diagnosis should be B20, Human immunodeficiency virus [HIV] disease, followed by additional diagnosis codes for all reported HIV-related conditions.

(b) Patient with HIV disease admitted for unrelated condition

If a patient with HIV disease is admitted for an unrelated condition (such as a traumatic injury), the code for the unrelated condition (e.g., the nature of injury code) should be the principal diagnosis. Other diagnoses would be B20 followed by additional diagnosis codes for all reported HIV-related conditions.

(c) Whether the patient is newly diagnosed

Whether the patient is newly diagnosed or has had previous admissions/encounters for HIV conditions is irrelevant to the sequencing decision.

(d) Asymptomatic human immunodeficiency virus

Z21, Asymptomatic human immunodeficiency virus [HIV] infection status, is to be applied when the patient without any documentation of symptoms is listed as being "HIV positive," "known HIV," "HIV test positive," or similar terminology. Do not use this code if the term "AIDS" is used or if the patient is treated for any HIV-related illness or is described as having any condition(s) resulting from his/her HIV positive status; use B20 in these cases.

(e) Patients with inconclusive HIV serology Patients with inconclusive HIV serology, but no definitive diagnosis or manifestations of the illness, may be assigned code R75, Inconclusive laboratory evidence of human immunodeficiency virus [HIV].

(f) Previously diagnosed HIV-related illness

Patients with any known prior diagnosis of an HIV-related illness should be coded to B20. Once a patient has developed an HIV-related illness, the patient should always be assigned code B20 on every subsequent admission/encounter. Patients previously diagnosed with any HIV illness (B20) should never be assigned to R75 or Z21, Asymptomatic human immunodeficiency virus [HIV] infection status.

(g) HIV Infection in Pregnancy, Childbirth and the Puerperium

During pregnancy, childbirth or the puerperium, a patient admitted (or presenting for a health care encounter) because of an HIV-related illness should receive a principal diagnosis code of O98.7-, Human immunodeficiency [HIV] disease complicating pregnancy, childbirth and the puerperium, followed by B20 and the code(s) for the HIV-related illness(es). Codes from Chapter 15 always take sequencing priority.

Patients with asymptomatic HIV infection status admitted (or presenting for a health care encounter) during pregnancy, childbirth, or the puerperium should receive codes of O98.7- and Z21.

(h) Encounters for testing for HIV

If a patient is being seen to determine his/her HIV status, use code Z11.4, Encounter for screening for human immunodeficiency virus [HIV]. Use additional codes for any associated high risk behavior.

If a patient with signs or symptoms is being seen for HIV testing, code the signs and symptoms. An additional counseling code Z71.7, Human immunodeficiency virus [HIV] counseling, may be used if counseling is provided during the encounter for the test.

When a patient returns to be informed of his/her HIV test results and the test result is negative, use code Z71.7, Human immunodeficiency virus [HIV] counseling.

If the results are positive, see previous guidelines and assign codes as appropriate.

b. Infectious agents as the cause of diseases classified to other chapters

Certain infections are classified in chapters other than Chapter 1 and no organism is identified as part of the infection code. In these instances, it is necessary to use an additional code from Chapter 1 to identify the organism. A code from category B95, Streptococcus, Staphylococcus, and Enterococcus as the cause of diseases classified to other chapters, B96, Other bacterial agents as the cause of diseases classified to other chapters, or B97, Viral agents as the cause of diseases classified to other chapters, is to be used as an additional code to identify the organism. An instructional note will be found at the infection code advising that an additional organism code is required.

c. Infections resistant to antibiotics

Many bacterial infections are resistant to current antibiotics. It is necessary to identify all infections documented as antibiotic resistant. Assign a code from category Z16, Resistance to antimicrobial drugs, following the infection code only if the infection code does not identify drug resistance.

d. Sepsis, Severe Sepsis, and Septic Shock

1) Coding of Sepsis and Severe Sepsis

(a) Sepsis

For a diagnosis of sepsis, assign the appropriate code for the underlying systemic infection. If the type of infection or causal organism is not further specified, assign code A41.9, Sepsis, unspecified organism.

A code from subcategory R65.2, Severe sepsis, should not be assigned unless severe sepsis or an associated acute organ dysfunction is documented.

(i) Negative or inconclusive blood cultures and sepsis

Negative or inconclusive blood cultures do not preclude a diagnosis of sepsis in patients with clinical evidence of the condition, however, the provider should be queried.

(ii) Urosepsis

The term urosepsis is a nonspecific term. It is not to be considered synonymous with sepsis. It has no default code in the Alphabetic Index.

Should a provider use this term, he/she must be queried for clarification.

(iii) Sepsis with organ dysfunction

If a patient has sepsis and associated acute organ dysfunction or multiple organ dysfunction (MOD), follow the instructions for coding severe sepsis.

(iv) Acute organ dysfunction that is not clearly associated with the sepsis

If a patient has sepsis and an acute organ dysfunction, but the medical record documentation indicates that the acute organ dysfunction is related to a medical condition other than the sepsis, do not assign a code from subcategory R65.2, Severe sepsis. An acute organ dysfunction must be associated with the sepsis in order to assign the severe sepsis code. If the documentation is not clear as to whether an acute organ dysfunction is related to the sepsis or another medical condition, query the provider.

(b) Severe sepsis

The coding of severe sepsis requires a minimum of 2 codes: first a code for the underlying systemic infection, followed by a code from subcategory R65.2, Severe sepsis. If the causal organism is not documented, assign code A41.9, Sepsis, unspecified organism, for the infection. Additional code(s) for the associated acute organ dysfunction are also required.

Due to the complex nature of severe sepsis, some cases may require querying the provider prior to assignment of the codes.

2) Septic shock

Septic shock generally refers to circulatory failure associated with severe sepsis, and therefore, it represents a type of acute organ dysfunction. For all cases of septic shock, the code for the underlying systemic infection should be sequenced first, followed by code R65.21, Severe sepsis with septic shock or code T81.12, Postprocedural septic shock. Any additional codes for the other acute organ dysfunctions should also be assigned. As noted in the sequencing instructions in the Tabular List, the code for septic shock cannot be assigned as a principal diagnosis.

Septic shock indicates the presence of severe sepsis. Code R65.21, Severe sepsis with septic shock, must be assigned if septic shock is documented in the medical record, even if the term severe sepsis is not documented.

3) Sequencing of severe sepsis

If severe sepsis is present on admission, and meets the definition of principal diagnosis, the underlying systemic infection should be assigned as principal diagnosis followed by the appropriate code from subcategory R65.2 as required by the sequencing rules in the Tabular List. A code from subcategory R65.2 can never be assigned as a principal diagnosis.

When severe sepsis develops during an encounter (it was not present on admission) the underlying systemic infection and the appropriate code from subcategory R65.2 should be assigned as secondary diagnoses.

Severe sepsis may be present on admission but the diagnosis may not be confirmed until sometime after admission. If the documentation is not clear whether severe sepsis was present on admission, the provider should be queried.

4) Sepsis and severe sepsis with a localized infection

If the reason for admission is both sepsis or severe sepsis and a localized infection, such as pneumonia or cellulitis, a code(s) for the underlying systemic infection should be assigned first and the code for the localized infection should be assigned as a secondary diagnosis. If the patient has severe sepsis, a code from subcategory R65.2 should also be assigned as a secondary diagnosis. If the patient is admitted with a localized infection, such as pneumonia, and sepsis/severe sepsis doesn't develop until after admission, the localized infection should be assigned first, followed by the appropriate sepsis/severe sepsis codes.

5) Sepsis due to a postprocedural infection

(a) Documentation of causal relationship

As with all postprocedural complications, code assignment is based on the provider's documentation of the relationship between the infection and the procedure.

(b) Sepsis due to a postprocedural infection

For such cases, the postprocedural infection code, such as, T80.2, Infections following infusion, transfusion, and therapeutic injection, T81.4, Infection following a procedure, T88.0, Infection following immunization, or O86.0, Infection of obstetric surgical wound, should be coded first, followed by the code for the specific infection. If the patient has severe sepsis the appropriate code from subcategory R65.2 should also be assigned with the additional code(s) for any acute organ dysfunction.

(c) Postprocedural infection and postprocedural septic shock

In cases where a postprocedural infection has occurred and has resulted in severe sepsis and postprocedural septic shock, the code for the precipitating complication such as code T81.4, Infection following a procedure, or O86.0, Infection of obstetrical surgical wound should be coded first followed by code R65.21, Severe sepsis with septic shock and a code for the systemic infection.

6) Sepsis and severe sepsis associated with a noninfectious process (condition)

In some cases a noninfectious process (condition), such as trauma, may lead to an infection which can result in sepsis or severe sepsis. If sepsis or severe sepsis is documented as associated with a noninfectious condition, such as a burn or serious injury, and this condition meets the definition for principal diagnosis, the code for the noninfectious condition should be sequenced first, followed by the code for the resulting infection. If severe sepsis, is present a code from subcategory R65.2 should also be assigned with any associated organ dysfunction(s) codes. It is not necessary to assign a code from subcategory R65.1, Systemic inflammatory response syndrome (SIRS) of non-infectious origin, for these cases.

If the infection meets the definition of principal diagnosis it should be sequenced before the non-infectious condition. When both the associated non-infectious condition and the infection meet the definition of principal diagnosis either may be assigned as principal diagnosis.

Only one code from category R65, Symptoms and signs specifically associated with systemic inflammation and infection, should be assigned. Therefore, when a non-infectious condition leads to an infection resulting in severe sepsis, assign the appropriate code from subcategory R65.2, Severe sepsis. Do not additionally assign a

2015 Draft ICD-10-CM

code from subcategory R65.1, Systemic inflammatory response syndrome (SIRS) of noninfectious origin.
See Section I.C.18. SIRS due to non-infectious process

7) Sepsis and septic shock complicating abortion, pregnancy, childbirth, and the puerperium
See Section I.C.15. Sepsis and septic shock complicating abortion, pregnancy, childbirth and the puerperium

8) Newborn sepsis
See Section I.C.16.f. Bacterial sepsis of Newborn

e. Methicillin Resistant Staphylococcus aureus (MRSA) Conditions

1) Selection and sequencing of MRSA codes

(a) Combination codes for MRSA infection
When a patient is diagnosed with an infection that is due to methicillin resistant Staphylococcus aureus (MRSA), and that infection has a combination code that includes the causal organism (e.g., sepsis, pneumonia) assign the appropriate combination code for the condition (e.g., code A41.02, Sepsis due to Methicillin resistant Staphylococcus aureus or code J15.212, Pneumonia due to Methicillin resistant Staphylococcus aureus). Do not assign code B95.62, Methicillin resistant Staphylococcus aureus infection as the cause of diseases classified elsewhere, as an additional code because the combination code includes the type of infection and the MRSA organism. Do not assign a code from subcategory Z16.11, Resistance to penicillins, as an additional diagnosis.
See Section C.1. for instructions on coding and sequencing of sepsis and severe sepsis.

(b) Other codes for MRSA infection
When there is documentation of a current infection (e.g., wound infection, stitch abscess, urinary tract infection) due to MRSA, and that infection does not have a combination code that includes the causal organism, assign the appropriate code to identify the condition along with code B95.62, Methicillin resistant Staphylococcus aureus infection as the cause of diseases classified elsewhere for the MRSA infection. Do not assign a code from subcategory Z16.11, Resistance to penicillins.

(c) Methicillin susceptible Staphylococcus aureus (MSSA) and MRSA colonization
The condition or state of being colonized or carrying MSSA or MRSA is called colonization or carriage, while an individual person is described as being colonized or being a carrier. Colonization means that MSSA or MSRA is present on or in the body without necessarily causing illness. A positive MRSA colonization test might be documented by the provider as "MRSA screen positive" or "MRSA nasal swab positive".
Assign code Z22.322, Carrier or suspected carrier of Methicillin resistant Staphylococcus aureus, for patients documented as having MRSA colonization. Assign code Z22.321, Carrier or suspected carrier of Methicillin susceptible Staphylococcus aureus, for patient documented as having MSSA colonization. Colonization is not necessarily indicative of a disease process or as the cause of a specific condition the patient may have unless documented as such by the provider.

(d) MRSA colonization and infection
If a patient is documented as having both MRSA colonization and infection during a hospital admission, code Z22.322, Carrier or suspected carrier of Methicillin resistant Staphylococcus aureus, and a code for the MRSA infection may both be assigned.

2. Chapter 2: Neoplasms (C00-D49)

General guidelines

Chapter 2 of the ICD-10-CM contains the codes for most benign and all malignant neoplasms. Certain benign neoplasms, such as prostatic adenomas, may be found in the specific body system chapters. To properly code a neoplasm it is necessary to determine from the record if the neoplasm is benign, in-situ, malignant, or of uncertain histologic behavior. If malignant, any secondary (metastatic) sites should also be determined.

Primary malignant neoplasms overlapping site boundaries

A primary malignant neoplasm that overlaps two or more contiguous (next to each other) sites should be classified to the subcategory/code .8 ('overlapping lesion'), unless the combination is specifically indexed elsewhere. For multiple neoplasms of the same site that are not contiguous such as tumors in different quadrants of the same breast, codes for each site should be assigned.

Malignant neoplasm of ectopic tissue

Malignant neoplasms of ectopic tissue are to be coded to the site of origin mentioned, e.g., ectopic pancreatic malignant neoplasms involving the stomach are coded to pancreas, unspecified (C25.9).

The neoplasm table in the Alphabetic Index should be referenced first. However, if the histological term is documented, that term should be referenced first, rather than going immediately to the Neoplasm Table, in order to determine which column in the Neoplasm Table is appropriate. For example, if the documentation indicates "adenoma," refer to the term in the Alphabetic Index to review the entries under this term and the instructional note to "see also neoplasm, by site, benign." The table provides the proper code based on the type of neoplasm and the site. It is important to select the proper column in the table that corresponds to the type of neoplasm. The Tabular List should then be referenced to verify that the correct code has been selected from the table and that a more specific site code does not exist.

See Section I.C.21. Factors influencing health status and contact with health services, Status, for information regarding Z15.0, codes for genetic susceptibility to cancer.

a. Treatment directed at the malignancy
If the treatment is directed at the malignancy, designate the malignancy as the principal diagnosis.
The only exception to this guideline is if a patient admission/encounter is solely for the administration of chemotherapy, immunotherapy or radiation therapy, assign the appropriate Z51.--code as the first-listed or principal diagnosis, and the diagnosis or problem for which the service is being performed as a secondary diagnosis.

b. Treatment of secondary site
When a patient is admitted because of a primary neoplasm with metastasis and treatment is directed toward the secondary site only, the secondary neoplasm is designated as the principal diagnosis even though the primary malignancy is still present.

c. Coding and sequencing of complications
Coding and sequencing of complications associated with the malignancies or with the therapy thereof are subject to the following guidelines:

1) Anemia associated with malignancy
When admission/encounter is for management of an anemia associated with the malignancy, and the treatment is only for anemia, the appropriate code for the malignancy is sequenced as the principal or first-listed diagnosis followed by the appropriate code for the anemia (such as D63.0, Anemia in neoplastic disease).

2) Anemia associated with chemotherapy, immunotherapy and radiation therapy
When the admission/encounter is for management of an anemia associated with an adverse effect of the administration of chemotherapy or immunotherapy and the only treatment is for the anemia, the anemia code is sequenced first followed by the appropriate codes for the neoplasm and the adverse effect (T45.1X5, Adverse effect of antineoplastic and immunosuppressive drugs).
When the admission/encounter is for management of an anemia associated with an adverse effect of radiotherapy, the anemia code should be sequenced first, followed by the appropriate neoplasm code and code Y84.2, Radiological procedure and radiotherapy as the cause of abnormal reaction of the patient, or of later complication, without mention of misadventure at the time of the procedure.

3) Management of dehydration due to the malignancy

When the admission/encounter is for management of dehydration due to the malignancy and only the dehydration is being treated (intravenous rehydration), the dehydration is sequenced first, followed by the code(s) for the malignancy.

4) Treatment of a complication resulting from a surgical procedure
When the admission/encounter is for treatment of a complication resulting from a surgical procedure, designate the complication as the principal or first-listed diagnosis if treatment is directed at resolving the complication.

d. Primary malignancy previously excised
When a primary malignancy has been previously excised or eradicated from its site and there is no further treatment directed to that site and there is no evidence of any existing primary malignancy, a code from category Z85, Personal history of malignant neoplasm, should be used to indicate the former site of the malignancy. Any mention of extension, invasion, or metastasis to another site is coded as a secondary malignant neoplasm to that site. The secondary site may be the principal or first-listed with the Z85 code used as a secondary code.

e. Admissions/Encounters involving chemotherapy, immunotherapy and radiation therapy

1) Episode of care involves surgical removal of neoplasm
When an episode of care involves the surgical removal of a neoplasm, primary or secondary site, followed by adjunct chemotherapy or radiation treatment during the same episode of care, the code for the neoplasm should be assigned as principal or first-listed diagnosis.

2) Patient admission/encounter solely for administration of chemotherapy, immunotherapy and radiation therapy
If a patient admission/encounter is solely for the administration of chemotherapy, immunotherapy or radiation therapy assign code Z51.0, Encounter for antineoplastic radiation therapy, or Z51.11, Encounter for antineoplastic chemotherapy, or Z51.12, Encounter for antineoplastic immunotherapy as the first-listed or principal diagnosis. If a patient receives more than one of these therapies during the same admission more than one of these codes may be assigned, in any sequence.
The malignancy for which the therapy is being administered should be assigned as a secondary diagnosis.

3) Patient admitted for radiation therapy, chemotherapy or immunotherapy and develops complications
When a patient is admitted for the purpose of radiotherapy, immunotherapy or chemotherapy and develops complications such as uncontrolled nausea and vomiting or dehydration, the principal or first-listed diagnosis is Z51.0, Encounter for antineoplastic radiation therapy, or Z51.11, Encounter for antineoplastic chemotherapy, or Z51.12, Encounter for antineoplastic immunotherapy followed by any codes for the complications.

f. Admission/encounter to determine extent of malignancy
When the reason for admission/encounter is to determine the extent of the malignancy, or for a procedure such as paracentesis or thoracentesis, the primary malignancy or appropriate metastatic site is designated as the principal or first-listed diagnosis, even though chemotherapy or radiotherapy is administered.

g. Symptoms, signs, and abnormal findings listed in Chapter 18 associated with neoplasms
Symptoms, signs, and ill-defined conditions listed in Chapter 18 characteristic of, or associated with, an existing primary or secondary site malignancy cannot be used to replace the malignancy as principal or first-listed diagnosis, regardless of the number of admissions or encounters for treatment and care of the neoplasm.
See section I.C.21. Factors influencing health status and contact with health services, Encounter for prophylactic organ removal.

h. Admission/encounter for pain control/management
See Section I.C.6. for information on coding admission/encounter for pain control/management.

i. Malignancy in two or more noncontiguous sites
A patient may have more than one malignant tumor in the same organ. These tumors may represent different primaries or metastatic disease, depending on the site. Should the documentation be unclear, the provider should be queried as to the status of each tumor so that the correct codes can be assigned.

j. Disseminated malignant neoplasm, unspecified
Code C80.0, Disseminated malignant neoplasm, unspecified, is for use only in those cases where the patient has advanced metastatic disease and no known primary or secondary sites are specified. It should not be used in place of assigning codes for the primary site and all known secondary sites.

k. Malignant neoplasm without specification of site
Code C80.1, Malignant (primary) neoplasm, unspecified, equates to Cancer, unspecified. This code should only be used when no determination can be made as to the primary site of a malignancy. This code should rarely be used in the inpatient setting.

l. Sequencing of neoplasm codes

1) Encounter for treatment of primary malignancy
If the reason for the encounter is for treatment of a primary malignancy, assign the malignancy as the principal/first-listed diagnosis. The primary site is to be sequenced first, followed by any metastatic sites.

2) Encounter for treatment of secondary malignancy
When an encounter is for a primary malignancy with metastasis and treatment is directed toward the metastatic (secondary) site(s) only, the metastatic site(s) is designated as the principal/first-listed diagnosis. The primary malignancy is coded as an additional code.

3) Malignant neoplasm in a pregnant patient
When a pregnant woman has a malignant neoplasm, a code from subcategory O9A.1-, Malignant neoplasm complicating pregnancy, childbirth, and the puerperium, should be sequenced first, followed by the appropriate code from Chapter 2 to indicate the type of neoplasm.

4) Encounter for complication associated with a neoplasm
When an encounter is for management of a complication associated with a neoplasm, such as dehydration, and the treatment is only for the complication, the complication is coded first, followed by the appropriate code(s) for the neoplasm.
The exception to this guideline is anemia. When the admission/encounter is for management of an anemia associated with the malignancy, and the treatment is only for anemia, the appropriate code for the malignancy is sequenced as the principal or first-listed diagnosis followed by code D63.0, Anemia in neoplastic disease.

5) Complication from surgical procedure for treatment of a neoplasm
When an encounter is for treatment of a complication resulting from a surgical procedure performed for the treatment of the neoplasm, designate the complication as the principal/first-listed diagnosis. See guideline regarding the coding of a current malignancy versus personal history to determine if the code for the neoplasm should also be assigned.

6) Pathologic fracture due to a neoplasm
When an encounter is for a pathological fracture due to a neoplasm, if the focus of treatment is the fracture, a code from subcategory M84.5, Pathological fracture in neoplastic disease, should be sequenced first, followed by the code for the neoplasm.
If the focus of treatment is the neoplasm with an associated pathological fracture, the neoplasm code should be sequenced first, followed by a code from M84.5 for the pathological fracture.

m. Current malignancy versus personal history of malignancy
When a primary malignancy has been excised but further treatment, such as an additional surgery for the malignancy, radiation therapy or chemotherapy is directed to that site, the primary malignancy code should be used until treatment is completed.
When a primary malignancy has been previously excised or eradicated from its site, there is no further treatment (of the malignancy) directed to that site, and there is no evidence of any existing primary malignancy, a code from category Z85, Personal history of malignant neoplasm,

should be used to indicate the former site of the malignancy.
See Section I.C.21. Factors influencing health status and contact with health services, History (of)

n. Leukemia, Multiple Myeloma, and Malignant Plasma Cell Neoplasms in remission versus personal history
The categories for leukemia, and category C90, Multiple myeloma and malignant plasma cell neoplasms, have codes indicating whether or not the leukemia has achieved remission. There are also codes Z85.6, Personal history of leukemia, and Z85.79, Personal history of other malignant neoplasms of lymphoid, hematopoietic and related tissues. If the documentation is unclear, as to whether the leukemia has achieved remission, the provider should be queried.
See Section I.C.21. Factors influencing health status and contact with health services, History (of)

o. Aftercare following surgery for neoplasm
See Section I.C.21. Factors influencing health status and contact with health services, Aftercare

p. Follow-up care for completed treatment of a malignancy
See Section I.C.21. Factors influencing health status and contact with health services, Follow-up

q. Prophylactic organ removal for prevention of malignancy
See Section I.C. 21, Factors influencing health status and contact with health services, Prophylactic organ removal

r. Malignant neoplasm associated with transplanted organ
A malignant neoplasm of a transplanted organ should be coded as a transplant complication. Assign first the appropriate code from category T86.-, Complications of transplanted organs and tissue, followed by code C80.2, Malignant neoplasm associated with transplanted organ. Use an additional code for the specific malignancy.

3. Chapter 3: Disease of the blood and blood-forming organs and certain disorders involving the immune mechanism (D50-D89)

Reserved for future guideline expansion

4. Chapter 4: Endocrine, Nutritional, and Metabolic Diseases (E00-E89)

a. Diabetes mellitus
The diabetes mellitus codes are combination codes that include the type of diabetes mellitus, the body system affected, and the complications affecting that body system. As many codes within a particular category as are necessary to describe all of the complications of the disease may be used. They should be sequenced based on the reason for a particular encounter. Assign as many codes from categories E08 – E13 as needed to identify all of the associated conditions that the patient has.

1) Type of diabetes
The age of a patient is not the sole determining factor, though most type 1 diabetics develop the condition before reaching puberty. For this reason type 1 diabetes mellitus is also referred to as juvenile diabetes.

2) Type of diabetes mellitus not documented
If the type of diabetes mellitus is not documented in the medical record the default is E11.-, Type 2 diabetes mellitus.

3) Diabetes mellitus and the use of insulin
If the documentation in a medical record does not indicate the type of diabetes but does indicate that the patient uses insulin, code E11, Type 2 diabetes mellitus, should be assigned. Code Z79.4, Long-term (current) use of insulin, should also be assigned to indicate that the patient uses insulin. Code Z79.4 should not be assigned if insulin is given temporarily to bring a type 2 patient's blood sugar under control during an encounter.

4) Diabetes mellitus in pregnancy and gestational diabetes
See Section I.C.15. Diabetes mellitus in pregnancy. See Section I.C.15. Gestational (pregnancy induced) diabetes

5) Complications due to insulin pump malfunction
(a) Underdose of insulin due to insulin pump failure An underdose of insulin due to an insulin pump failure should be assigned to a code from subcategory T85.6, Mechanical complication of other specified internal and external prosthetic devices, implants and grafts, that specifies the type of pump malfunction, as the principal or first-listed code, followed by code T38.3x6-, Underdosing of insulin and oral hypoglycemic [antidiabetic] drugs. Additional codes for the type of diabetes mellitus and any associated complications due to the underdosing should also be assigned.
(b) Overdose of insulin due to insulin pump failure The principal or first-listed code for an encounter due to an insulin pump malfunction resulting in an overdose of insulin, should also be T85.6-, Mechanical complication of other specified internal and external prosthetic devices, implants and grafts, followed by code T38.3x1-, Poisoning by insulin and oral hypoglycemic [antidiabetic] drugs, accidental (unintentional).

6) Secondary Diabetes Mellitus
Codes under categories E08, Diabetes mellitus due to underlying condition, and E09, Drug or chemical induced diabetes mellitus, identify complications/manifestations associated with secondary diabetes mellitus, and E13, Other specified diabetes mellitus,. Secondary diabetes is always caused by another condition or event (e.g., cystic fibrosis, malignant neoplasm of pancreas, pancreatectomy, adverse effect of drug, or poisoning).
(a) Secondary diabetes mellitus and the use of insulin
For patients who routinely use insulin, code Z79.4, Long-term (current) use of insulin, should also be assigned. Code Z79.4 should not be assigned if insulin is given temporarily to bring a patient's blood sugar under control during an encounter.
(b) Assigning and sequencing secondary diabetes codes and its causes
The sequencing of the secondary diabetes codes in relationship to codes for the cause of the diabetes is based on the Tabular List instructions for categories E08 and E09, and E13.
(i) Secondary diabetes mellitus due to pancreatectomy
For postpancreatectomy diabetes mellitus (lack of insulin due to the surgical removal of all or part of the pancreas), assign code E89.1, Postprocedural hypoinsulinemia. Assign a code from category E13 and a code from subcategory Z90.41-, Acquired absence of pancreas, as additional codes.
(ii) Secondary diabetes due to drugs
Secondary diabetes may be caused by an adverse effect of correctly administered medications, poisoning or sequela of poisoning.
See section I.C.19.e for coding of adverse effects and poisoning, and section I.C.20 for external cause code reporting.

5. Chapter 5: Mental and behavioral disorders (F01 – F99)

a. Pain disorders related to psychological factors
Assign code F45.41, for pain that is exclusively related to psychological disorders. As indicated by the Excludes 1 note under category G89, a code from category G89 should not be assigned with code F45.41.
Code F45.42, Pain disorders with related psychological factors, should be used following the appropriate code from category G89, Pain, not elsewhere classified, if there is documentation of a psychological component for a patient with acute or chronic pain.
See Section I.C.6. Pain

b. Mental and behavioral disorders due to psychoactive substance use
1) In Remission
Selection of codes for "in remission" for categories F10-F19, Mental and behavioral disorders due to psychoactive substance use (categories F10-F19 with -.21) requires the provider's clinical judgment. The appropriate codes for "in remission" are assigned only on the basis of

provider documentation (as defined in the *Official Guidelines for Coding and Reporting*).

2) Psychoactive Substance Use, Abuse And Dependence When the provider documentation refers to use, abuse and dependence of the same substance (e.g. alcohol, opioid, cannabis, etc.), only one code should be assigned to identify the pattern of use based on the following hierarchy:
   - If both use and abuse are documented, assign only the code for abuse
   - If both abuse and dependence are documented, assign only the code for dependence
   - If use, abuse and dependence are all documented, assign only the code for dependence
   - If both use and dependence are documented, assign only the code for dependence.

3) Psychoactive Substance Use as with all other diagnoses, the codes for psychoactive substance use (F10.9-, F11.9-, F12.9-, F13.9-, F14.9-, F15.9-, F16.9-) should only be assigned based on provider documentation and when they meet the definition of a reportable diagnosis (*see Section III, Reporting Additional Diagnoses*). The codes are to be used only when the psychoactive substance use is associated with a mental or behavioral disorder, and such a relationship is documented by the provider.

6. Chapter 6: Diseases of Nervous System and Sense Organs (G00-G99)

a. Dominant/nondominant side

Codes from category G81, Hemiplegia and hemiparesis, and subcategories, G83.1, Monoplegia of lower limb, G83.2, Monoplegia of upper limb, and G83.3, Monoplegia, unspecified, identify whether the dominant or nondominant side is affected. Should the affected side be documented, but not specified as dominant or nondominant, and the classification system does not indicate a default, code selection is as follows:

- For ambidextrous patients, the default should be dominant.
- If the left side is affected, the default is non-dominant.
- If the right side is affected, the default is dominant.

b. Pain - Category G89

1) General coding information

Codes in category G89, Pain, not elsewhere classified, may be used in conjunction with codes from other categories and chapters to provide more detail about acute or chronic pain and neoplasm-related pain, unless otherwise indicated below.

If the pain is not specified as acute or chronic, postthoracotomy, postprocedural, or neoplasm-related, do not assign codes from category G89.

A code from category G89 should not be assigned if the underlying (definitive) diagnosis is known, unless the reason for the encounter is pain control/ management and not management of the underlying condition.

When an admission or encounter is for a procedure aimed at treating the underlying condition (e.g., spinal fusion, kyphoplasty), a code for the underlying condition (e.g., vertebral fracture, spinal stenosis) should be assigned as the principal diagnosis. No code from category G89 should be assigned.

(a) Category G89 Codes as Principal or First-Listed Diagnosis

Category G89 codes are acceptable as principal diagnosis or the first-listed code:

- When pain control or pain management is the reason for the admission/encounter (e.g., a patient with displaced intervertebral disc, nerve impingement and severe back pain presents for injection of steroid into the spinal canal). The underlying cause of the pain should be reported as an additional diagnosis, if known.
- When a patient is admitted for the insertion of a neurostimulator for pain control, assign the appropriate pain code as the principal or first-listed diagnosis. When an admission or encounter is for a procedure aimed at treating the underlying condition and a neurostimulator is inserted for pain control during the same admission/encounter, a code for the underlying condition should be assigned as the principal diagnosis and the appropriate pain code should be assigned as a secondary diagnosis.

(b) Use of Category G89 Codes in Conjunction with Site Specific Pain Codes

(i) Assigning Category G89 and Site-Specific Pain Codes

Codes from category G89 may be used in conjunction with codes that identify the site of pain (including codes from chapter 18) if the category G89 code provides additional information. For example, if the code describes the site of the pain, but does not fully describe whether the pain is acute or chronic, then both codes should be assigned.

(ii) Sequencing of Category G89 Codes with Site-Specific Pain Codes

The sequencing of category G89 codes with site-specific pain codes (including chapter 18 codes), is dependent on the circumstances of the encounter/admission as follows:

If the encounter is for pain control or pain management, assign the code from category G89 followed by the code identifying the specific site of pain (e.g., encounter for pain management for acute neck pain from trauma is assigned code G89.11, Acute pain due to trauma, followed by code M54.2, Cervicalgia, to identify the site of pain).

If the encounter is for any other reason except pain control or pain management, and a related definitive diagnosis has not been established (confirmed) by the provider, assign the code for the specific site of pain first, followed by the appropriate code from category G89.

2) Pain due to devices, implants and grafts

See Section I.C.19. Pain due to medical devices

3) Postoperative Pain

The provider's documentation should be used to guide the coding of postoperative pain, as well as *Section III. Reporting Additional Diagnoses* and *Section IV. Diagnostic Coding and Reporting in the Outpatient Setting.*

The default for post-thoracotomy and other postoperative pain not specified as acute or chronic is the code for the acute form.

Routine or expected postoperative pain immediately after surgery should not be coded.

(a) Postoperative pain not associated with specific postoperative complication

Postoperative pain not associated with a specific postoperative complication is assigned to the appropriate postoperative pain code in category G89.

(b) Postoperative pain associated with specific postoperative complication

Postoperative pain associated with a specific postoperative complication (such as painful wire sutures) is assigned to the appropriate code(s) found in Chapter 19, Injury, poisoning, and certain other consequences of external causes. If appropriate, use additional code(s) from category G89 to identify acute or chronic pain (G89.18 or G89.28).

4) Chronic pain

Chronic pain is classified to subcategory G89.2. There is no time frame defining when pain becomes chronic pain. The provider's documentation should be used to guide use of these codes.

5) Neoplasm Related Pain

Code G89.3 is assigned to pain documented as being related, associated or due to cancer, primary or secondary malignancy, or tumor. This code is assigned regardless of whether the pain is acute or chronic.

This code may be assigned as the principal or first-listed code when the stated reason for the admission/encounter is documented as pain control/pain management. The underlying neoplasm should be reported as an additional diagnosis.

When the reason for the admission/encounter is management of the neoplasm and the pain associated with the neoplasm is also documented, code G89.3 may be assigned as an additional diagnosis. It is not necessary to assign an additional code for the site of the pain.

See Section I.C.2 for instructions on the sequencing of neoplasms for all other stated reasons for the admission/encounter (except for pain control/pain management).

6) Chronic pain syndrome

Central pain syndrome (G89.0) and chronic pain syndrome (G89.4) are different than the term "chronic pain," and therefore codes should only be used when the provider has specifically documented this condition.

See Section I.C.5. Pain disorders related to psychological factors

7. Chapter 7: Diseases of Eye and Adnexa (H00-H59)

a. Glaucoma

1) Assigning Glaucoma Codes

Assign as many codes from category H40, Glaucoma, as needed to identify the type of glaucoma, the affected eye, and the glaucoma stage.

2) Bilateral glaucoma with same type and stage

When a patient has bilateral glaucoma and both eyes are documented as being the same type and stage, and there is a code for bilateral glaucoma, report only the code for the type of glaucoma, bilateral, with the seventh character for the stage.

When a patient has bilateral glaucoma and both eyes are documented as being the same type and stage, and the classification does not provide a code for bilateral glaucoma (i.e. subcategories H40.10, H40.11 and H40.20) report only one code for the type of glaucoma with the appropriate seventh character for the stage.

3) Bilateral glaucoma stage with different types or stages

When a patient has bilateral glaucoma and each eye is documented as having a different type or stage, and the classification distinguishes laterality, assign the appropriate code for each eye rather than the code for bilateral glaucoma.

When a patient has bilateral glaucoma and each eye is documented as having a different type, and the classification does not distinguish laterality (i.e. subcategories H40.10, H40.11 and H40.20), assign one code for each type of glaucoma with the appropriate seventh character for the stage.

When a patient has bilateral glaucoma and each eye is documented as having the same type, but different stage, and the classification does not distinguish laterality (i.e. subcategories H40.10, H40.11 and H40.20), assign a code for the type of glaucoma for each eye with the seventh character for the specific glaucoma stage documented for each eye.

4) Patient admitted with glaucoma and stage evolves during the admission

If a patient is admitted with glaucoma and the stage progresses during the admission, assign the code for highest stage documented.

5) Indeterminate stage glaucoma

Assignment of the seventh character "4" for "indeterminate stage" should be based on the clinical documentation. The seventh character "4" is used for glaucomas whose stage cannot be clinically determined. This seventh character should not be confused with the seventh character "0", unspecified, which should be assigned when there

8. Chapter 8: Diseases of Ear and Mastoid Process (H60-H95)

Reserved for future guideline expansion

9. Chapter 9: Diseases of Circulatory System (I00-I99)

a. Hypertension

1) Hypertension with Heart Disease

Heart conditions classified to I50.- or I51.4-I51.9, are assigned to, a code from category I11, Hypertensive heart disease, when a causal relationship is stated (due to hypertension) or implied (hypertensive). Use an additional code from category I50, Heart failure, to identify the type of heart failure in those patients with heart failure.

The same heart conditions (I50.-, I51.4-I51.9) with hypertension, but without a stated causal relationship, are coded separately. Sequence according to the circumstances of the admission/encounter.

2) Hypertensive Chronic Kidney Disease

Assign codes from category I12, Hypertensive chronic kidney disease, when both hypertension and a condition classifiable to category N18, Chronic kidney disease (CKD), are present. Unlike hypertension with heart disease, ICD-10-CM presumes a cause-and-effect relationship and classifies chronic kidney disease with hypertension as hypertensive chronic kidney disease. The appropriate code from category N18 should be used as a secondary code with a code from category I12 to identify the stage of chronic kidney disease.

See Section I.C.14. Chronic kidney disease.

If a patient has hypertensive chronic kidney disease and acute renal failure, an additional code for the acute renal failure is required.

3) Hypertensive Heart and Chronic Kidney Disease

Assign codes from combination category I13, Hypertensive heart and chronic kidney disease, when both hypertensive kidney disease and hypertensive heart disease are stated in the diagnosis. Assume a relationship between the hypertension and the chronic kidney disease, whether or not the condition is so designated. If heart failure is present, assign an additional code from category I50 to identify the type of heart failure.

The appropriate code from category N18, Chronic kidney disease, should be used as a secondary code with a code from category I13 to identify the stage of chronic kidney disease.

See Section I.C.14. Chronic kidney disease.

The codes in category I13, Hypertensive heart and chronic kidney disease, are combination codes that include hypertension, heart disease and chronic kidney disease. The Includes note at I13 specifies that the conditions included at I11 and I12 are included together in I13. If a patient has hypertension, heart disease and chronic kidney disease then a code from I13 should be used, not individual codes for hypertension, heart disease and chronic kidney disease, or codes from I11 or I12.

For patients with both acute renal failure and chronic kidney disease an additional code for acute renal failure is required.

4) Hypertensive Cerebrovascular Disease

For hypertensive cerebrovascular disease, first assign the appropriate code from categories I60-I69, followed by the appropriate hypertension code.

5) Hypertensive Retinopathy

Subcategory H35.0, Background retinopathy and retinal vascular changes, should be used with a code from category I10-I15, Hypertensive disease, to include the systemic hypertension. The sequencing is based on the reason for the encounter.

6) Hypertension, Secondary

Secondary hypertension is due to an underlying condition. Two codes are required: one to identify the underlying etiology and one from category I15 to identify the hypertension. Sequencing of codes is determined by the reason for admission/encounter.

7) Hypertension, Transient

Assign code R03.0, Elevated blood pressure reading without diagnosis of hypertension, unless patient has an established diagnosis of hypertension. Assign code O13.-, Gestational [pregnancy-induced] hypertension without significant proteinuria, or O14.-, Pre-eclampsia, for transient hypertension of pregnancy.

8) Hypertension, Controlled
This diagnostic statement usually refers to an existing state of hypertension under control by therapy. Assign the appropriate code from categories I10-I15, Hypertensive diseases.

9) Hypertension, Uncontrolled
Uncontrolled hypertension may refer to untreated hypertension or hypertension not responding to current therapeutic regimen. In either case, assign the appropriate code from categories I10-I15, Hypertensive diseases.

b. Atherosclerotic Coronary Artery Disease and Angina
ICD-10-CM has combination codes for atherosclerotic heart disease with angina pectoris. The subcategories for these codes are I25.11, Atherosclerotic heart disease of native coronary artery with angina pectoris and I25.7, Atherosclerosis of coronary artery bypass graft(s) and coronary artery of transplanted heart with angina pectoris.
When using one of these combination codes it is not necessary to use an additional code for angina pectoris. A causal relationship can be assumed in a patient with both atherosclerosis and angina pectoris, unless the documentation indicates the angina is due to something other than the atherosclerosis.
If a patient with coronary artery disease is admitted due to an acute myocardial infarction (AMI), the AMI should be sequenced before the coronary artery disease.
See Section I.C.9. Acute myocardial infarction (AMI)

c. Intraoperative and Postprocedural Cerebrovascular Accident
Medical record documentation should clearly specify the cause-and-effect relationship between the medical intervention and the cerebrovascular accident in order to assign a code for intraoperative or postprocedural cerebrovascular accident. Proper code assignment depends on whether it was an infarction or hemorrhage and whether it occurred intraoperatively or postoperatively. If it was a cerebral hemorrhage, code assignment depends on the type of procedure performed.

d. Sequelae of Cerebrovascular Disease

1) Category I69, Sequelae of Cerebrovascular disease
Category I69 is used to indicate conditions classifiable to categories I60-I67 as the causes of sequela (neurologic deficits), themselves classified elsewhere. These "late effects" include neurologic deficits that persist after initial onset of conditions classifiable to categories I60-I67.
The neurologic deficits caused by cerebrovascular disease may be present from the onset or may arise at any time after the onset of the condition classifiable to categories I60-I67.
Codes from category I69, Sequelae of cerebrovascular disease, that specify hemiplegia, hemiparesis and monoplegia identify whether the dominant or nondominant side is affected. Should the affected side be documented, but not specified as dominant or nondominant, and the classification system does not indicate a default, code selection is as follows:
- For ambidextrous patients, the default should be dominant.
- If the left side is affected, the default is non-dominant.
- If the right side is affected, the default is dominant.

2) Codes from category I69 with codes from I60-I67
Codes from category I69 may be assigned on a health care record with codes from I60-I67, if the patient has a current cerebrovascular disease and deficits from an old cerebrovascular disease.

3) Codes from category I69 and Personal history of transient ischemic attack (TIA) and cerebral infarction (Z86.73)
Codes from category I69 should not be assigned if the patient does not have neurologic deficits.
See Section I.C.21. 4. History (of) for use of personal history codes

e. Acute myocardial infarction (AMI)

1) ST elevation myocardial infarction (STEMI) and non ST elevation myocardial infarction (NSTEMI)
The ICD-10-CM codes for acute myocardial infarction (AMI) identify the site, such as anterolateral wall or true posterior wall. Subcategories I21.0-I21.2 and code I21.4 are used for ST elevation myocardial infarction (STEMI). Code I21.4, Non-ST elevation (NSTEMI) myocardial infarction, is used for non ST elevation myocardial infarction (NSTEMI) and nontransmural MIs.
If NSTEMI evolves to STEMI, assign the STEMI code. If STEMI converts to NSTEMI due to thrombolytic therapy, it is still coded as STEMI.
For encounters occurring while the myocardial infarction is equal to, or less than, four weeks old, including transfers to another acute setting or a postacute setting, and the patient requires continued care for the myocardial infarction, codes from category I21 may continue to be reported. For encounters after the 4 weeks time frame and the patient is still receiving care related to the myocardial infarction, the appropriate aftercare code should be assigned, rather than a code from category I21. For old or healed myocardial infarctions not requiring further care, code I25.2, Old myocardial infarction, may be assigned.

2) Acute myocardial infarction, unspecified
Code I21.3, ST elevation (STEMI) myocardial infarction of unspecified site, is the default for the unspecified term acute myocardial infarction. If only STEMI or transmural MI without the site is documented, query the provider as to the site, or assign code I21.3.

3) AMI documented as nontransmural or subendocardial but site provided
If an AMI is documented as nontransmural or subendocardial, but the site is provided, it is still coded as a subendocardial AMI.
See Section I.C.21.3 for information on coding status post administration of tPA in a different facility within the last 24 hours.

4) Subsequent acute myocardial infarction
A code from category I22, Subsequent ST elevation (STEMI) and non ST elevation (NSTEMI) myocardial infarction, is to be used when a patient who has suffered an AMI has a new AMI within the 4 week time frame of the initial AMI. A code from category I22 must be used in conjunction with a code from category I21. The sequencing of the I22 and I21 codes depends on the circumstances of the encounter.

10. Chapter 10: Diseases of the Respiratory System (J00-J99)

a. Chronic Obstructive Pulmonary Disease [COPD] and Asthma

1) Acute exacerbation of chronic obstructive bronchitis and asthma
The codes in categories J44 and J45 distinguish between uncomplicated cases and those in acute exacerbation. An acute exacerbation is a worsening or a decompensation of a chronic condition. An acute exacerbation is not equivalent to an infection superimposed on a chronic condition, though an exacerbation may be triggered by an infection.

b. Acute Respiratory Failure

1) Acute respiratory failure as principal diagnosis
A code from subcategory J96.0, Acute respiratory failure, or subcategory J96.2, Acute and chronic respiratory failure, may be assigned as a principal diagnosis when it is the condition established after study to be chiefly responsible for occasioning the admission to the hospital, and the selection is supported by the Alphabetic Index and Tabular List. However, chapter-specific coding guidelines (such as obstetrics, poisoning, HIV, newborn) that provide sequencing direction take precedence.

2) Acute respiratory failure as secondary diagnosis
Respiratory failure may be listed as a secondary diagnosis if it occurs after admission, or if it is present on admission, but does not meet the definition of principal diagnosis.

3) Sequencing of acute respiratory failure and another acute condition
When a patient is admitted with respiratory failure and another acute condition, (e.g., myocardial infarction, cerebrovascular accident, aspiration pneumonia), the principal diagnosis will not be the same in every situation. This applies whether the other acute condition is a respiratory or nonrespiratory condition. Selection of the principal diagnosis will be dependent on the circumstances of admission. If both the respiratory

failure and the other acute condition are equally responsible for occasioning the admission to the hospital, and there are no chapter-specific sequencing rules, the guideline regarding two or more diagnoses that equally meet the definition for principal diagnosis (Section II, C.) may be applied in these situations.

If the documentation is not clear as to whether acute respiratory failure and another condition are equally responsible for occasioning the admission, query the provider for clarification.

c. Influenza due to certain identified influenza viruses

Code only confirmed cases of influenza due to certain identified influenza viruses (category J09), and due to other identified influenza virus (category J10). This is an exception to the hospital inpatient guideline *Section II, H. (Uncertain Diagnosis).*

In this context, "confirmation" does not require documentation of positive laboratory testing specific for avian or other novel influenza A or other identified influenza virus. However, coding should be based on the provider's diagnostic statement that the patient has avian influenza, or other novel influenza A, for category J09, or has another particular identified strain of influenza, such as H1N1 or H3N2, but not identified as novel or variant, for category J10.

If the provider records "suspected" or "possible" or "probable" avian influenza, or novel influenza, or other identified influenza, then the appropriate influenza code from category J11, Influenza due to unidentified influenza virus, should be assigned. A code from category J09, Influenza due to certain identified influenza viruses, should not be assigned nor should a code from category J10, Influenza due to other identified influenza virus.

d. Ventilator associated Pneumonia

1) Documentation of Ventilator associated Pneumonia

As with all procedural or postprocedural complications, code assignment is based on the provider's documentation of the relationship between the condition and the procedure.

Code J95.851, Ventilator associated pneumonia, should be assigned only when the provider has documented ventilator associated pneumonia (VAP). An additional code to identify the organism (e.g., Pseudomonas aeruginosa, code B96.5) should also be assigned. Do not assign an additional code from categories J12-J18 to identify the type of pneumonia.

Code J95.851 should not be assigned for cases where the patient has pneumonia and is on a mechanical ventilator and the provider has not specifically stated that the pneumonia is ventilator-associated pneumonia.

If the documentation is unclear as to whether the patient has a pneumonia that is a complication attributable to the mechanical ventilator, query the provider.

2) Ventilator associated Pneumonia Develops after Admission

A patient may be admitted with one type of pneumonia (e.g., code J13, Pneumonia due to Streptococcus pneumonia) and subsequently develop VAP. In this instance, the principal diagnosis would be the appropriate code from categories J12-J18 for the pneumonia diagnosed at the time of admission. Code J95.851, Ventilator associated pneumonia, would be assigned as an additional diagnosis when the provider has also documented the presence of ventilator associated pneumonia.

11. Chapter 11: Diseases of the Digestive System (K00-K94)

Reserved for future guideline expansion

12. Chapter 12: Diseases of the Skin and Subcutaneous Tissue (L00-L99)

a. Pressure ulcer stage codes

1) Pressure ulcer stages

Codes from category L89, Pressure ulcer, are combination codes that identify the site of the pressure ulcer as well as the stage of the ulcer.

The ICD-10-CM classifies pressure ulcer stages based on severity, which is designated by stages 1-4, unspecified stage and unstageable.

Assign as many codes from category L89 as needed to identify all the pressure ulcers the patient has, if applicable.

2) Unstageable pressure ulcers

Assignment of the code for unstageable pressure ulcer (L89.-0) should be based on the clinical documentation. These codes are used for pressure ulcers whose stage cannot be clinically determined (e.g., the ulcer is covered by eschar or has been treated with a skin or muscle graft) and pressure ulcers that are documented as deep tissue injury but not documented as due to trauma. This code should not be confused with the codes for unspecified stage (L89.--9). When there is no documentation regarding the stage of the pressure ulcer, assign the appropriate code for unspecified stage (L89.--9).

3) Documented pressure ulcer stage

Assignment of the pressure ulcer stage code should be guided by clinical documentation of the stage or documentation of the terms found in the Alphabetic Index. For clinical terms describing the stage that are not found in the Alphabetic Index, and there is no documentation of the stage, the provider should be queried.

4) Patients admitted with pressure ulcers documented as healed

No code is assigned if the documentation states that the pressure ulcer is completely healed.

5) Patients admitted with pressure ulcers documented as healing

Pressure ulcers described as healing should be assigned the appropriate pressure ulcer stage code based on the documentation in the medical record. If the documentation does not provide information about the stage of the healing pressure ulcer, assign the appropriate code for unspecified stage.

If the documentation is unclear as to whether the patient has a current (new) pressure ulcer or if the patient is being treated for a healing pressure ulcer, query the provider.

6) Patient admitted with pressure ulcer evolving into another stage during the admission

If a patient is admitted with a pressure ulcer at one stage and it progresses to a higher stage, assign the code for the highest stage reported for that site.

13. Chapter 13: Diseases of the Musculoskeletal System and Connective Tissue (M00-M99)

a. Site and laterality

Most of the codes within Chapter 13 have site and laterality designations. The site represents the bone, joint or the muscle involved. For some conditions where more than one bone, joint or muscle is usually involved, such as osteoarthritis, there is a "multiple sites" code available. For categories where no multiple site code is provided and more than one bone, joint or muscle is involved, multiple codes should be used to indicate the different sites involved.

1) Bone versus joint

For certain conditions, the bone may be affected at the upper or lower end, (e.g., avascular necrosis of bone, M87, Osteoporosis, M80, M81). Though the portion of the bone affected may be at the joint, the site designation will be the bone, not the joint.

b. Acute traumatic versus chronic or recurrent musculoskeletal conditions

Many musculoskeletal conditions are a result of previous injury or trauma to a site, or are recurrent conditions. Bone, joint or muscle conditions that are the result of a healed injury are usually found in chapter 13. Recurrent bone, joint or muscle conditions are also usually found in chapter 13. Any current, acute injury should be coded to the appropriate injury code from chapter 19. Chronic or recurrent conditions should generally be coded with a code from chapter 13. If it is difficult to determine from the documentation in the record which code is best to describe a condition, query the provider.

c. Coding of Pathologic Fractures

7th character A is for use as long as the patient is receiving active treatment for the fracture. Examples of active treatment are: surgical treatment, emergency department encounter, evaluation and treatment by a new physician. 7th character, D is to be used for encounters after the patient has completed active treatment. The other 7th characters, listed under each subcategory in the Tabular List, are to be used for subsequent encounters for treatment of problems associated with the healing, such as malunions, nonunions, and sequelae. Care for complications of surgical treatment for fracture repairs during the healing or recovery phase should be coded with the appropriate complication codes. *See Section I.C.19. Coding of traumatic fractures.*

d. Osteoporosis

Osteoporosis is a systemic condition, meaning that all bones of the musculoskeletal system are affected. Therefore, site is not a component of the codes under category M81, Osteoporosis without current pathological fracture. The site codes under category M80, Osteoporosis with current pathological fracture, identify the site of the fracture, not the osteoporosis.

1) Osteoporosis without pathological fracture

Category M81, Osteoporosis without current pathological fracture, is for use for patients with osteoporosis who do not currently have a pathologic fracture due to the osteoporosis, even if they have had a fracture in the past. For patients with a history of osteoporosis fractures, status code Z87.310, Personal history of (healed) osteoporosis fracture, should follow the code from M81.

2) Osteoporosis with current pathological fracture

Category M80, Osteoporosis with current pathological fracture, is for patients who have a current pathologic fracture at the time of an encounter. The codes under M80 identify the site of the fracture. A code from category M80, not a traumatic fracture code, should be used for any patient with known osteoporosis who suffers a fracture, even if the patient had a minor fall or trauma, if that fall or trauma would not usually break a normal, healthy bone.

14. Chapter 14: Diseases of Genitourinary System (N00-N99)

a. Chronic kidney disease

1) Stages of chronic kidney disease (CKD)

The ICD-10-CM classifies CKD based on severity. The severity of CKD is designated by stages 1-5. Stage 2, code N18.2, equates to mild CKD; stage 3, code N18.3, equates to moderate CKD; and stage 4, code N18.4, equates to severe CKD. Code N18.6, End stage renal disease (ESRD), is assigned when the provider has documented end-stage-renal disease (ESRD).

If both a stage of CKD and ESRD are documented, assign code N18.6 only.

2) Chronic kidney disease and kidney transplant status

Patients who have undergone kidney transplant may still have some form of chronic kidney disease (CKD) because the kidney transplant may not fully restore kidney function. Therefore, the presence of CKD alone does not constitute a transplant complication. Assign the appropriate N18 code for the patient's stage of CKD and code Z94.0, Kidney transplant status. If a transplant complication such as failure or rejection or other transplant complication is documented, *see section I.C.19.g for information on coding complications of a kidney transplant.* If the documentation is unclear as to whether the patient has a complication of the transplant, query the provider.

3) Chronic kidney disease with other conditions

Patients with CKD may also suffer from other serious conditions, most commonly diabetes mellitus and hypertension. The sequencing of the CKD code in relationship to codes for other contributing conditions is based on the conventions in the Tabular List. *See I.C.9. Hypertensive chronic kidney disease. See I.C.19. Chronic kidney disease and kidney transplant complications.*

15. Chapter 15: Pregnancy, Childbirth, and the Puerperium (O00-O9A)

a. General Rules for Obstetric Cases

1) Codes from chapter 15 and sequencing priority

Obstetric cases require codes from chapter 15, codes in the range O00-O9A, Pregnancy, Childbirth, and the Puerperium. Chapter 15 codes have sequencing priority over codes from other chapters. Additional codes from other chapters may be used in conjunction with chapter 15 codes to further specify conditions. Should the provider document that the pregnancy is incidental to the encounter, then code Z33.1, Pregnant state, incidental, should be used in place of any chapter 15 codes. It is the provider's responsibility to state that the condition being treated is not affecting the pregnancy.

2) Chapter 15 codes used only on the maternal record

Chapter 15 codes are to be used only on the maternal record, never on the record of the newborn.

3) Final character for trimester

The majority of codes in Chapter 15 have a final character indicating the trimester of pregnancy. The timeframes for the trimesters are indicated at the beginning of the chapter. If trimester is not a component of a code it is because the condition always occurs in a specific trimester, or the concept of trimester of pregnancy is not applicable. Certain codes have characters for only certain trimesters because the condition does not occur in all trimesters, but it may occur in more than just one.

Assignment of the final character for trimester should be based on the provider's documentation of the trimester (or number of weeks) for the current admission/encounter. This applies to the assignment of trimester for pre-existing conditions as well as those that develop during or are due to the pregnancy. The provider's documentation of the number of weeks may be used to assign the appropriate code identifying the trimester.

Whenever delivery occurs during the current admission, and there is an "in childbirth" option for the obstetric complication being coded, the "in childbirth" code should be assigned.

4) Selection of trimester for inpatient admissions that encompass more than one trimesters

In instances when a patient is admitted to a hospital for complications of pregnancy during one trimester and remains in the hospital into a subsequent trimester, the trimester character for the antepartum complication code should be assigned on the basis of the trimester when the complication developed, not the trimester of the discharge. If the condition developed prior to the current admission/encounter or represents a pre-existing condition, the trimester character for the trimester at the time of the admission/encounter should be assigned.

5) Unspecified trimester

Each category that includes codes for trimester has a code for "unspecified trimester." The "unspecified trimester" code should rarely be used, such as when the documentation in the record is insufficient to determine the trimester and it is not possible to obtain clarification.

6) Fetal Extensions

Where applicable, a 7th character is to be assigned for certain categories (O31, O32, O33.3 -O33.6, O35, O36, O40, O41, O60.1, O60.2, O64, and O69) to identify the fetus for which the complication code applies.

Assign 7th character "0":

- For single gestations
- When the documentation in the record is insufficient to determine the fetus affected and it is not possible to obtain clarification.
- When it is not possible to clinically determine which fetus is affected.

b. Selection of OB Principal or First-listed Diagnosis

1) Routine outpatient prenatal visits

For routine outpatient prenatal visits when no complications are present, a code from category Z34, Encounter for supervision of normal pregnancy, should be used as the first-listed diagnosis. These codes should not be used in conjunction with chapter 15 codes.

2) Prenatal outpatient visits for high-risk patients

For routine prenatal outpatient visits for patients with high-risk pregnancies, a code from category O09, Supervision of high-risk pregnancy, should be used as the first-listed diagnosis. Secondary chapter 15 codes may be used in conjunction with these codes if appropriate.

3) Episodes when no delivery occurs

In episodes when no delivery occurs, the principal diagnosis should correspond to the principal complication of the pregnancy which necessitated the encounter. Should more than one complication exist, all of which are treated or monitored, any of the complications codes may be sequenced first.

4) When a delivery occurs
When a delivery occurs, the principal diagnosis should correspond to the main circumstances or complication of the delivery. In cases of cesarean delivery, the selection of the principal diagnosis should be the condition established after study that was responsible for the patient's admission. If the patient was admitted with a condition that resulted in the performance of a cesarean procedure, that condition should be selected as the principal diagnosis. If the reason for the admission/encounter was unrelated to the condition resulting in the cesarean delivery, the condition related to the reason for the admission/encounter should be selected as the principal diagnosis.

5) Outcome of delivery
A code from category Z37, Outcome of delivery, should be included on every maternal record when a delivery has occurred. These codes are not to be used on subsequent records or on the newborn record.

c. Pre-existing conditions versus conditions due to the pregnancy
Certain categories in Chapter 15 distinguish between conditions of the mother that existed prior to pregnancy (pre-existing) and those that are a direct result of pregnancy. When assigning codes from Chapter 15, it is important to assess if a condition was pre-existing prior to pregnancy or developed during or due to the pregnancy in order to assign the correct code.
Categories that do not distinguish between pre-existing and pregnancy-related conditions may be used for either. It is acceptable to use codes specifically for the puerperium with codes complicating pregnancy and childbirth if a condition arises postpartum during the delivery encounter.

d. Pre-existing hypertension in pregnancy
Category O10, Pre-existing hypertension complicating pregnancy, childbirth and the puerperium, includes codes for hypertensive heart and hypertensive chronic kidney disease. When assigning one of the O10 codes that includes hypertensive heart disease or hypertensive chronic kidney disease, it is necessary to add a secondary code from the appropriate hypertension category to specify the type of heart failure or chronic kidney disease.
See Section I.C.9. Hypertension.

e. Fetal Conditions Affecting the Management of the Mother

1) Codes from categories O35 and O36
Codes from categories O35, Maternal care for known or suspected fetal abnormality and damage, and O36, Maternal care for other fetal problems, are assigned only when the fetal condition is actually responsible for modifying the management of the mother, i.e., by requiring diagnostic studies, additional observation, special care, or termination of pregnancy. The fact that the fetal condition exists does not justify assigning a code from this series to the mother's record.

2) In utero surgery
In cases when surgery is performed on the fetus, a diagnosis code from category O35, Maternal care for known or suspected fetal abnormality and damage, should be assigned identifying the fetal condition. Assign the appropriate procedure code for the procedure performed.
No code from Chapter 16, the perinatal codes, should be used on the mother's record to identify fetal conditions. Surgery performed in utero on a fetus is still to be coded as an obstetric encounter.

f. HIV Infection in Pregnancy, Childbirth and the Puerperium
During pregnancy, childbirth or the puerperium, a patient admitted because of an HIV-related illness should receive a principal diagnosis from subcategory O98.7-, Human immunodeficiency [HIV] disease complicating pregnancy, childbirth and the puerperium, followed by the code(s) for the HIV-related illness(es).
Patients with asymptomatic HIV infection status admitted during pregnancy, childbirth, or the puerperium should receive codes of O98.7- and Z21, Asymptomatic human immunodeficiency virus [HIV] infection status.

g. Diabetes mellitus in pregnancy
Diabetes mellitus is a significant complicating factor in pregnancy. Pregnant women who are diabetic should be assigned a code from category O24, Diabetes mellitus in pregnancy, childbirth, and the puerperium, first, followed by the appropriate diabetes code(s) (E08-E13) from Chapter 4.

h. Long term use of insulin
Code Z79.4, Long-term (current) use of insulin, should also be assigned if the diabetes mellitus is being treated with insulin.

i. Gestational (pregnancy induced) diabetes
Gestational (pregnancy induced) diabetes can occur during the second and third trimester of pregnancy in women who were not diabetic prior to pregnancy. Gestational diabetes can cause complications in the pregnancy similar to those of pre-existing diabetes mellitus. It also puts the woman at greater risk of developing diabetes after the pregnancy. Codes for gestational diabetes are in subcategory O24.4, Gestational diabetes mellitus. No other code from category O24, Diabetes mellitus in pregnancy, childbirth, and the puerperium, should be used with a code from O24.4
The codes under subcategory O24.4 include diet controlled and insulin controlled. If a patient with gestational diabetes is treated with both diet and insulin, only the code for insulin-controlled is required. Code Z79.4, Long-term (current) use of insulin, should not be assigned with codes from subcategory O24.4.
An abnormal glucose tolerance in pregnancy is assigned a code from subcategory O99.81, Abnormal glucose complicating pregnancy, childbirth, and the puerperium.

j. Sepsis and septic shock complicating abortion, pregnancy, childbirth and the puerperium
When assigning a chapter 15 code for sepsis complicating abortion, pregnancy, childbirth, and the puerperium, a code for the specific type of infection should be assigned as an additional diagnosis. If severe sepsis is present, a code from subcategory R65.2, Severe sepsis, and code(s) for associated organ dysfunction(s) should also be assigned as additional diagnoses.

k. Puerperal sepsis
Code O85, Puerperal sepsis, should be assigned with a secondary code to identify the causal organism (e.g., for a bacterial infection, assign a code from category B95-B96, Bacterial infections in conditions classified elsewhere). A code from category A40, Streptococcal sepsis, or A41, Other sepsis, should not be used for puerperal sepsis. If applicable, use additional codes to identify severe sepsis (R65.2-) and any associated acute organ dysfunction.

l. Alcohol and tobacco use during pregnancy, childbirth and the puerperium

1) Alcohol use during pregnancy, childbirth and the puerperium
Codes under subcategory O99.31, Alcohol use complicating pregnancy, childbirth, and the puerperium, should be assigned for any pregnancy case when a mother uses alcohol during the pregnancy or postpartum. A secondary code from category F10, Alcohol related disorders, should also be assigned to identify manifestations of the alcohol use.

2) Tobacco use during pregnancy, childbirth and the puerperium
Codes under subcategory O99.33, Smoking (tobacco) complicating pregnancy, childbirth, and the puerperium, should be assigned for any pregnancy case when a mother uses any type of tobacco product during the pregnancy or postpartum. A secondary code from category F17, Nicotine dependence, or code Z72.0, Tobacco use, should also be assigned to identify the type of nicotine dependence.

m. Poisoning, toxic effects, adverse effects and underdosing in a pregnant patient
A code from subcategory O9A.2, Injury, poisoning and certain other consequences of external causes complicating pregnancy, childbirth, and the puerperium, should be sequenced first, followed by the appropriate injury, poisoning, toxic effect, adverse effect or underdosing code, and then the additional code(s) that specifies the condition caused by the poisoning, toxic effect, adverse effect or underdosing.
See Section I.C.19. Adverse effects, poisoning, underdosing and toxic effects.

n. Normal Delivery, Code O80

1) Encounter for full term uncomplicated delivery
Code O80 should be assigned when a woman is admitted for a full-term normal delivery and delivers a single, healthy infant without any complications antepartum, during the delivery, or postpartum during the

delivery episode. Code O80 is always a principal diagnosis. It is not to be used if any other code from chapter 15 is needed to describe a current complication of the antenatal, delivery, or perinatal period. Additional codes from other chapters may be used with code O80 if they are not related to or are in any way complicating the pregnancy.

2) Uncomplicated delivery with resolved antepartum complication
Code O80 may be used if the patient had a complication at some point during the pregnancy, but the complication is not present at the time of the admission for delivery.

3) Outcome of delivery for O80
Z37.0, Single live birth, is the only outcome of delivery code appropriate for use with O80.

o. The Peripartum and Postpartum Periods

1) Peripartum and Postpartum periods
The postpartum period begins immediately after delivery and continues for six weeks following delivery. The peripartum period is defined as the last month of pregnancy to five months postpartum.

2) Peripartum and postpartum complication
A postpartum complication is any complication occurring within the six-week period.

3) Pregnancy-related complications after 6 week period
Chapter 15 codes may also be used to describe pregnancy-related complications after the peripartum or postpartum period if the provider documents that a condition is pregnancy related.

4) Admission for routine postpartum care following delivery outside hospital
When the mother delivers outside the hospital prior to admission and is admitted for routine postpartum care and no complications are noted, code Z39.0, Encounter for care and examination of mother immediately after delivery, should be assigned as the principal diagnosis.

5) Pregnancy associated cardiomyopathy
Pregnancy associated cardiomyopathy, code O90.3, is unique in that it may be diagnosed in the third trimester of pregnancy but may continue to progress months after delivery. For this reason, it is referred to as peripartum cardiomyopathy. Code O90.3 is only for use when the cardiomyopathy develops as a result of pregnancy in a woman who did not have pre-existing heart disease.

p. Code O94, Sequelae of complication of pregnancy, childbirth, and the puerperium

1) Code O94
Code O94, Sequelae of complication of pregnancy, childbirth, and the puerperium, is for use in those cases when an initial complication of a pregnancy develops a sequelae requiring care or treatment at a future date.

2) After the initial postpartum period
This code may be used at any time after the initial postpartum period.

3) Sequencing of Code O94
This code, like all sequela codes, is to be sequenced following the code describing the sequelae of the complication.

q. Termination of Pregnancy and Spontaneous Abortions

1) Abortion with Liveborn Fetus
When an attempted termination of pregnancy results in a liveborn fetus, assign code Z33.2, Encounter for elective termination of pregnancy and a code from category Z37, Outcome of Delivery.

2) Retained Products of Conception following an abortion
Subsequent encounters for retained products of conception following a spontaneous abortion or elective termination of pregnancy are assigned the appropriate code from category O03, Spontaneous abortion, or codes O07.4, Failed attempted termination of pregnancy without complication and Z33.2, Encounter for elective termination of pregnancy. This advice is appropriate even when the patient was discharged previously with a discharge diagnosis of complete abortion.

3) Complications leading to abortion
Codes from Chapter 15 may be used as additional codes to identify any documented complications of the pregnancy in conjunction with codes in categories in O07 and O08.

r. Abuse in a pregnant patient
For suspected or confirmed cases of abuse of a pregnant patient, a code(s) from subcategories O9A.3, Physical abuse complicating pregnancy, childbirth, and the puerperium, O9A.4, Sexual abuse complicating pregnancy, childbirth, and the puerperium, and O9A.5, Psychological abuse complicating pregnancy, childbirth, and the puerperium, should be sequenced first, followed by the appropriate codes (if applicable) to identify any associated current injury due to physical abuse, sexual abuse, and the perpetrator of abuse.
See Section I.C.19.f. Adult and child abuse, neglect and other maltreatment.

16. Chapter 16: Newborn (Perinatal) Guidelines (P00-P96)

For coding and reporting purposes the perinatal period is defined as before birth through the 28th day following birth. The following guidelines are provided for reporting purposes

a. General Perinatal Rules

1) Use of Chapter 16 Codes
Codes in this chapter are never for use on the maternal record. Codes from Chapter 15, the obstetric chapter, are never permitted on the newborn record. Chapter 16 codes may be used throughout the life of the patient if the condition is still present.

2) Principal Diagnosis for Birth Record
When coding the birth episode in a newborn record, assign a code from category Z38, Liveborn infants according to place of birth and type of delivery, as the principal diagnosis. A code from category Z38 is assigned only once, to a newborn at the time of birth. If a newborn is transferred to another institution, a code from category Z38 should not be used at the receiving hospital.
A code from category Z38 is used only on the newborn record, not on the mother's record.

3) Use of Codes from other Chapters with Codes from Chapter 16
Codes from other chapters may be used with codes from chapter 16 if the codes from the other chapters provide more specific detail. Codes for signs and symptoms may be assigned when a definitive diagnosis has not been established. If the reason for the encounter is a perinatal condition, the code from chapter 16 should be sequenced first.

4) Use of Chapter 16 Codes after the Perinatal Period
Should a condition originate in the perinatal period, and continue throughout the life of the patient, the perinatal code should continue to be used regardless of the patient's age.

5) Birth process or community acquired conditions
If a newborn has a condition that may be either due to the birth process or community acquired and the documentation does not indicate which it is, the default is due to the birth process and the code from Chapter 16 should be used. If the condition is community-acquired, a code from Chapter 16 should not be assigned.

6) Code all clinically significant conditions
All clinically significant conditions noted on routine newborn examination should be coded. A condition is clinically significant if it requires:

- clinical evaluation; or
- therapeutic treatment; or
- diagnostic procedures; or
- extended length of hospital stay; or
- increased nursing care and/or monitoring; or
- has implications for future health care needs

Note: The perinatal guidelines listed above are the same as the general coding guidelines for "additional diagnoses", except for the final point regarding implications for future health care needs. Codes should be assigned for conditions that have been specified by the provider as having implications for future health care needs.

b. Observation and Evaluation of Newborns for Suspected Conditions not Found
Reserved for future expansion

c. Coding Additional Perinatal Diagnoses

1) Assigning codes for conditions that require treatment
Assign codes for conditions that require treatment or further investigation, prolong the length of stay, or require resource utilization.

2) Codes for conditions specified as having implications for future health care needs
Assign codes for conditions that have been specified by the provider as having implications for future health care needs.
Note: This guideline should not be used for adult patients.

d. Prematurity and Fetal Growth Retardation
Providers utilize different criteria in determining prematurity. A code for prematurity should not be assigned unless it is documented. Assignment of codes in categories P05, Disorders of newborn related to slow fetal growth and fetal malnutrition, and P07, Disorders of newborn related to short gestation and low birth weight, not elsewhere classified, should be based on the recorded birth weight and estimated gestational age. Codes from category P05 should not be assigned with codes from category P07.
When both birth weight and gestational age are available, two codes from category P07 should be assigned, with the code for birth weight sequenced before the code for gestational age.
A code from P05 and codes from P07.2 and P07.3 may be used to specify weeks of gestation as documented by the provider in the record.

e. Low birth weight and immaturity status
Codes from category P07, Disorders of newborn related to short gestation and low birth weight, not elsewhere classified, are for use for a child or adult who was premature or had a low birth weight as a newborn and this is affecting the patient's current health status.
See Section I.C.21. Factors influencing health status and contact with health services, Status.

f. Bacterial Sepsis of Newborn
Category P36, Bacterial sepsis of newborn, includes congenital sepsis. If a perinate is documented as having sepsis without documentation of congenital or community acquired, the default is congenital and a code from category P36 should be assigned. If the P36 code includes the causal organism, an additional code from category B95, Streptococcus, Staphylococcus, and Enterococcus as the cause of diseases classified elsewhere, or B96, Other bacterial agents as the cause of diseases classified elsewhere, should not be assigned. If the P36 code does not include the causal organism, assign an additional code from category B96. If applicable, use additional codes to identify severe sepsis (R65.2-) and any associated acute organ dysfunction.

g. Stillbirth
Code P95, Stillbirth, is only for use in institutions that maintain separate records for stillbirths. No other code should be used with P95. Code P95 should not be used on the mother's record.

17. Chapter 17: Congenital malformations, deformations, and chromosomal abnormalities (Q00-Q99)

Assign an appropriate code(s) from categories Q00-Q99, Congenital malformations, deformations, and chromosomal abnormalities when a malformation/deformation or chromosomal abnormality is documented. A malformation/deformation/or chromosomal abnormality may be the principal/first-listed diagnosis on a record or a secondary diagnosis.

When a malformation/deformation/or chromosomal abnormality does not have a unique code assignment, assign additional code(s) for any manifestations that may be present.

When the code assignment specifically identifies the malformation/deformation/or chromosomal abnormality, manifestations that are an inherent component of the anomaly should not be coded separately. Additional codes should be assigned for manifestations that are not an inherent component.

Codes from Chapter 17 may be used throughout the life of the patient. If a congenital malformation or deformity has been corrected, a personal history code should be used to identify the history of the malformation or deformity. Although present at birth, malformation/deformation/or chromosomal abnormality may not be identified until later in life. Whenever the condition is diagnosed by the physician, it is appropriate to assign a code from codes Q00-Q99.

For the birth admission, the appropriate code from category Z38, Liveborn infants, according to place of birth and type of delivery, should be sequenced as the principal diagnosis, followed by any congenital anomaly codes, Q00-Q99.

18. Chapter 18: Symptoms, signs, and abnormal clinical and laboratory findings, not elsewhere classified (R00-R99)

Chapter 18 includes symptoms, signs, abnormal results of clinical or other investigative procedures, and ill-defined conditions regarding which no diagnosis classifiable elsewhere is recorded. Signs and symptoms that point to a specific diagnosis have been assigned to a category in other chapters of the classification.

a. Use of symptom codes
Codes that describe symptoms and signs are acceptable for reporting purposes when a related definitive diagnosis has not been established (confirmed) by the provider.

b. Use of a symptom code with a definitive diagnosis code
Codes for signs and symptoms may be reported in addition to a related definitive diagnosis when the sign or symptom is not routinely associated with that diagnosis, such as the various signs and symptoms associated with complex syndromes. The definitive diagnosis code should be sequenced before the symptom code.
Signs or symptoms that are associated routinely with a disease process should not be assigned as additional codes, unless otherwise instructed by the classification.

c. Combination codes that include symptoms
ICD-10-CM contains a number of combination codes that identify both the definitive diagnosis and common symptoms of that diagnosis. When using one of these combination codes, an additional code should not be assigned for the symptom.

d. Repeated falls
Code R29.6, Repeated falls, is for use for encounters when a patient has recently fallen and the reason for the fall is being investigated.
Code Z91.81, History of falling, is for use when a patient has fallen in the past and is at risk for future falls. When appropriate, both codes R29.6 and Z91.81 may be assigned together.

e. Coma scale
The coma scale codes (R40.2-) can be used in conjunction with traumatic brain injury codes, acute cerebrovascular disease or sequelae of cerebrovascular disease codes. These codes are primarily for use by trauma registries, but they may be used in any setting where this information is collected. The coma scale codes should be sequenced after the diagnosis code(s).
These codes, one from each subcategory, are needed to complete the scale. The 7th character indicates when the scale was recorded. The 7th character should match for all three codes.
At a minimum, report the initial score documented on presentation at your facility. This may be a score from the emergency medicine technician (EMT) or in the emergency department. If desired, a facility may choose to capture multiple Glasgow coma scale scores.
Assign code R40.24, Glasgow coma scale, total score, when only the total score is documented in the medical record and not the individual score(s).

f. Functional quadriplegia
Functional quadriplegia (code R53.2) is the lack of ability to use one's limbs or to ambulate due to extreme debility. It is not associated with neurologic deficit or injury, and code R53.2 should not be used for cases of neurologic quadriplegia. It should only be assigned if functional quadriplegia is specifically documented in the medical record.

g. SIRS due to Non-Infectious Process
The systemic inflammatory response syndrome (SIRS) can develop as a result of certain non-infectious disease processes, such as trauma, malignant neoplasm, or pancreatitis. When SIRS is documented with a noninfectious condition, and no subsequent infection is documented, the code for the underlying condition, such as an injury, should be assigned, followed by code R65.10, Systemic inflammatory response syndrome (SIRS) of non-infectious origin without acute organ dysfunction, or code R65.11, Systemic inflammatory response syndrome (SIRS) of non-infectious origin with acute organ dysfunction. If an associated acute organ dysfunction is documented, the appropriate code(s) for the specific type of organ dysfunction(s) should be assigned in addition to code R65.11. If acute organ dysfunction is documented, but it cannot be determined if the acute organ dysfunction is associated with SIRS or due to another condition (e.g., directly due to the trauma), the provider should be queried.

h. Death NOS
Code R99, Ill-defined and unknown cause of mortality, is only for use in the very limited circumstance when a patient who has already died is brought into an emergency department or other healthcare facility and is pronounced dead upon arrival. It does not represent the discharge disposition of death.

19. Chapter 19: Injury, poisoning, and certain other consequences of external causes (S00-T88)

a. Code Extensions

Most categories in chapter 19 have a 7th character requirement for each applicable code. Most categories in this chapter have three 7th character values (with the exception of fractures): A, initial encounter, D, subsequent encounter and S, sequela. Categories for traumatic fractures have additional 7th character values.

7th character "A", initial encounter is used while the patient is receiving active treatment for the condition. Examples of active treatment are: surgical treatment, emergency department encounter, and evaluation and treatment by a new physician.

7th character "D" subsequent encounter is used for encounters after the patient has received active treatment of the condition and is receiving routine care for the condition during the healing or recovery phase. Examples of subsequent care are: cast change or removal, removal of external or internal fixation device, medication adjustment, other aftercare and follow up visits following treatment of the injury or condition.

The aftercare Z codes should not be used for conditions such as injuries or poisonings, where 7th characters are provided to identify subsequent care. For example, for aftercare of an injury, assign the acute injury code with the 7th character "D" (subsequent encounter).

7th character "S", sequela, is for use for complications or conditions that arise as a direct result of an condition, such as scar formation after a burn. The scars are sequelae of the burn. When using 7th character "S", it is necessary to use both the injury code that precipitated the sequela and the code for the sequela itself. The "S" is added only to the injury code, not the sequela code. The 7th character "S" identifies the injury responsible for the sequela. The specific type of sequela (e.g. scar) is sequenced first, followed by the injury code.

b. Coding of Injuries

When coding injuries, assign separate codes for each injury unless a combination code is provided, in which case the combination code is assigned. Code T07, Unspecified multiple injuries should not be assigned in the inpatient setting unless information for a more specific code is not available. Traumatic injury codes (S00-T14.9) are not to be used for normal, healing surgical wounds or to identify complications of surgical wounds.

The code for the most serious injury, as determined by the provider and the focus of treatment, is sequenced first.

1) Superficial injuries

Superficial injuries such as abrasions or contusions are not coded when associated with more severe injuries of the same site.

2) Primary injury with damage to nerves/blood vessels

When a primary injury results in minor damage to peripheral nerves or blood vessels, the primary injury is sequenced first with additional code(s) for injuries to nerves and spinal cord (such as category S04), and/or injury to blood vessels (such as category S15). When the primary injury is to the blood vessels or nerves, that injury should be sequenced first.

c. Coding of Traumatic Fractures

The principles of multiple coding of injuries should be followed in coding fractures. Fractures of specified sites are coded individually by site in accordance with both the provisions within categories S02, S12, S22, S32, S42, S49, S52, S59, S62, S72, S79, S82, S89, S92 and the level of detail furnished by medical record content.

A fracture not indicated as open or closed should be coded to closed. A fracture not indicated whether displaced or not displaced should be coded to displaced.

More specific guidelines are as follows:

1) Initial vs. Subsequent Encounter for Fractures

Traumatic fractures are coded using the appropriate 7th character extension for initial encounter (A, B, C) while the patient is receiving active treatment for the fracture. Examples of active treatment are: surgical treatment, emergency department encounter, and evaluation and treatment by a new physician. The appropriate 7th character for initial encounter should also be assigned for a patient who delayed seeking treatment for the fracture or nonunion.

Fractures are coded using the appropriate 7th character extension for subsequent care for encounters after the patient has completed active treatment of the fracture and is receiving routine care for the fracture during the healing or recovery phase. Examples of fracture aftercare are: cast change or removal, removal of external or internal fixation device, medication adjustment, and follow-up visits following fracture treatment.

Care for complications of surgical treatment for fracture repairs during the healing or recovery phase should be coded with the appropriate complication codes.

Care of complications of fractures, such as malunion and nonunion, should be reported with the appropriate 7th character extensions for subsequent care with nonunion (K, M, N,) or subsequent care with malunion (P, Q, R).

A code from category M80, not a traumatic fracture code, should be used for any patient with known osteoporosis who suffers a fracture, even if the patient had a minor fall or trauma, if that fall or trauma would not usually break a normal, healthy bone.

See Section I.C.13. Osteoporosis.

The aftercare Z codes should not be used for aftercare for traumatic fractures. For aftercare of a traumatic fracture, assign the acute fracture code with the appropriate 7th character.

2) Multiple fractures sequencing

Multiple fractures are sequenced in accordance with the severity of the fracture.

d. Coding of Burns and Corrosions

The ICD-10-CM makes a distinction between burns and corrosions. The burn codes are for thermal burns, except sunburns, that come from a heat source, such as a fire or hot appliance. The burn codes are also for burns resulting from electricity and radiation. Corrosions are burns due to chemicals. The guidelines are the same for burns and corrosions.

Current burns (T20-T25) are classified by depth, extent and by agent (X code). Burns are classified by depth as first degree (erythema), second degree (blistering), and third degree (full-thickness involvement). Burns of the eye and internal organs (T26-T28) are classified by site, but not by degree.

1) Sequencing of burn and related condition codes

Sequence first the code that reflects the highest degree of burn when more than one burn is present.

a. When the reason for the admission or encounter is for treatment of external multiple burns, sequence first the code that reflects the burn of the highest degree.

b. When a patient has both internal and external burns, the circumstances of admission govern the selection of the principal diagnosis or first-listed diagnosis.

c. When a patient is admitted for burn injuries and other related conditions such as smoke inhalation and/or respiratory failure, the circumstances of admission govern the selection of the principal or first-listed diagnosis.

2) Burns of the same local site

Classify burns of the same local site (three-character category level, T20-T28) but of different degrees to the subcategory identifying the highest degree recorded in the diagnosis.

3) Non-healing burns

Non-healing burns are coded as acute burns. Necrosis of burned skin should be coded as a non-healed burn.

4) Infected Burn

For any documented infected burn site, use an additional code for the infection.

5) Assign separate codes for each burn site

When coding burns, assign separate codes for each burn site. Category T30, Burn and corrosion, body region unspecified is extremely vague and should rarely be used.

6) Burns and Corrosions Classified According to Extent of Body Surface Involved

Assign codes from category T31, Burns classified according to extent of body surface involved, or T32, Corrosions classified according to extent of body surface involved, when the site of the burn is not specified or when there is a need for additional data. It is advisable to use category T31 as additional coding when needed to provide data for evaluating burn mortality, such as that needed by burn units. It is also advisable to use category T31 as an additional code for reporting purposes when there is mention of a third-degree burn involving 20 percent or more of the body surface.

Categories T31 and T32 are based on the classic "rule of nines" in estimating body surface involved: head and neck are assigned nine percent, each arm nine percent, each leg 18 percent, the anterior trunk 18 percent, posterior trunk 18 percent, and genitalia one percent. Providers may change these percentage assignments where necessary to accommodate infants and children who have proportionately larger heads than adults, and patients who have large buttocks, thighs, or abdomen that involve burns.

7) Encounters for treatment of late effects of burns

Encounters for the treatment of the late effects of burns or corrosions (i.e., scars or joint contractures) should be coded with a burn or corrosion code with the 7th character "S" for sequela.

8) Sequelae with a late effect code and current burn

When appropriate, both a code for a current burn or corrosion with 7th character "A" or "D" and a burn or corrosion code with 7th character "S" may be assigned on the same record (when both a current burn and sequelae of an old burn exist). Burns and corrosions do not heal at the same rate and a current healing wound may still exist with sequela of a healed burn or corrosion.

9) Use of an external cause code with burns and corrosions

An external cause code should be used with burns and corrosions to identify the source and intent of the burn, as well as the place where it occurred.

e. Adverse Effects, Poisoning, Underdosing and Toxic Effects

Codes in categories T36-T65 are combination codes that include the substances that was taken, as well as the intent. No additional external cause code is required for poisonings, toxic effects, adverse effects and underdosing codes.

A code from categories T36-T65 is sequenced first, followed by the code(s) that specify the nature of the adverse effect, poisoning, or toxic effect. Note: This sequencing instruction does not apply to underdosing codes (fifth or sixth character "6", for example T36.0x6-).

1) Do not code directly from the Table of Drugs

Do not code directly from the Table of Drugs and Chemicals.

Always refer back to the Tabular List.

2) Use as many codes as necessary to describe

Use as many codes as necessary to describe completely all drugs, medicinal or biological substances.

3) If the same code would describe the causative agent

If the same code would describe the causative agent for more than one adverse reaction, poisoning, toxic effect or underdosing, assign the code only once.

4) If two or more drugs, medicinal or biological substances

If two or more drugs, medicinal or biological substances are reported, code each individually unless a combination code is listed in the Table of Drugs and Chemicals.

5) The occurrence of drug toxicity is classified in ICD-10-CM as follows:

(a) Adverse Effect

When coding an adverse effect of a drug that has been correctly prescribed and properly administered, assign the appropriate code for the nature of the adverse effect followed by the appropriate code for the adverse effect of the drug (T36-T50). The code for the drug should have a 5th or 6th character "5" (for example T36.0X5-) Examples of the nature of an adverse effect are tachycardia, delirium, gastrointestinal hemorrhaging, vomiting, hypokalemia, hepatitis, renal failure, or respiratory failure.

(b) Poisoning

When coding a poisoning or reaction to the improper use of a medication (e.g., overdose, wrong substance given or taken in error, wrong route of administration), first assign the appropriate code from categories T36-T50. The poisoning codes have an associated intent as their 5th or 6th character (accidental, intentional self-harm, assault and undetermined). Use additional code(s) for all manifestations of poisonings.

If there is also a diagnosis of abuse of or dependence on the substance, the abuse or dependence is assigned as an additional code.

Examples of poisoning include:

(i) Error was made in drug prescription Errors made in drug prescription or in the administration of the drug by provider, nurse, patient, or other person.

(ii) Overdose of a drug intentionally taken If an overdose of a drug was intentionally taken or administered and resulted in drug toxicity, it would be coded as a poisoning.

(iii) Nonprescribed drug taken with correctly prescribed and properly administered drug If a nonprescribed drug or medicinal agent was taken in combination with a correctly prescribed and properly administered drug, any drug toxicity or other reaction resulting from the interaction of the two drugs would be classified as a poisoning.

(iv) Interaction of drug(s) and alcohol When a reaction results from the interaction of a drug(s) and alcohol, this would be classified as poisoning.

See Section I.C.4. if poisoning is the result of insulin pump malfunctions.

(c) Underdosing

Underdosing refers to taking less of a medication than is prescribed by a provider or a manufacturer's instruction. For underdosing, assign the code from categories T36-T50 (fifth or sixth character "6").

Codes for underdosing should never be assigned as principal or first-listed codes. If a patient has a relapse or exacerbation of the medical condition for which the drug is prescribed because of the reduction in dose, then the medical condition itself should be coded.

Noncompliance (Z91.12-, Z91.13-) or complication of care (Y63.61, Y63.8-Y63.9) codes are to be used with an underdosing code to indicate intent, if known.

(d) Toxic Effects

When a harmful substance is ingested or comes in contact with a person, this is classified as a toxic effect. The toxic effect codes are in categories T51-T65.

Toxic effect codes have an associated intent: accidental, intentional self-harm, assault and undetermined.

f. Adult and child abuse, neglect and other maltreatment

Sequence first the appropriate code from categories T74.-(Adult and child abuse, neglect and other maltreatment, confirmed) or T76.-(Adult and child abuse, neglect and other maltreatment, suspected) for abuse, neglect and other maltreatment, followed by any accompanying mental health or injury code(s).

If the documentation in the medical record states abuse or neglect it is coded as confirmed (T74.-). It is coded as suspected if it is documented as suspected (T76.-).

For cases of confirmed abuse or neglect an external cause code from the assault section (X92-Y08) should be added to identify the cause of any physical injuries. A perpetrator code (Y07) should be added when the perpetrator of the abuse is known. For suspected cases of abuse or neglect, do not report external cause or perpetrator code.

If a suspected case of abuse, neglect or mistreatment is ruled out during an encounter code Z04.71, Encounter for examination and observation following alleged physical adult abuse, ruled out, or code Z04.72, Encounter for examination and observation following alleged child physical abuse, ruled out, should be used, not a code from T76.

If a suspected case of alleged rape or sexual abuse is ruled out during an encounter code Z04.41, Encounter for examination and observation following alleged physical adult abuse, ruled out, or code Z04.42, Encounter for examination and observation following alleged rape or sexual abuse, ruled out, should be used, not a code from T76.

See Section I.C.15.r Abuse in a pregnant patient.

g. Complications of care

1) General guidelines for complications of care

(a) Documentation of complications of care

See Section I.B.16. for information on documentation of complications of care.

2) Pain due to medical devices

Pain associated with devices, implants or grafts left in a surgical site (for example painful hip prosthesis) is assigned to the appropriate code(s) found in Chapter 19, Injury, poisoning, and certain other consequences of external causes. Specific codes for pain due to medical devices are found in the T code section of the ICD-10-CM. Use additional code(s) from category G89 to identify acute or chronic pain due to presence of the device, implant or graft (G89.18 or G89.28).

3) Transplant complications

(a) Transplant complications other than kidney

Codes under category T86, Complications of transplanted organs and tissues, are for use for both complications and rejection of transplanted organs. A transplant complication code is only assigned if the complication affects the function of the transplanted organ. Two codes are required to fully describe a transplant complication: the appropriate code from category T86 and a secondary code that identifies the complication.

Pre-existing conditions or conditions that develop after the transplant are not coded as complications unless they affect the function of the transplanted organs.

See I.C.21.c.3 for transplant organ removal status See I.C.2.r for malignant neoplasm associated with transplanted organ.

(b) Chronic kidney disease and kidney transplant complications

Patients who have undergone kidney transplant may still have some form of chronic kidney disease (CKD) because the kidney transplant may not fully restore kidney function. Code T86.1- should be assigned for documented complications of a kidney transplant, such as transplant failure or rejection or other transplant complication. Code T86.1- should not be assigned for post kidney transplant patients who have chronic kidney (CKD) unless a transplant complication such as transplant failure or rejection is documented. If the documentation is unclear as to whether the patient has a complication of the transplant, query the provider.

Conditions that affect the function of the transplanted kidney, other than CKD, should be assigned a code from subcategory T86.1, Complications of transplanted organ, Kidney, and a secondary code that identifies the complication.

For patients with CKD following a kidney transplant, but who do not have a complication such as failure or rejection, *see section I.C.14. Chronic kidney disease and kidney transplant status.*

4) Complication codes that include the external cause

As with certain other T codes, some of the complications of care codes have the external cause included in the code. The code includes the nature of the complication as well as the type of procedure that caused the complication. No external cause code indicating the type of procedure is necessary for these codes.

5) Complications of care codes within the body system chapters

Intraoperative and postprocedural complication codes are found within the body system chapters with codes specific to the organs and structures of that body system. These codes should be sequenced first, followed by a code(s) for the specific complication, if applicable.

20. Chapter 20: External Causes of Morbidity (V01-Y99)

The external causes of morbidity codes should never be sequenced as the first-listed or principal diagnosis.

External cause codes are intended to provide data for injury research and evaluation of injury prevention strategies. These codes capture how the injury or health condition happened (cause), the intent (unintentional or accidental; or intentional, such as suicide or assault), the place where the event occurred the activity of the patient at the time of the event, and the person's status (e.g., civilian, military).

There is no national requirement for mandatory ICD-10-CM external cause code reporting. Unless a provider is subject to a state-based external cause code reporting mandate or these codes are required by a particular payer, reporting of ICD-10-CM codes in Chapter 20, External Causes of Morbidity, is not required. In the absence of a mandatory reporting requirement, providers are encouraged to voluntarily report external cause codes, as they provide valuable data for injury research and evaluation of injury prevention strategies.

a. General External Cause Coding Guidelines

1) Used with any code in the range of A00.0-T88.9, Z00-Z99

An external cause code may be used with any code in the range of A00.0-T88.9, Z00-Z99, classification that is a health condition due to an external cause. Though they are most applicable to injuries, they are also valid for use with such things as infections or diseases due to an external source, and other health conditions, such as a heart attack that occurs during strenuous physical activity.

2) External cause code used for length of treatment

Assign the external cause code, with the appropriate 7th character (initial encounter, subsequent encounter or sequela) for each encounter for which the injury or condition is being treated.

3) Use the full range of external cause codes

Use the full range of external cause codes to completely describe the cause, the intent, the place of occurrence, and if applicable, the activity of the patient at the time of the event, and the patient's status, for all injuries, and other health conditions due to an external cause.

4) Assign as many external cause codes as necessary

Assign as many external cause codes as necessary to fully explain each cause. If only one external code can be recorded, assign the code most related to the principal diagnosis.

5) The selection of the appropriate external cause code

The selection of the appropriate external cause code is guided by the Alphabetic Index of External Causes and by Inclusion and Exclusion notes in the Tabular List.

6) External cause code can never be a principal diagnosis

An external cause code can never be a principal (first-listed) diagnosis.

7) Combination external cause codes

Certain of the external cause codes are combination codes that identify sequential events that result in an injury, such as a fall which results in striking against an object. The injury may be due to either event or both. The combination external cause code used should correspond to the sequence of events regardless of which caused the most serious injury.

8) No external cause code needed in certain circumstances

No external cause code from Chapter 20 is needed if the external cause and intent are included in a code from another chapter (e.g. T36.0x1- Poisoning by penicillins, accidental (unintentional)).

b. Place of Occurrence Guideline

Codes from category Y92, Place of occurrence of the external cause, are secondary codes for use after other external cause codes to identify the location of the patient at the time of injury or other condition.

A place of occurrence code is used only once, at the initial encounter for treatment. No 7th characters are used for Y92. Only one code from Y92 should be recorded on a medical record. A place of occurrence code should be used in conjunction with an activity code, Y93.

Do not use place of occurrence code Y92.9 if the place is not stated or is not applicable.

c. Activity Code

Assign a code from category Y93, Activity code, to describe the activity of the patient at the time the injury or other health condition occurred.

An activity code is used only once, at the initial encounter for treatment. Only one code from Y93 should be recorded on a medical record. An activity code should be used in conjunction with a place of occurrence code, Y92.

The activity codes are not applicable to poisonings, adverse effects, misadventures or late effects.

Do not assign Y93.9, Unspecified activity, if the activity is not stated.

A code from category Y93 is appropriate for use with external cause and intent codes if identifying the activity provides additional information about the event.

d. Place of Occurrence, Activity, and Status Codes Used with other External Cause Code

When applicable, place of occurrence, activity, and external cause status codes are sequenced after the main external cause code(s). Regardless of the number of external cause codes assigned, there should be only one place of occurrence code, one activity code, and one external cause status code assigned to an encounter.

e. If the Reporting Format Limits the Number of External Cause Codes

If the reporting format limits the number of external cause codes that can be used in reporting clinical data, report the code for the cause/intent most related to the principal diagnosis. If the format permits capture of additional external cause codes, the cause/intent, including medical misadventures, of the additional events should be reported rather than the codes for place, activity, or external status.

f. Multiple External Cause Coding Guidelines

More than one external cause code is required to fully describe the external cause of an illness or injury. The assignment of external cause codes should be sequenced in the following priority:

- If two or more events cause separate injuries, an external cause code should be assigned for each cause. The first-listed external cause code will be selected in the following order:
- External codes for child and adult abuse take priority over all other external cause codes.

  See Section I.C.19., Child and Adult abuse guidelines.
- External cause codes for terrorism events take priority over all other external cause codes except child and adult abuse.
- External cause codes for cataclysmic events take priority over all other external cause codes except child and adult abuse and terrorism.
- External cause codes for transport accidents take priority over all other external cause codes except cataclysmic events, child and adult abuse and terrorism.
- Activity and external cause status codes are assigned following all causal (intent) external cause codes.
- The first-listed external cause code should correspond to the cause of the most serious diagnosis due to an assault, accident, or self-harm, following the order of hierarchy listed above.

g. Child and Adult Abuse Guideline

Adult and child abuse, neglect and maltreatment are classified as assault. Any of the assault codes may be used to indicate the external cause of any injury resulting from the confirmed abuse.

For confirmed cases of abuse, neglect and maltreatment, when the perpetrator is known, a code from Y07, Perpetrator of maltreatment and neglect, should accompany any other assault codes.

See Section I.C.19. Adult and child abuse, neglect and other maltreatment

h. Unknown or Undetermined Intent Guideline

If the intent (accident, self-harm, assault) of the cause of an injury or other condition is unknown or unspecified, code the intent as accidental intent. All transport accident categories assume accidental intent.

1) Use of undetermined intent

External cause codes for events of undetermined intent are only for use if the documentation in the record specifies that the intent cannot be determined.

i. Sequelae (Late Effects) of External Cause Guidelines

1) Sequelae external cause codes

Sequela are reported using the external cause code with the 7th character extension "S" for sequela. These codes should be used with any report of a late effect or sequela resulting from a previous injury.

2) Sequela external cause code with a related current injury

A sequela external cause code should never be used with a related current nature of injury code.

3) Use of sequela external cause codes for subsequent visits

Use a late effect external cause code for subsequent visits when a late effect of the initial injury is being treated. Do not use a late effect external cause code for subsequent visits for follow-up care (e.g., to assess healing, to receive rehabilitative therapy) of the injury when no late effect of the injury has been documented.

j. Terrorism Guidelines

1) Cause of injury identified by the Federal Government (FBI) as terrorism

When the cause of an injury is identified by the Federal Government (FBI) as terrorism, the first-listed external cause code should be a code from category Y38, Terrorism. The definition of terrorism employed by the FBI is found at the inclusion note at the beginning of category Y38. Use additional code for place of occurrence (Y92.-). More than one Y38 code may be assigned if the injury is the result of more than one mechanism of terrorism.

2) Cause of an injury is suspected to be the result of terrorism

When the cause of an injury is suspected to be the result of terrorism a code from category Y38 should not be assigned. Suspected cases should be classified as assault.

3) Code Y38.9, Terrorism, secondary effects

Assign code Y38.9, Terrorism, secondary effects, for conditions occurring subsequent to the terrorist event. This code should not be assigned for conditions that are due to the initial terrorist act.

It is acceptable to assign code Y38.9 with another code from Y38 if there is an injury due to the initial terrorist event and an injury that is a subsequent result of the terrorist event.

k. External cause status

A code from category Y99, External cause status, should be assigned whenever any other external cause code is assigned for an encounter, including an Activity code, except for the events noted below. Assign a code from category Y99, External cause status, to indicate the work status of the person at the time the event occurred. The status code indicates whether the event occurred during military activity, whether a non-military person was at work, whether an individual including a student or volunteer was involved in a non-work activity at the time of the causal event.

A code from Y99, External cause status, should be assigned, when applicable, with other external cause codes, such as transport accidents and falls. The external cause status codes are not applicable to poisonings, adverse effects, misadventures or late effects.

Do not assign a code from category Y99 if no other external cause codes (cause, activity) are applicable for the encounter.

An external cause status code is used only once, at the initial encounter for treatment. Only one code from Y99 should be recorded on a medical record.

Do not assign code Y99.9, Unspecified external cause status, if the status is not stated.

21. Chapter 21: Factors influencing health status and contact with health services (Z00-Z99)

Note: The chapter specific guidelines provide additional information about the use of Z codes for specified encounters.

a. Use of Z codes in any healthcare setting

Z codes are for use in any healthcare setting. Z codes may be used as either a first-listed (principal diagnosis code in the inpatient setting) or secondary code, depending on the circumstances of the encounter. Certain Z codes may only be used as first-listed or principal diagnosis.

b. Z Codes indicate a reason for an encounter
Z codes are not procedure codes. A corresponding procedure code must accompany a Z code to describe any procedure performed.

c. Categories of Z Codes

1) Contact/Exposure

Category Z20 indicates contact with, and suspected exposure to, communicable diseases. These codes are for patients who do not show any sign or symptom of a disease but are suspected to have been exposed to it by close personal contact with an infected individual or are in an area where a disease is epidemic.

Category Z77, indicates contact with and suspected exposures hazardous to health.

Contact/exposure codes may be used as a first-listed code to explain an encounter for testing, or, more commonly, as a secondary code to identify a potential risk.

2) Inoculations and vaccinations

Code Z23 is for encounters for inoculations and vaccinations. It indicates that a patient is being seen to receive a prophylactic inoculation against a disease. Procedure codes are required to identify the actual administration of the injection and the type(s) of immunizations given. Code Z23 may be used as a secondary code if the inoculation is given as a routine part of preventive health care, such as a well-baby visit.

3) Status

Status codes indicate that a patient is either a carrier of a disease or has the sequelae or residual of a past disease or condition. This includes such things as the presence of prosthetic or mechanical devices resulting from past treatment.

A status code is informative, because the status may affect the course of treatment and its outcome. A status code is distinct from a history code. The history code indicates that the patient no longer has the condition.

A status code should not be used with a diagnosis code from one of the body system chapters, if the diagnosis code includes the information provided by the status code. For example, code Z94.1, Heart transplant status, should not be used with a code from subcategory T86.2, Complications of heart transplant. The status code does not provide additional information. The complication code indicates that the patient is a heart transplant patient.

For encounters for weaning from a mechanical ventilator, assign a code from subcategory J96.1, Chronic respiratory failure, followed by code Z99.11, Dependence on respirator [ventilator] status.

The status Z codes/categories are:

Z14 Genetic carrier
Genetic carrier status indicates that a person carries a gene, associated with a particular disease, which may be passed to offspring who may develop that disease. The person does not have the disease and is not at risk of developing the disease.

Z15 Genetic susceptibility to disease
Genetic susceptibility indicates that a person has a gene that increases the risk of that person developing the disease.
Codes from category Z15 should not be used as principal or first-listed codes. If the patient has the condition to which he/she is susceptible, and that condition is the reason for the encounter, the code for the current condition should be sequenced first. If the patient is being seen for follow-up after completed treatment for this condition, and the condition no longer exists, a follow-up code should be sequenced first, followed by the appropriate personal history and genetic susceptibility codes. If the purpose of the encounter is genetic counseling associated with procreative management, code Z31.5, Encounter for genetic counseling, should be assigned as the first-listed code, followed by a code from category Z15. Additional codes should be assigned for any applicable family or personal history.

Z16 Resistance to antimicrobial drugs
This code indicates that a patient has a condition that is resistant to antimicrobial drug treatment. Sequence the infection code first.

Z17 Estrogen receptor status

Z18 Retained foreign body fragments

Z21 Asymptomatic HIV infection status
This code indicates that a patient has tested positive for HIV but has manifested no signs or symptoms of the disease.

Z22 Carrier of infectious disease
Carrier status indicates that a person harbors the specific organisms of a disease without manifest symptoms and is capable of transmitting the infection.

Z28.3 Underimmunization status

Z33.1 Pregnant state, incidental
This code is a secondary code only for use when the pregnancy is in no way complicating the reason for visit. Otherwise, a code from the obstetric chapter is required.

Z66 Do not resuscitate
This code may be used when it is documented by the provider that a patient is on do not resuscitate status at any time during the stay.

Z67 Blood type

Z68 Body mass index (BMI)

Z74.01 Bed confinement status

Z76.82 Awaiting organ transplant status

Z78 Other specified health status
Code Z78.1, Physical restraint status, may be used when it is documented by the provider that a patient has been put in restraints during the current encounter. Please note that this code should not be reported when it is documented by the provider that a patient is temporarily restrained during a procedure.

Z79 Long-term (current) drug therapy
Codes from this category indicate a patient's continuous use of a prescribed drug (including such things as aspirin therapy) for the long-term treatment of a condition or for prophylactic use. It is not for use for patients who have addictions to drugs. This subcategory is not for use of medications for detoxification or maintenance programs to prevent withdrawal symptoms in patients with drug dependence (e.g., methadone maintenance for opiate dependence). Assign the appropriate code for the drug dependence instead.
Assign a code from Z79 if the patient is receiving a medication for an extended period as a prophylactic measure (such as for the prevention of deep vein thrombosis) or as treatment of a chronic condition (such as arthritis) or a disease requiring a lengthy course of treatment (such as cancer). Do not assign a code from category Z79 for medication being administered for a brief period of time to treat an acute illness or injury (such as a course of antibiotics to treat acute bronchitis).

Z88 Allergy status to drugs, medicaments and biological substances
Except: Z88.9, Allergy status to unspecified drugs, medicaments and biological substances status

Z89 Acquired absence of limb

Z90 Acquired absence of organs, not elsewhere classified

Z91.0- Allergy status, other than to drugs and biological substances

Z92.82 Status post administration of tPA (rtPA) in a different facility within the last 24 hours prior to admission to a current facility
Assign code Z92.82, Status post administration of tPA (rtPA) in a different facility within the last 24 hours prior to admission to current facility, as a secondary diagnosis when a patient is received by transfer into a facility and documentation indicates they were administered tissue plasminogen activator (tPA) within the last 24 hours prior to admission to the current facility.
This guideline applies even if the patient is still receiving the tPA at

the time they are received into the current facility.

The appropriate code for the condition for which the tPA was administered (such as cerebrovascular disease or myocardial infarction) should be assigned first.

Code Z92.82 is only applicable to the receiving facility record and not to the transferring facility record.

Z93 Artificial opening status

Z94 Transplanted organ and tissue status

Z95 Presence of cardiac and vascular implants and grafts

Z96 Presence of other functional implants

Z97 Presence of other devices

Z98 Other postprocedural states

Assign code Z98.85, Transplanted organ removal status, to indicate that a transplanted organ has been previously removed. This code should not be assigned for the encounter in which the transplanted organ is removed. The complication necessitating removal of the transplant organ should be assigned for that encounter.

See section I.C19.g.3. for information on the coding of organ transplant complications.

Z99 Dependence on enabling machines and devices, not elsewhere classified

Note: Categories Z89-Z90 and Z93-Z99 are for use only if there are no complications or malfunctions of the organ or tissue replaced, the amputation site or the equipment on which the patient is dependent.

4) History (of)

There are two types of history Z codes, personal and family. Personal history codes explain a patient's past medical condition that no longer exists and is not receiving any treatment, but that has the potential for recurrence, and therefore may require continued monitoring.

Family history codes are for use when a patient has a family member(s) who has had a particular disease that causes the patient to be at higher risk of also contracting the disease.

Personal history codes may be used in conjunction with follow-up codes and family history codes may be used in conjunction with screening codes to explain the need for a test or procedure. History codes are also acceptable on any medical record regardless of the reason for visit. A history of an illness, even if no longer present, is important information that may alter the type of treatment ordered.

The history Z code categories are:

Z80 Family history of primary malignant neoplasm

Z81 Family history of mental and behavioral disorders

Z82 Family history of certain disabilities and chronic diseases (leading to disablement)

Z83 Family history of other specific disorders

Z84 Family history of other conditions

Z85 Personal history of malignant neoplasm

Z86 Personal history of certain other diseases

Z87 Personal history of other diseases and conditions

Z91.4- Personal history of psychological trauma, not elsewhere classified

Z91.5 Personal history of self-harm

Z91.8- Other specified personal risk factors, not elsewhere classified

Exception:

Z91.83 Wandering in diseases classified elsewhere

Z92 Personal history of medical treatment

Except: Z92.0, Personal history of contraception

Except: Z92.82, Status post administration of tPA (rtPA) in a different facility within the last 24 hours prior to admission to a current facility

5) Screening

Screening is the testing for disease or disease precursors in seemingly well individuals so that early detection and treatment can be provided for those who test positive for the disease (e.g., screening mammogram).

The testing of a person to rule out or confirm a suspected diagnosis because the patient has some sign or symptom is a diagnostic examination, not a screening. In these cases, the sign or symptom is used to explain the reason for the test.

A screening code may be a first-listed code if the reason for the visit is specifically the screening exam. It may also be used as an additional code if the screening is done during an office visit for other health problems. A screening code is not necessary if the screening is inherent to a routine examination, such as a pap smear done during a routine pelvic examination.

Should a condition be discovered during the screening then the code for the condition may be assigned as an additional diagnosis.

The Z code indicates that a screening exam is planned. A procedure code is required to confirm that the screening was performed.

The screening Z codes/categories:

Z11 Encounter for screening for infectious and parasitic diseases

Z12 Encounter for screening for malignant neoplasms

Z13 Encounter for screening for other diseases and disorders

Except: Z13.9, Encounter for screening, unspecified

Z36 Encounter for antenatal screening for mother

6) Observation

There are two observation Z code categories. They are for use in very limited circumstances when a person is being observed for a suspected condition that is ruled out. The observation codes are not for use if an injury or illness or any signs or symptoms related to the suspected condition are present. In such cases the diagnosis/symptom code is used with the corresponding external cause code.

The observation codes are to be used as principal diagnosis only. Additional codes may be used in addition to the observation code but only if they are unrelated to the suspected condition being observed.

Codes from subcategory Z03.7, Encounter for suspected maternal and fetal conditions ruled out, may either be used as a first-listed or as an additional code assignment depending on the case. They are for use in very limited circumstances on a maternal record when an encounter is for a suspected maternal or fetal condition that is ruled out during that encounter (for example, a maternal or fetal condition may be suspected due to an abnormal test result). These codes should not be used when the condition is confirmed. In those cases, the confirmed condition should be coded. In addition, these codes are not for use if an illness or any signs or symptoms related to the suspected condition or problem are present. In such cases the diagnosis/symptom code is used.

Additional codes may be used in addition to the code from subcategory Z03.7, but only if they are unrelated to the suspected condition being evaluated.

Codes from subcategory Z03.7 may not be used for encounters for antenatal screening of mother.

See Section I.C.21.c.5, Screening.

For encounters for suspected fetal condition that are inconclusive following testing and evaluation, assign the appropriate code from category O35, O36, O40 or O41. The observation Z code categories:

Z03 Encounter for medical observation for suspected diseases and conditions ruled out

Z04 Encounter for examination and observation for other reasons

Except: Z04.9, Encounter for examination and observation for unspecified reason

7) Aftercare

Aftercare visit codes cover situations when the initial treatment of a disease has been performed and the patient requires continued care during the healing or recovery phase, or for the long-term consequences of the disease. The aftercare Z code should not be used if treatment is directed at a current, acute disease. The diagnosis code is to be used in these cases. Exceptions to this rule are codes Z51.0, Encounter for antineoplastic radiation therapy, and codes from subcategory Z51.1, Encounter for antineoplastic chemotherapy and immunotherapy. These codes are to be first-listed, followed by the diagnosis code when a patient's encounter is solely to receive radiation therapy, chemotherapy, or immunotherapy for the treatment of a neoplasm. If the reason for the encounter is more than one type of antineoplastic therapy, code Z51.0 and a code from subcategory Z51.1 may be assigned together, in which case one of these codes would be reported as a secondary diagnosis.

The aftercare Z codes should also not be used for aftercare for injuries. For aftercare of an injury, assign the acute injury code with the appropriate 7th character (for subsequent encounter).

The aftercare codes are generally first-listed to explain the specific reason for the encounter. An aftercare code may be used as an additional code when some type of aftercare is provided in addition to the reason for admission and no diagnosis code is applicable. An example of this would be the closure of a colostomy during an encounter for treatment of another condition.

Aftercare codes should be used in conjunction with other aftercare codes or diagnosis codes to provide better detail on the specifics of an aftercare encounter visit, unless otherwise directed by the classification. Should a patient receive multiple types of antineoplastic therapy during the same encounter, code Z51.0, Encounter for antineoplastic radiation therapy, and codes from subcategory Z51.1, Encounter for antineoplastic chemotherapy and immunotherapy, may be used together on a record. The sequencing of multiple aftercare codes depends on the circumstances of the encounter.

Certain aftercare Z code categories need a secondary diagnosis code to describe the resolving condition or sequelae. For others, the condition is included in the code title.

Additional Z code aftercare category terms include fitting and adjustment, and attention to artificial openings.

Status Z codes may be used with aftercare Z codes to indicate the nature of the aftercare. For example code Z95.1, Presence of aortocoronary bypass graft, may be used with code Z48.812, Encounter for surgical aftercare following surgery on the circulatory system, to indicate the surgery for which the aftercare is being performed. A status code should not be used when the aftercare code indicates the type of status, such as using Z43.0, Encounter for attention to tracheostomy, with Z93.0, Tracheostomy status.

The aftercare Z category/codes:

Z42 Encounter for plastic and reconstructive surgery following medical procedure or healed injury
Z43 Encounter for attention to artificial openings
Z44 Encounter for fitting and adjustment of external prosthetic device
Z45 Encounter for adjustment and management of implanted device
Z46 Encounter for fitting and adjustment of other devices
Z47 Orthopedic aftercare
Z48 Encounter for other postprocedural aftercare
Z49 Encounter for care involving renal dialysis
Z51 Encounter for other aftercare

8) Follow-up

The follow-up codes are used to explain continuing surveillance following completed treatment of a disease, condition, or injury. They imply that the condition has been fully treated and no longer exists. They should not be confused with aftercare codes, or injury codes with a 7th character for subsequent encounter, that explain ongoing care of a healing condition or its sequelae. Follow-up codes may be used in conjunction with history codes to provide the full picture of the healed condition and its treatment. The follow-up code is sequenced first, followed by the history code.

A follow-up code may be used to explain multiple visits. Should a condition be found to have recurred on the follow-up visit, then the diagnosis code for the condition should be assigned in place of the follow-up code.

The follow-up Z code categories:

Z08 Encounter for follow-up examination after completed treatment for malignant neoplasm
Z09 Encounter for follow-up examination after completed treatment for conditions other than malignant neoplasm
Z39 Encounter for maternal postpartum care and examination

9) Donor

Codes in category Z52, Donors of organs and tissues, are used for living individuals who are donating blood or other body tissue. These codes are only for individuals donating for others, not for self-donations. They are not used to identify cadaveric donations.

10) Counseling

Counseling Z codes are used when a patient or family member receives assistance in the aftermath of an illness or injury, or when support is required in coping with family or social problems. They are not used in conjunction with a diagnosis code when the counseling component of care is considered integral to standard treatment.

The counseling Z codes/categories:

Z30.0- Encounter for general counseling and advice on contraception
Z31.5 Encounter for genetic counseling
Z31.6- Encounter for general counseling and advice on procreation
Z32.2 Encounter for childbirth instruction
Z32.3 Encounter for childcare instruction
Z69 Encounter for mental health services for victim and perpetrator of abuse
Z70 Counseling related to sexual attitude, behavior and orientation
Z71 Persons encountering health services for other counseling and medical advice, not elsewhere classified
Z76.81 Expectant mother prebirth pediatrician visit

11) Encounters for Obstetrical and Reproductive Services

See Section I.C.15. Pregnancy, Childbirth, and the Puerperium, for further instruction on the use of these codes.

Z codes for pregnancy are for use in those circumstances when none of the problems or complications included in the codes from the Obstetrics chapter exist (a routine prenatal visit or postpartum care). Codes in category Z34, Encounter for supervision of normal pregnancy, are always first-listed and are not to be used with any other code from the OB chapter.

Codes in category Z3A, Weeks of gestation, may be assigned to provide additional information about the pregnancy. The date of the admission should be used to determine weeks of gestation for inpatient admissions that encompass more than one gestational week.

The outcome of delivery, category Z37, should be included on all maternal delivery records. It is always a secondary code. Codes in category Z37 should not be used on the newborn record.

Z codes for family planning (contraceptive) or procreative management and counseling should be included on an obstetric record either during the pregnancy or the postpartum stage, if applicable.

Z codes/categories for obstetrical and reproductive services:

Z30 Encounter for contraceptive management
Z31 Encounter for procreative management
Z32.2 Encounter for childbirth instruction
Z32.3 Encounter for childcare instruction
Z33 Pregnant state
Z34 Encounter for supervision of normal pregnancy
Z36 Encounter for antenatal screening of mother
Z3A Weeks of gestation

2015 Draft ICD-10-CM

Z37 Outcome of delivery
Z39 Encounter for maternal postpartum care and examination
Z76.81 Expectant mother prebirth pediatrician visit

12) Newborns and Infants
See Section I.C.16. Newborn (Perinatal) Guidelines, for further instruction on the use of these codes.
Newborn Z codes/categories:
Z76.1 Encounter for health supervision and care of foundling
Z00.1- Encounter for routine child health examination
Z38 Liveborn infants according to place of birth and type of delivery

13) Routine and administrative examinations
The Z codes allow for the description of encounters for routine examinations, such as, a general check-up, or, examinations for administrative purposes, such as, a pre-employment physical. The codes are not to be used if the examination is for diagnosis of a suspected condition or for treatment purposes. In such cases the diagnosis code is used. During a routine exam, should a diagnosis or condition be discovered, it should be coded as an additional code. Pre-existing and chronic conditions and history codes may also be included as additional codes as long as the examination is for administrative purposes and not focused on any particular condition.
Some of the codes for routine health examinations distinguish between "with" and "without" abnormal findings. Code assignment depends on the information that is known at the time the encounter is being coded. For example, if no abnormal findings were found during the examination, but the encounter is being coded before test results are back, it is acceptable to assign the code for "without abnormal findings." When assigning a code for "with abnormal findings," additional code(s) should be assigned to identify the specific abnormal finding(s).
Pre-operative examination and pre-procedural laboratory examination Z codes are for use only in those situations when a patient is being cleared for a procedure or surgery and no treatment is given.
The Z codes/categories for routine and administrative examinations:
Z00 Encounter for general examination without complaint, suspected or reported diagnosis
Z01 Encounter for other special examination without complaint, suspected or reported diagnosis
Z02 Encounter for administrative examination
Except: Z02.9, Encounter for administrative examinations, unspecified
Z32.0- Encounter for pregnancy test

14) Miscellaneous Z codes
The miscellaneous Z codes capture a number of other health care encounters that do not fall into one of the other categories. Certain of these codes identify the reason for the encounter; others are for use as additional codes that provide useful information on circumstances that may affect a patient's care and treatment.
Prophylactic Organ Removal
For encounters specifically for prophylactic removal of an organ (such as prophylactic removal of breasts due to a genetic susceptibility to cancer or a family history of cancer), the principal or first-listed code should be a code from category Z40, Encounter for prophylactic surgery, followed by the appropriate codes to identify the associated risk factor (such as genetic susceptibility or family history).
If the patient has a malignancy of one site and is having prophylactic removal at another site to prevent either a new primary malignancy or metastatic disease, a code for the malignancy should also be assigned in addition to a code from subcategory Z40.0, Encounter for prophylactic surgery for risk factors related to malignant neoplasms. A Z40.0 code should not be assigned if the patient is having organ removal for treatment of a malignancy, such as the removal of the testes for the treatment of prostate cancer.
Miscellaneous Z codes/categories:
Z28 Immunization not carried out
Except: Z28.3, Underimmunization status
Z40 Encounter for prophylactic surgery
Z41 Encounter for procedures for purposes other than remedying health state
Except: Z41.9, Encounter for procedure for purposes other than remedying health state, unspecified
Z53 Persons encountering health services for specific procedures and treatment, not carried out
Z55 Problems related to education and literacy
Z56 Problems related to employment and unemployment
Z57 Occupational exposure to risk factors
Z58 Problems related to physical environment
Z59 Problems related to housing and economic circumstances
Z60 Problems related to social environment
Z62 Problems related to upbringing
Z63 Other problems related to primary support group, including family circumstances
Z64 Problems related to certain psychosocial circumstances
Z65 Problems related to other psychosocial circumstances
Z72 Problems related to lifestyle
Z73 Problems related to life management difficulty
Z74 Problems related to care provider dependency
Except: Z74.01, Bed confinement status
Z75 Problems related to medical facilities and other health care
Z76.0 Encounter for issue of repeat prescription
Z76.3 Healthy person accompanying sick person
Z76.4 Other boarder to healthcare facility
Z76.5 Malingerer [conscious simulation]
Z91.1- Patient's noncompliance with medical treatment and regimen
Z91.83 Wandering in diseases classified elsewhere
Z91.89 Other specified personal risk factors, not elsewhere classified

15) Nonspecific Z codes
Certain Z codes are so non-specific, or potentially redundant with other codes in the classification, that there can be little justification for their use in the inpatient setting. Their use in the outpatient setting should be limited to those instances when there is no further documentation to permit more precise coding. Otherwise, any sign or symptom or any other reason for visit that is captured in another code should be used.
Nonspecific Z codes/categories:
Z02.9 Encounter for administrative examinations, unspecified Z04.9 Encounter for examination and observation for unspecified reason
Z13.9 Encounter for screening, unspecified
Z41.9 Encounter for procedure for purposes other than remedying health state, unspecified
Z52.9 Donor of unspecified organ or tissue
Z86.59 Personal history of other mental and behavioral disorders
Z88.9 Allergy status to unspecified drugs, medicaments and biological substances status
Z92.0 Personal history of contraception

16) Z Codes That May Only be Principal/First-Listed Diagnosis
The following Z codes/categories may only be reported as the principal/first-listed diagnosis, except when there are multiple encounters on the same day and the medical records for the encounters are combined:
Z00 Encounter for general examination without complaint, suspected or reported diagnosis
Z01 Encounter for other special examination without complaint, suspected or reported diagnosis
Z02 Encounter for administrative examination
Z03 Encounter for medical observation for suspected diseases and conditions ruled out

Z04 Encounter for examination and observation for other reasons
Z33.2 Encounter for elective termination of pregnancy
Z31.81 Encounter for male factor infertility in female patient
Z31.82 Encounter for Rh incompatibility status
Z31.83 Encounter for assisted reproductive fertility procedure cycle
Z31.84 Encounter for fertility preservation procedure
Z34 Encounter for supervision of normal pregnancy
Z39 Encounter for maternal postpartum care and examination
Z38 Liveborn infants according to place of birth and type of delivery
Z42 Encounter for plastic and reconstructive surgery following medical procedure or healed injury
Z51.0 Encounter for antineoplastic radiation therapy
Z51.1- Encounter for antineoplastic chemotherapy and immunotherapy
Z52 Donors of organs and tissues Except: Z52.9, Donor of unspecified organ or tissue
Z76.1 Encounter for health supervision and care of foundling
Z76.2 Encounter for health supervision and care of other healthy infant and child
Z99.12 Encounter for respirator [ventilator] dependence during power failure

Section II. Selection of Principal Diagnosis

The circumstances of inpatient admission always govern the selection of principal diagnosis. The principal diagnosis is defined in the Uniform Hospital Discharge Data Set (UHDDS) as "that condition established after study to be chiefly responsible for occasioning the admission of the patient to the hospital for care."

The UHDDS definitions are used by hospitals to report inpatient data elements in a standardized manner. These data elements and their definitions can be found in the July 31, 1985, *Federal Register* (Vol. 50, No, 147), pp. 31038-40.

Since that time the application of the UHDDS definitions has been expanded to include all non-outpatient settings (acute care, short term, long term care and psychiatric hospitals; home health agencies; rehab facilities; nursing homes, etc).

In determining principal diagnosis the coding conventions in the ICD-10-CM, the Tabular List and Alphabetic Index take precedence over these official coding guidelines.

(See Section I.A., Conventions for the ICD-10-CM)

The importance of consistent, complete documentation in the medical record cannot be overemphasized. Without such documentation the application of all coding guidelines is a difficult, if not impossible, task.

A. Codes for symptoms, signs, and ill-defined conditions

Codes for symptoms, signs, and ill-defined conditions from Chapter 18 are not to be used as principal diagnosis when a related definitive diagnosis has been established.

B. Two or more interrelated conditions, each potentially meeting the definition for principal diagnosis.

When there are two or more interrelated conditions (such as diseases in the same ICD-10-CM chapter or manifestations characteristically associated with a certain disease) potentially meeting the definition of principal diagnosis, either condition may be sequenced first, unless the circumstances of the admission, the therapy provided, the Tabular List, or the Alphabetic Index indicate otherwise.

C. Two or more diagnoses that equally meet the definition for principal diagnosis

In the unusual instance when two or more diagnoses equally meet the criteria for principal diagnosis as determined by the circumstances of admission, diagnostic workup and/or therapy provided, and the Alphabetic Index, Tabular List, or another coding guidelines does not provide sequencing direction, any one of the diagnoses may be sequenced first.

D. Two or more comparative or contrasting conditions.

In those rare instances when two or more contrasting or comparative diagnoses are documented as "either/or" (or similar terminology), they are coded as if the diagnoses were confirmed and the diagnoses are sequenced according to the circumstances of the admission. If no further determination can be made as to which diagnosis should be principal, either diagnosis may be sequenced first.

E. A symptom(s) followed by contrasting/comparative diagnoses

When a symptom(s) is followed by contrasting/comparative diagnoses, the symptom code is sequenced first. However, if the symptom code is integral to the conditions listed, no code for the symptom is reported. All the contrasting/comparative diagnoses should be coded as additional diagnoses.

F. Original treatment plan not carried out

Sequence as the principal diagnosis the condition, which after study occasioned the admission to the hospital, even though treatment may not have been carried out due to unforeseen circumstances.

G. Complications of surgery and other medical care

When the admission is for treatment of a complication resulting from surgery or other medical care, the complication code is sequenced as the principal diagnosis. If the complication is classified to the T80-T88 series and the code lacks the necessary specificity in describing the complication, an additional code for the specific complication should be assigned.

H. Uncertain Diagnosis

If the diagnosis documented at the time of discharge is qualified as "probable", "suspected", "likely", "questionable", "possible", or "still to be ruled out", or other similar terms indicating uncertainty, code the condition as if it existed or was established. The bases for these guidelines are the diagnostic workup, arrangements for further workup or observation, and initial therapeutic approach that correspond most closely with the established diagnosis.

Note: This guideline is applicable only to inpatient admissions to short-term, acute, long-term care and psychiatric hospitals.

I. Admission from Observation Unit

1. Admission Following Medical Observation

   When a patient is admitted to an observation unit for a medical condition, which either worsens or does not improve, and is subsequently admitted as an inpatient of the same hospital for this same medical condition, the principal diagnosis would be the medical condition which led to the hospital admission.

2. Admission Following Post-Operative Observation

   When a patient is admitted to an observation unit to monitor a condition (or complication) that develops following outpatient surgery, and then is subsequently admitted as an inpatient of the same hospital, hospitals should apply the Uniform Hospital Discharge Data Set (UHDDS) definition of principal diagnosis as "that condition established after study to be chiefly responsible for occasioning the admission of the patient to the hospital for care."

J. Admission from Outpatient Surgery

When a patient receives surgery in the hospital's outpatient surgery department and is subsequently admitted for continuing inpatient care at the same hospital, the following guidelines should be followed in selecting the principal diagnosis for the inpatient admission:

- If the reason for the inpatient admission is a complication, assign the complication as the principal diagnosis.
- If no complication, or other condition, is documented as the reason for the inpatient admission, assign the reason for the outpatient surgery as the principal diagnosis.
- If the reason for the inpatient admission is another condition unrelated to the surgery, assign the unrelated condition as the principal diagnosis.

K. Admissions/Encounters for Rehabilitation

When the purpose for the admission/encounter is rehabilitation, sequence first the code for the condition for which the service is being performed. For example, for an admission/encounter for rehabilitation for right-sided dominant hemiplegia following a cerebrovascular infarction, report code I69.351, Hemiplegia and hemiparesis following cerebral infarction affecting right dominant side, as the first-listed or principal diagnosis.

If the condition for which the rehabilitation service is no longer present, report the appropriate aftercare code as the first-listed or principal diagnosis. For example, if a patient with severe degenerative osteoarthritis of the hip, underwent hip replacement and the current encounter/admission is for rehabilitation, report code Z47.1, Aftercare following joint replacement surgery, as the first-listed or principal diagnosis.

See Section I.C.21.c.7, Factors influencing health states and contact with health services, Aftercare.

Section III. Reporting Additional Diagnoses

GENERAL RULES FOR OTHER (ADDITIONAL) DIAGNOSES

For reporting purposes the definition for "other diagnoses" is interpreted as additional conditions that affect patient care in terms of requiring:

- clinical evaluation;
- or therapeutic treatment;
- or diagnostic procedures;
- or extended length of hospital stay;
- or increased nursing care and/or monitoring.

The UHDDS item #11-b defines Other Diagnoses as "all conditions that coexist at the time of admission, that develop subsequently, or that affect the treatment received and/or the length of stay. Diagnoses that relate to an earlier episode which have no bearing on the current hospital stay are to be excluded." UHDDS definitions apply to inpatients in acute care, short-term, long term care and psychiatric hospital setting. The UHDDS definitions are used by acute care short-term hospitals to report inpatient data elements in a standardized manner. These data elements and their definitions can be found in the July 31, 1985, *Federal Register* (Vol. 50, No, 147), pp. 31038-40.

Since that time the application of the UHDDS definitions has been expanded to include all non-outpatient settings (acute care, short term, long term care and psychiatric hospitals; home health agencies; rehab facilities; nursing homes, etc).

The following guidelines are to be applied in designating "other diagnoses" when neither the Alphabetic Index nor the Tabular List in ICD-10-CM provide direction. The listing of the diagnoses in the patient record is the responsibility of the attending provider.

A. Previous conditions

If the provider has included a diagnosis in the final diagnostic statement, such as the discharge summary or the face sheet, it should ordinarily be coded. Some providers include in the diagnostic statement resolved conditions or diagnoses and status-post procedures from previous admission that have no bearing on the current stay. Such conditions are not to be reported and are coded only if required by hospital policy.

However, history codes (categories Z80-Z87) may be used as secondary codes if the historical condition or family history has an impact on current care or influences treatment.

B. Abnormal findings

Abnormal findings (laboratory, x-ray, pathologic, and other diagnostic results) are not coded and reported unless the provider indicates their clinical significance. If the findings are outside the normal range and the attending provider has ordered other tests to evaluate the condition or prescribed treatment, it is appropriate to ask the provider whether the abnormal finding should be added.

Please note: This differs from the coding practices in the outpatient setting for coding encounters for diagnostic tests that have been interpreted by a provider.

C. Uncertain Diagnosis

If the diagnosis documented at the time of discharge is qualified as "probable", "suspected", "likely", "questionable", "possible", or "still to be ruled out" or other similar terms indicating uncertainty, code the condition as if it existed or was established. The bases for these guidelines are the diagnostic workup, arrangements for further workup or observation, and initial therapeutic approach that correspond most closely with the established diagnosis.

Note: This guideline is applicable only to inpatient admissions to short-term, acute, long-term care and psychiatric hospitals.

Section IV. Diagnostic Coding and Reporting Guidelines for Outpatient Services

These coding guidelines for outpatient diagnoses have been approved for use by hospitals/ providers in coding and reporting hospital-based outpatient services and provider-based office visits.

Information about the use of certain abbreviations, punctuation, symbols, and other conventions used in the ICD-10-CM Tabular List (code numbers and titles), can be found in Section IA of these guidelines, under "Conventions Used in the Tabular List." Section I.B. contains general guidelines that apply to the entire classification. Section I.C. contains chapter-specific guidelines that correspond to the chapters as they are arranged in the classification. Information about the correct sequence to use in finding a code is also described in Section I.

The terms encounter and visit are often used interchangeably in describing outpatient service contacts and, therefore, appear together in these guidelines without distinguishing one from the other.

Though the conventions and general guidelines apply to all settings, coding guidelines for outpatient and provider reporting of diagnoses will vary in a number of instances from those for inpatient diagnoses, recognizing that:

The Uniform Hospital Discharge Data Set (UHDDS) definition of principal diagnosis applies only to inpatients in acute, short-term, long-term care and psychiatric hospitals.

Coding guidelines for inconclusive diagnoses (probable, suspected, rule out, etc.) were developed for inpatient reporting and do not apply to outpatients.

A. Selection of first-listed condition

In the outpatient setting, the term first-listed diagnosis is used in lieu of principal diagnosis.

In determining the first-listed diagnosis the coding conventions of ICD-10-CM, as well as the general and disease specific guidelines take precedence over the outpatient guidelines.

Diagnoses often are not established at the time of the initial encounter/visit. It may take two or more visits before the diagnosis is confirmed.

The most critical rule involves beginning the search for the correct code assignment through the Alphabetic Index. Never begin searching initially in the Tabular List as this will lead to coding errors.

1. Outpatient Surgery

   When a patient presents for outpatient surgery (same day surgery), code the reason for the surgery as the first-listed diagnosis (reason for the encounter), even if the surgery is not performed due to a contraindication.

2. Observation Stay

   When a patient is admitted for observation for a medical condition, assign a code for the medical condition as the first-listed diagnosis.

   When a patient presents for outpatient surgery and develops complications requiring admission to observation, code the reason for the surgery as the first reported diagnosis (reason for the encounter), followed by codes for the complications as secondary diagnoses.

B. Codes from A00.0 through T88.9, Z00-Z99

The appropriate code(s) from A00.0 through T88.9, Z00-Z99 must be used to identify diagnoses, symptoms, conditions, problems, complaints, or other reason(s) for the encounter/visit.

C. Accurate reporting of ICD-10-CM diagnosis codes

For accurate reporting of ICD-10-CM diagnosis codes, the documentation should describe the patient's condition, using terminology which includes specific diagnoses as well as symptoms, problems, or reasons for the encounter. There are ICD-10-CM codes to describe all of these.

D. Codes that describe symptoms and signs

Codes that describe symptoms and signs, as opposed to diagnoses, are acceptable for reporting purposes when a diagnosis has not been established (confirmed) by the provider. Chapter 18 of ICD-10-CM, Symptoms, Signs, and Abnormal Clinical and Laboratory Findings Not Elsewhere Classified (codes R00-R99) contain many, but not all codes for symptoms.

E. Encounters for circumstances other than a disease or injury

ICD-10-CM provides codes to deal with encounters for circumstances other than a disease or injury. The Factors Influencing Health Status and Contact with Health Services codes (Z00-Z99) are provided to deal with occasions when circumstances other than a disease or injury are recorded as diagnosis or problems. See Section I.C.21. Factors influencing health status and contact with health services.

F. **Level of Detail in Coding**

1. ICD-10-CM codes with 3, 4, 5, 6 or 7 characters ICD-10-CM is composed of codes with 3, 4, 5, 6 or 7 characters. Codes with three characters are included in ICD-10-CM as the heading of a category of codes that may be further subdivided by the use of fourth, fifth, sixth or seventh characters to provide greater specificity.
2. Use of full number of characters required for a code A three-character code is to be used only if it is not further subdivided. A code is invalid if it has not been coded to the full number of characters required for that code, including the 7th character extension, if applicable.

G. **ICD-10-CM code for the diagnosis, condition, problem, or other reason for encounter/visit**

List first the ICD-10-CM code for the diagnosis, condition, problem, or other reason for encounter/visit shown in the medical record to be chiefly responsible for the services provided. List additional codes that describe any coexisting conditions. In some cases the first-listed diagnosis may be a symptom when a diagnosis has not been established (confirmed) by the physician.

H. **Uncertain diagnosis**

Do not code diagnoses documented as "probable", "suspected," "questionable," "rule out," or "working diagnosis" or other similar terms indicating uncertainty. Rather, code the condition(s) to the highest degree of certainty for that encounter/visit, such as symptoms, signs, abnormal test results, or other reason for the visit.

Please note: This differs from the coding practices used by short-term, acute care, long-term care and psychiatric hospitals.

I. **Chronic diseases**

Chronic diseases treated on an ongoing basis may be coded and reported as many times as the patient receives treatment and care for the condition(s)

J. **Code all documented conditions that coexist**

Code all documented conditions that coexist at the time of the encounter/visit, and require or affect patient care treatment or management. Do not code conditions that were previously treated and no longer exist. However, history codes (categories Z80-Z87) may be used as secondary codes if the historical condition or family history has an impact on current care or influences treatment.

K. **Patients receiving diagnostic services only**

For patients receiving diagnostic services only during an encounter/visit, sequence first the diagnosis, condition, problem, or other reason for encounter/visit shown in the medical record to be chiefly responsible for the outpatient services provided during the encounter/visit. Codes for other diagnoses (e.g., chronic conditions) may be sequenced as additional diagnoses.

For encounters for routine laboratory/radiology testing in the absence of any signs, symptoms, or associated diagnosis, assign Z01.89, Encounter for other specified special examinations. If routine testing is performed during the same encounter as a test to evaluate a sign, symptom, or diagnosis, it is appropriate to assign both the Z code and the code describing the reason for the non-routine test.

For outpatient encounters for diagnostic tests that have been interpreted by a physician, and the final report is available at the time of coding, code any confirmed or definitive diagnosis(es) documented in the interpretation. Do not code related signs and symptoms as additional diagnoses.

Please note: This differs from the coding practice in the hospital inpatient setting regarding abnormal findings on test results.

L. **Patients receiving therapeutic services only**

For patients receiving therapeutic services only during an encounter/visit, sequence first the diagnosis, condition, problem, or other reason for encounter/visit shown in the medical record to be chiefly responsible for the outpatient services provided during the encounter/visit. Codes for other diagnoses (e.g., chronic conditions) may be sequenced as additional diagnoses.

The only exception to this rule is that when the primary reason for the admission/encounter is chemotherapy or radiation therapy, the appropriate Z code for the service is listed first, and the diagnosis or problem for which the service is being performed listed second.

M. **Patients receiving preoperative evaluations only**

For patients receiving preoperative evaluations only, sequence first a code from subcategory Z01.81, Encounter for pre-procedural examinations, to describe the pre-op consultations. Assign a code for the condition to describe the reason for the surgery as an additional diagnosis. Code also any findings related to the pre-op evaluation.

N. **Ambulatory surgery**

For ambulatory surgery, code the diagnosis for which the surgery was performed. If the postoperative diagnosis is known to be different from the preoperative diagnosis at the time the diagnosis is confirmed, select the postoperative diagnosis for coding, since it is the most definitive.

O. **Routine outpatient prenatal visits**

See Section I.C.15. Routine outpatient prenatal visits.

P. **Encounters for general medical examinations with abnormal findings**

The subcategories for encounters for general medical examinations, Z00.0-, provide codes for with and without abnormal findings. Should a general medical examination result in an abnormal finding, the code for general medical examination with abnormal finding should be assigned as the first-listed diagnosis. A secondary code for the abnormal finding should also be coded.

Q. **Encounters for routine health screenings**

See Section I.C.21. Factors influencing health status and contact with health services, Screening

Appendix I Present on Admission Reporting Guidelines (Effective with 2011 update)

Introduction

These guidelines are to be used as a supplement to the ICD-10-CM Official Guidelines for Coding and Reporting to facilitate the assignment of the Present on Admission (POA) indicator for each diagnosis and external cause of injury code reported on claim forms (UB-04 and 837 Institutional).

These guidelines are not intended to replace any guidelines in the main body of the ICD-10-CM Official Guidelines for Coding and Reporting. The POA guidelines are not intended to provide guidance on when a condition should be coded, but rather, how to apply the POA indicator to the final set of diagnosis codes that have been assigned in accordance with Sections I, II, and III of the official coding guidelines. Subsequent to the assignment of the ICD-10-CM codes, the POA indicator should then be assigned to those conditions that have been coded.

As stated in the Introduction to the ICD-10-CM Official Guidelines for Coding and Reporting, a joint effort between the healthcare provider and the coder is essential to achieve complete and accurate documentation, code assignment, and reporting of diagnoses and procedures. The importance of consistent, complete documentation in the medical record cannot be overemphasized. Medical record documentation from any provider involved in the care and treatment of the patient may be used to support the determination of whether a condition was present on admission or not. In the context of the official coding guidelines, the term "provider" means a physician or any qualified healthcare practitioner who is legally accountable for establishing the patient's diagnosis.

These guidelines are not a substitute for the provider's clinical judgment as to the determination of whether a condition was/was not present on admission. The provider should be queried regarding issues related to the linking of signs/symptoms, timing of test results, and the timing of findings.

General Reporting Requirements

All claims involving inpatient admissions to general acute care hospitals or other facilities that are subject to a law or regulation mandating collection of present on admission information.

Present on admission is defined as present at the time the order for inpatient admission occurs – conditions that develop during an outpatient encounter, including emergency department, observation, or outpatient surgery, are considered as present on admission.

POA indicator is assigned to principal and secondary diagnoses (as defined in Section II of the Official Guidelines for Coding and Reporting) and the external cause of injury codes.

Issues related to inconsistent, missing, conflicting or unclear documentation must still be resolved by the provider.

If a condition would not be coded and reported based on UHDDS definitions and current official coding guidelines, then the POA indicator would not be reported.

Reporting Options

Y	Yes
N	No
U	Unknown
W	Clinically undetermined
Unreported/ Not used (or "1" for Medicare usage)	(Exempt from POA reporting)

Reporting Definitions

Y	present at the time of inpatient admission
N	not present at the time of inpatient admission
U	documentation is insufficient to determine if condition is present on admission
W	provider is unable to clinically determine whether condition was present on admission or not

Timeframe for POA Identification and Documentation

There is no required timeframe as to when a provider (per the definition of "provider" used in these guidelines) must identify or document a condition to be present on admission. In some clinical situations, it may not be possible for a provider to make a definitive diagnosis (or a condition may not be recognized or reported by the patient) for a period of time after admission. In some cases it may be several days before the provider arrives at a definitive diagnosis. This does not mean that the condition was not present on admission. Determination of whether the condition was present on admission or not will be based on the applicable POA guideline as identified in this document, or on the provider's best clinical judgment.

If at the time of code assignment the documentation is unclear as to whether a condition was present on admission or not, it is appropriate to query the provider for clarification.

Assigning the POA Indicator

Condition is on the "Exempt from Reporting" list Leave the "present on admission" field blank if the condition is on the list of ICD-10-CM codes for which this field is not applicable. This is the only circumstance in which the field may be left blank.

POA Explicitly Documented

Assign "Y" for any condition the provider explicitly documents as being present on admission.

Assign "N" for any condition the provider explicitly documents as not present at the time of admission.

Conditions diagnosed prior to inpatient admission

Assign "Y" for conditions that were diagnosed prior to admission (example: hypertension, diabetes mellitus, asthma)

Conditions diagnosed during the admission but clearly present before admission

Assign "Y" for conditions diagnosed during the admission that were clearly present but not diagnosed until after admission occurred.

Diagnoses subsequently confirmed after admission are considered present on admission if at the time of admission they are documented as suspected, possible, rule out, differential diagnosis, or constitute an underlying cause of a symptom that is present at the time of admission.

Condition develops during outpatient encounter prior to inpatient admission

Assign "Y" for any condition that develops during an outpatient encounter prior to a written order for inpatient admission.

Documentation does not indicate whether condition was present on admission Assign "U" when the medical record documentation is unclear as to whether the condition was present on admission. "U" should not be routinely assigned and used only in very limited circumstances. Coders are encouraged to query the providers when the documentation is unclear.

Documentation states that it cannot be determined whether the condition was or was not present on admission

Assign "W" when the medical record documentation indicates that it cannot be clinically determined whether or not the condition was present on admission.

Chronic condition with acute exacerbation during the admission

If a single code identifies both the chronic condition and the acute exacerbation, see POA guidelines pertaining to combination codes.

If a single code only identifies the chronic condition and not the acute exacerbation (e.g., acute exacerbation of chronic leukemia), assign "Y."

Conditions documented as possible, probable, suspected, or rule out at the time of discharge

If the final diagnosis contains a possible, probable, suspected, or rule out diagnosis, and this diagnosis was based on signs, symptoms or clinical findings suspected at the time of inpatient admission, assign "Y."

If the final diagnosis contains a possible, probable, suspected, or rule out diagnosis, and this diagnosis was based on signs, symptoms or clinical findings that were not present on admission, assign "N".

Conditions documented as impending or threatened at the time of discharge

If the final diagnosis contains an impending or threatened diagnosis, and this diagnosis is based on symptoms or clinical findings that were present on admission, assign "Y".

If the final diagnosis contains an impending or threatened diagnosis, and this diagnosis is based on symptoms or clinical findings that were not present on admission, assign "N".

Acute and Chronic Conditions

Assign "Y" for acute conditions that are present at time of admission and N for acute conditions that are not present at time of admission.

Assign "Y" for chronic conditions, even though the condition may not be diagnosed until after admission.

If a single code identifies both an acute and chronic condition, *see the POA guidelines for combination codes.*

Combination Codes

Assign "N" if any part of the combination code was not present on admission (e.g., COPD with acute exacerbation and the exacerbation was not present on admission; gastric ulcer that does not start bleeding until after admission; asthma patient develops status asthmaticus after admission)

Assign "Y" if all parts of the combination code were present on admission (e.g., patient with acute prostatitis admitted with hematuria)

If the final diagnosis includes comparative or contrasting diagnoses, and both were present, or suspected, at the time of admission, assign "Y".

For infection codes that include the causal organism, assign "Y" if the infection (or signs of the infection) was present on admission, even though the culture results may not be known until after admission (e.g., patient is admitted with pneumonia and the provider documents pseudomonas as the causal organism a few days later).

Same Diagnosis Code for Two or More Conditions

When the same ICD-10-CM diagnosis code applies to two or more conditions during the same encounter (e.g. two separate conditions classified to the same ICD-10-CM diagnosis code):

Assign "Y" if all conditions represented by the single ICD-10-CM code were present on admission (e.g. bilateral unspecified age-related cataracts).

Assign "N" if any of the conditions represented by the single ICD-10-CM code was not present on admission (e.g. traumatic secondary and recurrent hemorrhage and seroma is assigned to a single code T79.2, but only one of the conditions was present on admission).

Obstetrical conditions

Whether or not the patient delivers during the current hospitalization does not affect assignment of the POA indicator. The determining factor for POA assignment is whether the pregnancy complication or obstetrical condition described by the code was present at the time of admission or not.

If the pregnancy complication or obstetrical condition was present on admission (e.g., patient admitted in preterm labor), assign "Y".

If the pregnancy complication or obstetrical condition was not present on admission (e.g., 2nd degree laceration during delivery, postpartum hemorrhage that occurred during current hospitalization, fetal distress develops after admission), assign "N".

If the obstetrical code includes more than one diagnosis and any of the diagnoses identified by the code were not present on admission assign "N".

(e.g., Category O11, Pre-existing hypertension with pre-eclampsia)

Perinatal conditions

Newborns are not considered to be admitted until after birth. Therefore, any condition present at birth or that developed in utero is considered present at admission and should be assigned "Y". This includes conditions that occur during delivery (e.g., injury during delivery, meconium aspiration, exposure to streptococcus B in the vaginal canal).

Congenital conditions and anomalies

Assign "Y" for congenital conditions and anomalies except for categories Q00-Q99, Congenital anomalies, which are on the exempt list. Congenital conditions are always considered present on admission.

External cause of injury codes

Assign "Y" for any external cause code representing an external cause of morbidity that occurred prior to inpatient admission (e.g., patient fell out of bed at home, patient fell out of bed in emergency room prior to admission)

Assign "N" for any external cause code representing an external cause of morbidity that occurred during inpatient hospitalization (e.g., patient fell out of hospital bed during hospital stay, patient experienced an adverse reaction to a medication administered after inpatient admission)

Categories and Codes Exempt from Diagnosis Present on Admission Requirement

Note: "Diagnosis present on admission" for these code categories are exempt because they represent circumstances regarding the healthcare encounter or factors influencing health status that do not represent a current disease or injury or are always present on admission

B90–B94	Sequelae of infectious and parasitic diseases
E64	Sequelae of malnutrition and other nutritional deficiences
I25.2	Old myocardial infarction
I69	Sequelae of cerebrovascular disease
O09	Supervision of high risk pregnancy
O66.5	Attempted application of vacuum extractor and forceps
O80	Encounter for full-term uncomplicated delivery
O94	Sequelae of complication of pregnancy, childbirth, and the puerperium
P00	Newborn (suspected to be) affected by maternal conditions that may be unrelated to present pregnancy
Q00 – Q99	Congenital malformations, deformations and chromosomal abnormalities
S00-T88.9	Injury, poisoning and certain other consequences of external causes with 7th character representing subsequent encounter or sequela
V00-V09	Pedestrian injured in transport accident Except V00.81-, Accident with wheelchair (powered) V00.83-, Accident with motorized mobility scooter
V10-V19	Pedal cycle rider injured in transport accident
V20-V29	Motorcycle rider injured in transport accident
V30-V39	Occupant of three-wheeled motor vehicle injured in transport accident
V40-V49	Car occupant injured in transport accident
V50-V59	Occupant of pick-up truck or van injured in transport accident
V60-V69	Occupant of heavy transport vehicle injured in transport accident
V70-V79	Bus occupant injured in transport accident
V80-V89	Other land transport accidents
V90-V94	Water transport accidents
V95-V97	Air and space transport accidents
V98-V99	Other and unspecified transport accidents
W09	Fall on and from playground equipment
W14	Fall from tree
W15	Fall from cliff
W17.0	Fall into well
W17.1	Fall into storm drain or manhole
W18.01	Striking against sports equipment with subsequent fall
W20.8	Other cause of strike by thrown, projected or falling object
W21	Striking against or struck by sports equipment
W30	Contact with agricultural machinery
W31	Contact with other and unspecified machinery
W32-W34	Accidental handgun discharge and malfunction
W35-W40	Exposure to inanimate mechanical forces
W52	Crushed, pushed or stepped on by crowd or human stampede
W56	Contact with nonvenomous marine animal
W58	Contact with crocodile or alligator
W61	Contact with birds (domestic) (wild)
W62	Contact with nonvenomous amphibians
W89	Exposure to man-made visible and ultraviolet light
X02	Exposure to controlled fire in building or structure
X03	Exposure to controlled fire, not in building or structure
X04	Exposure to ignition of highly flammable material
X52	Prolonged stay in weightless environment
X71	Intentional self-harm by drowning and submersion
X72	Intentional self-harm by handgun discharge
X73	Intentional self-harm by rifle, shotgun and larger firearm discharge
X74	Intentional self-harm by other and unspecified firearm and gun discharge
X75	Intentional self-harm by explosive material
X76	Intentional self-harm by smoke, fire and flames
X77	Intentional self-harm by steam, hot vapors and hot objects
X81	Intentional self-harm by jumping or lying in front of moving object
X82	Intentional self-harm by crashing of motor vehicle
X83	Intentional self-harm by other specified means
Y03	Assault by crashing of motor vehicle
Y07	Perpetrator of assault, maltreatment and neglect
Y08.8	Assault by strike by sports equipment
Y21	Drowning and submersion, undetermined intent
Y22	Handgun discharge, undetermined intent
Y23	Rifle, shotgun and larger firearm discharge, undetermined intent
Y24	Other and unspecified firearm discharge, undetermined intent
Y30	Falling, jumping or pushed from a high place, undetermined intent
Y32	Assault by crashing of motor vehicle, undetermined intent
Y35	Legal intervention
Y37	Military operations
Y36	Operations of war
Y38	Terrorism
Y92	Place of occurrence of the external cause
Y93	Activity code
Y99	External cause status
Z00	Encounter for general examination without complaint, suspected or reported diagnosis
Z01	Encounter for other special examination without complaint, suspected or reported diagnosis
Z02	Encounter for administrative examination
Z03	Encounter for medical observation for suspected diseases and conditions ruled out
Z08	Encounter for follow-up examination following completed treatment for malignant neoplasm
Z09	Encounter for follow-up examination after completed treatment for conditions other than malignant neoplasm
Z11	Encounter for screening for infectious and parasitic diseases
Z11.8	Encounter for screening for other infectious and parasitic diseases
Z12	Encounter for screening for malignant neoplasms
Z13	Encounter for screening for other diseases and disorders
Z13.4	Encounter for screening for certain developmental disorders in childhood
Z13.5	Encounter for screening for eye and ear disorders
Z13.6	Encounter for screening for cardiovascular disorders
Z13.83	Encounter for screening for respiratory disorder NEC
Z13.89	Encounter for screening for other disorder (inclusion term) Encounter for screening for genitourinary disorders)
Z13.89	Encounter for screening for other disorder
Z14	Genetic carrier
Z15	Genetic susceptibility to disease
Z17	Estrogen receptor status
Z18	Retained foreign body fragments
Z22	Carrier of infectious disease
Z23	Encounter for immunization
Z28	Immunization not carried out and underimmunization status
Z28.3	Underimmunization status

2015 Draft ICD-10-CM

Z30	Encounter for contraceptive management
Z31	Encounter for procreative management
Z34	Encounter for supervision of normal pregnancy
Z36	Encounter for antenatal screening of mother
Z37	Outcome of delivery
Z38	Liveborn infants according to place of birth and type of delivery
Z39	Encounter for maternal postpartum care and examination
Z41	Encounter for procedures for purposes other than remedying health state
Z42	Encounter for plastic and reconstructive surgery following medical procedure or healed injury
Z43	Encounter for attention to artificial openings
Z44	Encounter for fitting and adjustment of external prosthetic device
Z45	Encounter for adjustment and management of implanted device
Z46	Encounter for fitting and adjustment of other devices
Z47.8	Encounter for other orthopedic aftercare
Z49	Encounter for care involving renal dialysis
Z51	Encounter for other aftercare
Z51.5	Encounter for palliative care
Z51.8	Encounter for other specified aftercare
Z52	Donors of organs and tissues
Z59	Problems related to housing and economic circumstances
Z63	Other problems related to primary support group, including family circumstances
Z65	Problems related to other psychosocial circumstances
Z65.8	Other specified problems related to psychosocial circumstances
Z67.1-Z67.9	Blood type
Z68	Body mass index (BMI)
Z72	Problems related to lifestyle
Z74.01	Bed confinement status
Z76	Persons encountering health services in other circumstances
Z77.110-Z77.128	Environmental pollution and hazards in the physical environment
Z78	Other specified health status
Z79	Long term (current) drug therapy
Z80	Family history of primary malignant neoplasm
Z81	Family history of mental and behavioral disorders
Z82	Family history of certain disabilities and chronic diseases (leading to disablement)
Z83	Family history of other specific disorders
Z84	Family history of other conditions
Z85	Personal history of primary malignant neoplasm
Z86	Personal history of certain other diseases
Z87	Personal history of other diseases and conditions
Z87.828	Personal history of other (healed) physical injury and trauma
Z87.891	Personal history of nicotine dependence
Z88	Allergy status to drugs, medicaments and biological substances
Z89	Acquired absence of limb
Z90.710	Acquired absence of both cervix and uterus
Z91.0	Allergy status, other than to drugs and biological substances
Z91.4	Personal history of psychological trauma, not elsewhere classified
Z91.5	Personal history of self-harm
Z91.8	Other specified risk factors, not elsewhere classified
Z92	Personal history of medical treatment
Z93	Artificial opening status
Z94	Transplanted organ and tissue status
Z95	Presence of cardiac and vascular implants and grafts
Z97	Presence of other devices
Z98	Other postprocedural states
Z99	Dependence on enabling machines and devices, not elsewhere classified

Web Links for Additional Information

www.icd10center.com—An ongoing supportive Blog

Note: Each State will have its own website for Worker's Compensation, *For example, California has the Department of Worker's Compensation, whose website is: http://www.dir.ca.gov/dwc/.*

www.noridianmedicare.com
Centers for Medicare & Medicaid Services: *cms.gov*
http://www.cms.gov/Medicare/Coverage/DeterminationProcess/LCDs.html

Other Products by Eugene Fukumoto

Want to learn more about how to use ICD-10?

Online Courses by Eugene Fukumoto
Sponsored by MF University

1. Conquering ICD-10: Module 1
2. Conquering ICD-10: Module 2—Advanced Concepts

For more info, visit Eugene at:
www.mededonline.myicourse.com
www.dctodconline.myicourse.com
www.legaledonline.myicourse.com

Other Books by Eugene Fukumoto
Conquering ICD-10—For Chiropractors
Conquering ICD-10—For Family Physicians and General Practice
Conquering ICD-10—Worker's Compensation and Personal Injury—First Edition
www.icd10center.com

Index

G

H

I

O

P

R

S

T

U

V

W

X

Z